CW01085868

Aging and disability
Research and clinical perspectives

International review board for this book

Eli Carmeli, BT, PhD, Senior lecturer, Department of Physical Therapy, Sackler Faculty of Medicine, Tel Aviv University, IL-69978 Ramat Aviv, Israel.

Trine Flensborg-Madsen, MSc (Public Hlth Sci), researcher, Institute of Preventive Medicine, Faculty of Health Sciences, Copenhagen, Denmark.

Mohammed Morad, MD, Lecturer, Department of Family Medicine, Faculty of Health Sciences, University of Ben Gurion, Beer-Sheva, Israel

Hatim A Omar, MD, Professor of Pediatrics and Obstetrics/Gynecology and Director, Adolescent Medicine, University of Kentucky, Lexington, USA.

Daniel TL Shek, PhD, Professor of Social Work, Social Welfare Practice and Research Centre, Department of Social Work, the Chinese University of Hong Kong, Shatin, Hong Kong.

Jacob Urkin, MD, MPH, Director, Primary Care Unit, Division of Commuity Health, Faculty of Health Sciences, University of Ben Gurion, Beer-Sheva, Israel

Søren Ventegodt, MD, Director, Quality of Life Research Center, Copenhagen, Denmark

This book has been peer-reviewed by the editors in collaboration with the international review board, published under the auspices of the National Institute of Child Health and Human Development in Israel and supported by the Israel Foundation for Human Development, New York.

Aging and disability
Research and clinical perspectives

TABLE OF CONTENTS

Aging and disability
Research and clinical perspectives

Aging and disability
Research and clinical perspectives

Aging and disability
Research and clinical perspectives

Aging and disability
Research and clinical perspectives

Aging and disability
Research and clinical perspectives

PART TWELFE: PUBLICATIONS

FOREWORD

Isack Kandel, Patricia Schofield and Joav Merrick

Modern medicine and technology with better standards of living have resulted in people living longer and in recent time we have also seen the emergence of a new and larger group of people, who due to congenital or childhood disability have lived with their disability surviving into old age. Secondary medical conditions, such as respiratory illness, renal failure, accidents, infections and depression and barriers to medical care prevented most of these people from experiencing their true life expectancy. The population of persons with life long disability, together with the general population getting older who as a result of old age now have a disability (or more than one), challenge the servive providers and planners, who now have to face the problem of aging with a disability. Both the general population aging and the person with a life long disability have common issues and would both profit from knowledge, experience and research in this field.

Research activity within health and social care has moved on at a tremendous pace over the last decade. We are increasingly seeing high quality publications within high quality research journals that reports the findings and processes of investigations conducted within the health and social care arena. These are exciting times as a whole range of research methodologies are adopted and applied.

Historically, it has been perceived that the most appropriate research philosophy was from the positivist paradigm with randomised controlled trials viewed as the "gold standard" methodological approach. Whilst, such studies are still crucial to test hypotheses and evaluate interventions, increasingly it is being acknowledged that other methodologies also have a contribution to make in terms of adding to the body of knowledge. As such we are seeing other types of study including surveys and correlations and interestingly we are seeing the non-positive approaches that emphasise the perspectives of the participants themselves and include a whole range of methodologies including; interviews, case studies, observational studies and narratives. This is good news for research as we now see good quality quantitative research complemented by qualitative studies that provide a broader perspective and together they enhance the evidence base.

This book presents a number of research projects that encompass the range of research methodologies in aging. Thus demonstrating how health and social care can be evaluated from many different perspectives.

We hope that this emerging field will benefit from this book and that students and researchers in the health, allied health profession and social welfare will find material they can learn from.

INTRODUCTION

Growing older

Amanda Clarke and Lorna Warren

In-depth life story research was conducted in the United Kingdom to examine the meanings of growing older for men and women aged between 60 and 96 years old, drawing on previous gerontological work about the experience of aging. The findings revealed that meaning as applied to age was not fixed chronologically, but held diverse meanings based on participants' feelings, experiences, and interactions with others, whilst also reflecting and resisting some of the commonly held and mainly negative, stereotypes about later life. The participants said that they did not feel old, but indicated that there had been times in their lives when they had felt old: times of illness, redundancy, and bereavement. They also associated aging with physical and mental decline and illness, whether or not this reflected their substantive experience. Although participants' stories revealed that the unpleasant aspects of growing older cannot be denied, they also indicated that attitudes, behavior, and actions can, to an extent, help later life to be a more positive experience.

INTRODUCTION

Relatively few research studies use a biographical approach to facilitate nuanced understandings of aging from the older person's point of view, when compared with research about the 'problems' of aging: this can perpetuate stereotypical and ambiguous images of later life. On the one hand, later life is seen as a time of unavoidable retreat in the face of hardship, of physical and mental decline, and of withdrawal into dependency (1,2). On the other hand, in post-modern culture, "the prospect of an endless life has been revived through consumer images of perpetual youth and a blurring of traditional life course boundaries" (3). Featherstone and Wernick refer to the ambiguous images of later life as "the tension between the pull towards over-simplifying stereo-types of older age and the opposite pull towards the discovery of increasing complexity and differentiation" (4). In an attempt to address this ambiguity, Clarke's (1) doctoral study sought to examine the views of 'ordinary' older people about aging (5-7); how they perceive themselves, and how they experience later life. A biographical approach was used because life stories reveal the way in which people's beliefs, attitudes, feelings, and experiences have been shaped over a lifetime (8). Such an approach involves exploring whether people respond to aging in different ways, as well as what is unique and what is shared about later life.

Participants' perceptions were expressed through the positive and negative meanings that they ascribed to the process of aging through a variety of representations and self-representations that were given fuller meaning when set in the context of their lives. For, as JB Priestly (9) explained, "The previous life of old people...acts as a background and context for their expectations and experiences of old age".

OUR STUDY

A purposive sample of older men and women was recruited from voluntary groups, faith groups and cultural organizations, social clubs, appeals in the local media, and referral by other participants. Requests for participants referred to 'older people' rather than chronological age; it was left to individuals to define themselves as 'old' This method resulted in 10 men and 13 women (18 white participants and 5 black participants, 3 Jamaican and 2 Bangladeshi), most of whom were not receiving support from health or social services. Three rounds of audio-taped interviews (n=55) were undertaken in participants' homes over a period of about 6 months; the aim of which was to obtain: (1) participants' life stories; (2) the compilation of in-depth personal accounts of growing older, following-up themes from the first interviews; (3) participants' views about the research process, checking, elaborating, and discussing emerging themes from rounds (1) and (2). Not all participants completed round (3) due to illness, death, or loss of contact.

The first stage of the analysis involved reading and re-reading the transcripts, examining each narrative as a whole (10). Following Mauthner and Doucet (11), the main events, characters and the subplots were scrutinized, looking for recurrent images and words in each story and writing an edited life story for each participant. A detailed coding frame for the interviews was developed to compare themes across and between each interview and categorized using NU*DIST (version four), a qualitative data analysis package. All participants were offered a copy of their audio-tapes, were given the opportunity to amend their edited life stories, and were encouraged to comment on the main themes.

Findings categorized under the theme of growing older emerged from the first and second interviews, when participants were asked specific questions about later life in the context of their overall lives, beginning with the question, "Can you tell me how you feel about growing older?" (12). Participants expressed a rich heterogeneity of views, from resoundingly stating that they did not feel old to describing times when older age was indeed salient. The main themes of 'I don't feel old' and "are described below.

'I don't feel old'

One way in which to look at age is in chronological terms; however, as Gubrium and Holstein (13) argue, chronological age (objective age) is not necessarily related to what age means to the individual (subjective age). When participants were asked: "How do you feel about growing older?" they were unanimous in their response: they did not always "feel old." What came over most forcibly from their stories was that there was no set of characteristics peculiar to a certain number of years; individuals gave their own meaning to whatever age they happened to be. This contradicted the commonly held perspective that tends to allocate certain characteristics, roles, and actions to people based on their age. Arber and Ginn (14) refer to this as social age; that is, age that is socially constructed. An example of how people of a certain age are ascribed common behaviors was revealed in this account by Gladys Peters (93 years):

> "One of my neighbours asked me to make her grandchildren flannels, instead of Easter eggs, and when she gave them to them their mother said, "You're not to use them, you're to hang them on hooks in the bath-room" and when the little one said, "Why?" she said, "Well, the lady who's made them is nearly a hundred." And this little girl said, "What are they like when they get to a hundred?" (laughs).

Clearly, this girl expected Centenarians to act in a specific and uniformed way. Indeed, Dorothy Twigg (82 years), Janice Roberts (64 years), and Peter White (72 years) said they preferred not to tell people their ages since they thought people would expect them to behave like an "old person." Dorothy Twigg commented, "There's only one or two people that actually know my age and you're one of them." She explained:

> "A young man came into the shop where I volunteer a few weeks ago, he was training to be a journalist and he asked me questions and questions. And I said, "Are you finished now?" He said, "No, can I ask your age?" I said, "You can ask, but I'm not telling." So he says, "Go on, give us a clue." So I said, "Thirty plus" (laughs). If anyone asks me I just say, "Thirty plus" and they say, "We don't believe you" so I say, "Well, put another plus on then"."

When asked why she did not like revealing her age, Dorothy replied,

> *"I feel that the groups that I'm mixing with now, especially in the volunteer shop, they are all a lot younger than me. And I feel that they are saying, you know, "Can you manage?" And I don't like that. I suppose it's because I've always been so active and done that for other people and now I feel that people are doing it for me I feel a bit, oh dear, granny..."*

In describing how she felt about growing older, Janice Roberts' (64 years) response was typical:

> *"It's very difficult for me to think that I am old. My age, would be, "I'm old", but inside I don't feel any different at all."*

Maureen Williams (81 years) thought that feeling and acting old was nothing to do with chronological age:

> *"I think you can be old at sixty-five and you can not be old at ninety."*

Lillian Grayson (83 years) said that she felt little different from when she had first met her husband over sixty years before:

> *"I don't feel much different to what I did when I first met him (laughs). I don't feel in my eighties to be quite frank."*

Peter White (72 years) described how other people's reactions affected the way he perceived himself. He recalled a holiday in his nephew's caravan in Whitby. When he met his nephew a few weeks afterwards, his nephew told him that the owners of the adjacent caravan had said that they had "met the nice old gentleman." Peter commented,

> *"Well, I know I'm old, but I don't think that I'm that nice you know. Having said that, I thought, "Old gentleman, I don't think I'm old" (laughs). You're as old as you feel. Keep imagining you're forty-two."*

Tom Howarth (77 years) felt that he reacted to things emotionally in the same way that he had done when he was younger:

> *"I haven't noticed growing older because a lot of me is still very young. I still react romantically to things which you wouldn't think an old man could. I can see a film and be very moved to tears very easily. I'm going through the same emotions that I went through when I was a young man and, in that respect, I haven't grown old."*

Also interesting to note is that neither Dipti Sur nor Abdur Rahman, who were originally from Bangladesh, were certain of their real age. They reflected that in Bangla-deshi culture, little importance is placed on chronological age.

That participants did not feel old might be seen as a denial of aging; however, it is also bound-up with what is meant by the word 'old'. As Palmore (15) points out, although it might be thought that the word 'old' is a neutral or even a positive term as the Latin roots, alere and alescere, mean 'to nourish' or 'to grow', most synonyms for old make it clear that the connotations are usually negative: for example, "antiquated, archaic, senile, worn, discarded, infirm, frail" (15). In the present study, although all participants said that they did not "feel old", when asked more specific questions, such as "how do any physical changes make you feel?" it was apparent that there were times when participants did think of themselves as old; for example, when they experienced physical decline, when they were ill, when they were made redundant, and at times of bereavement.

When older age is salient

Regardless of whether participants felt that they were old and despite their own experience often to the contrary, older age was associated particularly with physical and mental decline.

Physical and mental decline/illness

George Daley (78 years) said that he first noticed that he was growing older when he could no longer physically carry out the things that he could when he was younger:

> "When you realize that there are certain things that you can't do that you used to be able to do, that's when I think you realize that you are old, or older. I'm not so strong, I can't do heavy, really heavy work like I could do when I was in my prime. That does from time to time strike you."

Also interesting to note is that George changed the word 'old' to the more subjective 'older', supporting his assertion that he did not feel old but concomitantly recognizing that everyone grows older in terms of chronological years. His use of the word 'prime' shows the more positive conno-tations associated with being younger. Brian Jenner, at 62 years, 16 years younger than George, appeared to agree:

> "I'm not really conscious of aging in a sense, you just feel the same in your head, don't you? Well, mostly I think. Well, you're conscious of not being so fit, I suppose. Doing physical things. You don't climb trees these days, you know (laughs), that sort of thing."

Brian's comment, 'you feel the same in your head' was reiterated by most participants. When Maureen Williams (81 years) was interviewed for the second time, she said that she had been poorly with a stomach upset for a couple of days previously and had, unusually for her, spent a day in bed:

"This week, I've said, "No, you're not getting old, you are old" (laughs). But I think illness… anybody, whatever age you are makes you feel…? Doesn't it? I think it comes home to you when you're taken ill. If you've got good health and you've got your faculties, I don't expect it hits you…"

Maureen repeatedly said in all her interviews that she did not feel old, but she said that at times she told her self that she 'must be getting old':

"Well I suppose you don't think of getting old until… well, you see your family getting married and children coming along and you think, "Oh, I must be getting older." Although again, I think it's an attitude of mind. I mean, some people are old, young, if you understand what I mean, and some people are never old (pauses). So I don't know when I started feeling old. I don't think that I feel old now."

Anne Daley (79 years) was terminally ill with a bone marrow deficiency at the time of her interview and in fact, died before what would have been her third interview. She felt that it was this illness that her 'aged' her; making her feel increasingly tired. She reflected, "It's aged me considerably, I know it has. I got much older quite quickly…"

Peter White (77 years) recalled that there were several times in his life when he had been conscious of aging:

"When I was made redundant, I thought, 'Well, what am I going to do with myself at my age?' At 56, I still thought I had nine good years of work left in me and I was fit at that time. I suppose that was one time when it struck me that I was getting old and perhaps the other time was when I had the two heart attacks in 1991, late '91. That made me realize that I was getting old and perhaps also, looking after my wife when she was very ill made me feel old. Basically, I suppose, because I was worried about what was going to happen to us both and whether I was still going to be able to cope. So yes, that made me feel old."

Janice Roberts (64 years) felt older when she was ill:

"I can't accept that I'm old, I can't really. I think that I can do everything that I've always done and I just don't think that I am old, except when I'm not well. And I still don't feel old and infirm. …I don't care if I live until I'm a hundred, as long as I've got my senses and I can walk about. I do worry about getting old and being ill."

She continued,

"I don't feel that I'm old, but yet I know I am and all the things come on to you and you think, "Oh dear"."

Janice's phrase, "all the things come on to you" referred to the physical problems that participants felt would invariably come with advancing years. Janice said that she could accept aging as long as she continued to be healthy and happy:

> "You just take it as it comes, as long as you're healthy and happy, that's the main thing and that's all that anybody can ask for. I think health is the main thing and your independence. If you can keep that, then you've won the battle, I think."

Similarly, Mabel Smith (91 years) said:

> "I don't feel old, mentally. If I'm stiff then I think, "Oh it must be old age." Some days I feel pleased that I have reached this age - providing I'm well."

Like Mabel, Hiron Balla Davi (70 years) related 'getting old' to 'aches and pains':

> "I'm getting old, but I don't feel that way; my mind is young and I want to keep it that way. I feel tired some-times, but I don't let that stop me doing things. I have aches and pains in my joints and muscles, but I've got to do things for myself and I do them."

Some participants were able to date the beginning of 'feeling old'. When Jim Caldwell (84 years) was asked when he first became conscious that he was getting older, he replied without hesitating, "When I had my first heart attack." Similarly, Lillian Grayson (83 years), talked about her husband's heart attack in relation to becoming more aware of age:

> "I think you're conscious of aging when you've got a serious illness, don't you? Ernest had a very bad heart attack when he was sixty-seven."

Ernest, her husband, agreed, "That's when you realize that you are getting older," and Lillian continued…

> "And I had the fear that I was going to lose my eyesight for years I had that you know because my eyes were so bad. But I said to him, 'We're getting old'. We feel us age now."

Lillian said that however a person felt, it was inevitable that age would 'catch up' on them and bring physical problems. In the extract below, she linked breathing difficulties specifically with aging, although she had said already that she had suffered from asthma for some time:

> "Your age catches up with you. When you're out walking you haven't got that strength in your legs that you had when you were young, you know. I

mean, I have a job getting on and off the buses now with this right leg and it keeps me awake at night. Ernest says it's rheumatism, but I don't think it is because I had small strokes a few years ago and I think it's after affects of that myself. You can't do all what you want to do, you get out of breath quick."

It is interesting to note that Lillian said that she and Ernest felt their age, but she did so in the context of talking about their medical conditions. Earlier in the interview, she had said that they did not feel old, later she said that their bodies told them otherwise: "Oh aye. The mind's willing but the body's not."

Whether or not participants had noticed changes in themselves physically, it was apparent that they expected to suffer either physical or mental decline or both as they aged. Brian Jenner (62 years) was very downbeat in his last interview (his mother had recently died). He associated his flu with older age:

(Coughs). "Crikey, I can't get my breath you know. Visible aging (laughs). I feel that sometimes, it's almost repulsive. But there is this aspect of oldness, of aging. Sometimes, well, I went to see my mother in this nursing home and there is this smell of piss, you know. ...I mean, it's quite sort of horrible really and it's no good denying it."

Brian continued,

"I just feel decrepit all of a sudden, it's funny that you should come round, you caught me on a good old person day. (Coughs). When they find I've got lung cancer or something... Nobody wants to be old do they really? You know, it's just inevitable, unless you die earlier, but I mean... No, I don't think it's anything to look forward to at all. It's downhill all the way I reckon. And you know, if you can just keep reasonable health it seems to me... and make a decent exit you know, slip off one night."

For Brian, a 'good old person' meant someone who showed 'visible signs' of aging; decrepitude, and illness. He reflected,

"It's (aging) essentially the result of being alive. You do these things and think, "What's next?' You know, you're a kid and then you ripen, you reach maturity and then you fruit, it's like an organic thing, like a tree, and then you stand around and things drop off (laughed) until you finally collapse."

He also associated later life with mental decline:

"Everybody when they're young says "I don't want to be old". It's like the famous rock quote "I don't want to live when I'm old" and I suspect the

nearer you get to it, you start to modify it a bit, "Well, when I'm a physical wreck, as long as I've got my brain", you start to talk like that yourself."

Brian's comment raises the paradox that although we do not want to age, we do want to live a long time (16).

Birthdays

In contrast to those participants who did not like to disclose their age (see above, 'I don't feel old'), it was apparent amongst older participants (those aged in their eighties and nineties) that they were proud to be the age they were; this attitude was most apparent when they described celebrating their birthdays. Gladys Roberts (93 years) talked extensively about her birthday celebrations:

"I had a party for my ninetieth birthday - we had prizes and games of bingo. My husband's niece sent me a cake and we had cherry and lemonade, port and brandy and then After Dinner Mints. I really enjoyed it."

Despite Dorothy Twigg (82 years) not liking to tell people her age, she did enjoy her annual 'birthday treat' to a musical or the theater in London. Betty Lomas had recently celebrated her ninetieth birthday—some of her cards were still on the mantelpiece; she said,

"Did I tell you I got seventy-three cards for my ninetieth birthday? Well, it speaks for itself. I'm lucky aren't I? We went to the Regency, for the party, because they've had it modernized, very nice. I were at the top with the Birthday cake and it was in the middle of us and there were lots of photographs taken."

Like Betty, Mabel Smith talked about celebrating her ninetieth birthday, a year before her interview:

"I like surprises myself, and I love to give people surprises. I've been very lucky really. I had a lovely ninetieth birthday. Granddaughter made me this lovely party."

At the age of 91, therefore, there were still things that could surprise Mabel. What was apparent in many participants' accounts was the belief that whatever their age, it was important to retain the ability to wonder and to look forward to events in the future. In later life, significant life events, such as major birthdays and anniversaries, continue, giving people the opportunity to express that innate human instinct—to celebrate (7,17).

DISCUSSION

It has been seen that participants presented a variety of meanings concerning growing older, based on their own perceptions and self-representations and by reflecting and resisting some commonly held and socially constructed views about later life. This observation suggests that there is no single definition of the word "old" nor a common way to grow old. On the one hand, participants said that they did not feel old; on the other hand, they described times in their lives when they do feel old. This disparity is echoed in other research studies (2,7,18-22). In the "Ageless Self", Kaufman (23) describes and analyses life story interviews with men and women aged sixty-five years and over who did not:

> "Speak of being old as meaningful in itself; that is, they do not relate to aging or chronological age as a category of experience or meaning. To the contrary, when old people talk about themselves, they express a sense of self that is age-less—an identity that maintains continuity despite the physical and social changes that come with old age."

Some participants in the present study suggested that they that did not think of themselves as old because the word 'old' has symbolic meaning that encompasses the negative stereotypical views about older people and therefore they wished to dissociate themselves from the category 'old.' This desire supports the view that older people's attitudes toward and experiences of later life are shaped not only by the interplay of social and physical constraints on their lives but also by their efforts to resist them. Research suggests that older people have been around long enough to assimilate society's devalued appraisal of later life (24,25). Tulle-Winton (26) argues,

> "At the present time, old age becomes a difficult label to apply to oneself because it is caught up in a network of images and pronouncements which the call to age success- fully forbids one to identify with. ...is it the onset of old age as an existential event or the modalities of its regulations which old people resist?"

Byteway (7) analyzed a panel of older people's written reflections about growing older and found that although they were willing to acknowledge chronological age in certain contexts that they thought appropriate, difficulties arose as a consequence of linking age with ambiguous statuses such as "middle-aged" and "elderly" (7). Byteway concludes that gerontologists should pay greater heed to the theoretical significance of chronological age and age-identity and less to age statuses.

Older people's resistance to age-defined labels is understandable given that western culture tends to "systematically devalue, marginalize, and discriminate" against older people (27). Thompson et al (2) study concludes that the myths of aging that we are fed in youth and middle age do not fit the lived experiences of many older people; hence, the grandparents in their study do not recognize themselves in the stereotypical images of later life. Saying 'I don't feel old' is "a cry of protest against a myth that causes pain and fear: a call for the recognition of human individuality and resourcefulness at any age". Further, Minichiello et al (28) in their Australian research into the meanings and experiences of ageism, found that older people themselves exhibit ageist attitudes; older participants' descriptions of oldness consisted of an extensive list of negative terms including: unattractive, burden, lonely, vulnerable, and unproductive. It is unsurprising, therefore, that older people themselves do not identify themselves with the word 'old'; as Andrews argues, "what rational, non-depressive person would?" (29).

In the present study, although participants said that they never pretended to be younger than they were, older age was associated with physical and mental decline. Expectations that older age necessarily involves illness and disability is a common idea (27), despite studies showing that functional impairment is less than what the stereotypes would suggest (22,30). The Bowling et al (22) survey of people aged 65 or over found that that physical health and functional status were the main predictors of subjective age and therefore advocate the use of a measure of subjective age, in addition to chronological age, to enhance sensitivity in aging research. Although participants in the present study said that they did not feel old, when they felt ill or tired, they became aware that their bodies were changing and tended to link this with aging (2,20). This supports Rae (32) who found that one of the most typical kinds of situations where the older woman may begin to think of herself as old was during a period of illness, disability, or 'general weariness'. Such a view is reflected by many people, what-ever their age. For example, in his column in the Times Magazine, John Diamond (33) described his declining physical state, brought on by cancer, as making him feel like an old person. Diamond writes,

> "Never mind middle age. I have skipped the better part of the premium-grade life-begins-at-years and jumped straight into decrepitude...".

Consistent with other research (2,28,34), what was clear is that regardless of whether participants had noticed changes in themselves physically, it was apparent that they expected to suffer either physical or mental decline or both as they aged. As Cremin (35) and Nilsson et al (10) also found, participants tended to draw a distinction between being old and feeling old. The former refers to chronological years—a physical state—the later to state of mind—a psychological state (36).

Such a distinction between mind and body has been explored through the concept of embodiment: "the experience of the lived body" (37). According to Merleau-Ponty (38), all human perception is embodied; we cannot perceive anything and our senses cannot function independently of our bodies. Yet we are not always conscious of our bodies, the body tends to be 'taken-for-granted' or 'absent', except in times when our bodies are not functioning as intended—such as when we are in pain, ill, or dying (34,39). In terms of later life, because we are more likely to experience ill health and disability as we age (40), in addition to visible changes in physical appearance, such as graying hair and wrinkles, understandably we become more aware of our bodies as we grow older. As Featherstone and Wernick(4) state, "It is a truism to say that aging is about the body". Encouragingly, Heikkinen (31) found that the 90-year-old men and women in her study no longer seemed troubled by personal anxieties and concerns and rarely mentioned their illnesses or pains.

   In our study, participants did not deny that they were growing older, but rather resisted the application of aging stereotypes to themselves. Participants' stories show that the unpleasant aspects of growing older cannot be denied; their comments, however, also indicate that their attitudes, behavior, and actions could to some extent, help later life to be a more positive experience. The oldest participants (over the ages of 80 and 90 years) took pride in their age as their stories about celebrating birthdays illustrate (7). Further, comments such as Brian's, that he was having an "older people's day" when interviewed, indicate that older people, like everyone, have some days that are better than others (41).

CONCLUSIONS

The results of this study suggest an ongoing dialogue between differing conceptions of what it is like to grow older and to be older; as Gilleard and Higgs (42) contest, in post-modern society:

> "Aging has become more complex, differentiated and ill defined, experienced from a variety of perspectives and expressed in variety of ways at different moments in people's lives."

Personal meanings of aging, as reflected in participants' narratives, revealed that aging is not one thing or another. Adopting a negative/positive stance to later life, therefore, is too simplistic; not taking into account that for all older people, "life's experiences are positioned somewhere on a continuum, with some good days and some bad days" (41). Everyone—whatever their age—can identify with such a sentiment; such experiences are not peculiar to later life.

   Perhaps we have to acknowledge that growing older is a normal and respectable, indeed an ordinary part of the human condition. As one participant, George Daley (79) reflected,

> "To me growing older is a continuation, it goes on all through life. I don't look upon old age as such as something separate and it certainly isn't something that I look upon as a bogey, it's just life."

ACKNOWLEDGEMENTS

This chapter is an updated version of an earlier published paper (Clarke A, Warren L. Growing older – the good, the bad and the ugly: Subjective views of aging. Int J Disabil Hum Dev 2006;5(1):61-7).

REFERENCES

1.   Clarke A. Looking back and moving forward: a bio-graphical approach to aging. Dissertation. Sheffield, UK: Dept Sociological Studies, Univ Sheffield, 2001.
2.   Thompson P, Itzin, C, Abendstern M. I don't feel old: the experience of later life. Oxford, UK: Oxford Univ Press, 1992.
3.   Katz S. Imagining the life-span. In: Featherstone M, Wernick A, eds. Images of aging. London, UK: Routledge, 1995:61-75.
4.   Featherstone M, Wernick A, eds. Images of aging. Cultural representations of later life. London, UK: Routledge, 1995.
5.   Midwinter E. Ten years before the mast of old age. Generations Rev 1991,1: 4-6.
6.   Hazan H. Old age Constructions and deconstructions. Cambridge, UK: Cambridge Univ Press, 1994.
7.   Bytheway, B Age-identities and the celebration of birthdays. Aging Soc 2005;16:613-21.
8.   Johnson ML. That was your life: a biographical approach to later life. In: Carver, V, Liddiard P, eds. Aging population. Sevenoaks: Hodder Stoughton, 1976.
9.   Featherstone M, Hepworth M. Aging and old age: reflections on the postmodern life course. In: Bytheway, B, Keil,T, Allat, P. Bryman, A. eds. Becoming and being old: Sociological approaches to later life. London, UK: Sage, 1989:143-57.
10.   Nilsson M, Sarvimaki, A, Ekman S. Feeling old: being in a phase of transition in later life. Nurs Inquiry 2001;7: 41-9.
11.   Mauthner N, Doucet, A. Reflections on voice-centred relational method: analysing maternal and domestic voices. In: Ribbens J, Edwards E, eds. Feminist dilemmas in qualitative research. Public knowledge and private lives. London, UK: Sage, 1998:119-46.
12.   Wengraf T. Qualitative research interviewing: Bio-graphic narrative and semi-structured methods. London, UK: Sage, 2001.
13.   Gubrium JF, Holstein JA. Aging and everyday life. Oxford, UK: Blackwell, 2000.
14.   Arber S, Ginn J. Health and illness in later life. In: Field D, Taylor S. eds. Sociological perspectives on health, illness and health care. London, UK: Blackwell, 1998.

15.   Palmore E. Guest editorial: Ageism in gerontological language. Gerontologist 2000;40:645.

16.   Minois G. The History of old age. Cambridge, UK: Polity Press, 1989.

17.   Jewell A, ed. Spirituality and aging. London, UK: Jessica Kingsley, 1999.

18.   Ågren M. Life at 85 and 92: A qualitative longitudinal study of how the oldest old experience and adjust to the increasing uncertainty of existence. Int J Aging Hum Dev 1998;47:105-17.

19.   Nilsson M, Ekman S, Sarvimaki, A. Aging with joy or resigning to old age: older people's experiences of their quality of life. Health Care Later Life 1998;3:94-110.

20.   Heikkinen RL. Patterns of experienced aging with a Finnish Cohort. Int J Aging Hum Dev 1993;36:269-77.

21.   O'Brien SJ, Conger PR. No time to look back: approaching the finish line of life's course. Int J Aging Hum Dev 1991;33:75-87.

22.   Bowling A, See-Tai, S, Ebrahim S, Gabriel Z, Solanki, P. Attributes of age-identity. Aging Soc 2005; 25:479-500.

23.   Kaufman SR. The ageless self: Sources of meaning in late life. Madison, WI, USA: Univ Wisconsin Press, 1986.

24.   Matthews S. The social world of old women. Beverly Hills, CA, USA: Sage, 1979.

25.   Bengston VL, Reedy MN, Gordon C. Aging and self-conceptions: personality processes and social contexts. In: Birren JE, Schaie KW, eds. Handbook of the psy-chology of aging. New York, NY, USA: Van Nostrand Reinhold, 1985.

26.   Tulle-Winton E. Growing old and resistance: towards a new cultural economy of old age? Aging Soc 1999; 19:281-99.

27.   Bernard M, Davies V. Our aging selves: reflections on growing older. In: Bernard M, Phillips, J, Machin L, Davies V, eds. Women aging: Changing identities, chal-lenging myths. London, UK: Routledge, 2000.

28.   Minichiello V, Browne J, Kendig H. Perceptions and consequences of ageism: views of older people. Aging Soc 2000;20:253-78.

29.   Andrews M. The seductiveness of agelessness. Aging Soc 1999; 19:301-18.

30.   Reed J, Clarke C. Nursing older people: constructing need and care. Nurs Inquiry 1999;6:208-15.

31.   Heikkinen R. The experience of aging and advanced old age: a ten-year follow up. Aging Soc 2004;24:567-82.

32.   Rae H. Older women and identity maintenance in later life. Can J Aging 1990;9:248-67.

33.   Diamond J. Untitled. Times Magazine August 29, 1998: 75.

34.   Heikkinen R. Aging in an autobiographical context. Aging Soc 2000;20:467-83.

35.   Cremin MC. Feeling old versus being old: views of troubled aging. Soc Sci Med 1992;34:1305-15.

36. Fairhurst E. Growing old gracefully as opposed to 'mutton dressed as lamb'. In: Nettleton S, Watson J, eds. The body in everyday life. London, UK: Routledge, 1998:258-75.

37. Lawler J. Knowing the body and embodiment: methodologies discourse and nursing. In: Lawler J, ed. The body in nursing. South Melbourne, Australia: Churchill Livingstone, 1997.

38. Merleau-Ponty M. Phenomenology of perception. London, UK: Routledge Kegan Paul, 1962.

39. Nettleton S, Watson J. eds. The body in everyday life. London, UK: Routledge, 1998.

40. Department of Health. National Service Framework for Older People. London, UK: HMSO, 2001.

41. Feldman S. 'Please don't call me 'dear' older women's narratives of health care. Nurs Inquiry 2001; 6(4):269-76.

42. Gilleard C, Higgs P. Cultures of aging: Self, citizen and the body. London, UK: Prentice Hall, 2000.

PART ONE:

QUALITY OF CARE IN RESIDENTIAL CARE CENTERS

CHAPTER 1
Positive events in care homes

Mark Faulkner, Sue Davies and Mike Nolan

The Combined Assessment of Residential Environments (CARE) profiling tool evaluates the frequency of positive events experienced by residents, relatives, and staff in care home settings. It is hoped that feedback from this tool will both reinforce good care home practice and identify areas for change based on the experiences of all major stakeholders. The development of CARE has been presented previously but in this chapter the process of analysis will be presented using data drawn from a single care home (residents, n=11; relatives, n=16; and staff, n=14). CARE was completed using one-to-one interviews (residents and staff) and a postal submission (relatives) yielding 41 completed questionnaires. Data analysis involved integrating the quantitative and qualitative aspects of the tool to generate a comprehensive profile of events at the home. This is displayed as two thematic profiles summarising the positive and negative experiences of those living and working in the home. The relevance of the profiles as a potential means of promoting change in the home are discussed with reference to the underlying theoretical rationale for the CARE profiles approach.

INTRODUCTION

As the levels of physical and cognitive frailty among older residents of care homes continue to rise, concerns about maintaining quality of life and quality of care remain (1,2). Despite recent legislative changes, there is still scope for significant improvement (3), but the challenges of introducing and sustaining change in care home settings are well documented (4-6). Emerging theory suggests that a positive 'culture of care' within care homes is far more likely when the needs of all major stakeholders, that is residents, relatives and staff, are identified and addressed (7). To this end, researchers at the University of Sheffield have developed the Combined Assessment of Residential Environments (CARE) profiles. This approach to practice development invites residents, relatives, and staff within a care home to assess how frequently they have encountered a series of 'positive events' during the previous month (two months in the case of relatives). These 'events' are everyday occur-rences within long-term care settings that are 'positive' in the sense that they elicit emotions such as happiness, joy and personal satisfaction (8-9). The purpose of the CARE profiles is to guide practice development by enhancing awareness of the needs of others, both within and between the key stakeholder groups. The CARE profiles are underpinned by two main theoretical approaches, one from the general psychological literature (positive events) and the other developed specifically from extensive previous work with older people and both paid and family carers (the senses framework).

The link between positive events—for example, enjoying exercise or social activities and well-being—is well established in the literature. Research has consistently shown that exposure to a greater number of positive events can enhance positive affect (or positive mood) (10-12) and self-esteem (12-14), whilst buffering the effects of negative events on daily self-esteem and depressive thinking (15-16). Others have suggested that experiencing positive events may act as 'breathers' from stress; 'sustainers' of coping effort; and 'restorers' for persons who suffer from chronic illnesses like arthritis (17). For example, Zautra and Smith (18) demonstrated that positive events, such as expressions of love and affection, receiving gifts, going out with friends and being praised, play an important role in buffering the relationship between perceived stress and pain for people with rheumatoid arthritis.

Clearly, therefore, experiencing positive events is likely to enhance the quality of life of residents within care homes. This is consistent with the person-centered approach to care that is currently being widely promoted in the United Kingdom (UK) in such initiatives as the National Service Framework for Older People (NSF) (19). Although the NSF provides useful guidance to those caring for older people, extensive empirical work has suggested the utility of a relationship-centered approach to care (20-21) underpinned by the Senses Framework (22-24). This view is predicated on the belief that in the best care environments all the major stakeholders experience 'six senses', these being:

- A sense of security—to feel safe
- A sense of belonging—to feel part of things
- A sense of continuity—to experience links and consistency
- A sense of purpose—to have a personally valuable goal or goals
- A sense of fulfillment—to make progress toward a desired goal or goals
- A sense of significance—to feel that 'you' matter

Evidence from the above studies suggests that if staff are to promote an environment that creates the senses for both residents and relatives, then they need to experience the senses themselves. The CARE-profiling approach was developed to identify positive events equating to the senses for each of the above groups and to generate a series of 'profiles' highlighting the positive features of living and working in a home setting, as well as areas in which improvements could be made.

Developing the CARE profiles

A variety of methods has been used to measure the frequency of positive events. Simpler approaches include asking participants to keep a diary (25-26), but there are also a number of questionnaires, e.g. the Life Experiences Scale (27); the Inventory of Small Life Events (28); the Adolescent Perceived Event Scale (29); and the Pleasant Events Schedule (30). Many of these tools were developed with younger people in mind and items may not be relevant to older generations. For example, the Life Experiences Survey includes events such as 'marriage' and 'the end of formal schooling', whilst the Pleasant Events Schedule includes 'being at a fraternity or sorority', 'rock climbing', and 'experiencing childbirth'. Another drawback is the length of questionnaires, with the Adolescent Perceived Event Scale having 164 items and the Pleasant Events Schedule 320 items. Consequently, authors have attempted to adapt these scales to suit their precise needs. This process has included removing items, adapting items for specific groups, and introducing new items. For instance, Logsdon and Teri's revision of the Pleasant Events Schedule for people with Alzheimer's disease contains just 20 of the 320 original items (31).

Given our desire to generate a series of positive events relevant to three differing stakeholder groups, we decided to generate a new series of questionnaires using an Event Frequency Approach adapted from earlier work by Faulkner (32). The Event Frequency Approach emphasizes the importance of involving representatives from all target-groups (e.g. residents, relatives, and staff) in the generation of questionnaire items (e.g. positive events). This process is conducted in two stages; 'event nomination' and 'event judgment'. During 'event nomination', positive events are solicited from the representatives of each target group. These events are then edited and placed into a list. Following this step, the representatives are asked to judge the relative importance of each event (event judgment), thus enabling the selection of only the most important events (items) for each questionnaire. In generating the CARE profiles questionnaire, the events nominated were consistent with the 'Senses Framework', which was used as a means of thematically balancing the questionnaires, thereby ensuring that a broad range of events were represented. To achieve this, events were initially categorized based on their most likely outcome in terms of the Senses Framework (21). Although this process required an extrapolation of outcome, most events related easily to a particular 'sense'. Once categorized, the five most important events following 'event judgment' (i.e. with the highest mean score) were selected for each of the six 'senses' to create a 30 item questionnaire. Examples of these items are presented in Figure 1 with the related 'sense' shown in parenthesis.

To determine event frequencies, an ordinal scale of "never, rarely, sometimes, usually and always" was selected, assuming that "always" represents an ideal frequency for the participant. The responses "Not applicable" and "Don't know" were also added to the response list in an attempt to classify missing data. The response categories were scored as:

Never = 0,
Rarely = 1,
Sometimes = 2,
Usually = 3, and
Always = 4,

producing a total score ranging from 0 to 120 (4 x 30 items) for each subscale. The CARE scores increase commensurate with a participant's exposure to positive events in the home setting. However, the ultimate goal is not to produce an overall score for each questionnaire but rather a 'profile' based on the median score for each of the 30 items. The timeframe over which frequencies of events were to be retrospectively judged was set at one month for residents and staff and two months for relatives. These timeframes were considered adequate for participants to have a feel for how often a particular event happened in a home.

CARE residents
- In the last month, were staff presentable? (significance)
- In the last month, did staff have time to talk with you? (belonging)

CARE Staff
- In the last month, was the home fully staffed for each shift? (continuity)
- In the last month, did staff have the skills to provide the care that residents needed? (security)

CARE relatives/visitors
- In the last two months, did staff appreciate your involvement in your relative's care? (achievement)
- In the last two months, could you take part in activities and games with your relative when you wanted? (purpose)

Response options
Never----Rarely----Sometimes----Usually----Always---//--N/A----Don't know

---

Figure 1. Examples of items from the three CARE questionnaires

In addition to the structured items, three open-ended questions give participants the opportunity to respond freely about their experiences in the home. Examples taken from the 'staff' questionnaire are as follows: "What do you enjoy most about working here?" (Item 31); "What do you enjoy least about working here?" (Item 32); and "Is there anything you would like to change about working here?" (Item 33). Similar questions are also provided in the residents' and relatives' questionnaires. Comments in response to these questions were found to be highly relevant to the environment being assessed and are important in the profiling process. A detailed account of the development of the CARE profiles themselves can be found in Faulkner et al (54).

To date, pilot studies have used CARE in four homes. The initial findings show that the questionnaire yields reliable information with alpha coefficients ranging from 0.70-0.89 for residents; 0.91-0.94 for relatives, and 0.78-0.92 for staff. More important, the feedback from home managers indicates that CARE profiles accurately capture events occurring in the home during the previous month. (The CARE profile questionnaires are reproduced in Appendixes 1, 2, and 3). Having provided a background to the purpose of CARE, we now describe a method of generating and interpreting the CARE profiles using data from a single care home. The work upon which this paper is based was undertaken between February 2004 and June 2005.

OUR STUDY

The chapter draws upon data collected from one of four privately owned nursing homes involved in the initial piloting of CARE. The home was based in the North of England and had 66 places for residents with a range of physical and cognitive disabilities. At the time of data collection, the home had failed to achieve 16 of the 33 minimum standards assessed at its most recent care-home inspection. Furthermore, four weeks before data collection, the home manager resigned leaving an acting manager from the regular staff in charge. The study was approved by the acting home manager, as well as by the local research ethics committee. Informed consent was sought from all prospective participants involved in this study.

The residents were selected by staff on the basis that they had been living in the home for at least one month and would be capable of answering a 30 item questionnaire. Consequently, 14 residents were approached, but two declined to participate and one was unable to complete the questionnaire. The 11 remaining participants included 7 females and 4 males, with a mean age of 78 years. Staff participants were selected on the basis that they had worked in the home for at least one month and were regular staff (i.e. not agency staff). Overall, 16 care staff were approached, with two declining to participate. The 14 remaining participants included 11 females and 3 males, with a mean age of 33 years (n = 10 Health Care Assistants; n = 4 Registered Nurses). All staff participants were involved in 'hands-on' care with residents.

Relatives/visitors were identified on the basis that they were the principal visitor and that they had visited the home on at least six occasions in the previous two months. As the addresses of relatives/visitors were confidential, the home assumed responsibility for posting out the CARE question-naires. Unfortunately, the home staff failed to record how many were sent, thus the response rates cannot be calculated. Nevertheless, 16 replies were received from nine females and seven males, with a mean age of 61 years.

For residents and staff, CARE was administered by one of the authors to preserve the anonymity of participants and to reduce the risk of bias. During administration, the question-naires were presented face-to-face in the cases of residents and staff, with residents preferring the items to be read to them. This prevented questionnaires, which may have been carrying sensitive information, from being overseen by others in the home if left unattended. It was also felt that this approach would enhance response rates and reduce the possibility of participants conferring on particular questions. Relatives' questionnaires were sent in the post for self-completion and return.

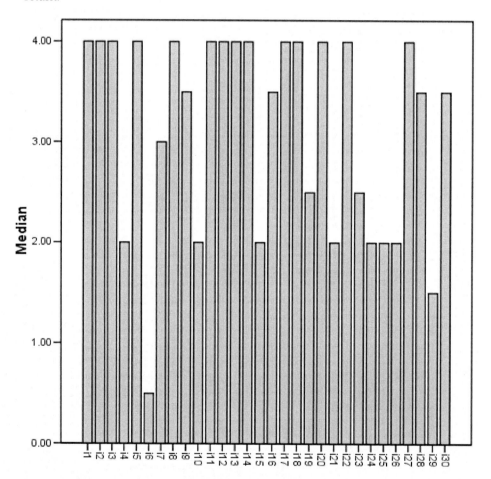

Figure 2. Frequencies of positive events experienced by residents

Activities

Low frequency events

Did the staff provide your relative with interesting things to do? (Relatives)

Were you involved in games and activities with residents during each shift?

(Staff)

Were mealtimes enjoyable? (Residents)

Were you provided with enjoyable things to do? (Residents)

Could you pursue your interests? (Residents)

Did staff encourage you to help yourself? (Residents)

Could you have food and drink when you wanted to? (Residents)

Comments from the open ended questions (items 32-33)

Lack of activities and stimulation (5) (Relatives):
- Should involve residents in making/creating/baking simple items
- Should allow residents to sit in the garden when sunny and warm
- Should sing-songs with old-time themes
- Should read a story or a few poems
- Food unimaginative: Low in fresh vegetables even when in season.

Field note: The activities coordinator recently left and has not been replaced.

Figure 3. Combined findings for the negative theme 'Activities'. The data were drawn from: (1) low frequency events (items 1-30); (2) least enjoyable experiences (item 32), and (3) suggested changes (item 33)

Following data collection, the participants' responses were entered onto the Statistical Package for the Social Sciences (SPSS) by group (residents, staff, relatives), using the scoring system mentioned previously. This system led to the construction of a profile of median item scores for each group, showing a snapshot of positive event frequencies for the month in question. Figure 2 shows the event profile for residents. Events showing the highest and lowest frequencies were then selected from each profile. A high frequency event is any event scoring 4. A low frequency event is any event scoring 2 or less. Thus the high frequency events from figure 2 (residents) are 1, 2, 3, 5, 8, 11, 12, 13, 14, 17, 18, 20, 22 and 27; and the low frequency events are 4, 6, 10, 15, 21, 24, 25, 26 and 29. Following this, the participants' responses from the final three 'open ended' questions were summarized as short phrases.

The quantitative and qualitative aspects of CARE (all groups combined) were then broken down into broadly positive and negative themes. Positive themes used data drawn from: (1) high frequency events (items 1-30); and (2) 'enjoyable' experiences (item 31): Negative themes used data drawn from: 1/ low frequency events (from items 1-30); 2/ 'least enjoyable' experiences (item 32); and 3/ suggested changes (item 33). Figure

3 presents findings for the negative theme 'Activities'. It commences with low frequency items from questions 1-30, which suggest that residents do not engage in stimulating activities in the home. Following this there is a summary of comments from the open-ended questions (items 32-33). It is evident that the lack of activities for residents in the home is a particular concern for relatives.

The final step in the analysis involved writing a short review for each of the above positive and negative themes. The review attempted to use language consistent with the responses of participants wherever possible. For example, if the median response to the residents' questionnaire item 'Did staff respond quickly when you asked for help?' was 2 (i.e. sometimes), then the review would say, "Residents sometimes felt that staff hadn't responded quickly to requests for help." Similarly, when using qualitative data, every attempt was made to preserve the meaning of a participant's original statement.

This analysis can also be extended using the 'senses framework' (21) to evaluate the potential ramifications of events on those living and working in a care home, by considering whether an event would be likely to enhance (or negate) an individual's sense of security, belonging, continuity, purpose, achievement and/or significance. Although the link between an individual's experience of 'events' and their experience of the 'senses' was not explicitly validated with participants, we feel that high-lighting the potential for particular events to create or inhibit possibilities for experiencing the senses can be a useful educational tool within the care home environment.

OUR FINDINGS

A review of positive and negative themes from the nursing home in question is provided in box 1-2. The positive themes review highlights promising aspects of the home, including the friendliness of staff, caring relationships, and the promotion of independence. The negative themes review, entitled 'areas for improvement,' highlights three primary areas of concern: poor staffing levels, resident activities, and communication. Themes are analyzed from the perspective of the senses framework throughout (see sections in italics).

A large section of the 'positive' themes review concerns structural aspects of the home, e.g. that residents' rooms are peaceful, tidy, and have a telephone. However, staff were also praised for their friendly and professional manner. Relatives found staff approachable and appreci-ative of the relatives' involvement as caregivers. Residents felt that staff encouraged them to be independent. These positive findings are important because they provide the assessor with an opportunity to provide constructive feed-back that emphasizes both the positive and the negative aspects of a home. CARE feedback ought to present an opportunity to celebrate what is good about a home as well as pointing the way toward future service development. The aim is to reinforce good practice and motivate staff toward providing even better standards of care in the future.

This opportunity will be missed completely if the feedback process produces demoralized staff.

Box 1. Summary of findings from use of CARE profiles in one nursing home

Positive themes review

The home environment

Residents found their rooms peaceful if they wanted to rest, and suitable to welcome visitors. Residents maintained the tidy appearance of their rooms with help from care staff and housekeepers. Furthermore, the presence of residents' own ornaments and occasionally furniture gave the room a familiar and homely feel. Residents had extra seating for guests in their room. Residents also had access to a telephone in their room, enabling them to contact family and friends when they wanted. [*The familiar surroundings in residents' rooms would help them to experience a 'sense of continuity', or an awareness of links and consistency. Furthermore, residents' attempts to maintain the appearance of their own rooms for visitors may provide them with a 'sense of purpose'*]. Relatives found the home clean and fragrant. They also commented that the rooms were a comfortable temperature, despite the hot weather. Both residents and relatives noted that the corridors and walkways were free from obstruction enabling them to travel safely around the home. [*This is conducive to residents and relatives experiencing a 'sense of security'*]. Both residents and relatives found that staff respected their belongings, especially residents' clothes, which were neatly put away rather than "shoved in a draw." [*This may promote a 'sense of significance;' by helping residents to feel recognised and valued as a person of worth*].

Friendly staff

Relatives found staff approachable and professional. When visiting the home, staff were welcoming and allowed them time with their loved one without unnecessary intrusion. Relatives also found staff appreciative of their involvement in their loved ones care [*These circumstances are conducive to relatives experiencing a 'sense of belonging', i.e. they will feel a part of things; a 'sense of significance', i.e. they will feel that they matter; and a 'sense of achievement', i.e. that staff have recognised their contribution to their loved one's care*].

Caring relationships

Residents suggested that staff treated them with respect ('like adults'), checking in on them regularly to make sure they were comfortable. Staff also appeared pleased when residents achieved things for themselves. It was also noted that staff were aware of residents' privacy needs. For example, they would knock before entering a residents' room and ensure that their privacy was maintained when performing a personal task like bathing or toileting. [*These circumstances are conducive to residents experiencing a 'sense of significance' and 'achievement'*]. Relatives felt that staff had the necessary skills to look after their loved one and trusted them with private (or confidential) information. [*These circumstances highlight that relatives feel 'secure' in their relationships with staff*].

Promoting independence

Residents indicated that they could please themselves what they did during the day. They were able to choose when to get up in the morning and could maintain their own appearance as they liked (e.g. choice of clothes etc). [*These circumstances are conducive with residents experiencing a 'sense of continuity'*]. Relatives were kept up-to-date with changes affecting their loved one. Staff would provide clear information and involve relatives in the decision making process. [*This is conducive with relatives experiencing a 'sense of purpose'*]. Relatives were also free to take part in their loved ones' care and could take them on trips outside the home, something that residents particularly enjoyed. Relatives also had opportunities to comment on the running of the home. Care staff found their work interesting and were encouraged to use their initiative.

The responses detailed above identify a range of positive features of the home. However, the profiles also suggested areas for improvement (see box 2).

Box 2. Summary of findings from use of CARE profiles in one nursing home (areas for improvement/causes of concern)

Areas for improvement/causes of concern
Poor staffing levels

This was a prominent theme emerging from the profiles. Staff found that they sometimes felt rushed when caring for residents. For example, one member of staff commented "Two carers to feed eight residents during mealtimes is unreasonable." Consequently, staff sometimes resented having to deliver what they perceived to be poorer standards of care purely because of time constraints. [*This may inhibit the potential for staff to experience a 'sense of achievement' which requires that staff are able to provide good care and feel satisfied with their efforts*]. Residents and relatives were also aware of the time constraints on staff. For example, residents felt that staff didn't always have enough time to talk with them. [*This may be contrary to residents experiencing a 'sense of significance'. That older people feel recognised and valued as a person of worth*]. Furthermore, residents noted that they didn't always know who would be looking after them from one day to the next (possibly due to the use of agency and other temporary staff). [*This may limit the extent to which residents experience a 'sense of continuity' which requires seamless consistent care delivered within an established relationship by known people*]. Staff commented that more carers, especially during periods of high occupancy and/or dependence in the home, would ease their pressure of work. This would allow them more one-to-one contact with residents and increase the continuity of the service they provided as a whole.

Resident activities

Residents, relatives and staff suggested that there was very little in the way of resident activities in the home. This might have been due to the recent departure of the activities coordinator. Furthermore, whilst staff generally enjoyed being involved in resident activities, they seem to have been unable to pursue this, possibly due to workload constraints [*This may be contrary to residents experiencing a 'sense of purpose' which requires that residents have opportunities to engage in purposeful activities in order to facilitate the constructive passing of time. Furthermore, if staff were unable to provide resident activities due to workload constraints, this could lead to them experiencing a diminished sense of achievement, i.e. they were unable to contribute towards therapeutic goals as appropriate*]. Several relatives made suggestions about the types of activities that their relatives would like, including baking, making/creating simple items, sing-along, stories/poems, and enjoying the garden in the summer (weather permitting). Some residents also suggested that they could not pursue their interests. A second issue related to mealtimes, which were not considered enjoyable by some residents. Unfortunately, the data provided few clues as to why this was, but one relative did point out that meals were low in fresh vegetables, even when in season.

Communication

Findings indicate that communication between residents, relatives and staff could be improved in several areas.

1/ Staff - Residents: Staff felt that they could not always have a meaningful conversation with residents (presumably due to a cognitive impairment). Residents, on the other hand, felt that staff did not always enjoy spending time with them (although they were always friendly) and showed a limited interested in their family and friends. Furthermore, residents felt that they were not always asked their opinion on things that affected them [*This may be contrary to residents experiencing several senses including: a 'sense of belonging', i.e. opportunities to maintain and form meaningful and reciprocal relationships; 'a sense of purpose', i.e. to exercise discretionary choice; and 'a sense of significance', i.e. to feel recognised and valued as a person of worth*]. Finally, two residents remarked that occasionally staff (especially at night) had poor English and they would struggle to understand them.

2/ Staff – Relatives: Staff felt that relatives were not always openly appreciative of their work [*thus missing opportunities to enhance their 'sense of achievement'*].

3/ Staff – Staff: Staff indicated that they were not always informed about matters affecting the home. Also, one member of staff suggested that the handover from night to day staff could have been better. [*This may be contrary to staff experiencing a sense of belonging, i.e. to feel part of a community of practitioners; and continuity, i.e. that expectations and standards of care are communicated clearly and consistently*].

MISCELLANEOUS REQUESTS
Prominent requests included remarks from both staff and residents that the staff wages should be increased, especially for care assistants. Several relatives also suggested that the home needed better air conditioning and a hot/cold drinks machine (evidently there used to be a drinks machine for relatives, but this was no longer available). Less prominent issues include a staff comment requesting basic training for all staff regarding dementia. There were also two minor comments from relatives, firstly that there was a need for a 'clear' relatives information pack and secondly that the taps in some of the rooms leaked and required maintenance.

Poor staffing levels and workload constraints feature prominently in the negative themes review. Evidence for this was provided by all stakeholder groups, in both the quantitative and the qualitative components of CARE. Consequently, several aspects of social care were com-promised including communal activities (e.g. games, sing-songs), and one-to-one staff/resident interactions (assisting with eating, socializing). Instead, it appears that an emphasis on simply 'getting the work done' has contributed to staff becoming dissatisfied with their work and socially detached from residents.

In taking initiatives for change forward, the Senses Framework seemed to be useful in highlighting the impact of positive/negative events on the subjective wellbeing of individuals within the stakeholder groups. For example, the 'negative themes profile' shows how residents were exposed to circumstances that failed to optimize five of the six senses (continuity, belonging, purpose, achievement, and significance). These circumstances have to be addressed through the development of strategies to enhance the senses, and thus optimize the residents' wellbeing. To assist this process, research by Nolan et al (24) described the context of care within which the senses flourish for all stakeholder groups. Thus, strategies to enhance belonging for residents ought to provide "opportunities to maintain and/or form meaningful and reciprocal relationships, to feel part of a community or group as desired." Whilst offering a therapeutic direction, this 'context of care' does not provide examples of actual strategies. Examples of strategies can be found in the work of Davies et al (23); yet, there is scope for more work in this area.

Providing feedback
The need to structure feedback to staff, residents, and relatives to explore such issues further is a potentially important part of the CARE profiling approach. Extensive work within care homes has shown that the Senses Framework provides an accessible means of providing feedback and enables stakeholders to recognize and to articulate the goals of care within a long-

term care setting (33-35). However, the most appropriate methods for providing feedback, together with the impact of such feedback on care experiences, has yet to be systematically identified. Experience within the current project suggests the importance of enabling all stakeholders to feel 'safe' in responding to feedback and negotiating the way in which this approach is managed is one way to achieve this goal. A range of options should be offered, including written summaries in an accessible format and verbal presentations to meetings of staff, residents, and relatives. The individuals responsible for collating and analyzing the responses to CARE should also make themselves available on a one-to-one basis, if necessary.

Concerning the feedback process, our experiences to date in four homes suggest the following guidelines:

- The feedback process must be negotiated at the outset
- The manager should have the opportunity to view the feedback before it is distributed throughout the home
- Both written and verbal feedback is desirable. Written feedback must be in plain language and large print to be accessible
- Participants should be encouraged to identify their own solutions and develop action plans with specific goals and targets
- Sustained change is more likely if problem areas are prioritized and one or two issues are worked on at a time
- Ideally, feedback would be channeled via an action group (34-35) with representatives of all stakeholders, who would take responsibility for implementing the changes. Existing mechanisms (staff meetings, relatives and residents groups) might also be useful in this respect.

DISCUSSION

The experiences of using CARE profiles within a single home highlight a number of issues that resonate with the wider literature on care homes. Although little literature is available on the effects of understaffing in nursing homes, that which does exist is evocative of the findings from this study. For example, Schnelle et al (36) compared the care provided by highly staffed nursing homes with moderately staffed and low-staffed homes. The authors found that the higher staffed homes performed significantly better on 13 of the 16 care processes assessed. The processes included (a) number of residents engaged in activities; (b) time spent assisting residents with feeding, toileting assists, and (c) exercise activities per hour. Understaffing has also been linked with a high staff turnover (37) and significant increases in staff injury, mostly incurred during moving and handling procedures (38).

Unfortunately, increasing staffing levels can be problematic for home managers, especially if operating under a 'one size fits all' policy determined by an external agency. Nevertheless, this is an important issue that clearly impacts on the culture of care within a home. Consequently, there may be a need to sensitize staffing policy to individual homes with consideration being given to the current staffing complement (including level of education and experience), resident dependency levels and room occupancy. Also noteworthy is that staffing levels tend to be determined to satisfy conditions of adequacy rather than excellence. There is a need to identify staffing levels that support a good quality of life for residents, not just resident safety. CARE profiling can be a helpful tool in identifying the impact of staff shortages on residents, on their families, and on other staff.

In relation to activities, recreation, social and community activities, and personal development are key domains in quality of life at all ages. Yet, despite evidence suggesting the protective effects of purposeful and meaningful activity for older individuals (39-41), observational studies suggest that older people living in care homes continue to spend much of the time without much to occupy them. According to Ballard et al (40), for example almost 50% of residents' time is spent asleep, socially withdrawn, or inactive, with only 14% being spent in some form of communication with others. Only 3% of their time involves constructive activity. Pruchno et al (42) found that the most frequent activities for residents were watching television (12% of waking hours) and resting (20%). Staff often lack awareness of the kinds of activities that frail older people, particularly those with cognitive impairment, will find enjoyable and meaningful. Additionally, there is an expectation that activities must be highly structured, usually involving groups of people. Advice and information about the range of activities that are appropriate can enable staff to be more creative in relation to day-to day events, increasing opportunities for meaningful engagement beyond those available in organized activities. Volunteers and family can also enrich the range of activities on offer (43). Raising awareness of this potential is an important component of the CARE profiling exercise.

Finally, a wealth of evidence suggests the importance of effective communication within care homes, in particular communication that supports shared decision-making and the development of reciprocal relationships (43-44). Staff may need support to enable very frail residents to make their views known (45). Staff may also need guidance that will enable them to see spending time simply talking with residents as a priority. A number of evaluation studies have demonstrated improvements in communication between staff and residents following structured intervention programs (46-48). Studies of staff job satisfaction in care homes suggest a relation between job satisfaction and a sense of being involved (49-50). Participation in decision-making by all grades of staff has also been associated with improved outcomes for residents on a range of measures (51-52). Raising awareness of these issues through use of the CARE profiles can suggest appropriate strategies for improving communication.

CONCLUSIONS

In conclusion, attempts to improve quality of life and quality of care within care homes are unlikely to succeed unless those involved are provided with strategies for achieving change. In the context of continuing concerns about whether care homes are meeting the needs of all stakeholders, this case study outlines the administration and analysis of the Combined Assessment of Residential Environments (CARE) profiles approach. (NB. An earlier publication considers the development of CARE and initial pilot data in more detail). The advantages of using CARE are that it is quick to administer, easy to use, and involves residents, relatives, and staff in the assessment process. An important drawback is that gaining sufficient numbers of 'resident' respondents can be difficult, especially when a home has a high proportion of cognitively impaired residents. Consequently, the experiences of such frail and vulnerable residents are not reflected in the CARE-assessment process as it currently stands. It is therefore proposed that an observational schedule focusing specifically on the experiences of cognitively impaired residents is developed to accompany the CARE questionnaires. However, in residential homes in which the majority of residents are capable of participation, CARE provides a valuable means of quality assurance.

A recent poll conducted for the Commission for Social Care Inspection (CSCI) suggested that older people support rigorous inspection of care services. However, the survey also found that older people want the balance of inspection to shift more toward talking to people using the service and their families and spending less time simply observing what goes on and checking paperwork (53). These findings suggest that the current inspection process may not be capturing all the issues of relevance to older people and their families. Recognizing the complexity of the organizations in which long-term care is provided suggests the need to think beyond the needs of individual residents to ensure that the most positive experiences are created (6,54). We suggest that the CARE profiles provide a valuable set of tools for drawing together the views and experiences of the main stakeholders within care home settings, which can then provide a basis for service development.

ACKNOWLEDGMENTS

This research was funded partly by the Department of Health and by the Department of Community, Ageing and Rehabilitation, School of Nursing and Midwifery, University of Sheffield, UK. This chapter is an updated version of an earlier published paper (Faulkner M, Davies S, Nolan M. Evaluating positive events in care homes: A case study using CARE profiling tool. Int J Disabil Hum Dev 2006;5(1):35-44).

REFERENCES

1.   Andrews GJ, Holmes D, Poland B, Lehoux P, Miller K, Pringle D, McGilton K. 'Airplanes are flying nursing homes' geographies in the concepts and locales of gerontological nursing practice. J Clin Nurs 2005; 14(S2):109-20.

2.   National Care Standards Commission. How do we care? The availability of registered care homes and children's homes in England and their performance against National Minimum Standards 2002-03. London, UK: TSO, 2004.

3.   Ashburner C, Meyer J, Johnson B, Smith C. Using action research to address loss of personhood in a continuing care setting. Illness Crisis Loss 2004; 12: 23-37.

4.   McCormack B, McKenna H. Challenges to quality monitoring systems in care homes. Qual Health Care 2001;10:200-1.

5.   Stanley D, Reed J. Opening up care: Achieving principled practice in health and social care institu-tions. London, UK: Arnold, 1999.

6.   Davies S, Nolan M. A relationship-centred approach to working with older people and their families. In: Hinchliff S, Norman S, Schober J, eds. Nursing Practice and Health Care, 4th ed. London, UK: Arnold, 2003.

7.   Diener E. Subjective well-being. Psychol Bull 1984; 93:542-75.

8.   Fisher MN, Snih SA, Ostir GV, Goodwin JS. Positive affect and disability among older Mexican Americans with arthritis. Arthritis Rheum 2004;51:34-9.

9.   David JP, Green PJ, Martin R, Suls J. Differential roles of neuroticism, extraversion and event desirability for mood in daily life: An integrative model of top-down and bottom-up influences. J Pers Soc Psychol 1997;73:150-9.

10.   Gable SL, Reis HT, Elliot AJ. Behavioural activation and inhibition in everyday life. J Pers Soc Psychol 2000;78:1135-49.

11.   Nezlek JB, Plesko RM. Affect and self-based models of relationships between daily events and daily well-being. Pers Soc Psychol Bull 2003;29:584-96.

12.   Butler AC, Hokanson JE, Flynn HA. A comparison of self-esteem liability and low trait self-esteem as vulnerability factors for depression. J Pers Soc Psychol 1994;66:166-77.

13.   Nezlek JB, Gable SL. Depression as a moderator of relationships between positive daily events and day-to-day psychological adjustment. Pers Soc Psychol Bull 2001;27:1692-1704.

14.   Cohen S, Hoberman HM. Positive events and social support as buffers of life change stress. J Appl Soc Psychol 1983;13:99-125.

15.   Dixon WA, Reid JK. Positive events as a moderator of stress-related depressive events. J Couns Dev 2000; 78:343-7.

16.   Folkman S, Moslowitz JT. Positive affect and the other side of coping. Am Psychol 2000;55:647-54.

17.   Zautra AJ, Smith BW. Depression and reactivity to Stress in older women with rheumatoid arthritis and osteoarthritis. Psychol Med 2001;63:6877-96.

18.   Department of Health. National Service Framework for Older People. London, UK: HMSO, 2001.

19.   Tresolini CP, Pew-Fetzer Task Force. Health pro-fessions education and relationships-centred care: A report of the Pew-Fetzer Task Force on advancing psychosocial education. San Francisco, California, USA: Pew Health Professions Commission, 1994.

20.   Nolan MR, Davies S, Brown J, Keady J, Nolan J. Beyond 'person centred' care: A new vision for ger-ontological nursing. J Clin Nur 2004;13:45-53.

21.   Nolan MR. Health and social care: what the future holds for nursing. Keynote address at Third Royal College of Nursing Older Person European Confer-ence and Exhibition, Harrogate, UK, 1997.

22.   Davies S, Laker S, Ellis L. Dignity on the ward: Promoting excellence in Care. good practice in acute hospital care for older people. London, UK: Help the Aged, 1999.

23.   Nolan MR, Davies S, Grant G. Working with older people and their families. Buckingham, UK: Open Univ Press, 2001.

24.   Stone AA. Event content in a daily survey is differentially associated with concurrent mood. J Pers Soc Psychol 1987;52:56-8.

25.   Langston CA. Capitalising on and coping with daily-life events: Expressive responses to positive events. J Pers Soc Psychol 1994;67:1112-25.

26.   Sarason IG, Johnson JH, Siegel JM. Assessing the impact of life changes: Development of the life ex-periences survey. J Consult Clin Psychol 1978; 46: 932-46.

27.   Zautra AJ, Guarnaccia CA, Dohrenwend BP. Measuring small life events. Am J Community Psychol 1986;14,629-55.

28.   Compas BE, Howell DC, Phares V, Williams RA, Ledoux N. Parent and child stress and symptoms: An integrative analysis. Dev Psychol 1989;25:550-9.

29.   MacPhillamy D, Lewinsohn PM. The pleasant events schedule. Eugene: Univ Oregon, USA, 1971.

30.   Logsdon RG, Teri L. The pleasant events schedule—AD: Psychometric properties and relationship to de-pression and cognition in Alzheimer's disease patients. Gerontologist 1997;37:40-5.

31.   Faulkner M. A measure of patient empowerment in hospital environments catering for older people. J Adv Nurs 2001;34:676-86.

32.   Aveyard B, Davies S. Moving forward together: evaluation of an Action Group involving staff and relatives within a nursing home for older people with dementia. Int J Older People Nurs 2006;1:95-104.

33.   Davies S, Darlington E, Powell A, Aveyard B. Developing partnerships at 67 Birch Avenue Nursing Home: The Support 67 action group. Qual Ageing 2003;4:32-7.

34.   Davies S, Powell A, Aveyard B. Developing con-tinuing care: towards a teaching nursing home. Br J Nurs 2002;11:1320-8.

35.   Schnelle JF, Simmons SF, Harrington C, Cadogan M, Garcia E, Bates-Jensen BM. Relationship of nursing home staffing to quality of care. Health Serv Res 2004;39:225-50.

36.   Kovner CT, Harrington C. Study: Correlation between staffing and quality. Am J Nurs 2002;102:65-6.

37.   Shogren E, Calkins A, Wilburn S. Restructuring may be hazardous to your health. Am J Nurs 1996;96:64-6.

38.   Baum CM. The contribution of occupation to function in persons with Alzheimer's disease. J Occup Sci 1995; 2:59-67.

39.   Ballard C, O'Brien J, James I, et al. Quality of life for people with dementia living in residential and nursing home care: the impact of performance on activities of daily living, behavioral and psychological symptoms, language skills, and psychotropic drugs. Int Psycho-geriatr 2001; 13:93-106.

40.   Kiely D, Flacker J. The protective effect of social engagement on 1-year mortality in a long-stay nursing home population. J Clin Epidemiol 2003;56:472-8.

41.   Pruchno RA, Rose MS. Time use by frail older people in different care settings. J Appl Gerontol 2002;21:5-23.

42.   Davies S, Brown-Wilson C. Creating community within care homes. In my home life. London, UK: Help the Aged, 2006.

43.   Davies S, Brown-Wilson C. Shared decision-making in care homes. In my home life. London, UK: Help the Aged, 2006.

44.   Murphy J, Tester S, Hubbard G, Downs M, Mac Donald C. Enabling frail older people with a com-munication difficulty to express their views: the use of Talking Mats[TM] as an interview tool. Health Soc Care Community 2005;1395-107.

45.   Williams K, Kemper S, Hummert ML. Practice con-cepts. Improving nursing home communication: an intervention to reduce elderspeak. Gerontologist 2003; 43:242-7.

46.   Dijkstra K, Bourgeois M, Burgio L, Allen R. Effects of a communication intervention on the discourse of nursing home residents with dementia and their nursing assistants. J Med Speech Lang Pathol 2002;10:143-57.

47.   Jordan FM, Worral LE, Hickson LM, Dodd BJ. The evaluation of intervention programmes for communi-catively impaired elderly people. Eur J Disord Commun 1993;28:63-85.

48.   Atkin M. Factors influencing staff turnover in long-term care. Report to Anchor Housing. Sheffield: Univ Sheffield, UK, 2005.

49.   Hall LM, McGilton KS, Krejci J, Pringle D, Johnston E, Fairley L, Brown M. Enhancing the quality of supportive supervisory behavior in long-term care facilities. J Nurs Adm 2005;35:181-7.

50.   Flesner MK, Rantz MJ. Mutual empowerment and respect: Effect on nursing home quality of care. J Nurs Care Qual 2004;19:193-6.

51.   Rantz MJ, Grando V, Conn V, Zwygart-Staffacher M, Hicks L, Flesner M, Scott J, Manion P, Minner D, Porter R, Maas M. Innovations in long-term care. Getting the basics right: care delivery in nursing homes. J Gerontol Nurs 2003;29:15-25.

52.   Commission for Social Care Inspection. When I get older: What people want from social care services and inspections as they get older. London, UK: CSCI, 2004.

53.   Anderson RA, Issel LM, McDaniel RR. Nursing homes as complex adaptive systems: relationship between management practice and resident outcomes. Nurs Res 2003;52:12-21.

54.   Faulkner M, Davies S, Nolan MR, Brown-Wilson C. Development of the Combined Assessment of Resi-dential Environments (CARE) Profiles. J Adv Nurs 2006;55(6):664-77.

CHAPTER 2
The role of the family in care homes

Isack Kandel and Joav Merrick

Admission to a nursing home for the elderly is a new and difficult phase of life, which can lead to changes in inter-family relationships. Family visits and interaction is often the only communication with the outside world and changes taking place in a society the elderly used to be part of. The visits reinforce the feeling that the family continue to love, care and support them despite their move to the nursing home. Family involvement in support of elderly nursing home residents is essential both in the initial stages of the move and later on. In this chapter we reviewed the literature to determine the contribution of a son/daughter visit to the elderly. We also attempted to examine views of multi-professional staff regarding family visits and whether the staff's attitude to the residents changed as a result of the visits.

INTRODUCTION

Life in a nursing home is a new and difficult phase of life. Moving to a nursing home often leads to changes in inter-family relationships. When elderly adults enter a nursing home, family visits become the pivotal point of their encounters with their relatives and sometimes even with the outer world. Expectations of the new relationship created between residents and their families are manifested in these visits. Family visits have covert participants as well - the nursing home staff.

This chapter examines the place of families in caring for elderly adults after placement in a nursing home. In addition, an attempt is made to reflect the views of elderly nursing home residents as well as of the staff, both nursing assistants and professionals, regarding the significance of family visits of elderly nursing home residents.

As a result of the gradually rising number of elderly adults aged 65 and older in Israel and elsewhere, many more people are moving from the community to nursing homes. Many studies have been conducted on the family contribution to the health and psychosocial well-being of the home-based elderly, but there is not much information on the role assumed by families in caring for elderly nursing home residents or family involvement in the nursing home. A few studies have been conducted on staff perception of the contribution of family involvement in nursing homes (1,2).

CHANGING ATTITUDES

In the past, the move to a nursing home was perceived in a negative manner. Some saw this as a process enforced on the elderly following pressure applied by family members. Elderly adults wished to remain in their family and in the community, while the family requested that they move to a nursing home, in order to relieve themselves of the burden of care and of the responsibilities. The family is supposed to serve as a system of mutual help, a system in which adult children care for their elderly parents. It is commonly assumed that placement of elderly adults in a nursing home marks the end of the family's need to care for them, and from now on the nursing home staff is responsible.

A study from 2001 (3) indicated elements related to the number of family visits and telephone conversations with elderly relatives immediately after moving to a nursing home. The study consisted of interviews with 1,441 significant relatives of elderly residents in a sample of nursing homes located in Maryland, United States. The results of the study indicated that the number of visits and calls declined by 50% after moving to a nursing home, compared to visits and calls reported for the period before the move. This study (3), conducted with a large number of subjects, found other variables which also affected the frequency of family visits. These included:

- Socioeconomic status. The higher the socioeconomic status of elderly residents and their families, the higher frequency of visits and calls
- Geographical proximity. There was a positive correlation between greater residential proximity to the nursing home and the number of visits
- Dementia. Demented elderly residents enjoyed less frequent visits.

Others found that the connection between elderly residents and their relatives continued after moving to a nursing home. They found that many families expressd a wish to continue caring for elderly parents and families believed that their care should be manifested not only in visits to the elderly, rather also in additional care (4).

PLACEMENT AND TRANSITION

When elderly adults move to a nursing home, both they and their families find it difficult. Some families report loss of control, guilt feelings, anger, anxiety, sadness, however also relief, when elderly relatives move to a nursing home. Sometimes family members feel that they have failed in their responsibility to care for the elderly and that they have broken their promise to avoid placement in a nursing home. These feelings linger with the family long after the elderly person has been placed in a nursing home (4,5).

Relatives' wish to keep in contact with the elderly and to care for them even after placement in a nursing home forms new challenges for them, for example how to form contact with the staff? How to maintain contact with the elderly? How to define their position within the new system? (4)

Albeck and Schreiber conducted an extensive study (6) examining the visiting patterns of sons and daughters of institutionalized elderly parents from the perspective of the elderly, the visitors and the staff. The purpose was to examine visiting characteristics of sons and daughters, who visited their elderly parents in nursing homes and identify the variables related to these characteristics from the visitors' perspective. In addition, the study examined the implications of the visit for the sons and daughters, and how prolonged coping with the care of an institutionalized elderly parent affected their views and attitudes. It was found that sons and daughters of elderly adults continued to provide them with support in various manners, due to their feeling of commitment and their feelings towards the elderly parent.

A number of scholars claimed that although the role assumed by the family underwent a transition when elderly adults were placed in a nursing home, relationships formed between the family and the elderly adults over many years would not change significantly. If the elderly adult and the family enjoyed a good relationship previously, this relationship would be maintained despite the move to a nursing home, and vice versa – if the relationship was bad, it will probably remain bad after moving to a nursing home (4).

It is customary to assume that the nursing home staff supply the residents' physical needs, while relatives offer psychological support. Early studies emphasized that relatives perform special functions for the elderly, functions that would not have been performed otherwise or by anyone else. This included: nurturing care, encouragement, heart to heart conversations, and socio-emotional help. In addition, was found that sometimes the family was involved in caring for the elderly by counseling the nursing home staff, with the aim of providing residents with individual and sensitive care, rather than by providing direct help (5).

It was found that the role of the family in caring for elderly adults living at home compared to those living at a nursing home, that relatives of elderly nursing home residents provided less help with activities of daily living (ADL) and instrumental activities of daily living (IADL)(5). Despite the hypothesis that families of elderly residents of nursing homes provide almost no physical help, they continued to provide significant quantities of help with activities of daily living (ADL) and instrumental activities of daily living (IADL) (5). Family members can be involved in caring for and maintaining contact with elderly residents of nursing homes in a number of manners. These include:

- Visiting the elderly

- Family events and festive ceremonies held at the nursing home
- Helping the nursing home staff with daily care during family visits
- Taking part in discussions and decisions concerning care
- Transmitting messages and needs of other residents to the nursing home staff
- Measuring and assessing the quality of care, residents' well-being and health (1)

Port et al indicated (3) additional variables that in their opinion affected family visits. Among these variables they stated the attitude of nursing home staff to family visits. In their opinion it is important for the staff to evoke an atmosphere that invites family involvement, with the aim of encouraging family visits.

FAMILY AND STAFF

It is necessary to anticipate struggles and conflicts between the staff, representing the formal institution and the family, due to the different motives of each group. Staff members are motivated by their professional duty, while families are motivated by their commitment to long-term help and love of the elderly. These conflicts might lead to tension between the staff and the families (7).

A negative relationship between the family and the nursing home staff may add to and exacerbate feelings of stress and distress and the family's difficult reactions to elderly adults' institutionalization (5). Poor relationships between staff and families have been found to predict depression, anxiety, and emotional stress among family members. Unsteady staff-family relationships result in a type of distress among nursing home staff (8).

A study conducted by Weman et al (9) examined the opinion of nurses on cooperation with relatives of elderly nursing home residents. 210 nurses responded from a sample of 314 nurses. All the nurses expressed their complete agreement with the need for full cooperation between nursing home staff and families. The nurses recommended to develop models that would deepen and improve cooperation between staff and families. Male nurses thought that families were a helping resource less than female nurses. Nurses with five and more years of seniority expressed the significance of family commitment towards the elderly residents. Moreover, they noted families' need to care for the affairs of the elderly adult. The study conducted in Sweden examined the attitude of nurses to families of elderly nursing home residents. Family members were perceived by nurses as a resource. The nurses thought that it was inappropriate to ask relatives to work together with the staff in caring for the elderly. They thought that help may be manifested in bringing the residents their personal belongings and in transmitting information from the residents to the staff. The nurses had positive feelings for the relatives, but they also claimed that relatives were demanding and that they took staff time. Although nurses thought that it was important for staff to communicate with resident families, they gave this issue a low priority. Nurses did not tend to initiate conversation with relatives and most conversation must be initiated by the family (10).

Studies comparing the nursing home staff definition of family involvement and care for elderly nursing home residents to family definition of the degree of involvement and responsibility showed that families consistently defined more responsibility in their care of elderly residents compared to nursing home staff definition of the families' responsibility (4).

The staff and the family may disagree regarding the role perception of each group. A study performed indicated that relatives often felt that nursing home staff did not recognize or allow for the family's opinion. This staff attitude gave relatives the feeling that they were being ignored and their opinions held no value. Relatives also claimed that staff focused only on technical care, while the family hoped that the staff also assumed responsibility for social and emotional aspects (7).

These disagreements often result from a lack of communication between staff and families. Many elderly nursing home patients, particularly those suffering from cognitive impairments are unable to report their condition and their nursing home experiences to their family. As a result, relatives become dependent on nursing home staff for receiving information about their loved ones. Work pressure at the nursing home makes it difficult and prevents the staff from holding long conversations with relatives, and social and cultural barriers also restrict communication between the groups. The families find themselves in a situation in which they do not receive sufficient information about their relatives and they have difficulty finding staff members with whom they can share their concerns. Some families hesitate to criticize or offer suggestions due to their concern that these remarks will have a negative effect on the staff care of their loved ones (7,8).

Another obstacle to staff-family cooperation are negative stereotypes held by each group. Relatives may not believe the staff and think that it is necessary to monitor the staff constantly. On the other hand, the staff may believe that relatives are unrealistic in their expectations of the help and care provided to elderly nursing home residents. Studies indicated that sometimes staff and families were angry at each other and ignored each other (8). Family involvement has the potential of being a positive contribution to the nursing home setting. This positive influence is manifested in the following areas: Improvement of residents' mental and psychosocial health with reduction of the burden of care imposed on the staff (3).

DISCUSSION

Abraham Harold Maslow (1908-1970) graded the existential needs of human beings in a hierarchy. There are basic needs such as food and accommodation, defense and security, belonging and love, appreciation and respect, and the need for self-fulfillment. Emotional and social needs complement physical needs and cannot substitute for them. Elderly adults' relationship with their family is supposed to provide partial fulfillment of their emotional and social needs.

Interpersonal relations are a significant and important resource for the elderly and they contribute to their mental and healthcare well-being. John Mostyn Bowlby (1907-1990), developer of the attachment theory, stated that the need for attachment continues throughout the entire life cycle. Attachment is an important resource for basic feelings of security. Attachment in old age has recently been studied by Bradley and Cafferty (11), who found that the attachment theory was particularly relevant in the case of elderly adults. The need for attachment leads to a feeling that there is someone close who can help in case of emergency. Attachment patterns of elderly people are related to a variety of results, such as adjustment to chronic illnesses, reaction to the death of a loved one, and mental health. Interpersonal relations represent for lonely and disabled elderly adults feelings of continuity, security, and love, and for this reason they continue to serve as an important source of life meaning.

Relatives' visiting of elderly people holds great significance. These visits contribute to the elderly resident's adjustment to the new setting. The visits reinforce elderly residents' feeling that the family continues to love them and support them despite their move to the nursing home. Family involvement in support of elderly nursing home residents is essential both in the initial stages of the move and later on. This pattern of visits helps elderly residents to adjust to the nursing home and improves their quality of life. Relatives also benefit from the visit, by improving their emotional well-being (5).

Elderly adults' subjective perception of their relationship with their relatives and their satisfaction with the relationship are significant for well-being in old age. These variables are even more important to health and mental well-being than visit frequency. Thus, visit frequency per se is not an exclusive indicator of the quality aspects of family relationships (12).

Studies have shown that there is a significant correlation between elderly loneliness and physical incapacity. Frequent contact with friends, sons and daughters, may reduce the risk of loneliness among the elderly. The data indicates that there is a correlation between functional capacity to perform activities of daily living (ADL) and relationships with relatives and friends and the feeling of loneliness among the elderly (13).

Research findings (14) have led to the conclusion that family is important to elderly nursing home residents. Researchers recommend that nurses organize activities that will include the families. In addition, researchers suggest that relatives take part in birthday celebrations and in organized outings. In their opinion, such activities will prevent the feeling of abandonment experienced by the elderly and provide additional opportunities for relatives to take part in nursing home activities.

Sometimes family visits are the only contact with the world outside the nursing home. The visiting relatives report to the elderly resident on events from the lives of common acquaintances and the more distant family. Reports received from relatives enables the elderly to preserve their connection with the world of the past despite the detachment caused by living in a nursing home.

In old age people experience a not insignificant number of changes and losses. When elderly adults decide on their own initiative or with the support of their family to move to a nursing home they become separated from the life they were used to. When moving to a nursing home, their relationship with relatives changes and is upset. Family visits are a microcosmos characterizing the condition of the elderly in the present. In this review we have attempted to determine the contribution of a son/daughter's visit to the elderly. We have also attempted to examine views of multi-professional staff regarding family visits and whether the staff's attitude to the residents changed as a result of the visits.

ACKNOWLEDGEMENTS

This paper is based upon research conducted by Ms. Yehudit Ostayev and Mr. Roslan Amirhanov at the Pinhas Rozen Nursing Home in Ramat Gan, managed by the "Central European Immigrants" Organization, for a seminar in health administration at the Academic College of Judea and Samaria in Ariel supervised by Isack Kandel.

REFERENCES

1. Port CL, Hebel JR, Gruber-Baldini AL, Baumgarten M, Burton L, Zimmerman S, Magaziner J. Measuring the frequency of contact between nursing home residents and their family and friends. Nurs Res 2003;52(1):52-6.

2. Hertzberg A, Ekman SL. 'We, not them and us?' Views on the relationships and interactions between staff and relatives of older people permanently living in nursing homes. J Adv Nurs 2000;31(3):614-22.

3. Port CL, Gruber-Baldini AL, Burton L, Baumgarten M, Hebel JR, Zimmerman SI, Magaziner J. Resident contact with family and friends following nursing home admission. Gerontologist 2001;41(5):589-96.

4. Ryan AA, Scullion HF. Family and staff perceptions of the role of families in nursing homes. J Adv Nurs 2000;32(3):626-34.

5. Gaugler JE, Anderson KA, Zarit SH, Pearlin LI. Family involvement in nursing homes: Effects on stress and well-being. Aging Mental Health 2004;8(1):65-75.

6. Albeck S, Schreiber R. Characteristics of son and daughter visits to elderly parents in nursing care homes. Gerontologia 2002;29(3):55-79.

7. Pillemer K, Hegeman CR, Albright B, Henderson C. Building bridges between families and nursing home staff: The Partners in Caregiving Program. Gerontologist 1998;38(4):499-503.

8. Pillemer K, Suitor JJ, Henderson CR, Meador R, Schultz L, Robison J, Hegeman C. A cooperative communication intervention for nursing home staff and family members of residents. Gerontologist 2003;43(2):96-106.

9.   Weman K, Kihlgren M, Fagerberg I. Older people living in nursing homes or other community care facilities: Registered nurses' views of their working situation and cooperation with family members. J Clin Nurs 2004;13(5):617-26.

10.   Hertzberg A, Ekman SL, Axelsson K. 'Relatives are a resource, but...': Registered nurses' views and experiences of relatives of residents in nursing homes. J Clin Nurs 2003;12(3): 431-41.

11.   Bradley JM, Cafferty TP. Attachment among older adults: Current issues and directions for future research. Attachment Hum Dev 2001;3(2):200-21.

12.   Weinberger M, Hiner SL, Tierney WM. Assessing social support in elderly adults. Soc Sci Med 1987;25(9):1049-55.

13.   Drageset J. The importance of activities of daily living and social contact for loneliness: A survey among residents in nursing homes. Scand J Caring Sci 2004;18(1):65-71.

14.   Tseng SZ, Wang RH. Quality of life and related factors among elderly nursing home residents in Southern Taiwan. Public Health Nurs 2001;18(5):304-11.

CHAPTER 3
Family visits and care staff attitude towards the elderly

Isack Kandel and Joav Merrick

Nursing home placement can affect the visiting pattern of the family to the older person. In this small study we wanted to investigate the benefits of family visits for elderly nursing home residents by comparing residents who received visits to residents who did not receive visits, to examine the views of multi-disciplinary staff regarding family visits of elderly residents and examine whether multi-disciplinary staff attitude to elderly nursing home residents changed as a result of family visits. This small sample from an Israeli nursing home indicated differences between the group of elderly residents who received family visits and those who did not. Those who received family visits reported better family relationships in the past and a higher frequency of visits before entering the nursing home. Those who did not receive visits reported never having been satisfied with the frequency of visits and strong feelings of longing at the conclusion of family visits. The multi-disciplinary staff members recognized the significance of family visits and tended to maintain an open policy towards family visits. The staff gave preference to the needs of the individual over the routine of the institution, albeit with certain limitations. No statistic significant correlations were found between the visit variable and staff attitude to residents. However it must be stated that the distribution of replies indicated that nursing home staff believed that there was a positive correlation between their attention to residents – and family visits.

INTRODUCTION

Moving to a nursing home often leads to changes in the relationship between the older person and the close and extended family. Tseng and Wang (1) examined variables that affect the quality of life of elderly nursing home residents in Taiwan. They found that social support from family had the greatest effect on the quality of life of the elderly. Elderly residents who enjoyed frequent interaction with their family received a higher score on the quality of life index. 25% of the elderly in that study preferred a weekly family visit frequency. The researchers recommended that nurses organize activities that will include resident families in order to prevent the feeling of abandonment and provide additional opportunities for relatives to take part in nursing home activities.

The present paper deals with the issue of family visits to elderly nursing home residents. In this study we related to the perceptions of family visits by two of the participants involved in these visits. These were the overt participant – the elderly resident, and the covert participant – the staff member. The study examined the qualitative aspect of family visits to the elderly. We examined which variables contribute to or detract from the elderly resident's satisfaction with the visit. In addition, the study also examined how nursing home staff perceives the visits as beneficial.

OUR PILOT STUDY

The purposes of our small pilot study were:

- To examine the benefits of family visits for elderly nursing home residents by comparing residents who received visits to residents who do not receive visits
- To examine the views of multi-disciplinary staff regarding family visits of elderly residents
- To examine whether multi-disciplinary staff's attitude to elderly nursing home residents changed as a result of family visits.

The data was gathered by two questionnaires composed by the researchers specifically for this study. One questionnaire on nursing home resident perception of family visits and another questionnaire on nursing home staff perception of family visits. These questionnaires were constructed specifically for the current study based on a literature review. The questionnaires were composed on the basis of principles of practical utility and relevance. The questionnaire on nursing home resident perception of family visits covered the following elements:

- Sociodemographic information concerning the elderly resident – age, sex
- Sociodemographic information concerning relatives – financial status
- Information on elderly resident expectation of the visit from two aspects – visit characteristics and visit contents
- Elderly resident satisfaction with family visits from two aspects – visit characteristics and visit contents
- Examination of elderly resident feelings following family visits.

The questionnaire on nursing home staff perception of family visits covered the following elements:

- Sociodemographic information concerning the staff member – sex, age, position, seniority, education
- Information about staff's expectations of the visit from two aspects – visit characteristics and visit contents
- Staff's views of the visit and its implications

The study was conducted through questionnaires completed by mutlidisciplinary staff and nursing home residents. The nursing home multidisciplinary staff included: nurses, nursing aides, a physician, a dietician, an occupational therapist. The questionnaires were distributed to the staff personally by a nurse who worked at the nursing home. Each participant received a general explanation of the study and its purposes. The participants completed the questionnaire personally without interviewers. The resident questionnaire was administered by only one interviewer for all residents in order to prevent bias. The interviewer remained true to the question wording and order. Each participating resident received a general explanation of the study and its purposes. The residents were assured that their responses would remain confidential. All the study participants gave their consent to participate in the study.

This study was conducted at the Pinhas Rosen nursing home located in Ramat Gan, Israel and established in 1951. This home is one of three belonging to the Central European Immigrant Organization. The Central European Immigrant Organization was founded in 1932 with the aim of helping German Jews to immigrate to Israel and settle. From its conception, the organization included a department for social affairs and a "mutual help enterprise" was founded, tasked with raising contributions and supporting members of the organization who lacked sufficient financial means. The mutual help enterprise is active to this very day. The Central European Immigrant Organization is legally recognized as a non-profit organization due to its social activities.

COMMENTS

We believed that this study could illuminate points that add to or detract from elderly nursing home resident satisfaction with family visits. Understanding elderly resident expectations of visits and acknowledging feelings that accompany visits will help all the visit participants – both overt and covert. Knowledge of resident expectations of visits will help relatives to carry out visits that provide a better response to resident needs. Thus it will be possible to produce the most benefit from the visit. This knowledge will facilitate the conclusion whether elderly residents develop realistic expectations of visits, and if not – it can help them develop realistic expectations. Understanding the significance of visits might help multidisciplinary staff cope with implications of the visit both for residents and for their environment. This study might help increase staff awareness of the significance of the sharing process – residents, family, staff.

Findings concerning staff views of family visits might lead to greater cooperation between relatives and staff with the goal of promoting residents' well-being. For example relatives will learn of the staff expectations of visit characteristics such as: location, visiting hours, frequency and will try to adjust themselves. This sharing process will help avoid disturbing staff work.

The purposes of this study were to examine the benefits of family visits for elderly nursing home residents, based on a comparison between elderly residents who received visits and those who did not receive visits, to examine the views of multi-disciplinary staff towards family visits of elderly residents and to examine whether the attitude of multi-disciplinary staff towards elderly nursing home residents changes as a result of family visits.

This discussion has two parts. The first part discusses the benefits of visits for elderly residents, referring to the differences between the group of residents who receive visits and those who do not receive visits. The second part discusses the views of multi-disciplinary staff concerning family visits, with special reference to staff attitude towards the group of residents who receive visits compared to those who do not receive visits.

Benefits of visits for elderly residents

This study indicated that there was a correlation between elderly resident satisfaction and pleasure as a result of family visits - and the nature of resident relationships with their children in the past and visit frequency prior to institutionalization. This finding supported the literature that claimed that cases of good past relationships between elderly residents and their relatives - this relationship will continue upon entering a nursing home, and vice versa – in cases of adverse relationships they will probably remain bad after moving to a nursing home (2).

Affectionate and mutual relationships between elderly adults and their relatives are often perceived as resulting from merits accumulated by the elderly adult in the past by providing assistance to the current caregiver. This commitment stems from gratitude and is manifested by the wish to repay the elderly relative for services provided in the past. This study does not support such findings as no statistically significant difference was found between elderly residents, who did not receive visits and those who did in regards to the assistance they received from their relatives.

This study found that elderly residents who did not receive family visits defined the financial status of their children as "average" compared to most of the elderly residents who did receive visits, who defined the financial status of their children as "above average". These findings supported those of Port et al (3), which indicated that the higher the socioeconomic status of elderly adults and their families, the higher the frequency of visits and attachment.

A statistically significant difference was found in the preference of most of the elderly residents who received visits to leave the nursing home with relatives, a preference that was only found among half of those residents who did not receive visits. The reason may be that elderly residents who usually do not receive visits would like to use the few encounters and the limited time with their family for solitary meetings and intimate conversations.

Half of the elderly residents who did not receive visits stated that they were never satisfied with the frequency of visits compared to most of the elderly residents who did receive visits and stated that they are usually satisfied with the frequency of visits. This finding reinforces the conclusions of the theory by Erik Homburger Erikson (1902–1994) on personality, where the eighth and last stage of human life completes the life cycle from a positive perspective and with feelings of achievement (maturity: 65 years until death, integrity versus despair and acceptance of your life.). People living in a nursing home, dependent on others and conscious of being in the last stage of their life, feel that this phase will be successfully completed if they can only ignore past struggles and rehabilitate their family relationships. Frequent encounters may facilitate successful closure of this final phase of life.

The study indicated that feelings of longing associated with visit conclusions were more acute among patients who did not receive visits. This finding supports findings stated in the literature regarding the strong need for attachment throughout the life cycle and particularly in old age. For lonely and disabled elderly adults, interpersonal relations represent feelings of continuity, security and love, and therefore they continue to be an important source of life meaning (4).

Family visits as viewed by multi-disciplinary staff

The sample consisted of 32 staff members from different sectors. For purposes of statistical processing, the sample was divided into two sub-populations: primary caregivers and staff from other sectors – therapists.

In this study all the subjects (aside from one caregiver) perceived maintaining relations between elderly residents and their relatives as very significant. This finding is compatible with the organizational culture at the Pinhas Rosen Nursing Home. The management of the nursing home encourages family involvement aimed at maintaining and nurturing contact between elderly residents and their families. The management finds that there is a role division between resident families and the institution, whereby the nursing home fulfills resident physical needs, while relatives offer psychological support.

Upon examining the motives behind family visits to the elderly, the staff believed that relatives came due to their wish to be with the residents and to help them. This finding is compatible with findings from other studies conducted in the United States, indicating that many families express a wish to continue caring for elderly parents and supporting them even after their institutionalization. According to the families, this care should be manifested not only by visits to the residents but also by performing additional support (2). Most of the staff members believed that the optimal visit frequency should be twice a week. It must be stated that nurse aides preferred a higher frequency – i.e. daily. This finding may indicate that the staff understands the significance of visits for residents' quality of life. The staff supports visits and gives preference to the needs of the individual over the routine of the institution.

The two visiting places stated as appropriate were the lounge and the lobby. This preference was compatible with that of the residents. Residents prefer to hold encounters with their relatives in public places, where others will see them with their family. Residents feel that this raises their personal and social prestige in the eyes of other residents and of the staff. It is interesting to state that staff members object to visits in the dining room and in the occupational room. Holding visits in these places might disturb the routine of the resident. It is possible that the staff's objection to visits in these places stems from their discomfort and concern of supervision and criticism.

The two activities selected as most important during visits were "talking with the residents" and "taking the resident on a walk". An interesting finding is that a small number of staff members and particularly nursing aides thought that one of the significant activities of relatives during visits was talking to the staff about the resident. In a study conducted in Sweden (5) registered nurses perceived relatives as a resource and recognized the significance of communication with the family for transmitting information about resident past to the staff, but nurses tended to leave the initiative to start a conversation to the family.

Two questions referred to staff attitude to elderly residents who received visits compared to those who did not receive visits. No statistic significant correlations were found between the visit variable and staff attitude to residents. However it must be stated that the distribution of replies indicated that nursing home staff believed that there was a positive correlation between their attention to residents – and family visits.

Study limitations

The population of elderly adults examined was a population originating from Central and Eastern Europe. This population has unique characteristics and thus distinct from other populations. Generalization from this study is therefore limited to this population. The questionnaire completed by the residents referred to their past relationships with sons/daughters. Answers to such questions may involve memory bias. The person examined was emotionally charged and this may be a problem of reporting reliability. Relationships may be idealized as the interviewees attempted to protect their son/daughter.

The number of elderly residents who did not receive visits was small, only four subjects and this may have distorted the results. The staff questionnaire might have involved social desirability. This might have caused staff to report a positive view of visits that did not reflect reality.

CONCLUSIONS

This study indicated that there were differences between the group of elderly residents who received family visits and those who did not receive family visits. Those who received family visits reported better family relationships in the past and a higher frequency of visits before entering the nursing home. Those who did not receive visits reported never having been satisfied with the frequency of visits and strong feelings of longing at the conclusion of family visits. In addition, nursing home staff believed that there was a positive correlation between their attention and family visits. In our opinion the staff must devote attention and time to this group of residents who did not receive visits. The staff is responsible for connecting between residents and their families in such cases with the aim of rehabilitating adverse relationships. Research has proven that it is important that staff form an atmosphere inviting family involvement with the goal of encouraging family visits.

The findings of this study proved that multi-disciplinary staff members recognized the significance of family visits. The staff tended to maintain an open policy towards family visits. The staff gave preference to the needs of the individual over the routine of the institution, albeit with certain limitations. These limitations included the place of visit and visit frequency. An important finding of this study is the limited number of multi-disciplinary staff members who stated that it was important for relatives to talk to the staff about the resident. In our opinion it is recommended to create an intervention program on this subject in order to change the staff approach to conversations with relatives. An intervention program is very important, particularly due to the fact that many nursing home residents, particularly those suffering from cognitive impairment, cannot report their condition and nursing home experiences to their family. As a result, family members become dependent on nursing home staff for receiving information about their loved ones. Family members can benefit from the findings of this study. Relatives of elderly residents can learn about multi-disciplinary staff expectations of visit characteristics from this study and thus cooperate with the staff and avoid disruption of staff work.

ACKNOWLEDGEMENTS

This chapter was based upon research conducted by Ms. Yehudit Ostayev and Mr. Roslan Amirhanov at the Pinhas Rozen Nursing Home in Ramat Gan, managed by the "Central European Immigrants" Organization, for a seminar in health administration at the Academic College of Judea and Samaria in Ariel supervised by Isack Kandel.

REFERENCES

1. Tseng SZ, Wang RH. Quality of life and related factors among elderly nursing home residents in Southern Taiwan. Public Health Nurs 2001;18(5):304-11.
2. Ryan AA, Scullion HF. Family and staff perceptions of the role of families in nursing homes. J Adv Nurs 2000;32(3): 626-34.
3. Port CL, Gruber-Baldini AL, Burton L, Baumgarten M, Hebel JR, Zimmerman SI, Magaziner J. Resident contact with family and friends following nursing home admission. Gerontologist 2001;41(5):589-96.

4.   Bradley JM, Cafferty TP. Attachment among older adults: Current ssues and directions for future research. Attachment Hum Dev 2001;3(2):200-21.

5.   Hertzberg A, Ekman SL, Axelsson K. 'Relatives are a resource, but...': Registered nurses' views and experiences of relatives of residents in nursing homes. J Clin Nurs 2003;12(3):431-41.

PART TWO:
HEALTHY ACTIVE AGING

CHAPTER 4
Culture and activity in aging

Josephine Tetley and Gail Mountain

The cumulative effects of illness and disability in older age can lead to individuals being less able to make positive decisions about involvement in activities for pleasure and socialization. This lowered self-efficacy can in turn lead to erosion of confidence and ultimately to social exclusion. Older tenants in sheltered housing schemes are at particular risk of isolation and exclusion as the move to age-specific housing is usually triggered by a sudden or gradual decline in ability and/or personal circumstances. In conjunction with this, assumptions that social networks naturally occur in communal retirement communities and that people will individually or collectively arrange activities can lead to peoples' aspirations for meaningful activities in later life being overlooked. This problem is further compounded as housing staff find their time is taken up building maintenance and ensuring that tenants receive basic housing and environmental services. This chapter reports on the findings from a needs analysis that aimed to identify the activities that older tenants in a sheltered housing scheme had enjoyed during their lifetime, were no longer able to do but wanted to resume, and any new interests they were interested in pursuing. This is followed by a description of a one-year activity and culture program developed out of this needs analysis, underpinned by previous work conducted in Sweden.

INTRODUCTION

Promoting healthy active aging is a key policy of the World Health Organisation (1). More specifically the WHO active aging framework recognizes that health promoting activities can maximize the capacities of older people, and enable them to continue making important contributions to the overall fabric of society (1). It is further argued that initiatives aimed at promoting health and activity through-out the life course should be regarded as a necessity, not a luxury, to prevent global aging putting untenable economic and societal demands on all countries (1). In the United

Kingdom (UK) the importance of healthy aging has been recognized in the National Service Framework (NSF) for Older People, with Standard 8 requiring health and social care services to promote 'health and active life in older age through a co-ordinated program of action' (2). The associated implementation milestone (Annex III) expected that by March 2004 'Strategic and operational plans would include a program to promote healthy aging and to prevent disease in older people' (2). A recent review of the NSF for older people identified that this target was not met across most of the UK (3). As a result, the most recent NSF implementation plan continues to emphasize the importance of healthy aging and has made this one its key themes (4). That health and social care practitioners have struggled to deliver programs of healthy aging is not surprising as although practice examples and case studies exist; questions remain about what constitutes effective preventive inter-vention (5). Moreover, models of preventive strategies for implementation in practice are poorly defined (6).

Further research investment is therefore required to demonstrate the contribution that preventative interventions can make toward maintaining health and well-being in later life. The existing evidence suggests that when older people engage in activities, self-reported well-being and life satis-faction are enhanced, morbidity rates are lowered, and mortality reduced (7,8). Significantly, these studies and others (9,10) have found that improvement in health status was not merely related to engagement in formal physical exercise, but that social, creative, and productive activities such as gardening, community work, and art-based sessions, also made a significant contribution toward health and well-being. In an attempt to foster preventive services, the UK Department of Health Partnership introduced a new strategy in 2005; the Partnerships for Older People Project initiative (POPP). This policy has provided funding for local councils to invest in service redesign, whereby health promotion and preventive services are embedded within the whole system of health and social care within their localities, with a shift away from the emphasis on acute service provision to enable this to take place (11).

Occupational therapists have traditionally led the development of activity programs for health (12-14). Other disciplines, such as nursing services, housing providers, physiotherapists, social services, however, now recognize that they must also undertake more creative partnership working outside of traditional networks and include workers from the arts, leisure, and voluntary sectors, if such health support staff are to promote health and well-being amongst older people and ensure continued community connectedness (15,16). The need to develop new and innovative ways of working in health and social care is supported by the work of Carter and Everitt (9), who evaluated two community projects that aimed to promote health with older people through the use of physical activities and the arts. The findings of this study identified that in practice, programs of activities can meet the needs of a diverse group of older people only by including a wide range of practitioners from health, social care, social work, housing, libraries, sports, recreation, adult education, and the arts.

A model of activity and culture

In Sweden, the concept of social activities as a means of improving the health and well-being of older people has been promoted. This approach has resulted in a wide range of activity and culture initiatives being established (17-20). Such projects are often located in community-based housing schemes for older people and offer programs of arts, music, activities, and entertainment to older tenants and to other older people living locally, who are encouraged to come to the housing scheme (17,19,20). An evaluation of these and other initiatives found that although the participants had restricted physical functions following disease or injury, participation in meaningful and enjoyable activities made a positive contribution to peoples' lives and improved individuals perceptions of their psychosocial functioning (17,19,21). These studies were of additional value as they presented varied descriptions and evaluations of activity models. For example, studies by Bodel (18), Lundvist and Liljeberg-Maack (19), and Samuelsson et al (20) described at local and national levels the ways in which work in day centers and specialist accommodations attempt to promote active aging within community-care settings. More specifically, Lundvist and Liljeberg-Maack described how they developed a weekly program of arts, literacy, physical exercise, gardening, and social activities to promote active and healthy aging. A study by Andersson-Sviden et al (17) however, looking more systematically at social and rehabili-tative activities, found that where these are offered through a social center, older people reported significantly improved psychsocial functioning. Drawing on these studies and examples from practice, the evidence was clear that well-developed models of activities could make a positive contribution to the overall health and well-being of older people.

Activity and age-specific housing

Community based activity programs for older people are delivered in a variety of settings including day centers, churches, and age-specific housing schemes (9,17,19,20). Locating activity programs in age-specific housing schemes is now perceived as increasingly important by policy makers because sheltered accommodation, private age-specific housing, and extra-care housing are used to reduce reliance on residential care or as a replacement for institutional provision (22,23). Moreover, if such activities can help tenants engage more fully with the external community and across generations, by taking people out and bring people in, then this approach can counteract the criticism that communal housing for older people tends to segregate them (24,25). Studies of older peoples' satisfaction with sheltered accommodation as a housing option have further revealed that people express greater levels of satisfaction when the environment is socially vibrant and can accommodate the very varied needs of tenants (15,23).

We wanted to look at how a multi-agency team of health, social care, and housing workers could work in partnership with workers from the arts, leisure, and recreation services and older people, who were resident in one local authority run sheltered housing scheme, to develop and implement a diverse program of activities. More specifically, drawing on a Swedish concept of activities for health, the project team hoped to explore with tenants the ways in which physical, recreational, arts, and social activities could contribute to their overall health and well-being.

OUR STUDY

Having identified the potential benefits of an activity program for older people, the project team approached a social housing agency that provided sheltered housing and put forward the idea of working with tenants to develop an activity and culture project. Following initial discussions, a sheltered housing scheme was identified as a pilot site for this work as the warden and the tenants expressed the greatest interest in taking part in this work.

Before commencing the study and interviewing the tenants, the research team obtained ethical and research governance approval. Once the study location had been agreed upon, all 27 tenants living in the scheme were sent a letter outlining the project and asking them to attend an introductory meeting. In addition, the warden passed information about the project to a married couple living in a nearby complex of flats, who regularly engaged in social activities within the sheltered housing complex.

Following this initial approach, 19 tenants, 3 men and 16 women aged 65 to 94 years, attended a meeting with the project leader, a second member of the research team, and the warden from their sheltered scheme. The meeting took place in the communal living area of the sheltered housing scheme as this was the area where people came together to socialize. Those present were given preliminary information about the proposed study and encouraged to ask questions. Drawing on reports of previous studies identified through the review of relevant literature, a list of examples was presented of the sort of activities that might be offered to facilitate understanding. These included creative activities such as painting and pottery sessions, physical activities such as chair aerobic sessions, a pedometer challenge, gardening, 'one off' challenging events such as an outdoor pursuits activity; social activities such as trips out to local areas of interest, film nights, musical activities; and literacy-based activities such as a book group. Local history and computer training 'silver surfer' projects were also suggested. Reflecting the findings from the literature, suggesting a wide range of activities to try and appeal to the diverse interests of the tenants was considered important (9). At the outset, the research team, older people, and housing providers agreed that should other tenants who were not initially interested later express an interest in the project, they would be given the opportunity in the activities. Tenants were also given the opportunity to join in the activities even if they did not wish to take part in the research activities associate with the project.

The initial proposals for the activity and culture center were positively received by the nineteen people who had attended the initial meetings. Following this, arrangements were made with each person to undertake needs analysis interviews (26) that would identify individual aspirations for the activity program. These interviews were semi-structured to explore how long each person had lived in the sheltered housing scheme; what promoted them to move there; where they had live before moving into sheltered housing; what sort of things they did in the week; what things they had enjoyed doing in the past and whether they were still able to do them; what they enjoy doing now; and any new things they would like to try.

Each person who agreed to be interviewed was given an information sheet that outlined what the interviews would entail and was asked to sign a consent form giving the researcher permission to undertake the interview and to tape record it. The taped interviews were transcribed and analyzed by the research team using content analysis (27). Each interview was analyzed separately in the first instance to identify the needs and interests of each individual. The results of this analysis were compared across the group to explore similarities and differences between participant's views.

OUR FINDINGS

The results of the initial exploration of needs for meaningful activity and analysis of the interviews revealed the following:

- the activities that people enjoy or had enjoyed in the past,
- the activities that people wanted to continue with or new activities that people wanted to try,
- the importance of social activities,
- the factors that affected peoples' abilities to continue with, or participate in activities.

The individual interviews also demonstrated that tenants were interested in pursuing or continuing activities that could be mapped against four main categories: physical, art and craft, cultural, and social.

Physical activities
Many tenants spoke about their past enjoyment of physical activities. For example, eleven of those interviewed said that they had enjoyed gardening in the past, in both home gardens and allotments. Since moving into the sheltered housing scheme, several people had tried to continue this activity by growing plants in the raised flower beds at the front of the housing scheme and by putting up hanging baskets. As Mr Broadfield explained:

I've just started some hanging baskets. I usually do them myself but it got a bit too much for me gathering all the stuff in, all the soil and growbags and that sort of thing.

As a consequence, he now bought pre-made baskets from a garden center to hang outside the main building. Other people described how they had previously participated in active games and sport such as table-tennis, bowls, walking, dancing, billiards, yoga, swimming, and exercise classes, but were now no longer engaged in such pursuits. The reasons given for disengagement were varied, but the interviews identified how changes to peoples' physical, sensory, and psychological health particularly affected their abilities to continue with these activities. For example, Mrs Lacey said that her son's death had affected her joining in the activities and she was no longer able to enjoy dancing:

I used to sing and dance, dance with anybody, and sing, but it's all gone. But the doctor said it will come back in time, but it's been an awful shock. …People used 'to call me the dancing queen because as soon as the music comes I'm up'. And when the Can-Can comes on, oh deary me…

As people's physical and sensory health deteriorated, such changes in combination with falling, or fear of falling, were identified as factors that affected people's abilities to continue with physical activities. Indeed, Mrs Cooke aged 93 years also described how she had 'danced and jived' on her ninetieth birthday, but went on to explain how a recent fall had slowed her down.

Although the tenants recognized that they were no longer able to continue with physical activities as they had in the past, or had given up activities, during the interviews, they identified new activities that they would like to try. Indeed, Mrs Smith described giving up yoga and swimming after her move into sheltered housing, but said that given the oppor-tunity she would like to try aquarobics and Tai Chi.

Art and craft activities

Art and craft were very popular with all those interviewed, and everyone described activities that they had enjoyed and wanted to continue or were continuing. For example, Mr Roberts described how in the past he had enjoyed silver-smithing and had done so for 13 years at night school. He showed the researcher examples of his work, a box, and a tankard and said, "I enjoyed that very much, very satisfying that".

Art, flower arranging, and needle crafts were also popular with the female tenants. One woman, Mrs McGill, explained how she had done a number of paintings in the past that she had hung on the corridor walls of the sheltered scheme. A number of the women described enjoying flower arranging and had displays of artificial flowers that they had put together themselves on show in their flats. Another woman, Mrs Smith, showed the researcher tapestries and knitting that were in progress, commenting that she thought that "doing the needlework had actually improved the dexterity of her hands."

Whilst general enthusiasm was expressed for trying new art and craft activities, loss of vision and physical health restrictions were raised as factors that restricted participation in such activities. All those interviewed had been affected by deteriorating vision, which affected their ability to continue with activities that involved small objects or fine detailed work like embroidery. One woman, Mrs Thrush, explained that she had lost her sight in her 60s and was now totally blind. She said that she had enjoyed art and craft activities and was now upset that she was no longer able to embroider or sew.

Cultural activities

All the tenants interviewed said that they were interested in music, the theatre, and/or literary-based activities. Music was important to the tenants for a number of reasons. Mrs Thrush had been a very active member of the Salvation Army and still attended the luncheon club and services. Others liked lighter musical entertainment and enjoyed the monthly visits from local musicians to the sheltered housing scheme. Mrs Cooke described 'the King' who visited once a month to entertain the tenants:

> Oh he's lovely. He's just our cup of tea. He laughs and talks to us and that, and sings.

Mrs North also enjoyed the visits from musical entertainers, explaining that in the past she had loved opera and going to the theatre to see musicals. She said,

> I like good singing. I were brought up among it You know when I was at school, the head master, he used to say I had the best singing voice.

Although musically based activities were popular, one woman, Miss Black, was particularly interested in formal art classes, literature, and poetry. She explained that she had always enjoyed reading, walking, and that after her father died, she started writing poetry. Miss Black said that whilst she had enjoyed this and won prizes for her poems, more recently she had struggled to write,

> I've not done any for a few years. I've got a lot that I've half done and want finishing, but I shall have to start and take it up again because it's a thing you miss. But you have a bit of writer's block sometimes.

When the researcher asked Miss Black if she would like a writing club she said,

I would indeed, I'd love a writing group again.

In direct contrast to the other tenants, although Miss Black enjoyed music, she did not enjoy the visits from the musical entertainers and didn't attend these events as she said that she "didn't like been sung at."

Social activities

Eighteen tenants described how they enjoyed meeting with one another at a weekly social club and on the afternoons and evenings when they met to play games with one another. The tenants also supported one another whilst they were taking part on these activities. For example, Mrs Day said she that she joined in "with everything that's [was] going on' at the scheme - the coffee morning, the social club and the bingo." Yet, she said that somebody had to "play her bingo for her" because of her poor eyesight. When she was asked if there were any particular activities that she would particularly like she said that she preferred things involving "mixing up with people" and went on to say,

> *I like to talk to people. I can sit on the corridor for hours looking for people coming up and down, men or women and I'm not bothered, you know.*

The oldest tenant in the sheltered housing scheme, Mrs Perkins, was 94 years old. She explained that she enjoyed the weekly club where she played bingo. It was interesting to note that whilst the bingo evenings were popular, comments from tenants indicated that it wasn't particularly the bingo but rather the social interaction that was important. Indeed, when Mrs Perkins was asked if she enjoyed bingo she said,

> *'Well put it this way, it gets me out among people.'*

Another tenant, Mrs Crookes, commented that she didn't particularly enjoy the bingo and that she mainly enjoyed the social contact. Mr Roberts also said that whilst he joined in many of the social activities he didn't join in the bingo as he didn't enjoy this.

Whereas the social activities that took place in a large group were popular, they were, however, difficult for certain people. Mrs White, a woman in her 90s, said that her general tiredness, poor eyesight, and poor hearing made it difficult for her to join in activities and that her deafness made her feel isolated…

> *If you feel you can't hear and you can't really see very well. I never thought I should go deaf like this. There's deaf and there's sight, and it's bad when you don't… when you're used to talking and doing, but then you can't.*

Interestingly, not everyone enjoyed the group social activities. Miss Black, who preferred the literary and art based activities, explained that she did not enjoy the bingo or large group activities explaining that

> *Women in the mass frighten me to death. Now that sounds horrid doesn't it. No, I'm not much of a company person at all. I don't mean to say I'm unsociable, perhaps folk think I am I don't know.*

She went on to clarify that she was

> *Not a clubby person, no. I don't mean unsociable altogether; I'm just not a socialite.*

Developing and implementing the program

Having identified the activities that the tenants enjoyed and the factors that appeared to affect their abilities to participate in these, a program of physical, arts and craft, cultural and social activities was put together that drew on the individual and collective interests highlighted by the needs analysis interviews. The proposals put forward to the tenants included the following:

- a greenhouse and gardening project,
- gentle exercise sessions such as chair aerobics, tai chi and accompanied walking,
- a pottery workshop,
- art-and-craft sessions led by a local artist,
- a falls-prevention workshop,
- trips out to the theater, local areas of interest such as the botanical gardens, and local sports events,
- themed social functions, which would include food and music.

These suggestions were positively received by the tenants. The research team then used funding acquired for the project to implement these. Again working on the principles of active participation by the tenants in the selection of the activities, local artists and workers from the city council's physical activities team were asked to come and meet with tenants to discuss their interests and to negotiate the exact nature of the activities. Two tenants also accompanied project team members on a trip to a local DIY warehouse to choose a greenhouse and general gardening equipment. When tenants, such as Miss Black, had specific interests, individual suggestions such as a supported visit to local literary events were put forward.

DISCUSSION

Although an active and engaged later life is seen as positive, the reasons for people choosing to continue with, or stopping, certain activities in older age are complex. The findings of the needs analysis presented here, consistent with other studies of activities in later life (28,29), found that older people of all ages take part in leisure-time activities that are not only enjoyable but also help them to maintain their health and to engage with others. However, changes to individual capacity (including disability, limited financial resources, low education, fatigue, attitudes, and habits), environmental constraints and or opportunities can easily erode their ability to participate (29,30). This limitation is compounded by outdated societal and service-provider assumptions about the needs and capacities of older people (6), which often leads to a stifling of interests and to restrictions being placed upon the nature of the activities offered. This assumption is often most keenly experienced by older people living in age-related accommodations who are also reliant upon others to help them to maintain participation. The needs analysis interviews identified that although tenants acknowledged being affected by changes to their physical health and sensory perception, they still wanted to continue with activities they had previously enjoyed or to try new activities.

Significantly, a UK study that developed an activity program to promote health in later life found that older people gained great pleasure from taking part in outward bound activities, but described sessions where they batted balls to each other and played with scarves as embarrassing and childish (9). So whilst activities may have to be adapted to compensate for the physical and sensory changes that occur in later life, if greater numbers of older people are to engage in and continue with activity programs, then such programs have to be diverse and workers have to be skilled facilitators of sessions that could otherwise be seen as patronizing.

This project also undertook individual needs analysis interviews to develop a program of activities in partnership with older tenants and ensure that the activities offered would be meaningful in the context of peoples lived experiences. This approach is important as older people affected by ill health and disabilities are traditionally offered rehabilitation and health-promoting activities through day hospitals. However, studies of rehabilitative and medically oriented day hospital care on community-based long-term care patients have found that these services do not reduce significantly the use of other health services, or improve the physical functioning of older people (31-33). Moreover, a Swedish study comparing rehabilitative day centers with social centers also found that social day centers had a more significant impact on people's perception of their psychosocial functioning because such centers offered activities regarded as meaningful to the people who attended (17).

It is also important that general assumptions are not made about potential interests based on broad indicators drawn from population data. This pilot project was based in a sheltered housing scheme located in the west of a large city in the North of England. In this location, 98.3% reported their ethnic background as white in the 2001 census (34). Unemployment levels are low, with most reporting employ-ment in manual, manufacturing, or transport-related work (34). This profile was consistent with the backgrounds reported by eighteen of the older people interviewed during the course of this study. Miss Black, however, was different—she had never married and had predominantly worked in the jewelry industry. Her interview revealed how her background and interests were distinctly different from those reported by other tenants. Therefore, working closely with as many older people as possible is important when developing an activity program to ensure that the diverse interests of a group, united by a physical location, are catered for.

CONCLUSION

In conclusion, for health promoting initiatives to support healthy aging successfully, it must be acknowledged that to have a positive impact on the health and well-being of older people, activity programs must be creative, must be based on individual and group needs, and must be developed in partnership with the older people who are the intended recipients.

ACKNOWLEDGMENTS

Grateful thanks are extended to Janet Wilson, Amanda Clarke, Chris Hockney, Julie Gamble, Janet James, and Emma Beeston, who helped with the data collection, analysis of the interviews, and supported the activities reported in this paper. This project has been supported by the Foundation of Nursing Studies' Developing Practice for Healthy Aging program in partnership with Pfizer Ltd, the Sheffield Health and Social Research Consortium and the British Council Grundtvig 2 programme. This chapter is an updated version of an earlier published paper (Tetley J, Mountain G. Activity and culture – the contribution to health and well-being in later life: A needs analysis. Int J Disabil Hum Dev 2006;5(1):45-51).

REFERENCES

1.   World Health Organisation. Active aging: a policy framework. Geneva: World Health Organisation, 2002.
2.   Department of Health. The national service frame-work for older people. London, UK: Department of Health, 2001.
3.   Commission for Healthcare Audit and Inspection. Living well in later life. A review of progress against the national service framework for older people. London, UK: Commission Healthcare Audit Inspection, 2006.
4.   Department of Health. A new ambition for old age. Next steps in implementing the national service framework for older people. A resource document. London, UK: Department Health, 2006.

5.   Little M. Improving older people's services: policy into practice. Inspection of Older People's Services. London, UK: SSI, 2002.

6.   Biley A. National service framework for older people: promoting health. Br J Nurs 2002;11:469-76.

7.   Glass TA, de Leon CM, Marottoli RA, Berkman LF. Population based study of social and productive activities as predictors of survival among elderly Americans. BMJ 1999;319:478-83.

8.   Litwin H, Shiovitz-Ezra S. The association between activity and well-being in later life: what really matters. Aging Soc 2006;26: 225-42.

9.   Carter P, Everitt A. Conceptualising practice with older people: friendship and conversation, Aging Soc 1998;18:79-99.

10.   Hurdle DE. Social support: A critical factor in women's health and health promotion. Health Soc Work 2001; 26(2):72-9.

11.   Dept Health Partnerships Older People Projects. A prospectus for grant applications. London, UK: Department Health, 2005.

12.   Clarke F, Azen A, Zemke R, Jackson J, Carlson M, Mandel D et al. Occupational therapy for independent- living older adults. JAMA 1997;278:1321-6.

13.   Clarke F, Parham D, Carlson M, Frank G, Jackson J, Pierce D et al. Occupational science: Academic inno-vation in the service of occupational therapy's future. Am J Occup Ther 1991; 45(4): 300-10.

14.   Rudman D, Cook J, Polatajko H. Understanding the potential of occupation: a qualitative exploration of seniors' perspectives on aging. Am J Occup Ther 1997;51:640-50.

15.   Percival J. Self-esteem and social motivation in age-segregated settings. Housing Studies 2001;16:827-40.

16.   Sanders K. Developing practice for healthy aging. Nurs Older People 2006;18:18-20

17.   Andersson-Svidén G, Tham K, Borell,, L. Elderly participants of social and rehabilitation day centers. Scand J Caring Sci 2004;18: 402-9.

18.   Bodel E. Cultural activities for seniors: Culture and health. A summary of a descriptive report. Umeå, Sweden: Municipality Umeå, 2004.

19.   Lundvist S, Liljeberg-Maack C. Aktivitets- och kulturcenterr på Bagaregårdens äldreboende. Gothenberg. Sweden: Örgryte Äldremsorg,   2002. http://www.orgryte.goteborg.se/prod/orgryte/dalis2.nsf/vyPubli cerade/02CA0CA84AA7610DC1256CE80030F5DE?OpenDocument [last accessed 2 July 2006].

20.   Samuelsson L, Malmberg B, Hansson J-H. Daycare for elderly people in Sweden: a national survey. Scand J Soc Welfare 1998;7: 310-9.

21.   Silverstein M, Parker M. Leisure activities and quality of life among the oldest old in Sweden. Res Aging 2002;24:473-8.

22.   King N. Models of very sheltered housing: re thinking housing for older people. Housing Care Support 2001; 4:22-5.

23.   Oldman C. Blurring the boundaries: A fresh look at housing and care provision for older people. York, UK: Joseph Rowntree Foundation, 2000.

24.   Fisk MJ. Older people's housing—the changing role of social housing providers. Generations Rev 2000; 10:8-10.

25.   Kingstone P, Bernard M, Briggs S, Nettleton H. Assessing the health impact of age-specific housing. Health Soc Care Community 2001; 9:228-34.

26.   Cooke J, Owen J, Wilson A. Research and develop-ment at the health and social care interface in primary care: a scoping exercise in one National Health Service region. Health Soc Care Community 2002; 10:435-44.

27.   Woods L, Priest H, Roberts P. An overview of three different approaches to the interpretation of qualitative data. Part 2: practical illustrations. Nurse Res 2002; 10:43-51.

28.   Midwinter E. Never too late to learn. Nurs Older People 2004;16: 10-2.

29.   Agahi N, Parker MG. Are today's older people more active than their predecessors? Participation in leisure-time activities in Sweden. Aging Soc 2005;25:925-41.

30.   Berger U, Der G, Mutrie N, Hannah MK The impact of retirement on physical activity. Aging Soc 2005; 25:181-95.

31.   Pitkala K. The effectiveness of day hospital care on home care patients. J Am Geriatr Soc 1998;46:1086-90.

32.   Forster A, Young J, Langhorne P. Systematic review of day hospital care for elderly people. The Day Hospital Group. BMJ 1999; 318(7187):837-41.

33.   Harwood RH, Ebrahim S. Measuring the outcomes of day hospital attendance: a comparison of the Barthel Index and London Handicap Scale. Clin Rehabil 2000; 14:527-31.

34.   National Statistics. Neighbourhood Statistics. Census 2001. London: HMSO, 2001. http://neighbourhood. statistics.gov.uk/ [last accessed 11 July 2006].

CHAPTER 5
Cardiorespiratory capacity, blood pressure, blood lipids and body composition over time in the elderly

Eli Carmeli, Pini Orbach, David T Lowenthal, Joav Merrick and Raymond Coleman

I t is generally recognized that physical activity levels in the elderly do not remain constant over time, and typically there is a marked reduction in physical activities in the elderly. The long-term benefits of regular physical training programs in the elderly are still not fully understood. This chapter describe a study of 55 elderly healthy subjects (over 65 years old) and re-evaluated for the effects of different physical activity patterns (sedentary, moderately active and highly active) on several physiological parameters (pre- and post-training) after a five year period (5.30 ± 1.14 years). Measurements included: body composition, blood lipid profiles, resting systolic and diastolic blood pressure, maximal oxygen uptake, and pulmonary function. Results indicated a larger decrease in maximal oxygen uptake (VO2max) in the group of elderly sedentary individuals (1.5±0.5 L/min) compared to the moderately active (1.7±0.6L/min) and the highly active groups (1.9±0.4 L/min). An active lifestyle was not sufficient to increase the physiological function of an individual. Our study could not clearly demonstrate favorable differences for the physically active groups over the sedentary group with regard to several important physiological factors over the five year follow-up and it appears that the recommendation for, and the initiation of adopting active lifestyles, may not be sufficient on their own to significantly increase an individual's physiological functioning.

INTRODUCTION

By the year 2030, it is estimated that the number of individuals aged 65 years or older will reach 70 million in the United States alone. Moreover, people aged 85 years or older will be the fastest growing segment of the population (1). Overall deterioration in physical activity and physiological functioning are commonly associated with aging in the elderly. The rate of aging is widely variable among individuals, and specific body systems within individuals may show a variable age-associated functional decline (2,3). There is some evidence that appropriate exercise training in healthy elderly persons may help maintain functional capacity and quality of life (4,5). The benefits of regular physical activity in improving health-related fitness and reducing the risk factors for coronary heart disease (CHD) have received considerable attention, especially in middle-aged males (6). The Heritage Family Study is the most recent study addressed the question of individual variation in responsiveness to regular exercise training (7). Regularly performed endurance exercise training may partially protect against the increase in body fat content with aging (8). Men and women undertaking a high level of endurance exercise training with advancing age, appear to avoid many of the undesirable changes in body composition, muscle strength and fat distribution that typically occur with aging (9). Adult men, who performed aerobic training for 20 weeks, showed significant improvements in VO2max, maximal expired ventilation (VEmax), and resting heart rate (HR) (10).

Other studies have also shown that active lifestyles can have beneficial effects with regard to CHD risk factors, not only in young adults, but also in middle-aged and older adults (10-12). Furthermore, the benefits of exercise in reducing CHD risk factors, such as elevated blood pressure (BP), elevated cholesterol levels, while increasing muscle strength (13), body weight (BW), working capacity, and respiration (VO2max and VEmax) have been demonstrated (14-16). Despite increasing evidence indicating the potential beneficial effects of regular physical activity on health and well-being in aging adults, there has been relatively little improvement in reducing sedentary behavioral patterns among aging adult Americans during the past 20 years.

Most of the current knowledge regarding the influence of modifying physical activity levels on related physiological functions and aerobic fitness has been derived from longitudinal studies of middle-aged and elderly individuals (17). In these studies, individual well-established physical activities patterns and exercise training protocols were relatively short or medium term (4-6 months) and make it difficult to draw conclusions regarding the long-term impact of changing physical activity status on cardiovascular functional capacity in the elderly. It is generally recognized that physical activity levels in adults and the elderly do not remain constant over time, and typically there is a marked reduction in physical activities in the elderly. The long-term benefits of regular physical training programs in the elderly are still not fully understood.

This chapter describes a longitudinal follow-up study in independently living men and women was designed to try and determine the impact of change or maintenance in physical activity status on body composition, cardio-respiratory fitness, and blood lipid profiles in a population of healthy people over the age of 65 years.

OUR STUDY

95 elderly subjects, aged 65 years or older from Gainesville, Florida area, volunteered to participate in our study. All participants had randomly participated in exercise or control groups in prior aging studies.

These previous series of studies were designed to try to evaluate the effects of exercise training on elderly individuals. In these earlier studies, aerobic training consisted of three sessions per week for 26 weeks. Training involved walking at 50% VO2max with intensity gradually increased until subjects could walk at 60-85% of their VO2max (18-20). All participants had mainly non-active behavior patterns prior to their initial participation (T1) in the training programs. Telephone screening was used to identify suitable healthy subjects for the exercise testing program and to determine that they did not suffer from cardiac disorders, peripheral vascular disease, pulmonary disease, or orthopedic limitations. On an initial visit all participants in the study provided signed informed consent, and completed questionnaires regarding their overall activity status, demographics and medical history. Subjects meeting the requirements were scheduled for a further screening visit.

In the longitudinal study all participants were evaluated prior to and following the five-year study period. Three sets of time-tables were defined: T1 initial evaluation; T2 at the end of a training program; and T3 five years after the completion of the training program. All testing procedures and instruments were identical at T1, T2, and T3.

Assessment of life quality

The general health related quality of life was measured at T1, T2, and T3. Subjects completed the SF-36 health questionnaire which includes eight physical and mental health scales of total of 36 items (21) and in addition the Stanford Usual Physical Activity Questionnaire was completed by each participant. Correlation coefficient of this questionnaire was found the best ($r=0.75$) compared with other validated measurements (22). Participants were given a list of typical activities divided into four activity categories: light, moderate, hard, and very hard. Activities were classified according to energy requirements and expressed in terms of metabolic equivalents. The metabolic equivalent values were multiplied by the number of hours spent in each activity level and summed across categories to estimate total energy expenditure in terms of Kcal/Kg of body weight/day (Kcal/Kg/day). Subjects scoring 35 Kcal/Kg/day or less were classified as sedentary (SED); scores between 35 to 40 Kcal/Kg/day were classified as moderately active (MOD); scores exceeding 40 Kcal/Kg/day were classified as highly active (HA).

Health screening

Participants underwent health screening in the laboratory after a minimum 3-hour fast, 12 hours abstinence from alcohol, decongestants, and tobacco products, and 24 hours without vigorous exercise. Participants underwent a general medical examination and physical health history. Tests included a resting standard 12-lead electrocardiogram (ECG), and a modified Naughton treadmill protocol for graded exercise test (GXT)(16). Before starting the test, supine and resting hyperventilation 12-lead ECG (Quinton Instrument Co., Seattle, Washington; model Q2000), resting systolic blood pressure (RSBP), and resting diastolic blood pressure (RDBP), were recorded. Standard criteria for exclusion from maximal GXT were used (1). This test was considered a diagnostic measure to determine patient suitability to continue further testing. The test was terminated if the subject was unable to continue or when symptoms of cardiovascular de-compensation became evident. Both a 12-lead ECG and heart rate were monitored continuously throughout the exercise and during seven minutes of recovery. The reliable testing (23) instruments and protocol kept constant over all testing periods. Diastolic blood pressure (DBP) and systolic blood pressure (SBP) were monitored pre-exercise, during exercise and during the recovery period. In addition, perceived exertion (RPE) was determined at the end of each minute during exercise and at the termination of exercise (24). 95 subjects were scheduled for the GXT screening and 36 were excluded from the study due to medical reasons and four subjects dropped out of the study.

Measurements and study design

The following measurements were taken from all subjects in four separate consecutive visits with a minimum of at least two full days rest between visits: (1st visit) height, body weight, skinfold thickness, VO2max; (2nd visit) resting heart rate (HR) and blood pressure, blood chemistry, pulmonary function test, VO2max; (3rd visit) resting HR and blood pressure, VO2max ; (4th visit) physical performance test and VO2max. Thus, VO2max was longitudinally assessed among the three activity groups.

Blood chemistry

Subjects reported to the laboratory after a minimum 12-hour fast. After 15 minutes sitting quietly, resting BP and HR were measured. Then, a 15 ml sample of venous blood (medial cubital vein) was taken for routine screening of blood cell count (BCC) and biochemistry profiles. All blood analyses were performed at the GlaxoSmithKline Clinical Laboratories (Tampa, FL).

Body weight

Body weight was measured shoeless on a digital scale (Detecto Scale Co., Webb City, Missouri; model #8430) to the nearest 0.1 kilogram.

Skinfold determinations

Body composition measurements were assessed from skinfold measurements on the right side of the body using a Lange skinfold caliper (Cambridge Scientific Industries, Cambridge, MD; model #68902). The following seven skinfold sites were used to determine body composition: chest, axilla, triceps, subscapula, abdomen, supra-iliac and thigh (18). The landmarks and techniques used for these measurements and for subsequent calculations of body composition were based on validation studies (25).

Maximal oxygen uptake test

The VO2max test was performed using the same protocol as described for the GXT for all subjects who performed less than 12 minutes in the initial GXT (16). However, for those who exercised >12 min on their initial GXT, the initial speed was 3, rather than 2 miles/h. The VO2max test was terminated when the subject was unable to continue or when signs or symptoms of cardiovascular abnormalities or distress became evident (see GXT). Subjects were excluded from the study if the test was terminated for anything other than subjective fatigue. Expired air was collected in meteorological balloons during the last 4-5 minutes of the test. The gas levels for oxygen (Model S-3A) and carbon dioxide (Model CD-3A) were determined with Ametek gas analyzers (Thermox Instruments Division, Pittsburgh, PA) calibrated with the use of precision tank gases. Volumes were measured with a Collins 120 liter chain compensated gasometer (Warren E. Collins Incorporated, Boston, MA). To ensure that a true VO2max had been achieved, two of the following criteria had to be met: an increase in VO2 <100 ml in the final minute of exercise, and HR considered to be maximal for a subject's age.

Resting blood pressure

Resting blood pressure (RBP) was measured in the left arm using a sphygmomanometer. Subjects were placed in a seated resting position in a quiet room for 15 minutes prior to having their RBP and resting HR measured. The average of three trials was used for statistical analysis.

Pulmonary function test

A flow-volume test was administered with the subject in a sedentary resting position in order to measure forced vital capacity (FVC) and forced expiratory volume for one second (FEV1.0) using a pulmonary function testing system (Med Graphics, St. Paul, MN, model #1070). The flow-volume loop test involved having the subject inspire to total capacity and perform a FVC maneuver by expiring maximally followed by a forced inspiration vital capacity maneuver. The average of three flow-volume loop tests was used for statistical analysis.

Physical performance test

The physical performance test (PPT) was administrated to subjects to provide a quantifiable measure of functional capacities to undertake common activities of daily living for subjects in different age and living status (26). Each subject was rated by the examiner according to nine tasks including: writing a sentence, simulated eating, turning 360 degrees, putting on a jacket, lifting a book and putting it on a shelf, picking up a coin from the floor, a 50-foot walk test, climbing a flight of stairs for speed, and climbing stairs for endurance.

The analysis was divided into three parts: Exercise training study (pre-training (T1) and post-training (T2) comparison, longitudinal studies, T1 to current (T3), and T2 to T3 comparisons, and a cross-sectional study of high (HA), moderate (MOD) and sedentary (SED) groups at T3. The data are presented as means (M) and standard deviation (SD) for all variables. All analyses used a significance level of $p < 0.05$. To evaluate the results of the post-training programs, multiple univariate one-way factorial ANOVAs with repeated measurement on the time of measurement (T1 and T2) were used. In longitudinal analyses, multiple univariate two-way 3 (activity level: HA, MOD, SED) x 2 (time of measurement: T1 and T3 testing; T2 and T3 testing) factorial ANOVAs with repeated measures on the last variable were used. Moreover, when initial significant differences among the groups at T1 and T2 were identified multiple univariate two-way 3 x 2 ANCOVAs with repeated measures on the second variable (time of measurement) were used. In the cross-sectional analysis (at T3) multiple univariate one-way (activity level: HA, MOD, SED) factorial ANOVAs were used. Gender interaction was evaluated by repeating the above described analyses with the addition of sex groups (female and male) in the model of interest. In the ANOVA and ANCOVA analyses from the longitudinal and cross-sectional studies, significant F ratios ($p < 0.05$) were analyzed using the Student Newman-Keuls test.

FINDINGS FROM OUR STUDY

No significant gender differences for dependent variables and time points were found, consequently combined results of both female and male subjects are presented. Out of the initial sample size of the 95 participants 36 were excluded from the study due to medical reasons and four subjects dropped out, leaving 55 persons in the study (males n=24, mean age 66.1±3.7, females n=31, mean age 67.5±4.2).

Effectiveness of prior training

Analysis of the previous training data indicated that subjects responded with a significant increase in relative VO2max (18%), absolute VO2max (L/min; AbVO2max) (10%), and VEmax (7%). In addition, RDBP (6%), RSBP

(4%), RHR (5%), body fat (5%), and sum of seven skinfolds (7%) were found to be lower after training (see table 1).

Table 1. Pre-training and post-training parameters

Variables	n	Pre-training (T1)	Post-training (T2)	p values
Age (years)	55	67.23 ± 4.4	---	---
Weight (kg)	55	71.0 ± 13.4	70.9 ± 14.4	0.832
Body fat (%)	54	29.5 ± 7.1	28.0 ± 7.4	0.009*
VO$_2$ (ml·kg^{-1}·min^{-1})	44	25.8 ± 5.4	29.0 ± 6.4	0.009*
VO$_2$ (L/min)	44	1.9 ± 0.5	2.1 ± 0.6	0.009*
HRmax (beats/min)	44	163 ± 12.9	164.8 ± 15	0.360
SBPmax (mm Hg)	44	192.6 ± 23.1	195.8 ± 25.6	0.103
DBPmax (mm Hg)	44	86.5 ± 12.6	84.3 ± 12.9	0.123
VEmax (L/min)	44	71.3 ± 23.6	75.6 ± 22.6	0.029*
RSBP (mm Hg)	55	123.3 ± 16.3	119.2 ± 16	0.004*
RDBP (mm Hg)	55	74.1 ± 8.2	69.8 ± 9.2	0.009*
RHR (beats/min)	55	66.1 ± 7.6	63 ± 7.1	0.009*
FEV/FVC (%)	25	78.5 ± 6	77.2 ± 5.8	0.063
FVC (L)	25	3.5 ± 0.8	3.5 ± 0.9	0.156
FEV1.0 (L)	25	2.9 ± 1.2	2.7 ± 0.6	0.315
Skinfold (mm)	54	164.9 ± 52.9	153.6 ± 54.7	0.009*

Note. Abbreviations are common for all tables presented. Data presented in all tables is for both genders combined. *Significance, $p < 0.05$. Number of observations (n). FEV1.0: forced expiratory volume in 1sec, FVC: forced vital capacity, RHR: resting heart rate in 1min, RDBP; HRmax: maximal heart rate in 1min: resting diastolic blood pressure, RSBP: resting systolic blood pressure, VO$_2$: maximal oxygen uptake, SBPmax: maximal systolic blood pressure, DBPmax: maximal diastolic blood pressure, VEmax: maximal expired ventilation, Skinfold = sum of seven measurements.

Pre-training and current comparison

Based on the Stanford 7-day recall questionnaire results, subjects were divided into three activity groups (HA, MOD, SED) for the analyses of dependent variables. No significant changes were observed in the HA group. Nevertheless, there was a non-significant trend indicating a decrease in relative VO2max (9%), % BF (8%), and a significant decrease in sum of seven skinfolds (14%) for T3 measurements (see table 2).

Table 2. Pre-training and current measurements for highly active subjects

Variables	n	Pre-training (T1)	Current (T3)	p
Age (years)	12	66.8 ± 3.2	71.9 ± 4.0	---
Weight (kg)	11	74.2 ± 8.1	73.6 ± 9.4	0.597
Body fat (%)	11	25.2 ± 4.8	23.3 ± 4.6	0.081
V02 (ml·kg^{-1}·min^{-1})	10	26.7 ± 5.7	24.2 ± 4.8	0.085
V02 (L/min)	10	2.1 ± 0.5	1.9 ± 0.4	0.090
HRmax (beats/min)	10	166.2 ± 12.4	161.8 ± 23	0.393
SBPmax (mm Hg)	10	198.1 ± 26.3	198 ± 19.0	0.990
DBPmax (mm Hg)	10	93.0 ± 14.0	91.0 ± 10.1	0.541
VEmax (L/min)	10	73.4 ± 18.1	77.3 ± 19.3	0.346
RSBP (mm Hg)	11	120.7 ± 19.3	118.5 ± 13.3	0.654
RDBP (mm Hg)	11	74.2 ± 9.4	73.3 ± 6.5	0.754
RHR (beats/min)	11	60.9 ± 7.4	59.9 ± 8.8	0.454
FEV/FVC (%)	6	75.2 ± 4.1	73.7 ± 4.7	0.423
FVC (L)	6	4.2 ± 0.7	4.1 ± 0.7	0.088
FEV1.0 (L)	6	3.2 ± 0.6	3 ± 0.6	0.132
Skinfold (mm)	11	138.1 ± 31.2	119.7 ± 28.3	0.022*
Cholesterol (total)	11	212.4 ± 27.2	206.9 ± 25.2	0.412
Triglycerides	10	117.0 ± 35.1	123.6 ± 46.2	0.528

*Significance, $p < 0.05$

Results from the MOD group indicated significant changes for % BF (12%), and relative VO2max (9%), revealing significant lower % BF and relative VO2max for T3 measurement (see table 3). For the MOD group, data analysis also indicated a significantly reduced AbVO2max (6%), and sum of seven skinfolds (18%) measurements for T3. Finally, T3 maximal SBP (SBPmax) was found to be higher (5%) for the MOD group.

Results from the SED group revealed a significant reduction in body fat (10%), and relative VO2max (18%) (see table 4). It was evident from the results that the SED group, not only had lower relative VO2max than MOD and HA groups, but also had a greater rate of decline in their VO2max. Results for the SED group also revealed a significant decrease in maximal HR (HRmax) (5%), AbVO2max (17%), FEV1.0 (11%), and sum of seven skinfolds (17%) for T3 measurements.

Post-training and current comparison

Results for the HA group indicated a significance decrease in relative VO2max (20%) from T2 to T3 (see Table 5). Current results for the HA

Table 3. Pre-training and current measurements for moderately active subjects

Variables	n	Pre-training (T1)	Current (T3)	p
Age (years)	27	68.2 ± 4.3	73.8 ± 4.4	---
Weight (kg)	27	66.0 ± 11.7	65.3 ± 12.5	0.2985
Body fat (%)	26	28.9 ± 7.0	25.7 ± 5.9	0.0003*
V0$_2$ (ml·kg^{-1}·min^{-1})	21	26.8 ± 5.9	24.6 ± 6.9	0.0141*
V0$_2$ (L/min)	21	1.8 ± 0.6	1.7 ± 0.6	0.011*
HRmax (beats/min)	21	163 ± 13.7	162.4 ± 15.3	0.825
SBPmax (mm Hg)	21	193.4 ± 22.9	201.8 ± 22.4	0.039*
DBPmax (mm Hg)	21	86.0 ± 11.1	89.4 ± 14.5	0.276
VEmax (L/min)	21	73.3 ± 26.5	70.6 ± 26.2	0.441
RSBP (mm Hg)	26	125.0 ± 16	128 ± 19.1	0.319
RDBP (mm Hg)	26	74.2 ± 8.2	75.7 ± 6.5	0.265
RHR (beats/min)	26	66.1 ± 6.3	66.2 ± 7.8	0.923
FEV/FVC (%)	8	80.0 ± 6.1	80.1 ± 3.8	0.811
FVC (L)	8	3.0 ± 0.5	2.8 ± 0.6	0.160
FEV1.0 (L)	8	3.1 ± 2.0	2.3 ± 0.5	0.243
Skinfold (mm)	26	157 ± 49.5	129.1 ± 40.1	0.0001*
Cholesterol (total)	23	210.9 ± 40.2	220.2 ± 40	0.197
Triglycerides	22	133.5 ± 52.8	135.0 ± 49.8	0.896

*Significance, $p < 0.05$

group showed smaller, but significant, decreases in AbVO2max (17%) than in MOD and SED groups. In addition, values for pulmonary function such as FVC (9%), and FEV1.0 (10%) were found to be reduced in a similar fashion as the MOD and SED groups. Additional T3 results for the HA group showed no significance change compared to T2. However, results for HA group indicated a substantially preferable shift in values for almost every category analyzed when compared to MOD and SED groups.

As in the HA group, results for the MOD group showed decreases in VO2max (20%), together with a significant decrease in % BF (6%) from T2 to T3 (see Table 6). Current results for the MOD group showed a significant decrease in VEmax (10%), AbVO2max (20%), FVC (10%), FEV1.0 (8%), and sum of seven skinfolds (12%) compared to T2 data.

Compared to the MOD and HA groups, results for the SED group showed a somewhat greater decrease in VO2max (28%), as well as a

Table 4. Pre-training and current measurements for sedentary subjects

Variables	n	Pre-training (T1)	Current (T3)	p
Age (years)	16	68.2 ± 4.3	73.8 ± 4.4	---
Weight (kg)	16	75.9 ± 16.7	76.8 ± 18.6	0.539
Body fat (%)	16	32.8 ± 7.1	29.8 ± 6.8	0.006*
V0$_2$				
(ml·kg^{-1}·min^{-1})	10	23.5 ± 4.1	19.1 ± 4.4	0.005*
V0$_2$ (L/min)	10	1.8 ± 0.5	1.5 ± 0.5	0.005*
HRmax				
(beats/min)	10	159.6 ± 8.8	151.5 ± 13.6	0.011*
SBPmax				
(mm Hg)	10	187.5 ± 18.3	194.1 ± 15.4	0.227
DBPmax				
(mm Hg)	10	82.1 ± 11.4	85.8 ± 15.4	0.524
VEmax (L/min)	10	61.6 ± 24	64.5 ± 23.1	0.219
RSBP (mm Hg)	16	121.8 ± 16.5	124.4 ± 10.1	0.484
RDBP (mm Hg)	16	73.4 ± 7.8	74.6 ± 5.1	0.487
RHR				
(beats/min)	16	69.1 ± 8.3	69.2 ± 8.7	0.973
FEV/FVC (%)	9	78.0 ± 5.5	81.6 ± 7.6	0.160
FVC (L)	9	3.5 ± 0.9	3.1 ± 0.8	0.002
FEV1.0 (L)	9	2.8 ± 0.7	2.5 ± 0.6	0.002*
Skinfold (mm)	16	190.3 ± 61.8	159.5 ± 50.5	0.006*
Cholesterol				
(total)	14	229.2 ± 55.5	222.8 ± 33.2	0.564
Triglycerides	14	119.0 ± 42.3	138.9 ± 60.5	0.155

Significance, $p < 0.05$

decrease in % BF (7%) for T3 measurements (see Table 7). Results for the SED group indicate a significant decrease in current HRmax (6%), AbVO2max (29%), FVC (12%), FEV1.0 (8%), and sum of seven skinfolds (14%). In addition, T3 results indicate an increase in RSBP (5%), RDBP (7%), RHR (6%), and FEV/FVC (6%).

Cross-sectional comparison

Mean body weight (BW) values were significantly different among groups ($p = 0.031$). When post-hoc analysis was performed significant differences were found between the SED and MOD groups, indicating heavier BW for the SED group than that found for the MOD group (see table 8). The mean relative VO2max values were borderline, but not significantly different, among groups ($p = 0.050$). Relative VO2max results, although borderline, again appeared favorable for the HA and the MOD groups, when compared to the SED group. In addition, results indicated the HA group to have significantly higher FVC values ($p = 0.036$) than MOD and SED groups. However, FEV1.0 and FEV/FVC results indicated no significant differences

Table 5. Post-training and current measurements for highly active subjects

Variables	n	Post-training (T2)	Current (T3)	p
Age (years)	12	66.8 ± 3.2	71.9 ± 4.0	---
Weight (kg)	10	74.2 ± 7.9	74.2 ± 9.3	1.000
Body Fat (%)	10	23.0 ± 5.4	22.6 ± 4.2	0.578
V02				
$(ml \cdot kg^{-1} \cdot min^{-1})$	9	31.1 ± 6.8	25.1 ± 4.2	0.009*
V02 (L/min)	9	2.4 ± 0.4	2.0 ± 0.3	0.010*
HRmax				
(beats/min)	9	164.8 ± 10.6	163.1 ± 23.9	0.818
SBPmax				
(mm Hg)	9	202.9 ± 22.5	198.7 ± 20.0	0.570
DBPmax				
(mm Hg)	9	91.8 ± 11.7	88.9 ± 11.7	0.288
VEmax (L/min)	9	80.1 ± 16.1	81.6 ± 14.8	0.703
RSBP (mm Hg)	10	111.3 ± 18.2	116.9 ± 12.7	0.256
RDBP (mm Hg)	10	67.8 ± 10.6	72.3 ± 6.0	0.172
RHR				
(beats/min)	10	57.3 ± 6.2	59.3 ± 9.1	0.313
FEV/FVC (%)	6	72.7 ± 3.3	73.2 ± 5.6	0.839
FVC (L)	6	4.5 ± 0.7	4.1 ± 0.7	0.049*
FEV1.0 (L)	6	3.3 ± 0.6	3.0 ± 0.6	0.006*
Skinfold (mm)	10	124.7 ± 33.5	117.1 ± 28.3	0.114

*Significance, $p < 0.05$

among groups ($p = 0.461$ and $p = 0.214$, respectively). Analysis of the sum of seven skinfold measurements detected significantly higher values for the SED group when compared to the HA and MOD groups. However, no significant differences were found between the MOD and HA group. The SED group had lower physical function as measured by the modified 9-item physical performance test (PPT) compared to the MOD and the HA groups ($p = 0.004$).

DISCUSSION

The primary finding of the present study was that the group of more physically active elderly individuals had maintained a better physiological status, when compared to sedentary individuals (SED) in both longitudinal as well as cross-sectional comparisons. Moreover, this study also found a decrease in important physiological measurements, such as VO2max, skinfold and % BF, in the HA (highly active) and MOD (moderately active) active categories.

Although active elderly individuals generally maintained, but not improved VO2max over the years (T1 to T3 comparison), results indicated that these elderly individuals have slightly decreased aerobic capacities. The

Table 6. Post-training and current measurements for moderately active subjects

Variables	n	Post-training (T2)	Current (T3)	p
Age (years)	27	68.2 ± 4.3	73.8 ± 4.4	---
Weight (kg)	27	65.6 ± 12.3	65.3 ± 12.5	0.149
Body fat (%)	26	27.3 ± 6.9	25.7 ± 5.9	0.032*
VO_2				
(ml·kg^{-1}·min^{-1})	21	30.2 ± 5.8	24.6 ± 6.9	0.000*
VO_2 (L/min)	21	2.1 ± 0.6	1.7 ± 0.6	0.000*
HRmax				
(beats/min)	21	164.7 ± 16.8	162.4 ± 15.3	0.307
SBPmax				
(mm Hg)	21	197.0 ± 26.2	201.8 ± 22.4	0.266
DBPmax				
(mm Hg)	21	83.1 ± 13.0	89.4 ± 14.5	0.045*
VEmax (L/min)	21	78.4 ± 24.9	70.6 ± 26.2	0.026*
RSBP (mm Hg)	26	122.1 ± 17.7	128.0 ± 19.1	0.069
RDBP (mm Hg)	26	70.1 ± 9.3	75.7 ± 6.5	0.003*
RHR				
(beats/min)	26	63.8 ± 7.0	66.2 ± 7.8	0.115
FEV/FVC (%)	8	79.0 ± 4.4	80.1 ± 3.8	0.540
FVC (L)	8	3.1 ± 0.6	2.8 ± 0.6	0.014*
FEV1.0 (L)	8	2.5 ± 0.5	2.3 ± 0.47	0.022*
Skinfold (mm)	26	145.3 ± 48.8	129.1 ± 40.1	0.006*

*Significance, $p < 0.05$

decrease in VO2max for MOD elderly individuals (9%), together with the trend of decline for HA elderly individuals, are in agreement with previous studies indicating that as sedentary men age their VO2max decreases at a rate of approximately 0.45 ml×kg-1×min-1 per year (27,28). The rate of decline in VO2max in MOD active elderly individuals agrees with other studies showing an age-related decline averaging 5 to 10% per decade (29). Furthermore, the greater decrease in relative VO2max observed for the T2 to T3 analysis is in agreement with some of the first longitudinal studies of VO2max (30-32). Dill et al (31) reported a greater rate of VO2max decline in highly trained men, who had not been training during the years preceding their retesting. Similarly, the rate of decline in VO2max observed for the SED group was only slightly different compared to the active groups and was somewhat in agreement with previous studies. Our results suggested that healthy sedentary men and women combined (see table 4) and separated (not published), who undergo natural aging processes demonstrate similar rates of decline in VO2max as their highly active counterparts with a progressive decline in VO2max expressed traditionally as Kg/BW generally occured with advancing age. This decline could be attributed to the age-associated increase in % BF and BW and the loss of metabolically active

Table 7. Post-training and current measurements for sedentary subjects

Variables	n	Post-training (T2)	Current (T3)	p
Age (years)	16	68.2 ± 4.3	73.8 ± 4.4	---
Weight (kg)	16	77.0 ± 18.3	76.8 ± 18.6	0.851
Body fat (%)	16	32.0 ± 7.8	29.8 ± 6.7	0.017*
VO$_2$ (ml·kg^{-1}·min^{-1})	9	26.0 ± 6.7	18.8 ± 4.6	0.001*
VEmax (L/min)	9	2.1 ± 0.6	1.5 ± 0.5	0.000*
HRmax (beats/min)	9	159.1 ± 10.2	150.7 ± 14.2	0.014*
SBPmax (mm Hg)	9	192.6 ± 28.9	196.6± 17.1	0.586
DBPmax (mm Hg)	9	80.2 ± 15.0	84.9 ± 16.0	0.437
VEmax (L/min)	9	72.1 ± 26.0	65.9 ± 24.1	0.084
RSBP (mm Hg)	16	118.3 ± 10.2	124.4 ± 10.1	0.009*
RDBP (mm Hg)	16	69.4 ± 8.6	74.6 ± 5.1	0.004*
RHR (beats/min)	16	65.4 ± 7.0	69.2 ± 8.7	0.037*
FEV/FVC (%)	9	77.2 ± 5.9	81.6 ± 7.6	0.029*
FVC (L)	9	3.5 ± 0.8	3.1 ± 0.8	0.002*
FEV1.0 (L)	9	2.7 ± 0.6	2.5 ± 0.6	0.016*
Skinfold (mm)	16	184.3 ± 65	159.5 ± 50.5	0.011*

*Significance, $p < 0.05$

tissue (i.e., muscles which decrease VO2max when normalized for weight). Muscle mass has been reported to decrease with age (10-12% per decade), even when total body mass is maintained, probably owing to increased fat mass. Furthermore, in both sexes, a large portion of the age-associated decline in VO2max in non-endurance-trained individuals can be explained by the loss of muscle mass (33). Since BW in this study was not found to change over time it is assumed that it did not account for the decreased VO2max observed. Furthermore, it is possible that the activity intensity performed by the MOD group, and to a certain degree by the HA group, was insufficient to prevent the moderate decrease in VO2max observed in this study.

Fat tissue accumulation and a loss of fat-free mass have been reported in advancing age resulting in an increase in BW. However, recent studies showed a consistent improvement in total BW and in skinfold measurements due to different training regimens (8). In the present study the longitudinal analysis of total body fat indicated an insignificant decrease (p<0.05) in % BF (12%) for MOD active elderly individuals as well as a mild decrease in % BF of HA elderly individuals. Therefore, our data indicate that staying physically active, (i.e., engaging in moderate and high activity levels), is an important lifestyle factor that may affect age-related changes in

Table 8. Cross-sectional comparison for current measurements

Variables	Highly active group	Moderately active group	Sedentary group	p
Age (years)	71.9 ± 4.0 (12)	72.0 ± 5.4 (27)	73.8 ± 4.4 (16)	---
Weight (kg)	73.6 ± 9.4 (11)	65.3 ± 12.5 (27)	76.8 ± 18.6 (16)	0.031*2
Body fat (%)	23.3 ± 4.6 (11)	25.7 ± 5.8 (27)	29.8 ± 6.8 (16)	0.018*1
V0$_2$ (ml·kg^{-1}·min^{-1})	24.3 ± 4.8 (10)	24.6 ± 6.9 (21)	19.1 ± 4.2 (10)	0.050
Hrmax (beats/min)	161.8 ± 23.0 (10)	162.4 ± 15.3(21)	151.5 ± 13.6 (10)	0.238
RSBP (mm Hg)	118.5 ± 13.3 (11)	128.0 ± 19.1 (26)	124.4 ± 10.1 (16)	0.556
RDBP (mm Hg)	73.3 ± 6.5 (11)	75.7 ± 6.5 (26)	74.6 ± 5.1(16)	0.920
FEV/FVC (%)	77.4 ± 10.0 (12)	81.0 ± 5.6 (27)	82.0 ± 6.3 (15)	0.214
FVC (L)	3.7 ± 0.9 (12)	3.0 ± 0.6 (27)	3.1 ± 0.9 (15)	0.036
FEV1.0 (L)	2.8 ± 0.7 (12)	2.6 ± 0.7 (27)	2.5 ± 0.6 (15)	0.461
Skinfold (mm)	119.7 ± 28.3 (11)	129.1 ± 39.3 (27)	159.5 ± 50.5(16)	0.027*1
TG	121.3 ± 44.5 (11)	131.0 ± 48.0 (26)	151.1 ± 70.7 (16)	0.343
LDL	137.7 ± 27.5 (11)	144.0 ± 37.4 (26)	136.8 ± 32.3 (16)	0.767
HDL	45.8 ± 9.5 (11)	55.3 ± 15.5 (26)	51.6 ± 17.5 (16)	0.222*3
CHOL	210.3 ± 26.7 (12)	215.5 ± 59.4 (26)	218.5 ± 34.3 (16)	0.900
PPT	27.3 ± 1.4 (12)	27.8 ± 1.8 (26)	24.8 ± 4.5 (16)	0.004 *

Note. * Post-hoc test- SED group were found to be significantly different from HA and MOD active groups (p < 0.05).   Post-hoc test- HA group was found to be significantly different from MOD and SED groups (p < 0.05).

*1 Post-hoc test- HA group is significantly different from SED (p < 0.05)

*2 Post-hoc test- SED group significantly different from MOD group (p < 0.05)

*3 Post-hoc test- HA group was found to be significantly different from MOD group

body composition. Nevertheless, it is important to note that the decrease in % BF for the HA elderly individuals was not statistically significant, although it is possible that this was due solely to the relatively small number of observations. Contrary to the notion that a decline in physical activity performed (reduced exercise-related energy expenditure) may contribute to age-associated elevations in body fat, our data indicate that whole body adiposity decreases with age in the sedentary individuals. It is possible that in the SED group the decrease in % BF was due to a higher initial value as a minimal increase in % BF occurs in individuals who are overweight. On the other hand, the lower overall % BF one has, the more difficult it is to lose BF. These results are similar to those supporting a maintenance of % BF with age, especially over age 60 (34,35) or a decrease in % BF in late old age (36). Furthermore, these results are also in accord with studies showing no change or minimal change in BW after early old age (over age 50) (37). Another possibility is that perhaps this group of sedentary individuals may have made dietary modifications, which largely influenced their % BF. However, dietary data collected in questionnaires were insufficient for meaningful analysis.

Hypertension is well recognized as the most potent, common, and determinable risk factor for cardiovascular disease in elderly individuals, whereas physical activity is widely recommended as a useful adjunct in primary and secondary prevention of hypertension in sedentary elderly individuals. In the HA group under study, results suggested that maintaining highly active lifestyles helped to preserve their initial (i.e., before the exercise training) resting and maximal BP. However, for the MOD active elderly individuals the results indicated a slight but significantly increased SBPmax (5%), maximal DBP (DBPmax) (8%) and RDBP (8%) over the follow-up period. These observations differ from the findings of a study showing six months of continuous endurance walking exercise training eliciting a beneficial effect in reducing RBP in elderly normotensive subjects (18). Studies have shown that elderly men and women with lower fitness levels have significantly higher average resting arterial BP than those in excellent fitness categories (38). In support of these studies, the present study indicated that the SED group averaged 6% elevation in RSBP and RDBP for the longitudinal analysis (T1 to T3 analysis). Furthermore, our data indicated that SED elderly individuals were able to somewhat maintain their RBP values similar to values recorded before training (T1). These data suggested that the nature of activity undertaken during the follow-up period was probably different from the one attained throughout the training studies. Thus, activity should be continued in order to maintain beneficial effects of exercise. It is important to mention, that the RBP, although slightly elevated, was continually far below 160/95 mm Hg, which is less than the RDBP value considered as a risk factor for CHD, therefore, reflecting reduced risk of CHD for all groups. Considering their lack of activity, it is possible that the SED group was able to maintain average normal RBP due to preferable genetic factors, possible modification of nutrition and maintenance of % BF and BW. In addition, one of the limitations of this study was that a normal RBP was initially necessary in order for the person to participate in the present study. Therefore, conclusions with regard to RBP and lifestyle status are limited.

Advanced age is associated with a decline in FEV/FVC for almost every sub-group with the rate of FEV1.0 decline accelerating in advancing years. The present longitudinal analysis showed a slight decrement (~ 10%) in pulmonary function for HA and MOD elderly individuals in agreement with the literature (35). As we anticipated, data indicated that sedentary individuals experienced even greater decreases in pulmonary function over time. In contrast, results for the SED group also indicated higher FEV/FVC values. Therefore, it would seem reasonable to speculate that these higher FEV/FVC values may be an indication for developing restrictive lung disease in these sedentary individuals. However, it is difficult to reach any clear conclusions regarding pulmonary measurements owing to the limited number of observations for the pulmonary variables. It is important to keep in mind that the same number of subjects for the HA and MOD groups yielded different results.

One of our main purposes in the present study was to evaluate current physiological status between the different study categories, since many studies support the finding that elderly individuals who maintain an active lifestyle have a healthier physiological profile and a more functional life than those who are significantly less active (39). If so, our physically active elderly individuals should have better physiological functioning compared to age-matched sedentary elderly individuals. Indeed, elderly individuals with habitual higher levels of physical activities, had better results on tests of % BF, PPT, and sum of seven skinfolds. However, no differences were found between groups for resting arterial blood pressure, blood lipids, aerobic capacity, and pulmonary function. Overall, VO2max, resting BP, PPT, and % BF were found to be consistently favorable for the HA and the MOD groups compared to the SED group. Our results are consistent with a study by Voorrips et al (40), who reported that elderly women with habitual higher physical activities had better endurance, resting BP and peak expiratory flow. Although resting SBP and DBP showed a tendency toward a small, but non-significant reduction for the HA group, it was considered unlikely that normotensive elderly subjects such as those in the present study would benefit from active lifestyles related to BP reduction observed in subjects with mild or borderline hypertension (41).

The role of regular physical activity in the etiology of chronic diseases associated with aging has been increasingly recognized over the past few decades. The daily functional capacity of individuals is reduced well before any physiological functional capacity is decreased and disease emerges. The physical performance test (PPT) is well accepted as a practical tool for estimating functional capacity through the ability to perform certain activities of daily living (26). In the present study sedentary elderly individuals had lower scores on the PPT test compared to the moderately active and highly active subjects. Thus, it appeared that the PPT should be used as a method of choice to estimate functional capacities of individuals.

Finally, an active lifestyle can result in higher levels of HDL and lower levels of LDL (42). In contrast to other measurements, LDL, HDL and cholesterol measurements were not influenced by activity levels in our study. It is possible that active lifestyles are very unlikely to improve plasma lipid profiles unless the activities are accompanied by substantial weight loss or changes in dietary habits.

One limitation of our study was the lack of quantifiable information about the activity status of the subjects during the period from the termination of the initial studies to the present investigation. It is certainly possible that a number of subjects had changed their activity levels during the 3 to 7 year interval from the initial to the present study.

CONCLUSIONS

In summary, the present study could not clearly demonstrate favorable differences for the active groups over the sedentary group with regard to several important physiological factors over the five year follow-up and it appears that the recommendation for, and the initiation of adopting active lifestyles, may not be sufficient on their own to significantly increase an individual's physiological functioning.

A striking and somehow unexpected finding of the present study was the demonstration that many important physiological parameters do not differ significantly between sedentary and active elderly individuals. Furthermore, given the preferable results for the active group on most tested variables, we suggest that misclassification is unlikely to have biased our results. Perhaps even more important, our data might suggest that the average elderly person does not participate in sufficiently high intensity exercise levels to provide most of the disease prevention benefits associated with increased physical activity levels shown in many training studies. Although the health benefits of regular physical activity regarding a variety of chronic disease areas, including cardiovascular disease, are now well established, many elderly people do not engage in regular physical activity. In addition, those who exercise do not perform it with appropriate frequency or intensity required to obtain positive physiological changes such as improved cardiovascular fitness. Moreover, these results suggest that unsupervised self-engaged physical activity may not always benefit elderly people.

ACKNOWLEDGEMENTS

This manuscript is dedicated to the memory of professor Michael L Pollock, PhD (1936-98). Michael L Pollock was the director of the University of Florida Center for Exercise Science and suffered an aneurysm while attending the annual meeting of the American College of Sports Medicine (ACSM). He had been responsible for new national exercise guidelines, updated every 10 to 12 years, based on committee reviews of published scientific papers. Pollock has chaired the ACSM sponsored group since its inception in 1972. His career research highlights includes   a 20-year study of master athletes 40 years and older that yielded information on the effects of aging on aerobic capacity, developing "exercise prescriptions" that hasten recovery after heart surgery, demonstrating that proper exercise programs can increase aerobic capacity 15 to 30 percent in people age 30 and older, determining low-impact exercises such as rapid walking to be better than jogging for the elderly, showing that building stronger bones through weight training can help prevent osteoporosis, determining that one set of weight-lifting exercises may be just as beneficial as the three-consecutive-set regime commonly performed. Pollock has been the recipient of several awards, including a Fellowship Award for Research from the Japan Society for the Promotion of Science, an Award of Excellence from the American Association of Cardiovascular and Pulmonary and the 1993 Scholar Award from the American College of Sports Medicine, Southeastern Region. He authored more than 275 articles, three books and two monographs on exercise physiology, physical fitness, cardiac rehabilitation and sports medicine. He was past president of the ACSM and a fellow of both the American College of Cardiology and the American Association of Cardiovascular and Pulmonary Rehabilitation. From 1972 to 1989, he served as a consultant to the President's Council on Physical Fitness and Sports. This chapter is an adapted version of an earlier published paper (Carmeli E, Orbach P, Lowenthal DT, Merrick J, Coleman R. Long-term effects of activity status in the elderly on cardiorespiratory capacity, blood pressure, blood lipids and body composition: A five year follow-up study.ScientificWorldJournal 2003;3:751-67).

REFERENCES

1.   Mazzeo RS, Cavanagh P, Evans,WJ, Fiatarone M, Hagberg J, McAuley E, Startzell J. ACSM position stand: exercise and physical activity for older adults. Med Sci Sports Exer 1998; 30: 992-1008.
2.   Allman BL, Rice CL. Neuromuscular fatigue and aging: central and peripheral factors. Muscle and Nerve, 2002;25: 785-96.
3.   Churchill JD, Galvez R, Colcombe S, Swain RA, Kramer AF, Greenough WT. Exercise, experience and aging brain. Neurobiol Aging, 2002;23: 941-55.
4.   Pollock ML, Graves JE, Swart DL, Lowenthal DT. Exercise training and prescription for the elderly. Southern Med J,1994; 87: S88-95.
5.   Hersey WC, Graves JE, Pollock ML, Gingerich R, Shireman,RB, Heath GW, Spierto F, McCole SD, Hagberg JM. (1994). Endurance exercise training improves body composition and plasma insulin responses in 70- to 79-year-old women. Metabol Clin Exper1994; 43: 847-54.
6.   Wallace ES, White JA, Downie A, Dalzell G, Doran D. Influence of exercise adherence level on modifiable coronary heart disease risk factors and functional-fitness level in middle-aged men. Brit J Sports Med 1993;27:101-6.
7.   Bouchard C, Rankinen T. Individual differences in response to regular physical activity. Med Sci Sports Exer,2001; 33: 446-51
8.   Kohrt WM, Malley MT, Dalsky GP, Holloszy JO. Body composition of healthy sedentary and trained, young and older men and women. Med Sci Sports Exer 1992;24: 832-7.
9.   Carmeli E, Coleman R, Reznick AZ. The biochemistry of aging muscle. Exp Gerontol 2002;37: 477-89.
10.   McGuire DK, Levine BD, Williamson JW, Snell PG, Blomqvist CG, Saltin B, Mitchell JH. A 30-year follow up of the Dallas Bed rest and Training study: II. Effect of age on cardiovascular response to exercise. Circulation,2001; 104: 1350-7.

11.   Cress ME, Buchner DM, Questad KA, Esselman PC, deLateur BJ, Schwartz RS. Exercise: effects on physical functional performance in independent older adults. J Gerontol Series A-Biol Sci Med Sci, 1999;54: M242-M248.

12.   Kasch FW, Boyer JL, Schmidt PK, Wells RH, Wallace JP, Verity LS, Guy H, Schneider D. Ageing of the cardiovascular system during 33 years of aerobic exercise. Age and Ageing, 1999; 28: 531-6.

13.   Carmeli E, Reznick AZ, Coleman R, Carmeli V. Muscle strength and mass of lower extremities in relation to functional abilities in elderly adults. Gerontology,2000; 46: 249-57.

14.   Young DR, Haskell,WL, Jatulis DE, Fortmann,SP. Associations between changes in physical activity and risk factors for coronary heart disease in a community-based sample of men and women: the Stanford Five-City Project. Am J Epidemiol 1991; 138: 205-16.

15.   Branch JD, Pate RR, Bourque SP. Moderate intensity training improves cardiorespiratory fitness in women. J Womens Health & Gender-based Med, 2000;9: 65-73.

16.   Vincent KR, Braith RW, Feldman RA, Kallas HE, Lowenthal DT. Improved cardiorespiratory endurance following 6 months of resistance exercise in elderly men and women. Arch Int Med 2002; 162: 673-8.

17.   Hubert HB, Eaker ED, Garrison RJ, Castelli WP. Life-style correlates of risk factor change in young adults: an eight-year study of coronary heart disease risk factors in the Framingham offspring. Am J Epidemiol 1987; 125: 812-31.

18.   Braith RW, Pollock ML, Lowenthal DT, Graves JE., Limacher MC. Moderate-and high-intensity exercise lowers blood pressure in normotensive subjects 60 to 79 years of age. Am J Cardiol, 1994; 73: 1124-8.

19.   Hagberg JM, Graves JE, Limacher M, Woods DR, Leggett SH, Cononie C, Gruber JJ, Pollock ML. Cardiovascular responses of 70- to 79-yr-old men and women to exercise training. J Appl Physiol 1989; 66: 2589-94.

20.   Jessup JV, Lowenthal DT, Pollock ML, Turner T. The effects of endurance exercise training on ambulatory blood pressure in normotensive older adults. Geriatr, Nephrol Urol 1998; 8:103-9.

21.   Ware JE, Gandek B, Kosinski M, Aaronson NK. The equivalence of SF-36 summary health scores estimated using standards and country-specific algorithms in 10 country: Results from the IQOLA project. J Clin Epidemiol 1998; 51:1167-70

22.   Bonnefoy M, Normand S, Pachiaudi C, Lacour JR, Laville M, Kostka T. Simultaneous validation of 10 physical activity questionnaires older men: a doubly labeled water study. J Am Geriat Soc 2001; 49: 28-35.

23.   Larsen GE, George JD, Alexander JL, Fellingham GW, Aldana SG, Parcell AC. Prediction of maximum oxygen consumption from walking, jogging, or running. Res Quart Exer Sports 2002; 73: 66-72.

24.   Lemura LM, Von Duvillard SP, Mookerjee,S. The effects of physical training of functional capacity in adults. Ages 46 to 90: a meta-analysis. J Sports Med Phys Fit, 2000; 40: 1-10.

25.   Jackson AS, Pollock ML. Research progress in validation of clinical methods of assessing body composition. Med Sci Sports Exer 1984; 16: 606-15.

26.   Reuben DB, Siu AL. An objective measure of physical function of elderly outpatients: The Physical Performance Test. J Am Geriatr Soc1990; 38:1105-12.

27.   Heath GW, Hagberg JM, Ehsani AA, Holloszy J.O. A physiological comparison of young and older endurance athletes. J Appl Physiol: Respiratory, Environmental and Exercise Physiology, 1981; 51:634-40.

28.   Taylor J, Tucker LA. Comparison of the CardiGlide, cross walk and treadmill walking in development of cardiovascular endurance, dynamic strength and flexibility in middle-aged men and women. Percepl Motor Skills,1996; 82: 875-82.

29.   Bell C, Paterson DH, Kowalchuk JM, Moy AP, Thorp DB, Noble EG, Taylor AW, Cunningham DA. Determinants of oxygen uptake kinetics in older humans following single-limb endurance exercise training. Exp Physiol 2001; 86: 659-65.

30.   Robinson S, Dill DB, Robinson RD, Tzankoff SP, Wagner JA. Physiological aging of champion runners. J Appl Physiol 1976; 41: 46-51.

31.   Dill DB, Hillyard SD, Miller J. Vital capacity, exercise performance, and blood gases at altitude as related to age. J Appl Physiol 1980;48:6-9

32.   Arsac LM, Locatelli E. Modeling the energetics of 100-m running by using speed curves of world champions. J Appl Physiol 2002; 92: 1781-8.

33.   Fleg JL, Lakatta E.G. Role of muscle loss in the age-associated reduction in VO2max. J Appl Physiol 1988; 65:1147-51.

34.   Gordon T, Kagan A, Garcia-Palmieri M, Kannel WB, Zukel WJ, Tillotson J, Sorlie P, Hjortland M. Diet and its relation to coronary heart disease and death in three populations. Circulation,1981; 63: 500-15.

35.   Burr ML, Phillips KM, Hurst DN. Lung function in the elderly. Thorax,1985; 40: 54-9.

36.   Silver AJ, Guillen CP, Kahl MJ, Morley J.E. Effect of aging on body fat. J Am Geriatr Soc 1993; 41: 211-3.

37.   Lesser GT, Markofsky J. Body water compartment with human aging using fat-free mass as the reference standard. Am J Physiol1979; 236: R215-20.

38.   LaMonte MJ, Durstine JL, Addy CL, Irwin ML, Ainsworth BE. Physical activity, physical fitness, and Framingham 10-year risk score: the cross cultural activity participation study. J Cardiopul Rehabil 2001; 21: 63-70.

39.   Blair SN, Connelly JC. How much physical activity should we do? The case for moderate amounts and intensities of physical activity. Re Quart Exer Sport, 1996; 67: 193-205.

40.   Voorrips LE, Lemmink KAPM, van Heuvelen MJP, Bult P, van Staveren WA. The physical condition of elderly women differing in habitual physical activity. Med Sci Sports Exer 1993; 25:1152-7.

41.   Kiyonaga A, Arakawa K, Tanaka H, Shindo M. Blood pressure and hormonal responses to aerobic exercise. Hypertension, 1985; 7: 125-31.

42.   Haskell WL. The influence of exercise training on plasma lipids and lipoproteins in health and disease. Acta Med Scand 1986; 711: 25-37.

CHAPTER 6
Older persons with intellectual disability and physical activity

Eli Carmeli, Shlomo Kessel and Joav Merrick

L onger life expectancy is resulting in increasing numbers of elderly adults with intellectual disability (ID). There has been the question whether persons with ID demonstrate early signs of aging before the general population. The aim of this chapter was to determine if persons with ID (with and without Down syndrome) showed premature aging changes compared with a control group. Elderly (n=24, average age of 61) from one residential care center in Israel and younger adults from another center (n=37, average age of 45) were compared with elderly residents without ID in an independent living facility. The study considered demographic data, medical data, anthropometric measurements, body fat and body mass index, flexibility and sensori-motor function tests. The results showed that the persons with ID had basically similar body composition to that of persons without ID, however the functional performance of elderly adults with ID was more impaired. We postulate that the slower functioning responses may be explained by a less physically active lifestyle, that may accelerate the onset of disease and result in symptoms associated with aging that are detrimental to health. It is therefore important that persons with ID participate in physical activity and exercises in order to promote health and prevent disease.

INTRODUCTION

In recent years aging has become an issue in the field of intellectual disability (ID), because longer life survival is resulting in increasing numbers of elderly adults with ID, which is also the case in Israel (1). Researchers investigating aging processes have generally found similar aging patterns for people with or without ID (2). Nonetheless, individuals with ID show some characteristics of premature aging resulting in a greater inclination to morbidity and deconditioning (3-5). Demographic aging, which refers to the increasing numbers of elderly adults within the overall population, is currently presenting major challenges for both health and social care services and for the immediate families.

Traditionally, intervention for aging persons with disabilities has focused on chronic physical impairment, functional capacity and mental condition. Several approaches have been used to try and minimize secondary conditions and reduce mortality rates. Comparative studies of elderly individuals, with and without ID, have raised several questions and have also revealed significant differences between the two groups.

The prevalence of various diseases (diabetes, hypertension), obesity, decrease of flexibility, and sedentary living can be used as indications of premature aging (6). Individual aging changes are very diverse and behavioral changes in day-to-day lifestyle have a major role in aging (7). The prevalence of physically debilitating symptoms in aging persons with ID, increases the demands for active diagnostic and therapeutic services. Such conditions include moderate to severe hearing loss and visual impairment (8,9), a high incidence of balance and gait dysfunction (10), arthritis and urinary incontinence (11), obesity (12) and non-ischemic heart disorders (13). Determination of premature aging may be indicated by a range of signs and symptoms (14). The evaluation and active screening of cognitive and functional capabilities are important in order to assess their specific needs and to determine appropriate rehabilitative and psychotherapeutic programs.

This chapter to evaluate and describe the physical and functional characteristics of elderly persons with ID in residential care and to compare their functional status and capabilities with a control population without ID, who lived in an independent living facility. Our study tried to focus on functional capability rather than on impairment in adults with ID and we believe that its implications could influence the decision making process in the welfare and health authorities.

OUR STUDY

A samle of elderly persons with intellectual disability (ID) was drawn from two redidential care centers in Israel, Neve Ram in the north (total population 197 persons) and Neve Natoa in the central part (total pop. 166 persons). The first group consisted of twenty-four elderly adults (out of 34), hereafter referred to as, Group A1, included two subgroups: a) with moderate ID and Down syndrome (DS) (n=10) and b) non-specified moderate ID (NSID) (n=14). The sample from the other center consisted of thirty seven (out of 46) younger adults, Group A2, included two subgroups: a) with moderate ID and DS (n=13) and b) the NSID (n=24). The participants through their legal guardians gave written informed consent to the study. All participants required minimal supervision for daily activities, and their daily activities regime was comparable.

The control group (CG) consisted of 31 (out of 42) older adults (aged 75.7 ± 5 years), who lived in independent living facilities located in Haifa in the north. All the participants of the control group provided informed consent to participate in the study. All participants with pre-existing conditions that could interfere with the results or could lead to co-morbidity (with non-age-related changes) were excluded from the study (i.e. blindness, amputation, severe osteoarthritis). Co-morbidity conditions included depression, and possible adverse drug reactions.

Kappa statistics (K) were used to determine the inter-rater reliability for the different evaluation procedures. The evaluation procedures on separate days were undertaken by two physical and occupational therapists, with four and 19 years of clinical experience as geriatric therapists. All medical assessments were undertaken by the physicians of the residential care centers, who provided medical services to the facility for the last seven years.

The following evaluation procedures were included in the assessment protocol for each participant: demographic data, medical data, body composition, and two sensorimotor function tests. Standard methods were used for anthropometric measurements including body weight (kg), height (cm), waist girth at the level of umbilicus, and thigh girth (at three points: the widest point, and seven cm and 14 cm above the base of the patella) using a cloth measuring tape. To determine the waist: hip ratio (WHR), the waist measurement was divided by the hip measurement at the widest point. Healthy females and males should have WHR less than 1.8 and 1.9, respectively. Studies showed that females and males with ratios greater than 1.8 and 1.9 tendedto have excessive fat around the waist. These measurements provide information about fat and muscle mass in the lower quadrant (i.e. pelvis and lower extremity) and serve as indicators for inclination to obesity, which are important because of their connection to health conditions such as heart disease, and muscle strength (15).

Body fat determination (TBF 611, Tanita Corp. USA) was based on a bio-electrical impedance analysis method (16). Bio-electrical impedance measures the length of time taken for an electrical impulse to travel from one place of the body (i.e. hand) to another place on the body (i.e. foot). The impulse requires less time to travel through muscle tissue than fat. Body mass index (BMI=weight(kg)/height(m2)) expresses the relationship of body weight to height. A BMI greater than 27.3, and 28.8 for females and males respectively, is an indication of obesity (17).

Flexibility of the lower trunk and hamstring muscles was measured by procedures adapted from Hoeger (18) and the functional reach test of Duncan et al. [19] in a modified long-sitting and forward reach test. The test requires that the subject reach forward in a long-sitting position, while keeping the legs straight. The best score of three trials was recorded.

Two sensoti-motor tests were performed: "timed-up and go" test (TUAG), and a three-minute distance walk test (3MDW). The "timed-up and go" test was used to measure the dynamic balance and gait speed (20). A participant was asked to rise from an armchair, walk three meters, and return to the chair. Times were measured using a manual stopwatch. The functional factors observed by the testers with this test include: path deviation, trunk sway, flexion of knees or back, abduction of arms, the use of a walking aid, sit-to-stand transfer, walk and turn. The target time period to complete this test for older adults with a good level of independence is between eight and ten seconds. The advantages of the test are: that it is simple, requires simple tools and quick to perform (less than 20 seconds including prior instructions), and can be performed by participants, who use assistive devices such as a walker, cane or crutches. The procedure was experimentally tested and found to be a highly reliable tool to measure balance function (21). The 3MDW test was used to determine the number of steps (at self-selected walking speeds) and the distance the participant can walk in three minutes (21). The test was performed in a quiet, obstacle-free outdoor area, 60 meters long and five meter wide. The participants walked between 10:00 and 11:00 a.m. in comfortable weather conditions (230C, 40% humidity). The monitor walked behind the participant so as not to influence the participant's pace, but as a safety precaution and to calculate the number of steps taken. Immediately after completing the walking test, the participant was seated and heart rate and blood pressure were evaluated.

All data were analyzed with SPSS 7.2 for Windows 97. Data are reported as mean ± one standard deviation. One sample independent t-tests were run to compare differences in demographic and medical data, body composition, body fat and sensorimotor tests between the groups. The critical value for statistical significance was assumed at an alpha level < 0.05.

OUR FINDINGS

Of the 28 elderly persons with intellectual disability (ID) initially selected for the evaluation from the first group, 24 (86%) were found eligible to participate in the study. Those dropped from the program had difficulties in complying with instructions or following specific orders.

Table 1 summarizes the demographic, body composition and medical characteristics of all the participants. Group A1a, the aged ID group with DS, as expected, as well as group A1b, the NSID group differed significantly from the control group in being younger, with a higher percentage of females and widows or unmarried. Yet, group A2a,b, the younger individuals with DS and with NSID were more comparable to the control group in terms of gender. In comparison with the control group, groups A1a,b and A2a,b were fairly similar with regard to both body composition, and medical problems with one exception, body weight was significantly lower (p < 0.05) from CG (control group), demonstrated a higher incidence of cardiac disease (p<0.005), and neurologic problems other than ID (p< 0.001). Group A1a also showed significantly shorter heights and stature (p<0.05). Individuals with DS showed more medical problems than individuals with NSID.

Table 2 shows the results of the flexibility and the two sensorimotor tests. Functional flexibility tests showed only slight and insignificant differences between the three groups. The ID study groups (A1 and A2 with DS and NSID) and the control group were able to bend forward in long-sitting positions for 18.7, 21.2, 20.3 and 22.6 cm respectively. Group A1 demonstrated significantly poorer performance in both sensorimotor tests

Table 1. Demographic, body composition, and medical characteristics of participants

	Study group A1 DS NSID	Study group A2 DS NSID	Control group (CG)	P value
Participants (number)	10 / 14	13 / 24	31	
Age (yr)	59±4 / 61± 3	44±3 / 45 ±4	75±7	<0.001
Gender (%) M/F	9/91 / 11/89	48/52 / 52/48	16/84	NS
Body weight (kg) M F M F	66.6±4.4 / 67.1±3.6 / 64.1± 4 / 63.4 ±4.3	70.4±5 / 69.8±7 / 68.4 ± 6 / 67.6 ± 6	65.2±4.9 / 65.3±4.4	<0.05 / NS / <0.05 / <0.05
Height (cm)	149.4±5.6 / 152 ± 4.9	158.7±6.2 / 160 ± 5.5	160.7±3.3	<0.05
Body fat (%)	21 / 20	21 / 19	20	NS
Waist girth (cm) M F M F	87.2±3.2 / 89.3±3.4 / 85.2 ± 2.5 / 86.6 ± 3.1	86.5±2.2 / 89.9±8.8 / 87.7 ± 7.2 / 86.4± 4.5	84.3±3.3 / 87.5±4.4	NS
Thigh girth (cm) M widest point M/F F M F	50.5±3.2 / 49.0±4.1 / 58.9± 3.6 / 51.3 ± 4.4	51.7±4.7 / 50.9±5.7 / 50.5± 5.1 / 51.7 ± 4.9	49.4±3.7 / 52.2±4.9	NS
Waist:Hip ratio M/F	1.7 / 1.8	1.7 / 1.7	1.7	NS
Body Mass index M F M F	26.1 / 26.8 / 26.2 / 26.3	25.9 / 25.6 / 25.4 / 25.7	25.2 / 25.9	NS
Single/widowed (%)	100 / 100	95 / 100	78	<0.001
Cardiac disease* (%)	39.7 / 11.9	30.4 / 2.3	26.4	<0.005 / <0.05
Hypertension (%)	38.8 / 21.3	28.2 / 3.3	31.8	NS / <0.05

Table 1 continued. Demographic, body composition, and medical characteristics of participants

	Study group A1 DS NSID	Study group A2 DS NSID	Control group (CG)	P value
Diabetes (%)	17.6	10.3	19.9	<0.005
	2.6	0		<0.05
Respiratory disease (COPD, asthma) (%)	27.3	25.5	24.5	<0.001
	20.1	13.5		<0.05
Hepatic disease (%)	10.6	5.0	11.1	<0.005
	0	0		<0.05
Neoplastic disease (benign & malignant tumors) (%)	3.6	0	4.1	<0.005
	0	0		<0.05
Renal disease (insufficiency and chronic UTI) (%)	9.6	7.3	10.6	<0.005
	0	0		<0.05
Neurologic disease (%)	40.7	37.6	11.5	<0.001
	45.8	51.2		
Vascular disease (%)	19.6	9.9	11.9	<0.005
	0	0		<0.05
GI diseases (%) (gastritis, duodenal ulcer, chronic constipation)	15.8	11.7	18.9	<0.005
	20.2	5.6		
Medication (no.)	3	4	4	NS
	4	2		

DS – Down Syndrome, NSID – non specified intellectual disability
N.S.- non-significant; M- male; F- female; p<0.05
* cardiac diseases include ischemic heart or congestive heart failure

than group A2 and the control group (p<0.05). Times longer than 12 seconds to perform the "timed-up and go" test may indicate some balance difficulties and increased risk for falling. In both the 3MDW test and the walking velocity test, group A1a,b walked significantly shorter distances at a slower pace (mean of 129 meters in 272 steps, average of 90 steps per minute) than A2a,b (mean of 162 meters in 340 steps, average of 116 steps per minute), CG (mean of 150 meters in 308 steps, average of 102 steps per minute), p<0.05.

Table 3 shows the inter-rater reliability results for specific evaluation items. The Kappa statistic was used to determine the amount of agreement between the therapists' assessment, thereby establishing the inter-rater reliability between them. The Kappa statistic was chosen, because it is applicable to categorical variables and because it assesses agreement beyond what may be expected based on chance alone. According to Landis and Koch (22), Kappa values greater than 0.75 represent excellent agreement between raters. The entire evaluation procedure took an average of 41 minutes to administer. The Kappa values for participant evaluations ranged from 0.66 to 0.94 as indicated in table 3. All items except medical history taken (0.69) were in excellent agreement.

Table 2. Sensorimotor tests

	A1 Group (n=24) *A2 Group (n=37)			Control Group: (n = 31)			
	Male (n=4) *n=16	Female (n=20) *n=21	Mean	CG Male (n=10)	CG Female (n=21)	Mean	Difference %
Flexibility (cm)	20 *21.4	18 *22	18.7 *21.2	CG 21	CG 19.4	20.3	**7.8
TUAG (seconds)	12.9 *7.2	13.3 *6.9	13.2 *7.0	CG 7.4	CG 7.2	7.3	**80.8
3MDW (meters/steps)	131/274 *165/349	128/270 *160/342	129/272 *162/340	CG 152/309	CG 149/307	CG 150/308	**14

CG - Control group; A1- elderly ID; A2 - younger ID
* A2
** p< 0.05 between A1 and CG

DISCUSSION

The main purpose of this study was to compare the clinical and functional characteristics between populations of aging adults with and without intellectual disability (ID). The study examined longitudinallly the test scores gained by different age cohort of old and younger adults with Down syndrome (DS) and with non-specific intellectual disability (NSID). As well as the study examined cross-sectionally the test scores gained by different age cohorts of adults without ID. Standard evaluations were used for elderly adults and younger with ID in residential care as compared with control group of elderly adults (CG) residing in independent care facilities, and the mean age of the control group was fourteen years older than that of the group A1. We were unable to use age-matched samples owing to the limited numbers of individuals with ID older than 63 year of age living in Israel. Moreover, the effects of long term residential care and the manifestation of institutionalisation were important in this study, but the number of non-ID instituionalized individuals was extremly limited and therefore there the match was not aged matched in this study, but rather accomodation-matched.

Table 3. Interrater reliability results for evaluation items for the group of older persons with ID (A1, DS and NSID) and control group (CG)

Evaluation Item	Study group (A1) (n=24)		Control groups (n = 31)		Kappa Study / Control group
	Agree	Disagree	Agree	Disagree	Study /CG
Weight	23	1	31	0	0.94 / 1.0
Height	23	1	30	1	0.94 / 0.94
Body fat	24	0	31	0	1.0 / 1.0
Thigh & Waist girth	22	2	29	2	0.79 / 0.80
Flexibility	23	1	29	2	0.79 / 0.80
Sensorimotor tests	22	2	30	1	0.79 / 0.89
Medical history taken	21	3	28	3	0.66 / 0.69

It is commonly believed that older adults with ID tend to demonstrate premature signs of aging, characterized by changes in body composition, functional decline and increased morbidity. How early in their life they present these signs is yet to be investigated, however in our study we could see that premature aging was not presenting in the younger group (45 years old). The relatively few previous aging investigations concerning elderly adults with ID have suggested that persons with ID develop some aging characteristics earlier than non-ID adults (23,24). The present study provides added support for the viewpoint of premature aging in persons with ID. Burt et al (25) examined the changes in functioning with aging in a longitudinal study in adults (22-56 years old) with Down syndrome and concluded that there is only minimal age-related declines in functioning. Their study did not support the idea that adults with Down syndrome show rapid age-related declines before age of 50. Our findings demonstrate that young individuals of 45 years old do not show earlier signs of aging.

The results of our study indicated that body composition of adults with ID (61 years old), including weight, height, BMI, WHR and body fat, are similar to those in our control group (CG, 75 years old). Changes in body composition represent one of the more dramatic biological markers of advanced age and are especially pronounced after the age of 70 years (26). Although Down syndrome individuals are generally of short stature, their height differences compared to the control group were insignificant. Although the mean age of the control group was 14 years greater than that of the A1 group, the study showed no significant differences between the two groups with regard to body composition. It seems to indicate that accelerating aging seen in the ID group might be indirectly reflected by body composition values. Age-associated loss of muscle mass, sarcopenia (27), with concomitant loss of strength and decreased joint flexibility and mobility, contribute to frailty in the older adults and expose these individuals to increased risk (28-32).

Our results lead us to assume that relative inactivity in adults may also lead to premature aging changes in body composition and may constitute increased risk for losing independence, and that the A1 group appears equally at risk to that of the older control group.

Most of the medical histories revealed non-significant differences between the A1 group and control group (CG) with two exceptions. Heart disorders were considerably more prevalent among individuals with ID. These heart disorders were often congenital, diagnosed early and well-treated. The incidence of neurological diseases in the A1 group (as demonstrated in table 1) supported the notion that these individuals will probably require more assistance and care in the future. An early onset of medical problems and prolonged poor health might accelerate the aging processes. It is noticiable that DS individuals possed more medical problems than individuals with NSID with only one execption of neurological diseases. This may reflect a predisposition to health problems among individuals with DS.

Functional flexibility of the trunk flexion and hamstring muscle stretching were similar in both groups. This indicated that both study groups and control group demonstrated similar degrees of soft tissue mobility and lumbar flexibility despite their differences in age. Loss of flexibility is one of the earliest noticeable changes occurring in elderly adults aged 70 years or older (33). The fact that 61 year old individuals with ID demonstrate similar degrees of flexibility to that of 75 year old non-ID individuals may possibly be a consequence of a more passive lifestyle. It may be associated with the constant help and assistance they receive in their daily living activities and may reflect a "use it or lose it" phenomenon. The flexibility results are somewhat surprising and merit special attention. Since individuals with Down syndrome often possess poor skeletal muscle tone with soft tissue elasticity, one might have expected a relative disadvantage with respect to flexibility as they aged, however, this was not the case. Since we did not evaluate muscle tone in the present study, we can only assume that a "lazy" lifestyle probably played a major role in determining flexibility levels at age 60 year among Down syndrome individuals compared to those of 75 year old individuals without ID.

The "timed-up and go" (TUAG) test is one of the more user-friendly functional assessment tests in the clinic, whereas the 3MDW test is an outdoor functional test used to assess the endurance capacity of the skeletal muscle of lower extremities, the heart and lungs (34). Group A1 scored lower in the functional tests, which may reflect on their general state of health or sedentary lifestyle and may indicate an increased mild risk for falling. The TUAG test was used to assess a person's ability to perform a task that is probably performed many times throughout the day by elderly adults. Adults, who take more than 20 seconds to complete the test are at high risk of falling and are not considered safe to be alone outside. This test can also supply further information about the participant's functional ability and rehabilitation requirements. Poor performance (slower than 20 seconds) may be used to justify therapy intervention as a preventive measure. Group A1 needed significantly more time to complete the test than the control group, but still finished the test within the normal timeframe. Ongoing follow-up is needed to detect, sooner rather than later, any deterioration in performing that specific task.

In the 3MDW test at self-selected walking speeds, A1 group covered shorter distances and were significantly slower than A2 group and the control group. According to Bohannon et al (35) a paced walking speed for elderly adults of 70 steps per minute is considered a slow walking velocity, and paced walking speed of 80 steps per minute is considered a slow-to-moderate walking speed. One explanation for our data may be that daily living and recreational activities of persons with ID in residential care do not provide sufficient stimuli to preserve functional mobility to the extent found in the control group. Consequently, results indicating low endurance capacity may conceivably reflect either poorer health conditions or less-intense life activities and a tendency for deconditioning (36,37).

Several improvements in the evaluation procedures may warrant consideration. For example, use of magnetic resonance imaging (MRI) as a reference method for quantifying the muscle mass is more accurate, but significantly more expensive and time-consuming (38).

CONCLUSIONS

Our findings showed that aged individuals with ID do present several indications of premature aging and in particular those with DS. The mechanisms, although still unknown, may be associated with physically inactive lifestyles, which in DS individuals may lead to acceleration of functional disabilities and overall less favorable health as they age. Further information concerning psychological and behavioral characteristics of inactive older adults will be useful for funneling diagnostic and preventive measures to the most vulnerable groups such as the individuals with ID.

ACKNOWLEDGEMENTS

This chapter is an adapted version of an earlier published paper (Carmeli E, Merrick J, Kessel S, Mashrawi Y, Carmeli V. Elderly persons with intellectual disability: A study of clinical characteristics, functional status and sensory capacity. ScientificWorldJornal 2003;3:298-307).

REFERENCES

1. Merrick J. Survey of Medical Clinics-2000. Jerusalem: Office Medical Director, Div Ment Retard, Min Soc Affairs, 2001.
2. Boyd R, Tedrick T. Aging adults with mental retardation and leisure. Research Update 1992;10:21-8.
3. Jacobson J, Sutton M, Janicki M. Demography and characteristics of aging and aged mentally retarded person. In: Janicki M, Wishiewski H, eds. Aging and developmental disabilities: issues and approaches. Baltimore, MD: Paul H Brookes, 1985:95-131.
4. Janicki MP, Jacobson J. Generational trends in sensory, physical and behavioral abilities among older mentally retarded persons. Am J Ment Defic 1986;90:490-500.
5. Ashman AF, Suttie JN. The medical health status of older people with mental retardation in Australia. J Appl Gerontol 1996;15: 57-73.
6. Cousins SO. Aging poorly with sedentary living. In: Cousins SO, ed. Exercise, aging and health. Philadelphia: Taylor Francis, 1998:1-13.
7. Nelson EA, Dannefer D. Aged heterogeneity: fact or fiction? The fate of diversity in gerontological research. Gerontologist 1992;32:17-23.
8. Evenhuis HM. Medical aspects of ageing in a population with intellectual disability: I. Visual impairment. J Intellect Disabil Res 1995;39:19-25.
9. Evenhuis HM. Medical aspects of ageing in a population with intellectual disability: II. Hearing impairment. J Intellect Disabil Res 1995;39:27-33.
10. Pilon W, Arsenault R. Characteristics of the populations at the Robert Giffard Psychiatric Hospital Center: people with intellectual deficiencies and people with mental disorders. Sante Mentale au Quebec 1997;22:115-36. [French]
11. Cooper SA. Clinical study of the effects of age on the physical health of adults with mental retardation. Am J Ment Retard 1998;102:582-9.
12. Rubin SS, Rimmer JH, Chicoine B, Braddock D, McGuire DE. Overweight prevalence in persons with Down syndrome. Ment Retard 1998;36:175-81.

13. Kapell D, Nightingale B, Rodriguez A,. Lee JH, Zigman WB, Schupf N. Prevalence of chronic medical conditions in adults with mental retardation: comparison with the general population. Ment Retard 1998;36:269-79.

14. National Advisory Council on Aging (NACA). Aging vignette, No. 2, 1993.

15. Martin AD, Spenst LF, Drinkwater DT, Clarys JP. Anthropometric estimation of muscle mass in men. Med Sci Sports Exerc 1990;22:729-33.

16. Thomas BJ, Cornish BH, Ward LC. Bioelectrical impedance analysis for measurement body fluid volume. J Clin Eng 1992;17:22-3.

17. Payne WA, Hahn DB. Understanding your health. St Louis, MO: Mosby, 1992:152-154.

18. Hoeger WK. Principles and labs for physical fitness and wellness. Englewood, CO: Morton, 1988:131-5.

19. Duncan P, Weiner DK, Chandler J, Stdenski S. Functional reach: a new clinical measure of balance. J Gerontol 1990;45:M192-6.

20. Mathias S, Nayak US, Isaacs B. Balance in elderly patient: the "get up and go" test. Arch Phyical Med Rehab 1986;67:387-9.

21. Berg K, Norman KE. Functional assessment of balance and gait. Clin Geriatr Med 1996;12:705-23.

22. Landis JR, Koch GG. The measurement of observer agreement for categorical data. Biometrics 1977; 33:159-74.

23. Prasher VP, Chowdhury TA, Rowe BR, Bain SC. ApoE genotype and Alzheimer's disease in adults with Down syndrome: meta-analysis. Am J Ment Retard 1997;102:103-10.

24. Crichton JU, Mackinnon M, White CP. The life-expectancy of persons with cerebral palsy. Dev Med Child Neurol 1995;37:1115-8.

25. Burt DB, Loveland KA, Chen YW, Chuang A, Lewis KR, Cherry L. (1995) Aging in adults with Down syndrome: report from a longitudinal study. Am J Ment Retard 1995;100:262-70.

26. Bemben MG, Massey BH, Bemben DA, Boileau RA, Misner JE. Age-related patterns in body composition for men aged 20-79 years. Med Sci Sports Exerc 1995;27:264-9.

27. Proctor DN, Balagopa P, Nair KS. Age-related sarcopenia in humans is associated with reduced synthetic rates of specific muscle proteins. J Nutr 1998;128 (Suppl):351S-5.

28. Voorrips LE, Lemmink APM, Van Heuvelen MJG, Bult P, van Staveren WA. The physical condition of elderly women differing in habitual physical activity. Med Sci Sports Exerc 1993;25:1152-7.

29. Evans WJ. Reversing sarcopenia: how weight training can build strength and vitality. Geriatric 1996;51:46-53.

30. Gallagher D, Visser M, De Meersman RE, Sepulveda D, Baumgartner RN, Pierson RN, Harris T, Heymsfield SB. Appendicular skeletal muscle mass: effects of age, gender and ethnicity. J Appl Physiol 1997; 83:229-39.

31.   Carmeli E, Coleman R, Llaguna HO, Cross DB. Do we allow elderly
        pedestriants sufficient time to cross the street in safety? J Aging Phys
        Act 2000; 8:51-8
32.   Carmeli E, Reznick AZ, Coleman R, Carmeli V. Muscle strength and
        mass of lower extremities in relation to functional abilities in elderly
        adults. Gerontology 2000;46:249-57.
33.   Chesworth BM, Vandervoort AA. Age and passive ankle stiffness in
        healthy women. Phys Ther 1989;69:217-24.
34.   Bendall MJ, Bassey EJ, Pearson MB. Factors affecting walking speed
        of elderly people. Age Ageing 1989;18:327-32.
35.   Bohannon RW, Andrews AW, Thomas MW. Walking speed:
        reference values and correlates for older adults. J Orthopedic Sports
        Phys Ther 1996;24: 86-90.
36.   Weinstein ND. The precaution adoption process. Health Psychol
        1998;74:335-86.
37.   Boyd R. Older adults with developmental disabilities: a brief
        examination of current knowledge. Act Adapt Aging 1997;21:7-27.
38.   Williams DP, Going SB, Milliken LA, Hall MC, Lohman TG.
        Practical techniques for assessing body composition in middle-aged
        and older adults. Med Sci Sports Exerc 1995;27:776-83.

CHAPTER 7
Assistive technology for persons with intellectual disability

Eli Carmeli, Carmit Cahana and Joav Merrick

People with intellectual disability (ID) require special support in order to achieve independence in their daily life. Persons with ID are less exposed to assistive technology, although studies have shown that the availability of aids afford an opportunity to reach independence and cooperation. This chapter is a national survey to examine the nature of the relationship between involvement of the physiotherapy (PT) team and the degree to which assistive technology was used. A questionnaire was sent to all PTs employed at all 54 residential care centers for persons with ID of the Division for Mental Retardation at the Ministry of Social Affairs in Israel. A significantly positive correlation was found between the degree of involvement of the physiotherapist and the utilization of assistive technology. Our study results may be summarized by stating that PTs demonstrated a great deal of involvements, particularly in relation to the extent of their work in the residential care centers. PT's awareness of the importance was indicated as the major reason to use assistive technology.

INTRODUCTION

The development of assistive technology is part of the effort made by society to cope with physical, cognitive, and sensory deficiencies causing disability, with the aim of improving and preserving quality of life (1). Unfortunately, it is generally acknowledged, though not empirically validated, that assistive technology aids are under-utilized by people with ID (2). The physiotherapist (PT) has an important role in the assessment, finding the right device, instruct, guide and supervise the person and the care staff on the use of assistive technology. People with intellectual disabilities (ID) have a greater need for support than other groups of people with disabilities, due to their mental, cognitive, and social limitation, in addition to their physical disabilities (3,4). The challenge of using assistive technology is not only technical, but rather aimed at promoting improvement of quality of life (5,6).

Previous publications indicated a number of reasons, why individuals with ID under-utilize assistive technology and explained the existing barriers to this outcome (7,8). On the other hand we do not know of any study published on the role of the PT in addressing assistive technology to people with ID. The PT, the direct-support staff member, and the user must know about the advantages and the limitations of the use of aids. For this purpose, it is important to evaluate the disability of the user and the support required of the technological aids. It is imperative for the PT to perform comprehensive functional diagnosis, proper instruction, encouragement, supervision, and support, upon receiving the instrument. A person with ID requires much attention and a longer period of practice and acclimation in order to know how to use the new instrument.

The aim of this chapter was to examine the nature of the relationship between involvement of the physiotherapy (PT) team and the degree to which assistive technology was used in residential care centers for persons with intellectual disability in Israel. Investigating this question may help the PT team to develop strategies of evaluation, instruction, supervision, and operation of treatment programs. The target would also be to use assistive technology aids, with the cooperation and direct support of the staff, to maximize implementation and the use of these aids in a daily schedule of people with ID.

OUR STUDY

A cross-sectional descriptive study was conducted in all the 54 residential care centers in Israel, with a total population of 6,000 people. We reviewed various questionnaires to identify themes that we believed should be part of an assistive technology survey for disabled people. From this review a questionnaire containing 38 closed items in two parts was developed. The first part had personal, demographic and professional questions, while the second part presented questions with five possible response categories (very regularly, regularly, occasionally, infrequently, never) in order to get information regarding the extent of the involvement of PT team and the degree to which assistive technology was used. The questionnaire was designed to be administrated by a PT and its context addressed questions regarding type of aids, way of usages and degree of satisfaction, existence of diagnosis process, evaluation, and guidance (i.e., documentation, reports, follow-up, maintenance and repair). Inter rater reliability between four experts was high (ICC = 0.91; r = 0.90). All four experts agreed that the content domains (i.e., assistive technology used) had been addressed adequately, thus content validity was supported. Percentage agreements (Kappa statistic for test-retest reliability) for categorical variables were ranged between 82% and 94%.

Data analysis was performed using SPSS version 10. Frequencies, means, and standard deviations were used to describe the data. Multiple regression analyses were conducted to explore variables that might predict patterns of PT involvement in which assistive technology was used. To analyse the relationship between single variables we used X2 tests. All tests were performed with a type I error rate of 5%.

OUR FINDINGS

Of 92 questionnaires mailed out to all physiotherapists, 70 were returned, however, five of those returned were partially blank. Therefore, we received 65 usable questionnaires, a 71% response rate based on the initial mailing. The degree of involvement in the workplace is a function of the extent of the PT position in each setting. Among the 65 PT respondents, who provided personal and professional information, were 75% women, 75% held BA degree, and 69% worked part time for at least three years in the residential care center (see table 1).

Table 1. Socio demographic data of the PT (n = 65), and residential care centers (n=54)

Variable	Outcomes	No	%	X²	P
Gender	Male	16	25	3.27	0.005
	Female	49	75		
Education	LPT	13	20	54.84	0.05
	BA in PT	35	75		
	MSc in PT	3	5		
Working Time (h/w)	Up 10	29	42	25.63	NS
	11-20	32	45		
	11 >	4	8		
Working Experience (months)	up to 12	22	30	33.28	
	12-36	35	58		0.05
	37 >	7	11		
Residential care center	Government	14	26		
	Public	17	31		
				4.1	0.05
	Private	23	43		

In Israel the Division for Mental Retardation (DMR) provide residential care service for all persons with intellectual disability through both government, public and private centers. The clients, the budget and the supervision is provided by the government (DMR), but the ownership of the center can be either government, public (non-for-profit) or private. Table 2 demonstrates the distribution of assistive technology in privately-owned and government-owned residential care centers. Most devices were significantly (p<0.05) in privately owned residential care centers. The majority of the participants (i.e. permanent residents) used either splints or corset along with one of the four walking aids.

Table 2. The distribution ration between assistive technology in private-owned vs government-owned residential care centers in Israel, (n = 6,000)

Variable	Total used (%)	Government (%)	Private (%)
Splint or Corset	60	0	100
St. Walker	48	80	20
Rollator	52	20	80
Arms rest walker	38	100	0
Quad cane	17	50	50
Limb Mobilizer	27	0	100
Other	32	20	80
P			0.05

From table 3 it can be seen that most of the PTs (45%) used the assistive technology for therapeutic gait, while only 5% used this technology for sensory stimulation.

Tables 4, 5 and 6 demonstrate the involvement of the PT and the mechanism used to promote assistive technology within the 54 residential care centers. The role of PT in residential care centers in assimilating rehabilitative technology is crucial. It includes screening (58%), analysis of findings, recording of documentation (50%), ordering the device, monitoring and supervising the on-going use (65%), and staff instructions, individually based (50%). Continued quality assurance (CQA) was the mechanism used for monitoring the implementation of assistive technology (table 4). A good correlation was found between use of the equipment and involvement of the PT ($r = 0.50$, $P < 0.001$), as well as, good correlation found between the degrees of recorded use of aids and the degrees to which aids were used in the residential care centers ($r = 0.63$, $P < 0.001$).

Table 3. Distribution of assistive technology main used purposes

Variable	Purposes (%)
Functional gait	20
Therapeutic gait	45
Preventive	20
Sensory stimulation	5
General activity	10

Table 4. The present mechanism of assistive technology

Variable	Outcome	%	X^2	P
Existing records				
	Updated/outdated	50/50	0.429	NS
Initial screening done by	Up to 50%	35		
	51% >	65	12.71	NS
Inservice*	PT	58		
	Non PT	42	6.08	NS
	Workshop	25		
	Single meeting	20	4.10	
	Individual	50		0.05
On-going maintenance responsibility*	Group	35		
	Administrator	28		
	Care giver	32	0.027	NS
On-going follow-up responsibility	Aide	25		
	PT	55		
	PT	62		0.05
Method of follow-up and supervision*	Non PT	48	33.11	
	CQA	65	0.78	0.05
	Randomized	35		
	Interview	30		

* The PT could mark two answers

Table 5 demonstrates the percentages used or not used of the assistive device and how PT were satisfied from the products. It seems that most residents actually used their aid, and the major reasons not to use them were environmental barriers (38%) and short treatment time (25%). The PT graded their overall satisfaction from the function and efficiency of the assistive aid as regularly (31%) i.e., it answers their expectations, and 13% answered that the assistive aid never satisfied them. A good correlation was found between the extent to which the use of aids was recorded and the involvement of the PT (r = 0.70; P<0.001).

Table 5. Characteristics of assistive technology used

Variable		Outcome (%)	X^2	P
Actual time-used by the Resident	Up to25%	20	2.78	
	26-50%	30		
	51-100%	50		0.05
Reason not to use*	environmental	38	19.70	NS
	treatment time	25		
	product deficiency	20		
	other	17		
Product satisfaction	very regularly	18	11.22	NS
	regularly	31		
	occasionally	16		
	infrequently	22		
	never	13		

* The PT could mark two answers

DISCUSSION

The total results of our study indicated a large degree of involvement by PT (physiotherapist) in assistive technology despite their limited number of work hours per week. This fact apparently explains the significance of the technology as seen by the PT team and the direct support staff in the residential setting in Israel. We believe that the significance of the issue of assistive technology as seen by PT probably stems from their academic background and professional training, but not necessarily from their years of experience. The variety of technology aids in residential setting for people with intellectual disability (ID), which included aids that were technologically simple and/or complex was interesting, because a literature review found that residents with ID were usually not sufficiently exposed to complex assistive technology equipment and therefore the use of these aids in this population limited and minimal (3,5). In contrast, our study found that most of the residents in residential settings in Israel used a variety of assistive aids, a fact indicating high awareness among the direct support staff on the one hand, and the resident's responsiveness to the personal accessory adapted to him/her, on the other hand.

According to our results, evidence showed that the maximal use of supportive equipment was aimed at purposes of mobility and gait. The majority of PTs reported high prevalence of therapeutic walking, indicating both individual therapy and the choice of a 'work tool', which is an assistive technological aid. In addition, it was found that the use of assistive technology had additional purpose not reported in the literature, such as preservation of existing status and treatment of in-voluntary movements.

Deficient documentation of findings and of the constant supervision was evident from the study results. The PTs were not strict about updating and recording their findings in the resident's file. We believe that the supervision and operation of a structured therapy program, through rehabilitative assistive technology, should usually be performed by staff from the health services professions, but we found that the supervision was often performed by people without a medical background, such as educational counselor or even a representative of the management of the residential setting. This phenomenon had implications for the monitoring stage of the daily use of aids. Thus the responsibility for continuous operation of rehabilitative technology falls almost equally on the management on the one hand, and the PT team on the other. This division however, did not have a negative effect on the use of rehabilitative aids and the degree of use among most of the residents.

An ethical aspect was raised from the study outcomes. The importance of paperwork has been extensively discussed and recommended by the American Physical Therapy Association (9). Documentation of the findings is indispensable in order to record milestones in the patient's condition, and to facilitate interdisciplinary communication. Moreover, a precise recording is a basic standard for provision of efficient and beneficial comprehensive rehabilitation. Deficient, outdated and imprecise recording is harmful to the quality of care. We believe that the introduction of a uniform system of recording for all stages of the PT involvement in the assimilation of rehabilitative technology may contribute to more efficient and beneficial use of the various aids.

The extent to which the residents used assistive technology aid was wide and varied. Our findings showed that the PT opinion for lack of use or barrier to utilization of assistive technology had multi-factorial reasons, such as insufficient support, inability to reach individual adaptation, and maintenance difficulties. Most PTs indicated that residents did not realize their maximal functional ability due to minimal use of aids. The reasons for minimal use of aids were varied and included, to a similar degree, environmental conditions that make it difficult to use them and organization of a therapy system (i.e, the time allocated to a therapy and practice unit). Topography of the residential setting and allocating accurate therapy time should expand the use of aids and thus improve the functional potential of the residents

Despite the technological development of instrumentation, there is still place for technical improvement of the specifications, such as the weight of the item, its stability or replacement of spare parts. Operating difficulties may cause lack of will and inability to use the equipment appropriately.

CONCLUSIONS

In light of the findings concerning the use of assistive technology aids in residential setting for people with ID in Israel, we recommend establishing a nationwide system with mechanism for the control and evaluation of the professional work of PT, also in the context of assimilating assistive technology. Introducing a structured system will help the process of assimilating assistive technology in residential care centers, increase its use, deepen the connection between the administrative staff and people in the clinical field, which may lower the direct and indirect financial costs related to the use of assistive equipment (10). Various institutions should take part of this system, including university affiliated facilities (11). Caregivers must not only provide for assistive device needs, but also consider a mechanism to ensure that persons with ID will be able to access and appropriately use the equipment they need in order to promote independence in their daily life (12).

ACKNOWLEDGEMENTS

We would like to thank Anne and Eli Shapira, Charitable Foundation, Portland Oregon USA for supporting this work. This chapter is an adapted version of an earlier published paper (Carmeli E, Cahana C, Merrick J. The assimilation of assistive technology in residential care centers for people with intellectual disabilities. ScientificWorldJournal 2004;4:178-85).

REFERENCES

1.   Edwards EIN, Jones DA. Ownership and use of assistive devices among older people in the community. Age Ageing 1998;27: 463-8.
2.   Parish SL. Federal income payments and mental retardation: The political and economic context. Ment Retard 2003;41:446-59.
3.   Wehmeyer ML. National survey of the use of assistive technology by adults with mental retardation. Ment. Retard 1998;36:44-51.
4.   Carmeli E, Coleman R. The clinical characteristics of aging adults with mental retardation. Phys Ther Rev 2001;6:267-71.
5.   Wehmeyer ML, Metzler CA. How self-determined are people with mental retardation? The Ntional Consumer Survey. Ment Retard 1995;33(2):111-9.
6.   Nilsson LM, Nyberg PJ. Driving to learn: a new concept for training children with cognitive disabilities in a powered wheelchair. Am J Occup Ther 2003;57:229-33.
7.   Berry BE, Ignash S. Assistive technology: Providing independence for individuals with disabilities. Rehab Nurs 2003;28: 6-14.

8.   Hammel J. Technology and the environment: supportive resource or
        barrier for people with developmental disabilities. Nurs Clin North
        Am 2003;38, 331-49.

9.   APTA. Guide for physical therapist practice. Am Phys Ther Ass
        1997;17(11):1620-31.

10.   Brodin J. Implementation of new technology for persons with
        mental retardation and the importance of staff education. Int J Rehab
        Res 1998;21:155-68.

11.   Merrick J, Kandel, I. Medical services for persons with intellectual
        disability in Israel. Public Health Rev 2003;31:45-68.

12.   Carmeli E, Levy R, Barchad S, Cahana C, Merrick J. Assistive
        technology and walking aid use by intellectual disabled older
        people in a residential care centers. Int J Disabil Hum Dev 2007,
        6(1):67-70.

PART THREE:
HEALTH ASPECTS

CHAPTER 8
Older persons with intellectual disability and their health needs

Joav Merrick, Isack Kandel and Mohammed Morad

People with developmental disability, mental retardation or intellectual disability are living longer and becoming prone to age related health problems and disease of old age like the general population. This worldwide trend is also seen in Israel, where today 44% of persons with intellectual disability in residential care are 40 years and above. There is a need for service and staff providers to receive training, a need for more research and better service for this aging population. This chapter presents health concerns for older persons with different levels of intellectual disability, health concerns in persons with Down syndrome and persons with epileptic seizures and cerebral palsy in relation to general practice and family medicine. This chapter is concluded with recommendations on health and aging in adults with intellectual disabilities and the call for formalized training in the topic for specialists in family medicine.

INTRODUCTION

Increased life expectancy for persons with intellectual disability (ID) that today is coming close to that of the general population, has resulted in a larger population of older persons with intellectual disability worldwide. One of the exceptions is persons with Down syndrome (DS), where the life expectancy today is 60 years or about twenty years below the general population.

Today in Israel (total population of over 7 million) the Division for Mental Retardation (DMR) is in contact with approximately 24,000 persons of all ages. Residential care is provided to about 7,000 persons in close to 60 residential care centers countrywide. In addition, 2,000 persons receive residential care in hostels or protected apartments within the community. More than 50 other settings provide vocational and educational services to 15,000 persons in day-care kindergartens, day-treatment centers, sheltered workshops or integrated care within the community.

Table 1. The population of persons with intellectual disability in residential care centers in Israel in 2005. Mean 116.36 (range 23-366) per center

Age in years	Males	Females	Total	Percent
0-9	101	58	159	2.36
10-19	428	359	787	11.66
20-39	1,660	1,164	2,824	41.84
40-49	746	624	1,370	20.30
50-59	575	569	1,144	16.95
> 60	241	224	465	6.89
Total	3,751	2,998	6,749	100.00
%	55.58	44.42	100.00	

Table 2. The level of intellectual disability (ID) in the population of persons with intellectual disability in residential care in Israel 2005. Mild MR: IQ 55-70, moderate: IQ 35-54, severe: IQ 20-34 and profound: IQ < 20. Other is 21 persons, who historically were placed in institutions for other reasons and preferred to stay on, because they regarded the institution as their home or persons under observation.

Age in years	Mild	Moderate	Severe	Profound	Other	Total	Percent
0-9	10	21	81	47	0	159	2,36
10-19	94	256	311	123	3	787	11.66
20-39	250	1,121	932	503	18	2,824	41.84
40-49	191	613	436	130	0	1,370	20.30
50-59	166	520	355	103	0	1,144	16.95
>60	58	256	112	39	0	465	6.89
Total	769	2,787	2,227	945	21	6,749	100,00
Percent	11.39	41.30	33.00	14.00	0.31	100.00	

The age distribution of 6,749 persons with ID in residential care centers from 2005 can be seen in table 1 (1), while the level of intellectual disability in residential care centers in Israel is seen in table 2 (1). In 2005 there were nine government operated residential care centers, 37 privately owned and 12 public with a mean of 116.36 persons in each center (range 23-366). It is worthy to note that the total expenditure is provided by the government, who also operate the government institutions. Private and public institution have their own independent administration, but receive funding, the clients and supervision by the government. The total expenditure of the DMR today is close to 200 million dollars per annum (for trends see (2)). The profile of the population in residential care centers is shown in table 3. In table 4 both community and residential care service is compared for the years 1990 and 2005. Here an increase in the number of persons served can be seen and also new services implemented over that period. Mortality in this population has been described elsewhere (3).

Table 3. Profile of the population in residential care 2005

Profile	Numbers	Percent
Educational	696	10.31
Treatment	1.615	23.93
Rehabilitation	462	6.85
Nursing	1.312	19.44
Intensive nursing	320	4.74
Challenging behavior	2.344	34.73
Total	**6,749**	**100.00**

With more persons with ID living longer comes an increase in age related health problems seen in the general population, such as heart disease, cardiovascular disease, cancer, visual and hearing impairment. Since many of the physicians and care staff involved with the health service of persons with ID came from the field of pediatrics, there will now be a need to take a long term view and involve the fields of family medicine and geriatrics in the care. The physician working in family medicine in the community in Israel has very little training or experience working with ID, inspite of more people with ID in Israel living today in the community compared to residential care (17,000 versus 6,000).

Table 4. Comparison between services in 1990-2005

Type of Service	1990	2005
Assessment Centers Total assessments	1,000	2,000
Kindergartens For nursing and treatment	900	2,800
Day-care for Mild MR	1,600	1,300
After hour care	700	1,100
Leisure	1,400	1,800
Home help assistance	150	250
Sheltered workshops	1,900	3,500
Long-day care	0	665
Integrated care in community (age 0-3 yrs)	0	150
Kindergarten for rehab (1-3 yrs)	0	125
TOTAL Community	7,650	13,690
TOTAL Residential	5,376	9,068
TOTAL Service DMR	13,026	22,758

In this chapter we would like to share some of our experiences on health related problems and needs of adult persons with intellectual disability relevant for family physicians or other allied professionals working with persons with ID both in residential care or in the community.

HEALTH CONCERNS IN PERSONS WITH MILD AND MODERATE INTELLECTUAL DISABILITY

The concerns will be the same as for the general aging population, but due to communication problems, lack of service, sometimes lack of interest or commitment from the service providers diagnosis or treatment can be ignored, overlooked or delayed for this population (4). This is unfortunate, because simple medical problems that could be solved will have adverse effects on the quality of life for the person with ID.

Cardiovascular disease was found to be less in persons with ID aged 65 years and older admitted to nursing homes than persons without ID (24.4% versus 56.5%)(5), but there are very few studies on the prevalence of heart disease in this population. A recent study from New York State (6) of 1,371 adult persons with ID living in the community showed that cardiovascular disease increased with increasing age and more likely among adults who were more functional, in adults with seizures and with the highest BMI. The incidence of death from cancer in the United Kingdom for persons with intellectual has been lower than the general population (11.7-17.5% versus 26%), but the incidence of cancer is now on the increase due to increased longevity (7,8). In New York State cancer increased significantly with age and was more likely to occur in females(6). Gastrointestinal cancer was proportionally higher than the general population (48-58.5% versus 25% of cancer deaths in the United Kingdom)(7,8). In a study of cancer and Down syndrome a statistically significant excess of leukemia was found and in addition an excess of gastric cancer in institutionalised males observed (9).

Women with ID are much less likely to undergo cervical smear tests than the general population (19% versus 77%)(10) and also less likely to have breast cancer examinations or receive mammography (11).

Visual and hearing impairment effect about half of the general population over 65 years and will also be seen in older persons with ID. Visual impairment was found seven times higher in adults with ID than the general population (12). Cataract, glaucoma, macular degeneration and diabetic retinopathy should be considered. Ocular and orbital abnormalities in persons with Down syndrome are numerous and reported with various occurrence: blepharitis (2-47 %), keratoconus (5-8 %), glaucoma (less than 1 %), iris anomalies (38-90 %), cataract (25-85 %), retinal anomalies (0-38 %), optic nerve anomalies (very few cases), strabismus (23-44 %), amblyopia (10-26 %), nystagmus (5-30 %) and refractive errors (18-58 %) (13). Deafness is also common in this population(14) and impairment increase with increasing age (6,14). Presbycusis (high pitched tones become harder to hear) and hearing loss is also seen in this population as a result of impacted earwax (15).

Constipation is seen frequent with this population and can be a lifelong problem, which increases with age due to decline in mobility and less bowel motility or movement. Medication can also be a factor in constipation. Caretakers need to be aware of this problem, because of the dangers to accumulation and sometimes even intestinal perforation and death (16).

In aging the bladder capacity and muscle tone will decrease and cause urinary incontinence and in men enlargement of the prostate gland can also restrict urinary flow.

Dental problems in surveys of this population have identified poor oral hygiene, high prevalence of gingival disease and untreated dental caries with dental care difficult to implement (17).

HEALTH CONCERNS IN PERSONS WITH SEVERE AND PROFOUND INTELLECTUAL DISABILITY

Many persons with severe and profound ID will have associated medical problems and disease. In our review of mortality in this population in Israel (3) for the 1991-97 period, 60% of the 450 cases were deaths before the age of 41 years and 68% in the severe-profound group. Cardiovascular reasons accounted for 35%, respiratory disease for 25% and infectious diseases for 9% of the cases. The group with severe and profound ID, who survived into old age will therefore have musculoskeletal problems, respiratory disease, problems with swallowing, some will need gastrostomy and therefore demand a high service level.

Osteoporosis and increased fractures should be kept in mind in this population (18) due to immobility, nutrition and lack of activity.

HEALTH CONCERNS IN DOWN SYNDROME

In the 1920s the life expectancy for persons with Down syndrome (DS) was only nine years, but this has now increased to 56-60 years, which is still twenty years less than the general population (19).

The Atzheimer disease (AD) was first described by professor Alois Alzheimer, Germany, in 1906 (20), when he reported the case of Auguste D, a 51-year old female patient, he had followed at a Frankfurt hospital since 1901 up until her death on April 8th, 1906. Even after her death he went on to study the neuropathological features of her illness. Shortly after her death he presented her case at the 37th Conference of German Psychiatrist in Tubingen on November 4th, 1906 in which he described her symptoms:

- Progressive cognitive impairment
- Focal symptoms
- Hallucinations
- Delusions
- Psychosocial incompetence
- Neurobiological changes found at autopsy: plaques, neurofibrillary tangles and artheriosclerotic changes

These symptoms are still the characteristics of AD today, which is the most common cause of dementia in western countries. Clinicaly AD most often presents with a subtle onset of memory loss followed by a slowly progressive dementia that has a course of several years. The duration of AD can be 3-10 years from diagnosis to death and this progress is more rapid in persons with DS and usually seizures will present itself at the end stage. Epilepsy is seen in about 5% of persons with DS, but the combination of DS and AD will produce epileptic seizures in 85% of the cases.

Besides from AD persons with DS are prone to other medical problems when aging. A recent study from Holland (21) of 96 adults with DS from an institution were investigated systematically over the period 1991-95 with cytogenetic diagnosis, mental functioning, dementia, ophthalmological and audiological assessments and thyriod function. Seventy (73%) were older that 40 years and only 4.3 % females. Three % were with mild ID, 82% moderate and severe ID and 15% profound ID. 19% had already dementia, but this number increased to 42% in persons above 50 years of age.

Epilepsy was present in 16.7 % of all the persons, but in 50% of those with dementia. Vision problems were frequent with only 17% with normal vision and here again increase of problems with increase in age. In the 50-59 year age group 44.8% had moderate to severe vision loss. Seventy percent had moderate, severe or very severe hearing loss, which was undiagnosed before systematic hearing tests were performed. 49% had thyroid dysfunction.

Besides from the above observed health problems persons with DS have increased obesity, premature aging of the immune system resulting in various diseases, increased sleep apnoa and musculoskeletal problems (22).

EPILEPSY AND CEREBRAL PALSY

Persons with intellectual disability (ID), epilepsy and seizures, who receive anti-epileptic drugs over long periods, will also be at an increased risk for premature mortality, increased risk of osteoporosis and increased risks of falls.

A study of risk factors for injuries and falls (23) among 268 adults with ID from 18 nursing homes in Chicago revealed that 11% (30 cases) had reported injuries 12 months prior to the follow-up study. Over 50% of the injuries were caused by falls and persons with a higher frequency of seizures, more destructive behavior and usage of anti-psychotic drugs had the highest risk of injuries. Further analysis of the data revealed that persons over 70 years, ambulatory and a higher frequency of seizures had the higest risk of injurious falls.

Studies of the effect of aging in persons with cerebral palsy (CP) are few and studies with persons with both ID and CP are even less. Reason would tell you that mobility would be decreased over the years, osteoporosis increased and increased dependency on care over the years.

INTELLECTUAL DISABILITY AND GENERAL PRACTICE

The number of persons with intellectual disability (ID) in general practice has been studied in Holland (24). A general practice database with 62,000 patients had 318 persons (or 0.65%) with ID, which together with persons in residential case showed a total prevalence of 0.82%.

Barriers to treatment in general practice has been studied in Australia among 912 randomly selected general practitioners (GP)(25), where communication diffuculties with patients and other health professionals, and problems in getting patient histories were the most significant barriers. Other difficulties were lack of training and experience, poor patient complience, consultation time limitations, difficulties in problem determination, examination difficulties, poor continuity of care and inadequate knowledge of services and resources.

Researchers in Cardiff, Wales have developed a health screening tool for persons with ID in general practice (26), which has also been used in general practice in New Zealand (27). Here the introduction of an annual health screen resulted in medical findings of 72.6% of the 1,311 persons screened, which afterward required follow-up interventions.

A survey conducted through all United States family practice residency directors (28) showed that 84% of the programs had provided residents with one or more experience about health care needs of persons with ID and 60% had instructed residents in that area. Holland in the year 2000 established a chair in intellectual disability at the University of Rotterdam Department of Family Medicine and started a three year sub-specialty in ID (29), where the first class of specialists in ID graduated in November 2003.

CONCLUSION

We have seen an increase in the population of persons with intellectual disability surviving into older age over recent years resulting in health problems emerging like in the general population, but sometimes at a much earlier stage, like Atzheimer disease in Down syndrome beginning in the early forties. There is therefore a need to provide more evidece based practice standards to enhance health status, longevity, functional capability and quality of life in this population (30).

A working group (Aging Special Interest Research Group) under the International Association for the Scientific Study of Intellectual Disabilities (IASSID) published recommendations for further research areas (30):

- The acquisition of additional clinical and epidemiological knowledge regarding specific syndromes with linkages to basic science research in biomolecular genetics and metabolism.

- The development of adapted diagnostic and therapeutic methods for people who have difficulties with cooperation or communication.

- The development and evaluation of interdisciplinary interventions for complicated conditions (like sensory impairment, dysphagia, communication and functional decline).

- The development of clinimetric measures in a number of areas (functional capability, quality of life, mental health, pain assessment and clinical diagnosis), that are sensitive and specific, easy to administer and applicable to persons with a wide range of mental and physical capabilities.

- The evaluation of clinical guidelines, including referral protocols, to support community based primary care physicians, within specific health care systems, to care for people with intellectual disabilities.

- The evaluation of the applicability of a new discipline of lifespan developmental medicine to lead in interdisciplinary care, health care education, service delivery and research for people with intellectual disability.

- The development of the knowledge base regarding the health status and needs of people with intellectual disabilities living in less developed countries.

In Israel we have over the past ten years embarked on several major studies of aging in the population of persons with ID and eventually we would like to follow the trend of our colleagues in Holland and establish a formalized sub-specialty.

REFERENCES

1.   Merrick J. Survey of medical clinics-2005. Jerusalem: Office Med Dir, Min Labour Social Affairs, 2006.
2.   Merrick, J. Trends in government expenditure for persons with intellectual disability in Israel. Int J Adolesc Med Health 2000;12(Suppl 1): S109-14.
3..   Merrick J. Mortality for persons with intellectual disability in residential care in Israel 1991-97. J. Intell. Dev. Disability 2002;27(4):265-72.
4.   Kerr AM, McCulloch D, Oliver K, McLean B, Coleman E, Law T, Beaton P, Wallace S, Newell E, Eccles T, Prescott RJ. Medical need of people with intellectual disability require regular reassessment and provision of client- an carer-held reports. J Intellect Disabil Res 2003;47:134-45.
5.   Anderson DJ. Health Issues. In: Sutton E et al, eds. Older adults with developmental disabilities. Baltimore: Paul Brookes, 1993:29-48.
6.   Janicki MP, Davidson PW, Henderson CM, McCallion P, Taets JD, Force LT, Sulkes SB, Frangenberg E, Ladrigan PM. Health characteristics and health services utilization in older adults with intellectual disability living in community residences. J Intellect Disabil Res 2002;46:287-98.
7.   Cooke LB. Cancer and learning disability. J Intellect Disabil Res 1997;41: 312-316.
8.   Duff M, Hoghton M, Scheepers M, Cooper M, Baddeley P. Helicobacter pylori: Has the killer escaped from the institution ? A possible cause of increased stomach cancer in a population with intellectual disability. J Intellect Disabil Res 2001;45:219-25.
9.   Boker LK, Merrick J. Cancer incidence in persons with Down syndrome in Israel. Down Syndr Res Pract 2002;8(1):31-6.

10.   Djuretic T, Laing-Morton T, Guy M, Gill M. Concerted effort is needed to ensure the women use preventive services. BMJ 1999;318: 536.

11.   Davies N, Duff M. Breast cancer screening for older women with intellectual disability living in community group homes. J Intellect Disabil Res 2001;45:253-7.

12.   Warburg M. Visual impairment among people with developmental delay. J Intellect Disabil Res 1994;38:423-32.

13.   Merrick J, Koslowe K. Refractive errors and visual anomalies in Down syndrome. Down Syndr Res Pract 2001;6(3):131-3.

14.   Evenhuis HM. Medical aspects of ageing in a population with intellectual disability: II. Hearing impairment. J. Intell. Disabil. Res 1995;39:27-33.

15.   Crandell CC, Roesser RJ. Incidence of excessive/impacted cerumen in individuals with mental retardation: A longitudinal investigation. Am J Ment Retard 1993;97:568-74.

16.   Bohmer CJM, Taminiau JAJM, Klinkenberg-Knol EC, Meuwissen SGM. The prevalence of constipation in institutionalized people with intellectual disability. J Intellect Disabil Res 2001;45:212-8.

17.   Walman HB, Perlman SP. Providing dental services for people with disabilities: Why is it so difficult ? Ment Retard 2002;40(4):330-3.

18.   Center J, Beange H, McElduff A. People with mental retardation have an increased prevalence of osteoporosis: A population study. Am J Ment Retard 1998;103(1):19-28.

19.   Merrick J. Aspects of Down syndrome. Int J Adolesc Med Health 2000;12(1): 5-17.

20.   Alzheimer A. Uber einen eigenartigen schweren Erkrankungsprozess der Hirnrinde. Neurol. Centralblatt 1906;23:1129-36. [German]

21.   Van Buggenhout GJCM., Trommelen JCM, Schoenmaker A, De Baal C, Verbeek JJMC, Smeets DFCM, Ropers HH, Devriendt K, Hamel BCJ, Fryns JP. Down syndrome in a population of elderly mentally retarded patients: Genetic-diagnostic survey and implications for medical care. Am J Med Genetics 1999;85:376-84.

22.   Merrick J, Ezra E, Josef B, Hendel D, Steinberg DM, Wientroub S. Musculoskeletal problems in Down syndrome. European Paediatric Orthopaedic Society Survey: The Israeli sample. J Pediatr Orthopaedics Part B 2000;9:185-92.

23.   Hsieh K, Heller T, Miller AB. Risk factors for injuries and falls among adults with developmental disabilities. J. Intell. Disabil. Res 2001;45: 76-82.

24.   van Schrojenstein Lantman-de Valk HMJ, Metsemakers JFM, Soomers-Turlings MJMSJG, Haveman MJ, Crebolder HFJM. People with intellectual disability in general practice: Case definition and case findings. J Intellect Disabil Res 1997;41:373-9.

25.   Lennox NG, Diggens JN, Ugoni AM. The general practice care of people with in tellectual disability: Barriers and solutions. J Intellect Disabil Res 1997;41:380-90.

26.   Jones RG, Kerr MP. A randomized control trial of an opportunistic health screening tool in primary care for people with intellectual disability. J Intellect Disabil Res 1997;41:409-15.

27.   Webb OJ, Rogers L. Health screening for people with intellectual disability: The New Zealand experience. J Intellect Disabil Res 1999;43:497-503.

28.   Tyler CV, Snyder CW, Zyzanski SJ. Caring for adults with mental retardation: Survey of family practice residency program directors. Ment Retard 1999;37(5):347-52.

29.   Evenhuis HM, van Praag PH, Wiersema MI, Huisman S. Curriculum for the medical specialist training for physicians for people with intellectual disability. Amsterdam: Dutch Society Physicians for People with Intellectual Disability (NVAZ), 1998.

30.   Evenhuis HM, Henderson CM, Beange H, Lennox N, Chicoine B. Healthy ageing in people with intellectual disability. Physical health issues. Geneva: World Health Organization, 2000.

CHAPTER 9
Medical services for persons with intellectual disability. Model of Israel

Joav Merrick and Isack Kandel

T he first school for children with intellectual disability (ID) was opened in Tel Aviv in 1929, the first boarding school for children with ID was established in Jerusalem in 1931, the first center for assessment of children with ID established in Tel Aviv in 1936 and with the establishment of the modern State of Israel 1948, there was a total of four residential care centers providing services for 150 children with ID. This chapter will describe in brief the history and development of the public health work with persons with intellectual disability from the birth of the modern State of Israel in 1948 until today with a focus on medical and nursing care with ideas for the future work with this population.

INTRODUCTION

The first school for children with intellectual disability (ID) was opened in Tel Aviv in 1929. The first residential care center or boarding school for children with ID was established in 1931 in Jerusalem and the first center for assessment of children with ID was established in Tel Aviv in 1936. The second residential care center, also established on private initiative, was opened in Herzliya in 1945 (1).

At the time of the establishment of the modern State of Israel 1948, there was a total of four residential care centers providing services for 150 children with ID. In addition, throughout the country there were 25 special education classes serving 350 students (1).

HISTORY OF THE DEVELOPMENT OF SERVICES

The history of the development of services has been reviewed and the changes divided into different time periods: between the years 1948-61, 1962-1976, 1977-1985 and 1986-1994 (1).

The 1948-61 period was a period of change and innovation (1). In 1950 the Ministry of Education established a separate department for special education with about 400 children registered. Official records from 1957 showed that on a countrywide basis there were 22 classes with 252 children with moderate ID and 276 classes with 5,284 children with mild ID. In 1951 the Israeli Parent Association for children with ID (called AKIM) was established in Tel Aviv and today they have 51 branches with a variety of services: Nurseries and kindergartens, support for families, respite care centers, hostels and apartments, community centers, employment programs, summer camps, sports (branch of Special Olympics), arts activities and guardianship. These activities are mainly funded by the government, but AKIM is also supported by fundraising and donations.

During this period welfare services for children with ID at the Ministry of Welfare were provided through the Child, Adolescent and Youth Protection Services. Residential care was provided by government (695 persons registered in 1962) or private institutions (469 persons registered in 1962)(1). The first sheltered workshop was opened in Jerusalem in 1955 by AKIM.

The 1962-1977 period saw the establishment of a separate service within the Ministry of Welfare for persons with intellectual disability in 1962 (1). This brought all services for both children and adults under one roof. This process was not easy, but both internal and external pressure and at the same time the efforts of President John F Kennedy in the United States to focus on mental retardation were helpful. Standards for residential care were established, criteria for placements were formulated and three assessment centers were opened in Jerusalem, Haifa and Tel Aviv. Kindergartens, day care centers and sheltered workshops for adults were established all over the country. In 1965 the "Residential Care Center Law" was passed in the Israeli Parliament to regulate supervision and in 1969 the "Welfare Law for persons with ID" came into effect. Training of care staff in residential care centers and community settings (hostels) was initiated in 1968, with the opening of the first certification course for caregiving professionals.

During the 1977-1985 period (1) the Ministry of Welfare merged with the Ministry of Labour (in 1977) to create the Ministry of Labour and Social Affairs (MoLSA). The Service for persons with Mental Retardation was upgraded and became the Division for Mental Retardation (DMR) in 1978. In 1977, the "father" of normalization and de-institutionalization, Niels Erik Bank-Mikkelsen from Denmark, came to Israel for a visit and his report on the situation in Israel with his recommendations, together with reports from the parent advocacy organization AKIM resulted in a period of reorganization and improvement of services. The DMR worked on a clear definition of the target population to who services would be provided, the principle of providing community based services was adopted, supervision of residential care was improved and several facilities were closed due to poor performance. In addition, clear policy concerning criminal acts carried out by persons with ID was formulated, mandatory education was introduced, laws were passed concerning guardianship, disability allowance, marriage and payment for productive employment. A public campaign to educate the Israeli public on mental retardation and intellectual disability was also put in effect.

During this period several universities became interested in the field of intellectual disability and several publications in the form of MA and PhD dissertations saw the light. These publications were solely in the fields of social work and psychology (1), whilst the nursing and medicine professions in Israel have as yet displayed little interest in the area of intellectual disability.

The 1986-1994 period (1) may be described as a period of significant development and expansion. The DMR now realised its responsibility for all persons with ID from infancy to old age and also started work with parents and families. Towards the end of this period, with the support of a new Minister in 1993, residential care centers were expanded and the long waiting list that has been in existence for years was totally abolished. This provided better choices for both parents and self advocates. Community services were also expanded and parents were encouraged to leave there children at home as long as possible. More power and responsibility was given to local authorities to take responsibility for community housing and placement.

DIVISION FOR MENTAL RETARDATION IN RECENT YEARS

Today in Israel (total population of over 7 million) the Division for Mental Retardation (DMR) is in contact with approximately 24,000 persons of all ages. Residential care is provided in residential care centers, hostels and protected apartments together with day-care kindergartens, day-treatment centers, sheltered workshops or integrated care within the community.

The age distribution, the level of intellectual disability and the resident profile in residential care centers in Israel (2) was described in chapter 6.

MEDICAL AND NURSING SERVICE

We have no data available when the first nurse or physician was employed and at which residential care center, but we know that the third residential care center (Makim in Ramle) established in Israel in 1954 was established and run by a nurse, who had survived the Holocaust (1).

Historically the development of medical services within the Ministry of Labour and Social Affairs (MOLSA) was not an overall planned process, but rather something that evolved along with the specific needs over time or as a consequence of personal interests or needs.

In the late 1960s, Moshe Kurtz, Director General of what was then known as the Ministry of Welfare, displayed unique foresight when he proposed to establish a medical service within the Ministry with the aim to provide answers to the significant needs and issues arising from the various services. The director of Rehabilitation, Michael Rosenberg, found a suitable candidate, who had shown interest in the medical and social aspects of the treatment of persons with ID at the Swedish Village in Jerusalem by bringing his medical students from Hadassah to learn on site. In 1970, Vlademir Sterk, a pediatrician and assistant professor of pediatrics, who had immigrated from Yugoslavia and earlier conducted research in metabolic disorders at Stanford University, was appointed the first medical director of the Ministry of Welfare on a fulltime basis. The intention of the Director General was to have a medical service and a medical director for all the medical aspects of the Welfare Ministry, but the medical director decided that his services were most needed within the Division for Mental Retardation and therefore concentrated his work within the service for persons with ID. Several years later the position of chief nurse was also created within the DMR to supervise and manage the work of nurses at the local institutional level.

In 2005 (2) there was the equivalent of 43 full time chief nurse positions, 276 full time nurse positions and 41 full time physician positions working in the residential care centers. Only a few nurses were employed in community settings (hostels and protected apartments), because medical service is usually provided in the community under the same conditions as for the general population.

MEDICAL AND NURSING CARE

The population in residential care centers was in 2005 characterized by 1,312 nursing patients and further 320 intensive nursing care patients (2). The total population in residental care centers is very much in need of nursing care and the medical profile or medical problems can be seen in table 1 (2).

Table 1. Profile of 6,749 persons with intellectual disability in residential care centers in Israel 2005 (2)

Profile	Numbers	Percent
Gastric tube feeding	14	0.47
Urinary catheter	25	0.37
Gastrostomy	177	2.62
Pressure sore (decubitus)	47	0.67
Dialysis	10	0.15
Oncology treatment	68	1.01
Down syndrome	586	8.68
Fragile X	70	1.04
Epilepsy	2,102	31.15
Diabetes Mellitus	341	5.05
Hypertension	459	6.80
Asthma	153	2.27
Phenylketonuria (PKU)	18	0.27
Self injurious behavior (SIB)	188	2.79
Blindness	324	4.80
Wheel chair (normal)	1,175	17.41
Wheel chair (electric)	38	0.56
Walkers	185	2.74

Table 2. Regular medication of 6,749 persons with intellectual disability in residential care centers in Israel 2005 (2)

Type of medication	Number of persons	Percent
Chronic medication	5,548	82.20
AED (for epilepsy)	2,043	30.27
Psychotropic	3,440	50.97

Besides from these specific problems this population is in need of daily medication three times a day (chronic medication). 82% (see table 2) received medication every day, 30% received anti epileptic drugs and 51% psychotropic medication (2). Over and above the daily medication there is also medication for acute problems, preventive medicine and vaccinations. Every year for example, nearly all residents receive the flu vaccination (in 2005 a total of 4,741 flu vaccinations (70%), even though we had a shortage of available vaccinations that year)(2).

Another important function of the nurse and the medical team in residential care centers is the performance of daily examinations of the residents. Daily a regular clinic is held, providing treatment to patients with complaints or problems during the previous night that needs to be seen by the physician, but also routine examinations. Our goal is that each resident is seen at least once a year by the physician and also undergoes a routine laboratory bloodtest annually. In table 3 the number of examinations for 2005 (2) can be seen. Blood is drawn in the residential care center, but send out to laboratories run by the HMOs in the specific catch-up area of the center.

Table 3. Number of medical examinations at all residential care centers in Israel in 2005 (6,749 residents)(2).

Examination	Total for 2005	Exams per person/year
Physician	87,375	12.95
Psychiatrist	20,900	3.10
Other physician	4,423	0.66
Physiotherapist	115,709	17.14
Bloodtest, urine, Stool, other	27,393	4.06

Table 4. Infectious diseases in all residential care centers in 2005 (6,749 residents) (2)

Disease	Number of cases
Septicemia	3
Viral hepatitis	19
Salmonellosis	6
Snake bites	1
Scorpion bites	0
Campylobacteriosis	1
Pertussis	1
Varicella	16
Scabies	735
Lice	197

Infectious disease is often seen in this population. We do not have statistics for the number of yearly pulmonary infections, but some statistics can be seen in table 4 (2). That year one residential care center suffered from 50 cases of MRSA infection.

Another function of the medical and nursing staff is to coordinate dental surveillence and treatment. We aim to have each resident seen by the dentist at least once a year. The nurse is responsible for keeping the dental appointments at one of our 12 dental clinics around the country. Each dental clinic is situated in a residential care center, usually in close proximity to the medical clinic. The number of dental visits for 2005 (2) can be seen in table 5.

Table 5. Dental treatment in all residential care centers in 2005 (6,749 persons) (2). GA=General Aneasthesia

Examination	Numbers	Percent
Dental examination	7,569	112.15
Dental hygienist	6,287	93.15
Treatment under GA	112	1.66

The medical clinics in our residential care centers are usually staffed with nurses (most are practical nurses) 24 hours every day. The physician makes visits during the day, but is not on call and therefore the medical clinic at the residential care center may send the resident to the emergency room or for hospitalization, should medical problems arise during the evening and nights. Some of the residential care centers have a small number of beds for observation (called internal institutional hospitalization in table 6).

Emergency and hospital utilization in 2005 is shown in table 6 (2) and as can be seen in table 7 the total somatic hospitalization discharge for our population was lower than the general population in spite of dealing with a population in residential care centers with a "heavy" medical profile, which resulted in more hospitalization days. Psychiatric hospitalization discharge was the same, but the number of hospitalization days in psychiatric care was much less than for the general population (3).

Table 6. Emergency room visits and hospitalizations for all residential care centers in 2005 (6,749 residents) (2)

Activity	Numbers	Number of days	Rate/1,000
Emergency Room	1,860	0	275.60
Internal Medicine	597	3,409	88.46
Pediatrics	170	1.193	25.19
Surgery	138	777	20.45
Other	169	958	25.04
Total somatic Hospitalization	1,074	6,337	159.13
Psychiatric	33	655	4.89
Total hosp.	1,107	6,992	164.02

Table 7. Comparison between somatic and psychiatric hospitalization discharges (rate per 1,000) and total hospitalization days of persons in residential care centers in Israel (DMR) 2005 (2) with the general Israeli population in 2004 (3)

Somatic hospitalization discharge 2004 in general population:	180.5
DMR 2005:	159.13
Psychaitric hospitalizations discharge 2004:	4.1
DMR 2005:	4.89
Total somatic hospitalization days 2004:	760.5
DMR 2005:	938.95
Total psychiatric hospitalization days 2004:	220.1
DMR 2005:	97.05

The physician in each residential care center is usually a family physician or a physician without specialization for the adult population and a pediatrician if a pediatric population. The residential care physician serves as the core physician for the resident. The local physician will often require specialist advice from physicians in hospital out-patient clinics or specialist medical centers in the area. The number of specialist referrals in 2005 is seen in table 8 and the number of special examination in laboratories or clinics outside the residential care center is seen in table 9.

Table 8. Utilization of ambulatory services outside the residential care centers in 2005 (6,749 residents)(2). Numbers and rate per 1,000 population.

Type of service	Number of visits in 2005	Rate/1,000
Surgery	823	121.9
Internal medicine	179	26.5
Eye	1,313	194.6
Optometrist	451	66.8
Dermatology	838	124.2
Orthopedics	930	137.8
Gynecology	769	113.9
Neurology	727	107.7
Oncology	70	10.4
ENT	892	132.2
Diabetes	231	34.2
Cardiology	188	27.9
Endocrinology	211	31.3
Pulmology	144	21.3
Child development	8	0.1
Urology	291	43.1
Gastroenterology	368	54.5
Hearing impairment	117	17.3
Proctology	75	11.1
Rehabilitation	95	14.1
Vascular	89	13.2
Hematology	114	16.9
Physiotherapy	117	17.3
Plastic surgery	89	13.2
Oral surgery	138	20.5
Hemodialysis	688	101.9
Psychiatrist	155	22.9
Other	332	49.2
TOTAL	12,302	1,822.8

All activities mentioned above require the cooperation and the involvement of the medical and nursing staff with other professionals (socialworker, psychologist, physiotherapist, nritritionist) and care givers in order to be properly performed. The nurse staff will often have to be involved to explain and calm down the resident and sometimes follow and participate with the resident at the out-patient clinic, dental visit or during hospitalization.

Table 9. Utilization of ambulatory laboratory services outside the residential care centers in 2005 (2). Number of examinations and rate per 1,000 population.

Type of laboratory	Number of exams	Rate/1,000
Chest X ray	577	85.5
Other X ray	772	114.4
Ultrasound	734	108.8
ECG	1,380	204.5
EEG	163	24.2
Mammography	310	45.9
ECHO	151	22.4
CT	256	37.9
MRI	45	6.7
Other	79	11.7
TOTAL	4,467	661.9

DISCUSSION

Medical services for persons with intellectual disability (ID) have come a long way, since the establishment of the modern State of Israel in 1948. Within the framework of the Division for Mental Retardation of the Ministry of Social Affairs (MSA), as it is called today, medical service is provided at an acceptable level, even with the lack of adequate manpower, but within the community there is a lack of relevant services.

We have over the years developed several dreams and wishes for the future. We would like to go in the direction of Holland (4) with a subspecialty for family physicians and pediatricians in intellectual disability. There is both a need for a raised level of care in the residential care centers, but most certainly also for the community, where today familiy physicians and pediatricians provide primary care to most, if not all, persons with intellectual disability living at home or in community based hostels or protected apartments.

We would also like to see more registered nurses coming to work with this special population. Unfortunately at present there is a shortage of nurses in Israel. In addition, our work place and conditions does not seem to be attractive to well trained quality nursing personnel or physicians. We have to compete with work opportunities in the hospital system or the HMOs and are not successful. Therefore, our initial goal has been that at least the chief nurses in all residential centers will be a registered nurse. This goal has nearly been reached today, but we certainly hope that over the next years all nurses will be registered nurses. In this effort we have been helped by the Ministry of Health, because practical nurses will soon be a thing of the past and by end 2007 this term will be abolished, which we all hope will be for the benefit of our residents also. With this development we would also like to see a subspecialty in intellectual disability for nurses, but again that has not materialized.

In order to facilitate such activities we would like to have university affiliation, where students in medicine and allied professions can be educated in our field of work, to have students on site in our residential care centers and to conduct joint research projects. A step in that direction was taken in 1999, when the National Institute of Child Health and Human Development (NICHD) was established as the research arm of the Office of the Medical Director (5). This institute is involved in research and education in the fields of child health, disability, intellectual disability and human development with many activities and publications, since its establishment (6), but we have not at this stage managed to accomplish university affiliation.

Many countries around the world have adapted the Scandinavian model of normalization and deinstitutionalization, which developed in the 1970s, where persons were transferred from large state institutions into services in the community. Several states in United States of America have completely closed down their institutions and today serve this population in the community. The transfer has not been without complications, such as earlier death, more health problems or lack of health and dental services and homelessness and therefore we believe that it is not a question of either or, but instead a combination of both residential care in small institutions and community settings. In Israel we would like to see the future development in a direction, where both community care and residential care for the population of persons with ID are combined (7,8). We would like to have the future "institution" for persons with ID established within selected areas around the country in order to provide service for persons unable to stay in the community or at home, but the residential care center should also function as the regional medical center for persons with ID living in the community or at home, since the present model for medical care is inaequate. The medical center at the area residential care center should provide prevention programs, rehabilitation, nursing care and treatment in the health field, dental health, nutrition, preventive medicine (vaccination, women health etc), physiotherapy and occupational therapy for the target population within the whole area assigned.

We would like to see special long-term nursing facilities for our intensive nursing care patients. Today there are 320 intensive nursing patients already in our facilities without the adequate staff, equipment or facilities (2). Several years ago a ministerial committee was set up by both the Minister of Health and the Minister of Social Affairs with participation of professionals from both ministries and the direction of thought was to establish four centers, one in each region in Israel, with about 100 long-term intensive nursing care beds for these chronically ill patients with the required staff according to current standard of the Ministry of Health. We hope that each regional center will not only treat the long-term intensive nursing patients, but also function as a regional multidisciplinary out-patient facility for all persons with ID in the region providing medical, dental, occupational and physiotherapy service, supervision, assessments, education and research. The first facility has been build with 50 beds at the Aleh Negev Village in the south of Israel (Ofakim), but has not yet been opened, which we hope will be soon, because the demand is great.

We would also like to see a Health Division established in the Ministry of Social Affairs (after the last election in 2003 the Ministry of Labour was abolished) as an independent division with its own administration, manpower and budget affiliated directly to the Minister and the Director General. The new division should be responsible for all medical, health care and allied professions within the entire Ministry and its government, public and private facilities working under license or auspices of the Ministry. It is suggested that this division should be established with the manpower and resourses already in existence in various parts of the Ministry with the budget for the division coming from a re-allocation of the budget from the various divisions (Division for Mental Retardation, Rehabilitation, Service for Children and Youth, Service of the Aged etc)(9).

So far the medical service or health care has been fragmented and spread around the Ministry with very little intercommunication and coordination (other than in cases of emergencies). Working as a nurse, physician or allied professional in MSA has not been an attractive position (we have to compete with better and interesting jobs like intensive care or surgery) and the result has been that the professionals we have in the various institutions are usually retired professionals, professionals who could not get a position in the traditional medical system in Israel or professionals who work full-time in the traditional system and come to us to work "on the side" and therefore not really part of our system. Continuity is very important in MSA with the clients and problems we deal with. Most of the medical care is with persons with disability, chronic illness or severe social problems, where it is very important with a long term perspective, contact, training and involvement. If the professionals change all the time, because the work (with f.ex intellectual disability or disability in general) is without possibilities for advancement, for credit, for training or for academic affiliation, the clients in the end are the ones who suffer (9).

The reform has to be done from within the MSA, because the traditional medical system is not interested in dealing with the work we do. Traditional medicine is interested in emergencies and short term hospitalizations and not in chronic illness, rehabilitation or long term chronic care. In MSA we are dealing with social medicine, but have not applied the model for our work. The establishment of a Health Division will make better management, better utilization of resources, better setting of priorities, better training and better research and development, when there will be a professional system and environment to work in. as in the traditional medical system to make it attractive for professionals to work in the Ministry (9). The Health Division will work on the level of the Ministry, the level of districts and the local institutional level. On one hand serve the Minister and Director General on all health and health related issues and on the other provide service, management and supervision to all the divisions, services and departments of the ministry.

At the district level or regional level work will be strengthened, when the four small medical centers (one in each region with 50-100 beds) for treatment of intensive nursing patients will be established. At the local level in each institution today (residential care centers of the Division for Mental Retardation, Division of Rehabilitation, Service for the Aged, Service for Children and Youth, Division for Youth Development etc) there are full- or part time physicians, psychiatrists, nurses sometimes in 24 hours service, physiotherapists, occupational therapists, speech therapists, pharmacists, dieticians, psychologists and social workers. All this manpower is not affiliated in an organized way to a central entity, but it is suggested that they will be with the establishment of a Health Division.

CONCLUSIONS

In this chapter we have tried to picture the history and development of the work with persons with intellectual disability from the birth of the modern State of Israel in 1948 until today. The focus has been on medical care with a stress on the often difficult and hard work carried out be the health care workers. Over the years there has not been time to think about further education, academic affiliation or research in nursing care or practice.

The work has been illustrated with data of the health profile, morbidity and mortality of the residents and we finalize the chapter with some wishes and dreams for the future.

We recommend the future development in Israel in a direction of combining both community care and institutional care for the population of persons with ID. We recommend to have the future residential care center for persons with ID established within selected areas or regions around the country in order to provide service for persons unable to stay in the community or at home, but the center should also function as the medical center for persons with ID living in the community or at home, because the present models are not adequate. The medical center at the regional level should provide prevention programs, rehabilitation and treatment in the health field, dental health, nutrition, preventive medicine (vaccination, women health etc), physiotherapy and occupational therapy for the target population within the whole area assigned.

ACKNOWLEDGEMENTS

This chapter is an updated and adapted version of a paper publisted earlier (Merrick J, Kandel I. Medical services for persons with intellectual disability in Israel. Public Health Rev 2003;31(1):45-68).

REFERENCES

1.   Hovav M, Ramot A. The development of welfare services for the mentally handicapped in Israel. Social Security 1998;5:142-62.

2.   Merrick J. Survey of medical clinics-2005. Jerusalem: Office Med Dir, Min Labour Social Affairs, 2006.

3.   Haklai Z, Gordon E, Stein N, Shteiman A, Hillel S, Ozeri R, Aburbeh M. Health in Israel. Selected data. Jerusalem: Health Information Dept, Min Health, 2005.

4.   Evenhuis HM, van Praag PH, Wiersema MI. Curriculum in medical specialist training for physicians for people with intellectual disability. Amsterdam, Holland: Dutch Society for Physicians of People with Intellectual Disability, 1998.

5.   Merrick J. Proposal for a National Institute of Child Health and Human Development. Jerusalem: Office Med Dir, Min Labour Soc Affairs, 1999. (Website: www.nichd-israel.com).

6.   Merrick J. Publication list 1999-2006. Israel National Institute of Child Health and Human Development. Jerusalem: Office Med Dir, Min Soc Affairs, 2007. (Website: www.nichd-israel.com).

7.   Kandel I. Services for persons with intellectual disability in Israel. Reflections on the future. In: Rimmerman A, Hovav M, Duvdevany I, Ramot A, eds. The developmental disabilities and mental retardation in Israel: Needs and responses. Jerusalem: Magness Press, 1997:156-65. [Hebrew]

8.   Merrick J, Cahana C. Giving the intellectually disabled a chance. Rehab Int 2000;10(1):22-4.

9.   Merrick J, Kandel I. Medical services for persons with intellectual disability in Israel. Public Health Rev 2003;31(1):45-68.

PART FOUR:
PAIN IN OLDER PEOPLE

CHAPTER 10
Where are we now in the assessment of pain in older people?

Patricia Schofield, Amanda Clarke, Mark Faulkner, Tony Ryan and Amanda Howarth

The purpose of this chapter is to present the findings of a review of the literature into pain and older people. The funded study was part of the development of an annotated bibliography published in August 2005. The review included all major databases and involved the collection of 214 papers between the dates of 1995 and 2005. The papers were divided into several major themes, which include experiences, management (pharmacological and non-pharmacological), assessment, and attitudes. Within this chapter, the results of the review into pain assessment will be discussed, which includes 42 of the collected papers. The chapter will discuss issues pertaining to the development of specific tools for older people, a discussion of tools already available, comparisons of staff versus older people's perceptions of pain scales, and articles with cognitive impairment as a focus. Recommendations for further study are made.

INTRODUCTION

Whilst the consequences of chronic pain are fairly well documented, the issue concerning chronic pain in the older adult has, in the past, received less attention. For example in 1991, Melding (1) highlighted that of the 4,000 papers published annually concerning chronic pain, less than 1% addressed the issue of chronic pain in the older adult. Furthermore, a review of eight geriatric textbooks high-lighted that they contained only 18 pages out of a possible 5,000 related to pain (1).

Only during the last decade have the issues pertaining to pain in the older adult started to be highlighted and primarily, much of this work has been carried out in the United States of America (USA). However, some United Kingdom (UK) studies are appearing, and recent develop-ments are making carers consider the older population and their needs in terms of pain. The recent National Service Framework (NSF) (2) for older people does highlight the need to address chronic pain in the older adult. Furthermore, it has been suggested that it is time for clinicians to "grasp the nettle" and provide services tailored to meet the needs of the older person, as their numbers are increasing, and a population explosion in the group by 2020 is anticipated (3).

Some researchers have suggested that 50% of older people living in the community are experiencing chronic pain, and this number increases to as high as 80% within the nursing home population (4). Whilst a recent investigation by Allcock (5) reported that 37% of nursing home residents were experiencing chronic pain and that 69% of homes did not have a policy regarding pain management. However, this study did rely only upon the reports of carers, and the investigator did not interview the residents themselves.

It has been suggested that 80% of those over the age of sixty-five suffer at least one chronic illness (6) and many such illnesses are associated with pain. For example, Brattberg et al (7) highlighted that 30% of men and 53% of women over the age of 55 experience peripheral joint pains.

Blomqvist (8) recently highlighted in her study of pain in a group of 150 older people that a range of potentially painful conditions exists, including; falls, leg ulcers, degen-erative joints, and cancer. Many of these conditions were well known and visible, yet the management of pain in this group was poor.

It has even been suggested that in this group, age-related changes occur that result in complex alterations in the processing of pain through the nervous system (1,9). Examples of this phenomenon are often seen whereby patients are admitted with silent myocardial infarctions (10) and abdominal catastrophes (11,12). However, despite the relevance of these studies, which have been questioned in practice, the belief is still widespread that aging decreases pain perception. An alternative perspective to this is the belief that older people get used to pain (13).

Whilst there have been major developments in the field of pain assessment and in particular with the introduction of the McGill Pain Questionnaire as a multidimensional pain tool (14). Many reasons have been cited as to why pain assessment is poor with the older age group (15). The purpose of this study was therefore to address the issues related to poor pain assessment in the older adult by reviewing the literature to date, to identify the evidence based pain assessment tools that are available for this group, and to determine where shortfalls exists to make recom-mendations for further reliability and validity testing or for developing new tools.

OUR SEARCH

All major databases were searched for articles published between the years of 1994 and 2004 (AHMED, CINAHL, MEDLINE, EMBASE, Science Citation Index, Psychlit, ageinfo, anchor housing, index for thesis, steinberg). We anticipated that the literature before this date would be sparse and out of date. Cochrane has been contacted and to date there is no systematic review of literature in this field nor are there any plans to carry out such a review in the near future. The process for the collection of the literature involved the following aspects:

Population

The population included older people and by definition this will include individuals between the ages of 60-100 years.

Interventions

The whole range of interventions were examined including, pharmacological, non-pharmacological, assessment methods and complementary approaches.

Outcomes

Studies were reviewed that highlighted the clinical outcomes of interventions such as quality of life or depression. Also socio-economic information were included.

Study designs

It is anticipated that there is limited experimental research in this area and as such all study designs were included. The following search terms were used: older people, elderly, pain, chronic pain, assessment, assessment tools, dementia. Each study was rated using an instrument that addresses the requirements of both qualitative and quantitative studies (16).

In total, 214 articles were collected. A preliminary review by the team excluded articles that were not research based or related to chronic pain and/or older people. At this stage, 78 articles were rejected. The literature obtained was organized into five main categories as follows:

1.   Socio-economic /Prevalence (8 articles)
2.   Attitudes (8 articles)
3.   Assessment (42 articles)
4.   Experiences (40 articles)
5.   Management (40 articles)

For the purpose of this chapter, the authors will discuss the articles related to assessment only. The articles were published in Sweden, USA, Australia, Canada, and The Netherlands, with only one article published in the UK (15). Only peer reviewed, research-based articles were included in the review. The authors of the publications used a range of clinical settings from community to residential care, nursing homes, and specialized geriatric care units. The oldest participants in the studies were 97 years, with the youngest being 17 years. Although, the latter included participants that were under the selection criteria age group, this study was included as the authors compared pain assessment in this group against an older age group.

The sample sizes in the studies ranged from 19 in the smallest sample to 758 in the largest sample, although some studies used staff and others used patients/residents. There was also a difference between the studies in terms of whether the investigators included those with cognitive impairment in their sample. For the purpose of the review, the literature has been divided into several major themes which will be discussed as follows:

Testing tools already available

Fifteen of the papers reviewed were designed to consider established pain tools that were already applied to adult care. For example, Blomqvist and Hallberg (17) looked at the use of verbal descriptors in residential care in Sweden. Other investigators actually compared a range of scales; for example, Closs et al (15) looked at five different scales across a range of care home settings in the UK and was able to conclude with her sample that the Verbal Rating Scale (VRS) was the most successful, followed by the numbers rating scale (NRS). The color scale (CS) and faces scale (FS) were not completed. Kaasalainen and Crook (18) supported this finding in their study in Canada, with the NRS being more popular and similar problems were associated with the FS.

Again in the USA, Krulewitch et al (19) found similar results in that the pain intensity scale (PIS) was more successful than other scales used with their group in the community. Clearly, the FS is not a popular choice with older adults based upon the literature reviewed. Although, in contrast to these findings, Taylor (20) evaluated the FS in a community setting with 39 black older adults and found that this was the most popular scale, with her sample suggesting that there may be some cultural differences in the preference of pain scales. Nevertheless, this sample was very small and all participants were cognitively intact compared with the samples in the other studies.

A number of the studies reviewed considered the use of the minimum data set (MDS). The minimum data set is a health assessment that is completed quarterly and includes measures of frequency and intensity of pain on a three point likert scale with verbal descriptors and can be completed by either the resident (if capable) or the licensed practical nurse (21). Although, some studies reviewed suggest that this scale tends to under-report pain in residents with cognitive impairment (21-23), which appears to be a consistent problem highlighted by many authors. Furthermore, Jenq et al (24) found that where the MDS was in place, pain was assessed quarterly, but seldom assessed daily, so it would seem that the assessment was carried out as a policy issue as opposed to enhancing patient care.

Other scales that have been evaluated in the literature include the NVPAT (23), the PPQ (21) and facial expression (25), which all authors suggested were appropriate for use in older people with cognitive impairment. However, the numbers in each of these studies was very small and they all suggest that further work has to be done.

It is evident from the review so far that many of the pain assessment scales have been used with older adults, but generally in small-scale studies with a whole range of confounding variables. Nevertheless, there is some sug-gestion about which may be more appropriate with this group and which may not. Clearly, a need exists to investigate the scales in a much larger multi-center study in which confounding variables may be controlled. As suggested by (24), many of these scales are being used with older people, but reliability and validity testing must be performed, and the needs of the older person with cognitive impairment must be addressed for true assessments of pain to be made (26).

Developing tools

The number of papers that actually developed tools was smaller; six papers in total were reviewed for this section. Ferrell et al (27) developed a pain questionnaire, which they tested against the McGill Pain Questionnaire in a group of 176 older adults. The authors reported some success with this geriatric pain measure, which consists of 24 items and provides an indication of the effects of pain upon activities of living. However, there may be some issues in terms of cross cultural use, and the scale does not measure intensity.

One of the earliest and most documented pain-assess-ment tools developed specifically for individuals with cognitive impairment was the DS Dat Scale (28). This scale was based upon behavioral indicators and was designed for use with persons with advanced Alzheimer's disease. The investigators were able to report some success with this scale in three units in the USA. However, they do not appear to have conducted any further validation or reliability studies.

Recently, a number of published papers have introduced new assessment tools. Warden (29) introduced the PAINAD scale, again based upon behaviors to measure pain in the advanced dementia group, which they tested in a patients dementia care unit in the USA. Unfortunately, this was a small scale study of only 19 participants, all of whom were males, which does mean that further work will have to be carried out. A promising Australian study conducted by Davis et al (30) and reported in two papers involves the development and validation of a behavioral scale for people with cognitive impairment. The authors based their work upon the tool of Hurley et al (28) and related literature followed by an expert panel review and testing in extended care units. The sample size was very small, and the authors found that the tool was not completed as the staff said that it was too complicated, therefore they recommended further refinement.

More recently, two interesting pain tools were developed by Abbey et al (31) and Wary (32). Both scales are based upon behaviors and both authors provide evidence of reliability and validity of their tools. It will be interesting to watch the developments with these pain scales in the future, and they can only serve to enhance the care of the cognitively impaired older adult. In conclusion, this section of the literature seems to have identified a number of pain scales that may be appropriately applied to older adults with varying degrees of cognitive impairment. The emphasis now will be to refine and test these scales as opposed to developing more scales.

Residents versus staff comparisons

Three papers were identified that explored the differences between residents and staff perceptions of pain. As highlighted earlier, a number of studies have explored the attitudes of staff in caring for the older adult in pain. These studies stem from the USA, Sweden, and the UK, and generally explore the barriers to effective pain management (5,33-35) with recommendations for further education and training in issues surrounding pain and management for staff working with older adults, however, the studies included in this paper focus upon issues surrounding pain assessment.

A study by Bergh and Sjostrum (36) conducted a structured interview of residents and staff of geriatric units in Sweden to compare nurses' and patients' assessments of pain. The authors used 39 patients for the study, although 4 were excluded because they were unable to complete the visual analogue scale due to cognitive impairments. Whilst 66 nurses were eligible to take part in the study, included were only the 39 that were in contact with the residents. The investigators were able to conclude that the nurses tended to overestimate mild pain but to underestimate severe pain. Furthermore, as there was a difference between the ratings of tolerance—nurses with more training were better at assessment—it was difficult to determine the methodology with this study. Although, the authors discuss the use of interviews, they do not describe what questions were actually asked.

A second study was designed to determine the most appropriate pain assessment tools to identify pain in older adults with cognitive impairment. Krulewitch et al (19) compared staff and older people's assessments in the community in USA. They used a sample of 156 dementia sufferers and found that both staff and patients tended to assess pain more succinctly and comparatively when using the pain intensity scale.

Only one study actually looked at non-nursing staff. Cohen-Mansfield and Lipson (37) looked at physician assessments of pain in a nursing home population. The authors found that geriatrician assessments of pain were both reliable and valid until the level of cognitive impairment in the resident increased. Unfortunately, the authors used only four geriatricians within this study, which is far to small to be generalizable.

The scarcity of research into carers' versus older persons' perceptions of pain and assessment does appear evident within this review. In particular, it would be interesting to compare assessments within various members of the MDT, for example, nurses, physicians, and possibly physiotherapists.

Cognitive impairment as the focus

A number of papers discussed earlier do include older people with cognitive impairments (CI) within their samples, and some papers demonstrate the development of assess-ment scales particularly for this group. Nine of the reviewed studies focused specifically on the needs of the older adult with CI, and these will be discussed within this section. Some of the early papers in this area suggest that a need exists to identify and develop behavioral pain assessment tools that are particularly appropriate for this group (38,39), and it could be suggested that at this stage, this work has actually been carried out. For example, as discussed previously, there appears to be a consistency in behaviors associated with pain, and scales produced by Abbey et al (31) and Wary (32) are now available for practice. Whilst further work may have to be done to validate such tools, we have moved on and we do recognize that pain in the cognitively impaired older adult is an issue.

Some of the work identifies the perspective that nurses do identify and treat pain better in the cognitively intact older adult (40), which again is fairly well acknowledged. Additionally, studies have identified that older adults with CI tend to have less pain medication than do cognitively intact residents (41), and that although CI residents tend to under-report pain, their reports are no less valid than their cognitively intact counterparts (42). Although, the study by Scherder et al (43) does contradict this finding in that they report that older adults with CI have less intense pain; others suggest that the ability to localize pain decreases with increasing CI (44). All of these are contentious issues.

It may be necessary to be more precise regarding the level of cognitive impairment to determine the focus of further study in this area. Many studies in the review use the Mini-Mental State Examination (MMSE) as a measure of cognitive function and some do not. There does have to be some consistency in the scales used, therefore a recognized level of CI may be identified that is consistent with all studies. For example, Kaasalainen and Crook (18) demonstrated with their study that the ability to complete various pain assessment scales varies according to the level of CI. Therefore, only severe CI adults would be unable to complete the traditional assessment scales. This finding again points to the issue of the further validation of recognized scales in adults having various levels of CI using a standard measure of CI status.

Miscellaneous

The final selection of papers is categorized as miscellaneous because they appear to fall outside of the other categories. For example, a small study carried out in Sweden by Hall-Lord et al (45) attempted to categorize the various aspects of pain into sensory, emotional, intellectual, and existential amongst a group of older adults. Although, an interesting study, the sample size (n = 42) was very small. A second study in this group carried out a telephone survey of directors of nursing in USA nursing homes and asked their views on pain assessment. Again, this was an interesting study but it could be suggested that the directors may not be aware of what is happening in their homes and they may not choose to give an honest response if it puts them in a bad light. Scherder et al (46) carried out a study looking at the cause of the most suffering within 68 care home residents in the Netherlands and concluded that chronic pain caused less suffering. This was a complicated paper and the sample size was small. A further paper by Yong et al (47) looked at the differences between younger and older adults in terms of stoicism and cautiousness and did demonstrate some interesting findings that would be worthy of further investigation. Finally an interesting study by Zarit et al (48) looked at the nature of pain in older people over time and found that pain increases with age but so too does adaptation to pain. Unfortunately, as with any longitudinal study, the sample size decreased significantly, but again this is a novel perspective with some potential for further study.

CONCLUSIONS

The aim of this review was to determine the assessment practice for dealing with older people and to consolidate published research and subsequently determine a way forward for future research in the field. Forty-two articles were found that appeared to meet the inclusion and exclusion criteria. From this total, 42,290 older people were studied in a range of community, nursing, and residential home settings in Europe, the USA, and Australia. The older people studied were experiencing various degrees of CI. Only 547 staff were actually included in the studies reviewed from a range of backgrounds, including registered nurses, managers, and unqualified caregivers. Twenty-two different pain assessment tools were tested in various settings, and some studies compared more than one tool. Within the literature, there were various perspectives on which are the best pain tools for use in this client group, with differences of opinion concerning the faces pain scale, verbal descriptors, and numerical pain scales. Eleven of the reviewed articles focused upon the discussion of issues surrounding intensity and quality of pain and whether this changes with increasing age. Overall, the investigators appear consistent in their belief that there are no changes. In terms of cognitive impairment, eleven pain assessment tools have been developed, all of which focus upon the presence of behaviors and the ability of the staff to identify and possibly rate such behaviors. Although, many of the assess-ment tools developed for this group were consistent in their choice of behaviors as being representative of pain, it appears that new tools have been developed as opposed to adapting or re-testing previously developed tools.

So what can be concluded from this review? Is there a direction that has to be taken to continue study in this area? Several conclusions can be drawn and conclusions made:

- There is a need to investigate the range of pain scales in a much larger multi-centre study in which confounding variables may be controlled. Many of the scales have been tested in small samples within specific cultural groups, it may be that no one pain assessment tool is appropriate for all older people, or it may be that there is a range that could be appropriate. Perhaps future direction could address this issue and test some of the tools in a larger multi-centre study.
- The emphasis now will be to refine and test behavioral scales as opposed to developing more scales. As there appears to be enough consistency in terms of behaviors, it is perhaps time to develop the reliability and validity of scales that already exist.
- It would be interesting to compare assessments within various members of the MDT, for example, nurses, physicians, and possibly physiotherapists. None of the studies has incorporated other specialists within their research, with the exception of one that looked at physicians' assessments of pain. It would be interesting to

see a more multidimensional perspective, and perhaps a lot can be learned from professions allied to medicine.

- There is an issue regarding measures of cognitive impairment. Many of the studies used the MMSE as a measure of level of CI, but some used other measures. This inconsistency again points to the issue of further validation of the recognized scales in adults with various levels of CI using a standard measure of CI status.

In conclusion, whilst a great deal of work has been done in this field over the last decade, clearly the time is right to consolidate and re-focus on what really has to be done.

ACKNOWLEDGMENTS

This chapter was supported by a University of Sheffield, School of Nursing and Midwifery Grant. This chapter is an adapted version of an earlier published paper (Schofield P, Clarke A, Faulkner M, Ryan T, Dunham M, Howarth A. Assessment of pain in older people. Where are we now and what needs to be done? Int j Disabil Hum Dev 2006;5(1):3-8).

REFERENCES

1. Melding PS. Is there such a thing as geriatric pain? Pain 1991;46:119-21.
2. Department of Health. National Service Framework for older people. Stationary Office HMSO London, UK, 2001.
3. Gibson S. Pain in older persons. Presentation at the World Pain Congress. San Diego, CA, USA. IASP, 2002.
4. American Geriatrics Society Panel on chronic pain in older persons. The Management of chronic pain in older persons. J Am Geriatr Soc 1998;46:635-51.
5. Allcock N, McGarry J, Elkan R. Management of pain in older people within a care home: a preliminary study. Health Soc Care Community 2002;10(6):464-71.
6. Kane RL, Ouslander JG, Abrass IB. Essentials of clinical geriatrics, 2nd Ed. New York, NY, USA: McGraw Hill, 1989.
7. Brattberg G Thorslund M, Wilkman A The prevalence of pain in a general population: the results of a postal survey in a county of Sweden. Pain 1988;37:215-22.
8. Blomqvist K, Edberg A. Living with persistent pain: experiences of older people receiving home care. J Adv Nurs 2002;40(3):297-306.
9. Melzack. R, Wall P. The challenge of pain. London, UK: Penguin, 1992.
10. Sherman ED Robillard E. Sensitivity to pain in relationship to age. J Am Geriatr Soc 1964;12:1037-44.
11. Bender JS. Approach to the acute abdomen. Med Clin North Am 1989;73:1413-22.

12.   Agency for Healthcare Policy and Research. Acute pain management: Opeations or medical procedures and trauma. Washington, DC, USA: AHPR Publ. No.92-0032, 1992.
13.   Harkins SW, Kwentus J, Price DD. Pain in the elderly. In: Benedict C, Chapman CR, Morica G, eds. Advances in pain research and therapy. New York, NY, USA: Raven, 1984:103-21.
14.   Herr K, Mobiliy P. Pain assessment in the elderly: clinical considerations. J Gerontol Nurs 1991;17:12-9.
15.   Closs SJ, Barr B, Briggs M, Cash K, Seers K. A comparison of five pain assessment scales for nursing home residents with varying degrees of cognitive impairment. J Pain Symptom Manage 2004;27(3): 196-205.
16.   Hawker S, Payne.S, Kerr C, Hardey M et al. Appraising the evidence: reviewing disparate data systematically. Qualitative Health Res 2002;12(9): 1284-99.
17.   Blomvist K, Hallberg IR Pain in older adults living in sheltered accommodation—agreements between assess- ments by older adults and staff. J Clin Nurs 1999; 8(2):159-69.
18.   Kaasalainen S, Crook J. An exploration of seniors ability to report pain. Clin Nurs Res 2004;13(3):199-215.
19.   Krulewitch A London M Skakel V et al. Assessment of pain in cognitively impaired older adults: a comparison of pain assessment tools and their use by nonprofessional caregivers. J Am Geriatr Soc 2000; 48(12):1607-11.
20.   Taylor LJ, Herr K. Pain intensity assessment: a comparison of selected pain intensity scales for use in cognitively intact and cognitively impaired African American older adults. Pain Manag Nurs 2003;4(2): 87-95.
21.   Fisher SE Burgio LD Thorn BE et al. Pain assessment and management in cognitively impaired nursing home residents: association of certified nursing assistant pain report, minimum data set report and analgesic medication use. J Am Geriatri Soc 2002; 50:152-6.
22.   Cohen-Mansfield J. The adequacy of the minimum data set assessment of pain in cognitively impaired nursing home residents. J Pain Sympt Manag 2004; 27(4):343-51.
23.   Fischer SM Kutner JS Maier J. Pain assessment in persons with advanced dementia. Poster Abstract, Am Geriatr Soc, 2003.
24.   Jenq GY Zhenchao G Drikamer M et al. Timing in the communication of pain among nursing home residents, nursing staff and clinicians. Arch Intern Med 2004;164(14):1508-12.
25.   Manfredi P Breuer B Meir D et al. Pain assessment in elderly patints with severe dementia. J Pain Sympt Manag 2003;25(1):48-52.
26.   Stolee P Hillier L Esbaugh J et al. Instruments for the assessment of pain in older persons with cognitive impairment. J Am Geriatr Soc 2005;53(2):319-26.

27.   Ferrell BA Stein W Beck JC. The geriatric pain measure: validity, reliability and factor analysis: Brief methodological reports. J Am Geriatr Soc 2000; 48(12):1669-73.

28.   Hurley AC, Volicer BJ, Hanrahan SH, Volicer L. Assessment of discomfort in advanced Alzheimer patients. Res Nurs Health 1992;15(3):369-77.

29.   Warden V, Hurley A, Volicer L Development and psychometric evaluation of the the pain assessment in advanced dementia scale (PAINAD). J Am Dir Assoc 2003;4:9-15.

30.   Davis E Male M Reimer V et al. Pain assessment and cognitive impairment. nursing standard. Personal communication, 2004.

31.   Abbey J Piller N DeBellis A et al. The Abbey pain scale: a 1-minute numerical indicator for people with end-stage dementia. Int J Palliat Nurs 2004;10(1):6-13.

32.   Wary B Filbet M Villard JF et al. Using doloplus with non-verbal cognitively impaired elderly patients, 2004. www.doloplus.com

33.   Blomquist K. Older people in persistent pain: nursing & paramedical staff perceptions and management. J Adv Nurs 2002;41(6):575-84.

34.   Vallerand A Hasenau S Templin T (2004) Barriers to pain management by home care nurses. Home Healthcare Nurse 2004;22(12):831-8.

35.   Weiner D Rudy T. Attitudinal barriers to effective treatment of persistent pain in nursing home residents. J Am Geriatr Soc 2002;50(12):2035-40.

36.   Bergh I Sjostrom B. A comparative study of nurses and elderly patients ratings of pain and pain tolerance. J Gerontol Nurs 1999;25(5):30-6.

37.   Cohen-Mansfield J. Pain in cognitively impaired nursing home residents: How well are physicians diagnosing it? J Am Geriatr Soc 2002;50(6):1039-44.

38.   Marzinski L. The tragedy of dementia: clinically assessing pain in the confused non-verbal elderly. J Gerontol Nurs 1991;17(6):25-8.

39.   Simons W Malabar R. Assessing pain in elderly patients who cannot respond verbally. J Adv Nurs 1995;22;663-9.

40.   Kenefick AL. Pain and the functional status of nursing home residents. Dissertation. Amherst Massachusetts, USA: Univ Massachusetts Amherst, 1999.

41.   Mezinskis P Keller A Luggen A. Assessment of pain in the cognitively impaired older adult in long-term care. Geriatr Nurs 2004;25(2):107-12.

42.   Parmalee P Smith B Katz I. Pain complaints and cognitive status among elderly institution residents J Am Geriatr Soc 1993;41:517-22.

43.   Scherder E Bouma A Slaets J et al. Repeated pain assessment in Alzheimer's Disease. Dement Geriatr Cogn Disord 2001;12:400-7.

44.   Schuler M Njoo N Hestermann M et al. Acute and chronic pain in geriatrics: Clinical characteristics of pain and the influence of cognition. Am Acad Pain Med 2004;5(3):253-62.

45.   Hall-Lord ML Larsson G Steen B. Chronic pain and distress among elderly in the community: comparison of patients' experiences with enrolled nurses' assess-ments. J Nurs Manag 1999;7(1):45-54.

46.   Scherder EJA Smit R Vuijk PJ et al. The acute versus chronic pain questionnaire (ACPQ) and actual pain experience in older people. Aging Ment Health 2002; 6(3):304-12.

47.   Yong H Gibson S Horne D et al. Development of a pain attitudes questionnaire to assess stoicism and cautiousness for possible age differences. J Gerontol 2001;56B(5):279-84.

48.   Zarit SH Griffiths PC Berg S. Pain perceptions of the oldest old: A longitudinal study. Gerontologist 2004; 44(4):459-68.

CHAPTER 11
Pain in older people. A view on assessment and management

Patricia Schofield

This chapter presents the findings of a systematic literature review carried out to determine the most appropriate strategies that could be performed for the assessment and management of pain in residents living in care homes. Five hundred and seventy-one papers were initially identified, of which 70 papers were found to be appropriate. The 70 papers were organized into five key themes: Assessment and behavioural Assessment, Barriers/Attitudes/Perceptions, Cognitive Behavioural Therapy, Complementary Therapies, and Education/ Guidelines. Most of the papers related to pain in this group were pharmacological, suggesting that health care professionals generally feel that pharmacological approaches are the only way to manage pain in this group. Nevertheless, the non-pharmacological papers do suggest that there are other methods of pain control, which should be considered. Recommendations for further research are made.

INTRODUCTION

Pain is the most common symptom of disease and the most common complaint reported to physicians. However, chronic pain can present a perplexing problem for healthcare workers, which has resulted in a widespread acceptance for the need for specialized chronic pain clinics within the western world (1). Although the consequences of chronic pain are well documented, issues concerning chronic pain in older people are less well documented. For example, Melding (2) found that of the 4,000 papers published annually relating to pain, less that 1% focused upon pain in the older population, and that a review of 8 geriatric textbooks showed that they contained only 18 of 5,000 pages on pain. The specific problems of pain management in older people have only begun to be addressed systematically over the last decade, Within the United Kingdom (UK), the recent National Service Frameworks (3) have highlighted the need to address chronic pain in older age groups. A presentation at the International Association for the Study of pain conference (4) suggested that it is time for clinicians to "grasp the nettle" and provide services tailored to meet the needs of the older person as numbers of older people in pain are increasing on an international level and will represent two thirds of the pain population by the year 2020.

Whilst it has been suggested that 50% of older people living in the community have chronic pain, it has been estimated that 45% to 80% of care home residents have pain (5). It is postulated that there are several reasons for this apparent lack of pain management. For example, Yates and Fentiman (6) highlighted problems surrounding residents reporting pain in a sample of ten. They found that residents tend to become resigned to the pain and are ambivalent about the benefits of any action. This finding has been reinforced by Ferrell (5), who highlights the problems associated with pharmacological management in the older population. Pharmacotherapy in the older person is complicated by the risk of adverse drug reactions in this population, which is two to three times higher than in younger age groups (7). For example, non-steroidal anti-inflammatory drugs are reported to cause a greater risk of gastric ulceration in the older age group (8,9), and compliance is another factor, which has been highlighted as low as 25$ to 50% (10).

Ferrell (5) goes on to suggest that the management of pain in this group should focus upon the use of a combination of pharmacological and non-pharmacological approaches. Such approaches can enhance quality of life, a philosophy that is reinforced in a study by Ross and Crook (11) who demonstrate the impact of pain upon care home residents in terms of mood, sleep disturbance, and function. The authors make recommendations for the contribution that can be made by nurses in the assessment and treatment of pain in this setting.

More recently Blomqvist and Edberg (12) highlighted the important role of the nurse in terms of listening, acting upon side effects, and emphasizing common approaches, such as distraction and mobility to manage pain.

A second problem associated with pain in this population appears to relate to the lack of education amongst care home staff. Poor understanding of the use and effects of pharmacological interventions, management strategies, and a lack of pain assessment and skills to identify pain behaviors have all been identified as possible reasons for poor pain management. Cohen-Mansfield and Lipson (13) highlighted recently that 22% of 79 care home residents had reported pain to staff, but this had not been documented. A recent investigation by Allcock et al (14) reported that 37% of care home residents were experiencing chronic pain and that 69% of the homes investigated did not have a policy regarding pain management. However, this study relied on the reports of formal carers and did not explore the pain from the residents' perspective. It is important also to consider pain from the residents' own reports because several studies have shown a mismatch between professionals' and patients' ratings of pain (15). This issue is compounded by the fact that many care home staff are health care assistants, and the homes often have limited resources and limited access to continual professional development.

A further problem associated with the recognition and management of pain in this group relates to the high incidence of cognitive impairment associated with the care home population. It has been suggested that more than 50% of care home residents are cognitively impaired (5), which consequently becomes problematic in terms of the identification of pain. Yet, a large study conducted by Parmalee et al (16) found no evidence that cognitive impairment 'masked' pain complaints in a population of 750 care home residents. Assessment tools have been developed that purport to measure pain in this group using behavioural indicators (17,18). However, how can we expect to assess and manage pain effectively in residents with cognitive impairment, when it is evident from the literature that we are still unable to deal effectively with pain problems in older people without cognitive impairment who are able to communicate their pain. It is evident that there is a need to identify pain characteristics in this group and then to clarify the most appropriate form of management that residents are willing to use, whilst developing the skills of care home staff to carry out assessment and management of pain in the cognitively impaired group.

OUR REVIEW

The first phase of the project was carried out to determine the level of knowledge that currently exists. A number of studies have been conducted that suggest the potential for distraction, relaxation, and heat/cold strategies. Further-more, a growing body of evidence suggests using a range of pain-assessment measures. This systematic review was conducted to enable a consolidation of knowledge and to develop best practice guidelines. The review questions were as follows:

- What are the methods of non-pharmacological management appropriate for dealing with pain in the older adult?
- What are the most appropriate pain assessment tools for the measurement of pain in the older adult

The population included within the review included both male and female older people, defined as over the age of 65 years and classified as experiencing chronic non-cancer pain. All methods of management were included with the exception of pharmacological approaches.

All electronic data bases were searched including CINAHL, MEDLINE, and EMBASE, along with hand searching of conference abstracts and key policy documents. Experts in the field were contacted including the British Pain Society, Jennifer Abbey, and Betty Ferrell. Inclusion and exclusion criteria were developed to exclude papers published before 1995 and those related to cancer pain or pharmacological management. Key words included older people, elderly, care home, residential home, residential care, long-term care, assessment tools, management, complementary therapies, non prescription interventions, self management. Only papers written in English were included. All studies were read independently by both researchers and graded according to the guidelines proposed by Hawker et al (19). All papers were then organized into themes. Statistical analysis was not performed because the number of papers of a similar intervention was insufficient to combine.

WHAT DID WE FIND?

The search identified 571 papers on management. Three rounds of discussions took place and in the first round we rejected 274 papers, in the second round 192 papers and in the third round 35 papers. Sixty-six were pharmacology papers and 22 were cancer related. From the 70 papers reviewed, only four studies were randomized controlled trials (RTCs). Nevertheless, the papers were organized according to the themes as follows:

- Assessment and Behavioral assessment
- Barriers/attitudes/perceptions
- Cognitive Behavioral therapy
- Complementary therapies
- Education/guidelines

Two RCTs examined Cognitive Behavioural Therapy (CBT) and two studies looked at complementary therapies. It was therefore impossible to analyze statistically the results of this review. The two CBT studies included a total of 51 and 43 participants randomly assigned into 2 groups. Thus, a total of 54 participants received CBT and for one study this was not full CBT, but one element that was 'biofeedback'. This prevents analysis by combining the results because the treatments approaches were different and the numbers too small to demonstrate any significant power. Within the complementary therapies section were three studies that carried out pretest/posttest designs. However, again, the numbers were very small and the approaches were different. For example, one study looked at the effects of relaxation training (n = 14), one study looked at aromatherapy (n = 4), and one study looked at "tender touch" (n = 71). Thus again, the approaches cannot be combined for the purpose of analysis.

Within this review, 70 papers were included and 501 were rejected. Six main themes were identified, and the papers fit into the themes as follows: assessment (31 papers), behavioral assessment tools (13 papers), attitudes (13 papers), management-psychological (4 papers), complementary therapies (6 papers), and educational initiatives/guidelines (3 papers).

Sixty-six articles were identified as pharmacological studies and these were not reviewed as they were not considered appropriate for this project. It is important to note that in the last decade, only 70 papers related to the pain management of older people, which is quite a small number and somewhat significant if compared with other groups. This observation further reinforces that lack of priority that is associated with pain in the older adult.

In terms of study designs, the papers on pain assessment were largely survey designs or interviews and/or observations of staff to determine perceptions of patients in pain. Fifteen of the papers looked at pre-designed tools and their application to the older adult and six papers actually designed tools from scratch. Thus, the majority of papers in this section were qualitative or correlational studies. The 13 papers around attitudes of staff were all surveys or inter-views. In terms of the interventional studies (13 papers), 4 were randomized controlled trials, 5 quasi-experiments, and the rest were case studies or mixed methods. The methodology is really no surprise because it would be expected that the only RCTs conducted would be around interventions, and the remaining themes would consist of exploratory work. Each theme will be discussed below.

Pain assessment

Fifteen of the papers reviewed were designed to consider established pain tools that were applied already to adult care. For example, Blomqvist and Hallberg (20) looked at the use of verbal descriptors in residential care in Sweden. Other investigators actually compared a range of scales such as Closs et al (21), who looked at five scales across a range of care home settings in the UK; the authors concluded that the Verbal Rating Scale (VRS) was the most successful of the five, followed by the numbers rating scale (NRS). The color scale (CS) and faces scale (FS) were not completed.

A number of the studies reviewed considered the use of the minimum data set (MDS). The MDS is a health assess-ment that is completed quarterly in the United States of America (USA), and includes measures of frequency and intensity of pain on a three-point likert scale with verbal descriptors. The MDS can be completed by either the resident (if capable) or the licensed practical nurse. Some of the studies reviewed suggest that this scale tends to under-report pain in residents with cognitive impairment, which appears to be a consistent problem highlighted by many authors. Furthermore, Jenq et al (22) found that where the MDS was in place, pain was assessed quarterly but seldom assessed daily. From this finding, it would seem that the assessment was carried in structured response to a policy rather than as an effective means by which to enhance patient care.

It is evident from the review so far that many of the pain assessment scales have been used with older adults but generally in small-scale studies having a wide range of confounding variables. There are some suggestions made about which scales may be more appropriate with this group and which may not. There is an evident need to investigate the scales in a much larger multi-center study in which confounding variables may be controlled

In terms of behavioral pain assessment scales, a total of 11 papers were identified. Each paper reported on evaluation of a different scale and all were very similar in the behaviors identified by the investigators as being indicative of pain. Such indicators included; facial expression, body movement, mood, and sleep disturbances, for example. The results of this section have been reported elsewhere (23). However, it can be concluded that further work does need to be done in this area, but the Abbey (24), DOLOPLUS-2 (25), and PACSLAC (26) appear to be the most reliable and valid.

Psychological interventions-cognitive-behavioral therapy

This section provided four papers, of which two were doctoral theses and two were unpublished. Psychological approaches for the management of pain have been developed and refined extensively since the introduction of the Gate Control Theory of Pain (27), in particular for the management of chronic pain in adults. One such approach is based upon the belief that by changing the individual's thoughts and beliefs about the pain, they can adopt more positive coping strategies and subsequently regain control and consequently cope with ongoing pain.

The first study in this group was a doctoral thesis that evaluated the effectiveness of CBT compared with attention support within a group of nursing home residents (28). The study was conducted in Canada and from a potential pool of 104 residents, 28 were recruited and assigned into 2 groups. Data were collected pre- and post-treatment and once again 4 months following intervention. Information was also collected from caregivers. The program was conducted over a period of 10 weeks and included teaching the residents a range of skills including education, reconceptualization, relaxation, imagery, diversion, and cognitive restructuring. The results of the study support the findings of others who demonstrated positive effects of psychologically based interventions. The author concluded that CBT can be applied to nursing home residents but that there is a need to be flexible to their needs and the group approach may not always be appropriate. The author suggests that although this approach can be time consuming for staff, it is an approach that care staff could apply and does have the potential to save care costs in terms of medication intake and nursing care related to pain.

More recently, Kerns et al (29) reported a case study of a 72-year-old man referred to a pain center and offered the opportunity to take part in CBT. The results of this study further support the positive findings suggested by Cook (28) and proposed that CBT is well suited to the treatment of older people with chronic pain.

Finally, 22 nursing home residents were invited to participate in a study by Strine (30), in which they were randomly assigned into a biofeedback or waiting list group and subsequently monitored for 10 weeks. The results of the study indicate that biofeedback has a potential efficacy for pain reduction amongst older people resident in the nursing homes. The main problem with this study, like others, is the small sample size. In addition, the investigators did not measure cognitive ability and therefore are unable to suggest that the cognitive ability needed by older people to ensure this approach is appropriate. Nevertheless, all the studies when viewed collectively appear to support the potential effectiveness of psychologically based programs for older populations in care homes, provided that resource issues and training can be addressed.

Complementary therapy

Complementary therapies are becoming increasingly popular within health care and within pain management. The rationale is that the therapies provide adjuvant care, and the increasing emphasis on a more holistic perspective to care is enhancing their popularity. The earliest paper in this group presents the findings of a one-year project investi-gating the effects of gentle massage in two groups of elderly nursing home residents suffering from chronic pain and dementia in New York. Of 71 residents, 59 completed the 12-week program, which was facilitated by a qualified massage therapist (31). Dementia and/or pain were identified using the MDS, and then the resident's carer and/ or family member was invited to take part in the training of "tender touch". Data were collected on pain and anxiety/ agitation during the 3-month study period. The nursing assistants commented that they used the strategy when walking residents and it helped to calm them down. Family members also made positive comments. Indeed, the paper contains some really moving accounts of family experiences. In conclusion, the authors found that the carers enjoyed using the approach, and pain and anxiety scores did reduce during the study period. Although, this approach could be perceived as time consuming, the study found that following 1-2 hours of training, the staff/carers could provide tender touch during periods of feeding or moving residents, and so it could potentially be incorporated into mainstream care tasks as opposed to being extra.

Another paper that examined the effects or aromatherapy/massage is that of Kunstler et al (32). The authors highlighted how in 1998 the American Geriatric Society issued guidelines for the management of pain in the elderly, in which they recommend both pharmacological and non-pharmacological management of pain. The authors used a multiple single-subject design within an 816 bed long term care facility. Four residents were recruited into the study, and the data collected included pain assessment and obser-vations/comments from the residents. Residents included in the study had to score >24 on the MMSE (Mini-mental state examination) and were able to sign the consent form.

The sessions were conducted by a certified therapeutic recreation specialist (CTRS) and consisted of a 30-minute hand massage and aromatherapy session in the early evening 3 times per week for 12 weeks. The authors reported the case studies, and were able to demonstrate a statistically significant reduction in the participants' pain perceptions during intervention and improved sleep patterns as well. Once again, the numbers in the study are small. However, the research does suggest a way forward for future investigation, and certainly no negative effects were seen amongst the participants, suggesting a safe and beneficial approach. Interestingly, part of the intervention within this study incorporated efforts to create a more positive environment in which relaxation could take place, this is similar to the findings of the authors own work (33-40).

In terms of relaxation, McBee et al (41) conducted a study in nursing homes in the USA that investigated the effects of a 10-week program of relaxation training. Fourteen residents participated in the study and were given a once-weekly session covering the principles of relaxation, along with the various different approaches that included meditation, music therapy, aromatherapy, yoga, and poetry readings. Group members were interviewed pre- and post-sessions about life satisfaction and their experiences of pain. Following the interventions, the group reported feeling "less sad" and did experience less pain, although this finding was not significantly significant. Whilst the numbers in the study were very small, again, this approach did not cause any harm, and positive comments from the residents themselves indicate that this is an approach worthy of further investigation.

A different perspective is that adopted within the study by Simmons et al (42), in which the authors investigated the impact of exercise on pain. The study involved the randomization of residents into a control group who received no treatment and the experimental group who participated in a 32-week exercise/endurance program. The program consisted of mobility training and stand ups. Data were collected using the Geriatric Pain Measure, and average mobility was measured before and following intervention. No significant changes in pain were observed with either group during the study, but the mobility of the experimental group did improve over time. However, the investigators concluded that this intervention was ineffective over time; furthermore it would appear to be rather labor intensive in terms of the staff commitment necessary to conduct the exercises 2 hours for 32 weeks.

A further study in this section involved a randomized controlled trial investigating the effects of Qi therapy in a group of older people in Korea. The principles behind the approach are based upon the Chinese philosophies of the vital energy that flows through the body, which can be restored through medical Qigong, similar to the laying on of hands or healing philosophies. For this study, 43 participants from a residential care community were randomly assigned into a control (general care) or Qi therapy group. Pain and mood was assessed pre-intervention and weekly post-intervention for six weeks. The results suggest that Qi therapy significantly reduced pain and improved mood in the experimental group. This was a small study with some promising results. However, further work would have to be carried out and issues regarding the employment of a Qi master would have to be addressed. Wider issues regarding each of the complementary therapy studies and psychological interventions that have been reviewed appear to be related to the issue of control. Control is generally perceived as a valuable strategy for coping with pain.

The final paper reviewed by Tse et al (43) aimed to explore interventions used by older people in a survey. Forty-four people living in a nursing home took part in the study, the majority of whom were experiencing pain (79%). This study identified issues within this population that appear to be fairly typical and have been discussed previously in terms of reluctance to report pain, fear of being labeled, and the assumption that pain is a natural part of aging. Interestingly, this study identified that residents self medicate with pharmacological and non-pharmacological interventions supplied by family including oils, massage, and gels. Although, the numbers were small and there may be some cultural differences, this study does support the fact that residents in care homes still want to be involved in decisions regarding their pain management. There is an issue regarding untreated pain, and this group is receptive to complementary or non-conventional approaches.

Education/guidelines

The first study in this group by Cronin (44) reported on an education program designed to provide participants with information about pain management to improve their skills and sensitivity in dealing with cognitively impaired patients in two long term nursing facilities. The staff in the facilities were given access to a seminar, and then the residents notes were monitored for treatment changes and staff were interviewed.

Several limitations were noted, which included inability of staff to attend due to time issues and interestingly, the majority of attendees were actually unqualified care assistants, which is an important point. Nevertheless, the project did demonstrate that sensitivity to pain improved with education.

The second study in this category was conducted in the USA (45) a few years later and involved a mixed-method study designed to explore the feasibility of introducing clinical practice guidelines for pain management in 23 long-term care facilities. Less than half of the facilities (45%) implemented the guidelines, despite the enthusiasm to do so in the first instance. The rationale for this lack of take up was based upon the fact that the guidelines were implemented without any underpinning education and they needed to be "short and sweet".

The final study reviewed was a quasi-experimental pretest/post-test that evaluated pain management education and training within 21 facilities in the USA (46).

Within each home, a quality-improvement team was set up and this was followed by six bimonthly education and training workshops attended by the quality improvement team. The group was then invited to audit pain management and feedback the results followed by the introduction of pain management guidelines and a tool kit of pain management strategies. Seventeen facilities completed the project, and the investigators demonstrated a 41% reduction in pain prevalence during the study. The success of this study appears to be due to the initial investment towards empowering the homes by setting up an individual quality-improvement team who appeared to have an investment in seeing the success of the project.

CONCLUSIONS

This systematic review has provided a useful insight into the state of the research around pain in care homes. It has helped to consolidate where most of the work has been carried out and to determine the focus for further research in this area. From this review, the authors are able to make several recommendations for practice and research. Clearly, the assessment scales are appropriate for the majority of older adults using numerical or verbal rating scales. These can be adopted where mild to moderate cognitive impairment is present. However, in the presence of severe cognitive impairment, a number of behavioral scales are well validated and highlight similar behavioral indicators. Furthermore, there is clearly a need to look more closely at the role and contribution of family carers as they can potentially provide valuable insight into the older adult's experience. A number of barriers exist amongst staff toward older adults in pain, but these can be improved by educating staff. This education should be complemented by the implementation of pain guidelines that all staff can follow as a treatment plan encompassing not only pharmacological approaches but also complementary and psychological based approaches, such as the environment. In terms of research, there is a need to carry out more research in this area, particularly to address the needs of older adults who are more vulnerable such as the cognitively impaired group. Furthermore, collaborative multimodal pain management should be investigated further in this group, for whom pharmacological approaches are less than ideal. Much work can still be done in both practice development and research to improve care for older adults in our society.

ACKNOWLEDGMENTS

This Project was funded by a research grant from the Burdett Trust for Nursing. This chapter is an adapted version of an earlier published paper (Schofield P, Reid D. The assessment and management of pain in older people: A systematic review of the literature. Int J Disabil Hum Dev 2006;5(1):9-15).

REFERENCES

1.   Ferrell BR. Pain management in elderly people. J Am Geriatr Soc 1991;39:64-73.
2.   Melding PS. Is there such a thing as geriatric pain? Pain 1991;46:119-21.
3.   Department of Health. National Service Framework for older people. London, UK: Stationary Office HMSO, 2001.
4.   Gibson S. Pain in older persons. Presentation at the World Pain Congress. San Diego, CA, USA. IASP, 2002.
5.   Ferrell BA, Ferrell BR, Rivera L. Pain in cognitively impaired nursing home patients. J Pain Sympt Manage 1995;10:591-8.
6.   Yates P, Dewar A, Fentiman B. Pain: The views of elderly people living in long-term residential care settings. J Adv Nurs 1995;21(4): 667-74.
7.   Portenoy RK. Management of chronic pain in the elderly: pharmacology of opioids and other analgesic drugs. In: Ferrell BA, Ferrell BR, eds. Pain in the elderly. Seattle, WA, USA: IASP Press,.1996:21-34.
8.   Loeb DS, Ahlquist DA, Talley NJ. Management of gastroduodenopathy associated with the use of non-steroidal anti-inflammatory drugs. Mayo Clinic 1992;67:354-64.

9.   Weinblatt ME. Nonsteroidal anti-inflammatory drug toxicity: increased risk in the elderly. Scand J Rheumatol 1991;91:9-17.

10.   Morrow D, Leirer V, Sheikh J. Adherence and medication instructions: review and recommendations. J Am Geriatr Soc 1988;36:1147-60.

11.   Ross M, Crook J. Elderly recipients of nursing home services: Pain disability and functional competence. J Adv Nurs 1998;27(6):1117-26.

12.   Blomqvist K, Edberg A. Living with persistent pain: experiences of older people receiving home care. J Adv Nurs 2002;40(3):297-306.

13.   Cohen-Mansfield J, Lipson S. Pain in cognitively impaired nursing home residents: How well are physicians diagnosing it? J Am Geriatr Soc 2002; 50(6):1039-44.

14.   Allcock N, McGarry J, Elkan R. Management of pain in older people within a care home: a preliminary study. Health Soc Care Community 2002;10(6):464-71.

15.   Hall-Lord ML, Larsson G, Steen B. Chronic pain and distress among elderly in the community: comparison of patients' experiences with enrolled nurses' assess-ments. J Nurs Manage 199;7(1):45-54.

16.   Parmalee P Smith B Katz I. Pain complaints and cognitive status among elderly institution residents. J Am Geriatr Soc 1993;41:517-22.

17.   Hurley AC, Volicer BJ, Hanrahan PA et al. Assessment of discomfort in advanced Alzheimer patients. Res Nurs Health 1992;15(5):369-77.

18.   Simons W, Malabar R. Assessing pain in elderly patients who cannot respond verbally. J Adv Nurs 1995;22:663-9.

19.   Hawker S, Payne.S, Kerr C, Hardey M et al. Appraising the evidence: reviewing disparate data systematically. Qual Health Res 2002;12(9):1284-99.

20.   Blomqvist K, Edberg A. Living with persistent pain: experiences of older people receiving home care. J Adv Nurs 2002;40(3):297-306.

21.   Closs SJ, Barr B, Briggs M, Cash K, Seers K. A comparison of five pain assessment scales for nursing home residents with varying degrees of cognitive impairment. J Pain Symptom Manage 2004;27(3): 196-205.

22.   Jenq GY, Zhenchao G, Drikamer M, Marotti RA, Carrington R. Timing in the communication of pain among nursing home residents, nursing staff and clinicians. Arch Intern Med 2004;164:1508-12.

23.   Schofield PA, Clarke A, Faulkner M, Ryan T, Dunham M, Howarth A. Assessment of pain in adults with cognitive impairment: A review of the tools. Int J Disabil Hum Dev (in press).

24.   Abbey J, Piller N, DeBellis A, Esterman A, Parker D, Giles L. The Abbey pain scale: a 1-minute numerical indicator for people with end stage dementia. Int J Palliat Nurs 2004;10(1):6-13.

25.   Lefebre-Chapiro S, DOLOPLUS group. The DOLO-PLUS-2 scale— evaluating pain in the elderly. Eur J Palliat Care 2001;8(5):191-4.

26.   Fuchs-Lacelle S, Hadjistavropoulis T. Development and preliminary validation of the pain assessment checklist for seniors with limited ability to communi-cate (PACSLAC). Pain Manage Nurs 2004;5(1):1-19.

27.   Melzack R, Wall P. Pain mechanisms: A new theory. Science 1965;50:971-9.

28.   Cook A. Cognitive–Behavioral pain management for elderly nursing home residents. Dissertation. Manitoba, Winnipeg: Univ Manitoba, 1995.

29.   Kerns R, Otis JD, Marcus KS. Cognitive-Behavioral therapy for chronic pain in the elderly. Clin Geriatr Med 2001;17(3):503-23.

30.   Strine GN. Self-reports of pain reduction through paced respiration and heart rate variability bio-feedback with nursing home residents. Dissertation. Chester, Pennsylvania: Widener Univ, 2002.

31.   Sansone P, Schmitt L. Providing tender touch massage to elderly nursing home residents: A demonstration project. Geriatr Nurs 2000;21(6):303-8.

32.   Kunstler R, Greenblatt F, Moreno N. Aromatherapy and hand massage: Therapeutic recreation interventions for pain management. Ther Recreation J 2004;38(2): 133-46.

33.   Schofield PA. Snoezelen: Its potential for people with chronic pain. Complement Ther Nurs Midwifery 1996; 2:9-12.

34.   Schofield PA, Davis B. Sensory deprivation: The concept as applied to chronic pain. Disabil Rehabil 1998;20(10):357-66.

35.   Schofield PA, Davis B. Snoezelen and chronic pain: developing a study to evaluate its use. Complement Ther Nurs Midwifery 1998;4: 66-72.

36.   Schofield PA, Davis B. Evaluating the use of Snoezelen and chronic pain: the findings of an investigation into its use (Part II). Complement Ther Nurs Midwifery 1998;4:137-43.

37.   Schofield PA, Davis B. Sensory stimulation (Snoezelen) versus relaxation for the management of chronic pain. Disabil Rehabil 2000;22(15):675-82.

38.   Schofield PA. The feasibility of using Snoezelen within palliative care. Int J Palliat Nurs 2002;3(5): 281-6.

39.   Schofield PA. Snoezelen: An alternative environment for relaxation in the management of chronic pain. Br J Nurs 2002;11(12):811-9.

40.   Schofield PA. An investigation into the prevalence and nature of pain in care home residents: A pilot study. Sheffield: Univ Sheffield, UK, Unpublished Report, 2004.

41.   McBee L, Westreich L, Likourezos A. A psycho-educational relaxation group for pain and stress management in the nursing home. J Soc Work Long Term Care 2004;3(1):15-28.

42.   Simmons SF, Ferrell BA, Schnelle JF. Effects of a controlled exercise trial on pain in nursing home residents. Clin J Pain 2002;18: 380-5.

43.   Tse MMY, Pun SPY, Benzie IFF. Pain relief strategies used by older people with chronic pain: an exploratory survey for planning patient-centred interventions. J Clin Nurs 2005;14:315-20.

44. Cronin S. An educational program designed to improve nursing personnel's pain management skills with cognitively impaired elderly residents in long term care facilities. Thesis. Kentucky: Allen and Donna Lansing School Nurs, 1999.

45. Resnick B, Quinn C, Baxter S. Testing the feasibility of implementation of clinical practice guidelines in long-term care facilities. J Am Med Dir Assoc 2004;5:1-8.

46. Baier RR, Gifford DR, Patry G, Banks S, Rochon T, DeSilva D, Teno J. Ameliorating pain in nursing homes: a collaborative quality improvement project. J Am Geriatr Soc 2004;52:1988-95.

CHAPTER 12
Talking to older people about pain

Patricia Schofield

Thi s chapter describes a qualitative study conducted within the care home setting to determine the pain experiences of residents, their preferred strategies, and the staff attitudes and understanding about pain. An exploratory cross sectional study within six care homes within one district was conducted using several methods of data collection. The residents and staff were interviewed and a questionnaire given to a random sample of staff. Several key themes were identified by residents, including a reluctance to report pain, acceptance that pain is normal and low expectations of help from medical interventions, fear of chemical or pharmacological interventions, age-related perceptions of pain, and lack of awareness of potential pain relieving strategies. Staff interviews highlighted that they wanted to know if the residents were in pain, wanting to do more, and an interest in using complementary therapies. Recommendations are made for further research in this area.

INTRODUCTION

The management of pain has evolved and improved over the last few decades, and a major contributing factor has been the introduction of the Gate Control Theory (1). This theory advocates the appreciation of many factors that contribute to the individuality of the pain experience and promotes multidimensional management as opposed to single specialist care (2). Developments in pain manage-ment since 1965 include the introduction of standard definitions of pain, pain services, and a widespread recognition that pain management requires a multi-dimensional perspective and therefore, a multidisciplinary approach.

Despite this theory, certain groups within society still do not appear to be adequately catered for, including people with learning disabilities or ethnic minorities. Such groups are not provided with services designed to address their specific needs. A further group in this category is older people; although they have been receiving more interest in recent years, there is still less research around their needs than those of the general adult population.

For example, a recent study investigated the educational requirements of nurses who care for the most vulnerable in this group living in care homes (3), and another study by Closs (4) highlighted the concerns regarding appropriate measurement of pain in the older population. Both studies recommended that further study was needed. The purpose of the current study was to investigate residents' and staff's perspectives regarding the prevalence of pain within the care home setting and to identify the views of older people in terms of their preferred pain management strategies.

Historically, pain has been viewed as a natural part of aging and therefore, considered something the person must learn to live with (5). However, it has been suggested that 80% of those over the age of 65 years suffer at least one chronic illness (6) and that 50% of cancers occur in the over 65 years age group. This view was reinforced in a recent study by Blomqvist (7), who highlighted that in a group of 150 older people, there was a range of potentially painful conditions including falls, leg ulcers, degenerative joints, and cancer, and that many of these were well known and visible. However, Blomqvist (7) noted that the management of pain in this group was very poor.

Some have suggested that there could be age related changes occurring in the older age group, resulting in complex alterations in the processing of pain through the nervous system. Examples of this can be seen in practice as in the work of Morrison and Siu (8), who reported patients' experiences of silent myocardial infarctions, or abdominal catastrophes, or the differences in response to fractures in dementia patients versus non dementia patients (8).

Major developments have also been made in terms of pain assessment, for example the introduction of the McGill Pain Questionnaire (9) as a multidimensional pain tool. This questionnaire has been translated into eighteen languages and used across the age spectrum. But the assessment of pain in the older age group still remains poor, and many reasons have been cited as to why this is so (4). Where assessment scales have been used, some success has been reported, with the visual analogue scale and the faces scale (10). Although Closs et al (10) highlight the difficulties encountered within the care home population when using these scales, in terms of visual, hearing and communication problems. Some researchers have attempted recently to address these issues and to develop scales that specifically rely upon the behaviors of patients instead of on verbal reports, and the investigators suggest some success with their measures (11-13).

A further issue highlighted in the literature suggests that older people do not wish to bother staff or complain, and they believe that the doctors and nurses are the experts and will "know" when they are in pain (14). However, the United Kingdom (UK) National Service Framework (15) advocates that older people should be more involved in making decisions involving their own treatment and, as such, staff should include them in the assessment process and enable older people to make informed decisions regarding treatment. Furthermore, the skills of the health care professionals can be questioned since pain is an intrinsic experience that is not readily obvious to the observer, and subsequently requires a level of expertise to identify.

According to Wittgenstein (16) we can only know, when we have pain and assume when others have pain based upon our observations. Furthermore, the assumption that doctors and nurses "know" when their patients are experiencing pain does rely upon a level of understanding and knowledge on their part, which is not always the case. As suggested by Cowan et al (17) such a level of understanding does not exist, and consequently patients receive poor pain management. Historically, education about pain for both doctors and nurses has been poor and although it is improving, the issue of Opiophobia (18) stills remains, and concerns regarding addiction, tolerance, and dependence prevent the appropriate administration of many analgesic drugs, including opioids. Furthermore, fears of adverse side effects exist for both staff and the older people themselves (19).

It is evident that a number of issues are highlighted within the literature that appear to explain why there is poor pain management in older people, but the topic has received little attention within the research field to date (20). Such issues are related to the older people themselves, and those who care for them; however, many concepts require further investigation. Therefore, to explore the issue of pain in older people in more detail would seem appropriate, with a particular emphasis upon the most vulnerable in this group—those living in care homes. This group is relatively powerless and relies on staff for their pain management. It would be interesting, therefore, to know if the management offered is that which they themselves would prefer.

OUR RESEARCH

Whilst others have investigated the educational requirements of staff and the assessment of pain in care homes, this chapter will describe the first study in the UK to examine the preferences of the residents themselves. Therefore, the study has three aims:

1.   To determine the incidence and nature of pain as it exists within a small sample of care homes in the north of England.
2.   To determine how the staff perceive residents pain and identify their preferred pain management strategies.
3.   To determine the preferred pain management strategies of the residents themselves.

An exploratory cross-sectional study within six care homes within one district was conducted using several methods of data collection. The residents and staff were interviewed and a questionnaire given to a random sample of staff. Data on demographic details were collected from the residents themselves. This chapter will present the findings of the qualitative data collection obtained by interviewing the residents.

The area selected for the study consists of a population of 374,200, of which 63,825 are over the age of 65 years. Within this area are 105 care homes. Six care homes were randomly selected from the pool of homes and were representative of nursing, residential, and mixed groups. Residents were selected by adhering to inclusion criteria, which included informed consent and completion of the mini-mental state questionnaire (MMSE) (21) For the purpose of the study, only those residents who scored >23 were included as they were considered capable of answering extensive questions regarding pain and its management. All members of staff, both qualified and unqualified, were invited to take part in a discussion group, and a random sample of staff was invited to complete a pain knowledge questionnaire.

The residents were interviewed using a semi-structured format, which consisted of asking questions regarding their past and current medical history and pain history, followed by questions about pain and any pain-producing problems like arthritis. Further questions were related to ways of coping with pain, and pharmacological interventions. A questionnaire was also used and given to qualified staff and consisted of thematic questions, on the following topics:

- Nursing role in pain assessment
- General knowledge about pain
- Knowledge of pharmacological management
- Knowledge of older people
- Barriers to effective pain management as perceived by them.

The method of analysis used for this chapter was content analysis (21). The qualitative information obtained from the residents' interviews and the staff discussion groups were transcribed verbatim and read through to highlight key issues. Further reading organized these issues into themes that were checked by the investigator and then verified by an independent reviewer. Ultimately, with content analysis the material could be analyzed quantitatively using frequencies, however, with the small numbers in the study this approach was not appropriate.

SOME FINDINGS OF OUR RESEARCH

A potential pool of 216 residents was identified from the six care homes, and from this number 26 were considered mentally competent to participate, according to the MMSE, and thus signed a consent form to take part in the study. The mean age of the residents was 82 years (SD 9.1 Range 65-100). This group contained 9 male and 16 female residents. At the time of interview, 85% were experiencing pain (n = 22). Despite this result, 50% (n=13) were not taking any analgesic medication, and the rest were taking Paracetamol (n = 9) or Co-analgesics (Codeine + Paracetamol) (n = 4). The range of pain conditions included arthritis, hip pain, multiple pains, and leg ulcers. Arthritis affected 45% (n = 12) of the sample.

The data obtained from the resident interviews were grouped into four themes as follows:

1.   A reluctance to report pain/acceptance that pain is normal and low
        expectations of help from medical interventions
2.   Fear of chemical or pharmacological interventions
3.   Age-related perceptions of pain
4.   Lack of awareness of potential pain relieving strategies

During the interview, the investigator asked the residents "if they were in
pain at the time"? Many residents were, but when asked why they had not
reported the pain to the staff, they commented that there was no need to as
there was probably nothing that anyone could do. For example, one patient
commented that:

> "it's not unbearable, it just reminds me that its there, but there is nothing
> anyone can do so I do not grumble" (resident 7)

Yates and Fentiman (22) found in their study that nursing home residents
accepted pain as a companion of old age and were therefore reticent of
seeking help. Furthermore, a more recent study by Weiner and Rudy (23)
suggested that older people appear to under-report pain, due to fears of
worsening dependence. Within the current study this was highlighted by
one resident who commented that:

> "what can you do? I just make the most of what I have at least I can still
> get around" (resident 6)

Many studies have reported the low expectations of help from medical
interventions (24-26), and the current study was no exception. For example,
when asked why she did not report her pain, resident 7 stated; "there is no
point telling the staff, there is nothing they can do" A similar comment was
made by resident 5 who said "there is nothing anyone can do to help"

Fear of chemical or pharmacological interventions

Many residents commented that they were fearful of using pharmacological
interventions and would prefer to manage without them. When the
investigator asked about taking tablets for pain, the residents would
comment that they would rather manage without or that nothing seemed to
help. One resident (resident 5) commented that:

> "she was living on drugs or tablets and did not really want to take
> anything else"

Weiner and Rudy (23) also highlighted such fears within their study, which
they attributed to fears of addiction and dependence. It could be that older
people have to accept their increasing dependence upon others when they
go into a care home, and succumbing to tablets signifies a worsening of their
dependence.

Many residents commented upon the side effects of the drugs and
highlighted problems such as constipation, dizziness, and sleepiness. It was

interesting to note within the study that many of the concerns related to drugs were expressed by the residents over the age of 75 years, and the investigator is curious whether this is related to the over 75 age group living before the inception of the national health service (NHS), and therefore have grown up with self management strategies.

Schumacher et al (27) found similar findings in their study in which older people were reluctant to take analgesics for their cancer pain as they perceived them as toxins. The patients in the Schumacher et al (27) study were younger (with a mean age of 63 years) and as it was an American study, were therefore within a different health care system. Additionally, the investigator does acknowledge that the numbers in the current study were very small and therefore, found it difficult to draw any firm conclusions

Age related perceptions of pain

Not only was the older age group reluctant to take analgesics but also were reluctant to actually admit having had pain. The residents under 75 years were more willing to voice their pain, and consequently to take analgesic drugs. These 'younger' residents commented that:

> *"one more tablet will not make any difference" (resident 2)*

or that

> *"I used to buy things from the chemist when I was at home, but they do not like you to do that in here, so you have to ask them it really annoys me, why should I ask for them, I know when I am in pain, not them" (resident 3)*

In contrast, the over 75 age group tended to listen to music or watch television and they avoided tablets, which they called "chemicals" A study by Dunn and Horgas (28) demonstrated with their sample of 200 older people that the participants accepted a range of coping strategies for pain management, including both pharmacologic and non-pharmacologic. However, this study investigated older people's methods of coping in the community and as highlighted by Weiner and Rudy (23) with their study of nursing home residents, taking medication could signify further dependence. A further study by Sheffield et al (29) suggested that older people actually become desensitized to the pain after living with it for so long which could be one explanation.

Lack of awareness of potential pain relieving strategies

The residents interviewed did appear to be keen to be involved in their own pain-management strategies. This was reflected in their comments of taking a hot bath or shower when the pain was bad, or "rubbing the affected area". But generally, the residents were unaware of approaches such as relaxation, massage, or distraction. The study by Dunn and Horgas (28) highlighted that the behavioral coping strategies used by their sample were in order of priority; reporting pain, medication, diversion, exercise and heat. Interestingly, these findings are different from those in the current study, in which the over 75 age group appeared to prefer self-management approaches, whilst the under 75s opted for reporting and medication. The study by Lumme-Sandt et al (19) demonstrated how the "oldest old" in their sample accepted pain as part of aging and held a high respect for the doctors and any prescriptions that they may or may not provide. The Lumme-Sande et al (19) sample were aged over 90 years, and there could be some cultural differences in relation to pain and coping, as demonstrated in the classic study by Zborowski (30) who highlighted the vast cultural differences that can exist and consequently influence the pain threshold.

Staff interviews
Interviews with staff revealed the following themes:

- Knowing the residents are in pain
- Doing more
- Complementary therapies
- Knowing the residents are in pain

The staff explained that they often know when the residents were in pain because they got to know the residents really well over a period of months or even years. One staff member said, "you just know when they have pain, it is because you get used to them, our residents have been here for years and we know how they behave and the signs of them not being happy" (Trained staff member 1).

A study by Weiner and Rudy (23) supported this belief amongst nursing home staff in that the staff reported certain behaviors consistently as being representative of pain. Such behaviors included; grimacing, guarding, whimpering, crying, and facial expression, along with agitation and aggression or as one staff member stated, "residents become irritable or confused and we know that there is something wrong, often this is pain" (Trained staff member 2).

An increasing number of pain assessment tools has been developed specifically for those who are cognitively impaired, all of which are based upon similar behaviors (31-34). A recent review identified eleven behavioral tools in total, but more testing is required to determine the psycho-metric properties of these tools (35).

Doing more
Many of the staff commented that they would like to do more, and this was related to both assessment and management strategies. Some staff have experienced the use of pain-assessment tools in the acute setting and would like to see them put into practice within the care home. Those who have studied staff perceptions in care home settings do support the concept that the staff are keen to improve the situation, as found within the current study, but often time was a limiting factor (23,36,37) and others suggested that education within the care home setting was poor for all levels of staff.

The current study described in this chapter did identify a fairly good level of basic knowledge amongst staff, which is different from the findings by the Allcock et al (3) study, but they did not appreciate the potential of simple strategies such as making residents laugh as effective pain management, an issue highlighted also by Blomqvist (7). Therefore, further education would be needed to increase staff awareness of their contribution. A project is currently ongoing to intro-duce distance learning education on "pain in the older adult" into the care home setting (38).

Complementary therapies

The staff appeared to have an awareness of complementary therapies and believed that they could make a valuable contribution to the care of the residents by gaining further education in the use of such therapies. The types of therapies mentioned included massage, aromatherapy, relaxation, distraction, and Snoezelen. One staff member stated that "we often use distraction without realising it when we are doing dressing changes we use music for example" (Trained staff member 4).

As mentioned previously, Blomqvist (7) also found in her study that staff performed simple pain-relieving strategies, without realizing it, as part of their everyday practice. Of course, the danger is that introducing new approaches may fail in an area where staff shortages are part of everyday life. Therefore, recommendations for changes in practice must take into account poor staffing levels within the care home setting.

DISCUSSION

The results obtained and described in this chapter must be viewed in light of the limitations. The sample of care homes was very small and could not therefore be considered representative of the care home population. Secondly, the investigator opted to interview residents without cognitive impairment, and others in the field have demonstrated that this group could be included (4) up to moderate levels of cognitive impairment. Furthermore, the sample of residents inter-viewed is also very small and as such does not represent the care home population per se. However, despite these limitations, some interesting issues were highlighted.

From the data we were able to conclude that for older people within the care home setting, pain is an issue that is not effectively recognized or dealt with by staff in a way that is acceptable for the residents. Furthermore, there are some staff misconceptions about pain in this population that need to be addressed. Viewed with these limitations in mind, the current study does demonstrate areas for further research.

For example, a further study identifying the older person's preferred pain-management strategies would inform practice and help to develop an education package for both qualified and unqualified staff within the care home setting.

The two distinct age groups that appear to exist is interesting, with the younger ones being more accepting of intervention, in particular pharmacologic intervention. This point has not been highlighted before by other authors, and it could be that the older group lived before the introduction of the NHS and therefore are more self-reliant than their younger counterparts. This notion would require further exploration in a larger study before any firm conclusions could be made. Clearly, whatever the reason, the findings do suggest that there must be a range of pain management approaches on offer, and carers should not always focus upon pharmacologic interventions.

The reticence of older people to acknowledge their pain is not something new, others within the literature have alluded to this (23), and it may be that the resident has grown tired of complaining, only to be told that nothing can be done, so that they have become conditioned to "not complain". An alternative perspective is that highlighted by Lumme-Sandt et al (19) in that some older people value stoicism, control, and fortitude or that of Dunn and Horgas (28), who demonstrated how some older people prefer to use their own religion as a way of coping. The issue of fear is not uncommon or unexpected. Many older people have a range of comorbidities that require pharmacologic inter-ventions and through experience may have learned that mixing tablets can cause unpleasant side effects. Alterna-tively, this could be an issue of lack of understanding or education, whereby the tablets have never actually been fully explained to the resident.

Finally, a lack of knowledge of alternative strategies is an interesting concept. Many healthcare professionals tend to focus upon pharmacologic management and when this fails, do not consider the other options. Therefore, the residents have probably never been given the choice of complementary or adjuvant approaches that could be used to enhance their current strategies.

CONCLUSIONS

This paper presented a small scale exploratory study, which when viewed in the light of the limitations, does appear to demonstrate some important issues. Much of the prior research has highlighted pain assessment issues with older people in care homes and recommended the need for education. Other studies do not appear to have explored pain management from the residents' perspective. The present study does highlight some important concerns amongst the residents themselves that have not been highlighted by staff. Such concerns have implications for the way that we approach the management of pain in care homes. Whilst a wealth of literature advocates tailoring pain management to each person, it does not appear to address the individual needs of older people. Perhaps older people have been conditioned to 'live' with pain or to accept that pharmacologic approaches are the only option. Furthermore, many authors have made recommendations regarding the educational needs of staff, but what happens when the majority of staff are untrained? No one has considered the important role that untrained staff could play in providing resident-focused strategies. Therefore, several recommend-ations can be made in the light of our current knowledge, as follows:

- Conduct further research to include residents with cognitive impairment and to determine their views and needs

- Identify other approaches to pain management from the literature (other than pharmacologic) and discuss these with residents to determine their willingness to use such approaches, and ultimately develop a resident focused pain management strategy
- Develop an education package specifically for un-qualified staff to be implemented under the direct supervision of the qualified staff to cover aspects of assessment and management of pain.

ACKNOWLEDGMENTS

The study was funded by the University of Sheffield, CAR departmental grant. This chapter is an adapted version of an earlier published paper (Schofield P. Talking to older people in care homes: Perceptions of their pain and their preferred management strategies. Results from a pilot study. Int J Disabil Hum Dev 206;5(1):53-9).

REFERENCES

1.   Melzack R, Wall P. Pain Mechanisms: A new theory. Science 1965;150:971-9.
2.   McCaffery M, Beebe D. Pain clinical manual for nursing practice St Louis, MO, USA: Mosby, 1989.
3.   Allcock N, McGarry J, Elkan R. Management of pain in older people within the nursing home: a preliminary study. Health Soc Care Community 2002;10(6):464-71.
4.   Closs SJ. Pain and elderly patients: a survey of nurses knowledge and experiences. J Adv Nurs 1996;23(2): 237-42.
5.   Yates P, Fentiman B. Pain: the views of elderly people living in long-term residential care settings. J Adv Nurs 1995;21(4):667-74.
6.   Kane RL, Ouslander JG, Abrass IB. Essentials of clinical geriatrics, 2nd ed. New York, NY, USA: McGraw Hill, 1989.
7.   Blomqvist K. Older people in persistent pain: nursing, and paramedical staff perceptions and pain manage-ment. J Adv Nurs 2003;4(6):575-84.
8.   Morrison RS, Siu AL. A comparison of pain and its treatment in advanced dementia and cognitively intact patients with hip fracture. J Pain Sympt Manage 2000; 19(4):240-8.
9.   Herr KL, Mobily PR. Comparison of selected pain assessment tools for use with the elderly. Applied Nurs Res 1991;6:39-45.
10.   Closs SJ, Barr B, Briggs M, Cash K, Seers K. A comparison of five pain assessment scales for nursing home residents with varying degrees of cognitive impairment. J Pain Symptom Manage 2004;27(3):196-205.
11.   Abbey J, Piller N, DeBellis A, Esterman A, Parker D, Giles L, Lowcay B. The Abbey Pain Scale: a 1-minute numerical indicator for people with end stage dementia. Int J Palliative Nurs 2004;10(1):6-13.
12.   Chapiro SL. The DOLOPLUS© 2 scale—evaluating pain in the elderly. Eur J Palliative Care 2001;8(5): 191-4.

13.   Warden V, Hurley A, Volicer L. Development and psychometric evaluation of the Pain Assessment in Advanced Dementia Scale (PAINAD). J Am Dir Assoc 2003;4:9-15.

14.   Ferrell BR. Pain management in elderly people. J Am Geriatr Soc 1991;39:64-73.

15.   Department of Health National Service Framework for older people. London, UK: HMSO, 2001.

16.   Wittgenstein L. The philosophical investigations. New York, NY, USA: Anchor Books, 1967.

17.   Cowan DT, Roberts JD, Fitzpatrick JM, White AE. The need for effective assessment and management of pain among older people in care homes. Rev Clin Gerontol 2003;13:335-41.

18.   Morgan JP. American opiophoba: customary under utilization of opioid analgesics. Adv Alcohol Subst Abuse 1985;5(1-2):163-73.

19.   Lumme-Sandt K, Hervonen A, Jylla M. Interpretive repertoires of medication among the oldest-old. Soc Sci Med 2000;50(12):1843-50.

20.   Folstein M, Folstein S, McHugh P. Mini-Mental state. A practical method for grading the cognitive state of patients for the clinician. J Psychiatr Res 1975;12: 189–98.

21.   Mayring P. Qualitative content analysis. In: Flick U, ed. A companion to qualitative research. London, UK: Sage, 2004.

22.   Yates P, Dewar A, Fentiman B. Pain: The views of elderly people living in long term residential care settings. J Adv Nurs 1994;21:667-74.

23.   Weiner J, Rudy TE. Attitudinal barriers to effective treatment of persistent pain in nursing home residents. J Am Geriatr Soc 2002;50(12):2035-40.

24.   Bergh I, Sjostrom B. A comparative study of nurses' and elderly patients' ratings of pain and pain tolerance. J Gerontol Nurs 1999;25(5):30-6.

25.   Hall Lord ML, Larsson G, Steen B. Chronic pain and distress among elderly in the community: a comparison of patients experiences with enrolled nurses assess-ments. J Nurs Manage 1999;7(1):45-54.

26.   Weiner D, Peterson B, Keefe F. Chronic pain asso-ciated behaviors in the nursing home: resident versus caregiver perceptions. Pain 1999;80(3):577-88.

27.   Schumacher KL, West C, Dodd M, Paul SM, Tripathy D, Koo P, Miaskowski CA. Pain management auto-biographies and reluctance to use Opioids for cancer pain management. Cancer Nurs 2002; 25(2):125-33.

28.   Dunn K, Horgas AL. Religious and nonreligious coping in older adults experiencing chronic pain. Pain Manage Nurs 2004;5(1):19-28.

29.   Sheffield D, Krittayaphong R, Go BM, Christy CG, Biles PL, Sheps DS. The relationship between resting systolic blood pressure and cutaneous pain perception in cardiac patients with angina pectoris and controls. Pain 1997;71:249-55.

30.   Zborowski M. People in pain. San Francisco, CA, USA: Jossey Bass, 1969.

31.   Hurley AC, Volicer BJ, Hanrahan PA, Houde S, Volicer L. Assessment of discomfort in advanced Alzheimer patients. Res Nurs Health 1992;15:369-77.
32.   Simons W, Malabar R. Assessing pain in elderly patients who cannot respond verbally. J Adv Nurs 1995;22:663-9.
33.   Sloman R, Ahern M, Wright A, Brown L. Nurses knowledge of pain in the elderly. J Pain Sympt Manage 2001;21(4):317-22.
34.   Jeng GY, Guo Z, Drickamer M, Marottoli RA, Reid MC. Timing in the communication of pain among nursing home residents, nursing staff and clinicians. Arch Intern Med 2004;164:1508-12.
35.   Schofield PA, Clarke A, Dunham M, Ryan T, Faulkner M, Howarth A. Assessment of pain in older People. Where are we now and what needs to be done? Int J Disabil Hum Dev 2006;5(1)3-8. [this issue]
36.   Lin CC. Barriers to analgesic management of cancer pain: a comparison of attitudes of Taiwanese patients and their family caregivers. Pain 2000;88:7-14.
37.   Larson PD. Effective pain management in older adults AORN J 2000;71(1):205-8.
38.   Schofield PA, Dunham M, Dowd C, Black C, Aveyard B, Miller L. A distance learning package for the management of older people. Shefield, UK: Univ Sheffield Press, 2005.

CHAPTER 13
Pain and older people with learning disability/intellectual disability and dementia

Diana Kerr and Heather Wilkinson

This chapter is base on a study that explored the detection, management, and understanding of pain amongst a range of professional groups involved in supporting people with a learning disability/intellectual disability, who have dementia. The study also recorded the experiences and views of some people with a learning disability who had dementia. People with a learning disability are living longer and this increased longevity brings with it the conditions and illnesses of older age; of which dementia is one. Amongst people in the general population who have dementia, pain recognition and treatment are known to be inadequate. The dilemmas and obstacles to effective pain management were explored and the findings also identified examples of good practice. We found that the pain experiences and management of people with a learning disability who have dementia mirror findings in relation to people in the general population. The research did identify, however, extra and compounding issues in relation to people with a learning disability. Drawing on this research, this article outlines recommendations for practitioners and service providers and discusses the key lessons for responding more effectively to pain in people with a learning disability and dementia.

INTRODUCTION

Increasing numbers of people with a learning disability (also called 'intellectual disability' internationally and 'mental retardation' in the United States) are now growing older (1,2) This demographic shift means that as people with a learning disability grow older, their needs and experiences include the onset of the conditions and illnesses associated with ageing, dementia being one in particular (1,3,4) Supporting people with a learning disability who develop illnesses that can often be painful is a growing concern for service providers across a range of community and health care settings (5).

In this chapter, we draw on recently completed research exploring responses to the pain needs of people with a learning disability and dementia to consider the key lessons that can be drawn from this research. We open with a short review of the demographic changes and their relevance to the changing health and social care needs of people with a learning disability; we then provide a description of the research study before moving into several sections that outline the key findings. These sections include a summary of the issues in relation to people with a learning disability that contributed to poor pain recognition and therefore poor treatment. These issues include attributing all changes to the impact of dementia (diagnostic overshadowing); focusing on behavior that challenges; communication difficulties associated with dementia; the influence of the person's previous history on current assessments; beliefs about pain thresholds; professional awareness of the impact of older age on people with a learning disability; and the use of 'as required' medication. In responding to the pain needs of people with a learning disability and dementia, a battery of useful non-pharmacologic interventions can be used effectively and a short section is included on these. The chapter ends with a discussion of the key lessons to be drawn from the work.

BACKGROUND

The rapid advances in the health and social care of people with a learning disability means that people with a learning disability now have a much higher life expectancy (3). The exact population statistics for people with a learning disability in the United Kingdom (UK) are limited: recent demographic figures for England estimate that ~25,000 people are aged 60 years and over (6), whereas for Scotland estimates are ~12,000 people with a learning disability (7). Also predicted is that population trends for people with a learning disability in the UK will continue to grow by over 1% per annum over the next 10 years (7). One result of this increased life expectancy is an increased incidence of the illnesses associated with older age (3,8).

Dementia is a particular example of one of these illnesses. Reports differ on actual numbers of people with a learning disability who develop dementia, ranging from 22% of older people with a learning disability in Britain (8) to a more recent American study that found a prevalence of dementia of 3% for people aged 40 years and older, 6% for people aged 60 years and older, and 12% for people aged 80 years and older (3). Trends are different for people with Down's syndrome, who show an increased prevalence of dementia of 3.4% in the age group 30 to 39 years, 10.3% in the age group 40 to 49 years, and a 40% increase in the age group 50 to 59 years (9). For those with Down's syndrome, estimates of incidence tend to vary from 75% for individuals aged 60 years and over (10) to 54.9% for people aged between 60 and 69 (11), and down to only 36% for the age group 50 to 59 years (12).

People with learning disabilities can experience more complex health needs when compared with the general population and critically, many of their health needs are unrecognized and unmet (13). Higher health needs and higher levels of unmet health needs than the general population means that a person with a learning disability is more likely to have a greater prevalence of pain (13-16).

In the general population, between 64% and 86% will experience chronic pain as a consequence of the onset of the conditions of older age (17). When older people develop dementia, their pain needs are not adequately met (18). One study of elderly residents with dementia in nursing homes found that only 12% received any pain relief (19).

Some claims suggest an altered or decreased sensitivity to pain for people with a learning disability, and the idea that people with a learning disability don't feel pain 'as much' as the general population is a commonly held assumption and generalization (14,16,20). Challenges to this assumption highlight pain as under-recognized, under-assessed, under-estimated, and under-treated, mostly due to the communication barriers experienced by people with a learning disability in expressing pain (21,22). An added layer of complexity can be the lack of understanding, skills and knowledge of clinical staff in recognizing and responding to people's pain (23-25) People with a learning disability have a long history of experiencing barriers to their health needs being met.

It has been consistently found that insufficient attention has been given to the health needs of people with learning disabilities. This deficiency includes a lack of basic health promotion, under-identification of ill health, and a deficit in meeting the health needs specific to people with learning disabilities. To suggest that persons with learning disabilities are already included in all health improvement policy and practice ignores their long history of unmet health needs, health needs specific to persons with learning disabilities, and the complex issues that prohibit access to and effective use of services and care (13).

The study reported in this chapter was based on the premise that the existence of a high level of un-recognized and, therefore, untreated pain among people with dementia in the general population (18) is likely to be replicated among people with a learning disability (5).

OUR RESEARCH

The study took place over a 16-month period, from July 2004 to October 2005. The main phase of the work involved six research sites located throughout the UK, chosen for their varying size and geographical spread, and included residential and non-residential service provision. In each site, interviews were conducted with three primary groups: older people with a learning disability and dementia; support staff; and members of the community learning disability team and GP (see table 1 for totals of each group inter-viewed).

The individuals with a learning disability and dementia became the central focus of a case study and, where possible, interviews or guided conversations were held with each case study participant. Time was also spent observing each person in their 'home' setting. For all other partici-pants (Staff, General Practitioners (GPs), Community Learning Difficulty

Team members), the interviews were conversational, observational, and informal in nature. The themes of the data gathered focused on belief systems about pain; the words, phrases, and non-verbal methods used to describe pain; views about how physical pain is managed; and views on how physical pain should be managed.

Table 1. Breakdown of total numbers of people interviewed

People interviewed	Number
Support staff	49
Psychiatrists	2
Psychologists	3
Managers	12
GPs	6
Community nurses	6
Occupational therapists	2
People with dementia	6
Total number of interviews	86

The data were collected using audiotape recordings and these were transcribed. The thematic analysis of verbatim transcripts was also supported by notes of observations and reflections made by the researchers immediately following the interviews. Analysis of the data was an iterative process and overlapped the period of interviewing. A collaborative approach was taken with research team members carrying out a detailed review of specific transcripts and then identifying key themes, concepts, and processes emerging from the data. The team then looked at these themes again to understand more fully the similarities and differences in the respondents' accounts (26).

OUR FINDINGS

The evidence showed that the knowledge that someone has a learning disability can often 'override and obscure physical illness' (27). Also recognized is that within the general population of people with dementia, the tendency is to attribute changes in the individual to the progression of their dementia, rather than to other causes (28). Indeed, challenging behavior is often seen as an inevitable part of dementia (29). Evidence in the latter study implied that people with both a learning disability and dementia experienced the impact of these responses leading to 'diagnostic over-shadowing'. In such cases the diagnosis of dementia was used as an explanation for all of the changes in the person's behavior, resulting in behaviors that were possibly pain related being attributed to the dementia rather than to pain. One of the key ways in which this finding was illustrated in the study was in relation to explanations given for nighttime disturbance amongst people with a learning disability and dementia.

Often people with dementia wake at night, partly because of the impact of disturbance to the circadian rhythm (30). As a result, the tendency amongst those supporting people with dementia is to attribute all nighttime disturbances to the impact of the dementia. However, it is evident that many non-dementia-related reasons can explain why someone may wake at night, with the existence of painful conditions being an important one of these. One painful condition that many people with a learning disability and dementia will experience is arthritis. This condition is particularly painful at night when joints stiffen. The study reported evidence of people, from their own descriptions, awakening at night with arthritic pain.

> 'Well it (knee) swells if maybe I'm lying in bed sleeping and I wake up stiff' (woman with dementia)

> 'Can't lie on that (hip)...feel it in bed' (women with dementia).

Staff were not picking up on the arthritis but rather were attributing the nighttime waking solely to the reason that the person had dementia, so they were not offering any pain relief.

Focusing on 'behavior that challenges'

People with a learning disability, for a variety of reasons, can more often present with behavior that challenges their carers and services than do their non-disabled, age-matched peers (31). Indeed 'challenging behavior' is often given a high priority among training courses for staff working with people with a learning disability. Although a vital aspect of staff learning and skill development, this approach can lead to staff wrongly attributing challenging behavior to causes other than pain, particularly when people with a learning disability develop dementia. If someone already has a history of behavior that others find challenging, then a pain-related behavior may possibly be seen as a repeat of previous behaviors. If staff are primed to see the behavior as 'challenging', then the possibility that it might be pain related can be overlooked.

Pain is positively associated with screaming, aggression, and verbal agitation in dementia (32). It is interesting to reflect on the types of behaviors that can result from pain experiences. Questionnaires to groups about their responses to pain elicit most of the following: increased irritation, moaning, withdrawal, crying, screaming, swearing, aggression, poor eating, anxiety, and hitting out if touched or threatened to be touched in the painful area. Many such behaviors are also labeled as challenging amongst people with a learning disability who have dementia. The misinterpretation of the meaning of the behavior is compounded by reports that often the primary response to 'challenging behavior' in people with dementia is treatment with antipsychotic medication (33) or sedation. These responses only serve to mask the symptoms and make the identification of pain less likely, as illustrated in the case study of Jane.

CASE STUDY 1

Jane is 51 years old, has Down's syndrome, and has been diagnosed with dementia. Every morning Jane screamed, shouted abuse, and hit out as staff helped her out of bed and along to the bathroom. There was some feeling that this behavior was because she did not want to get out of bed and face the day. She was seen as 'being stubborn'. This seemed to be confirmed by the fact that the screaming and hitting stopped after the bathing was done and as the day progressed. The morning procedure became increasingly distressing for everyone concerned. Jane had arthritis. Arthritis is a painful condition that is worse in the mornings after the person stiffens up during the night. A decision was made to give Jane paracetamol 20 minutes before she got out of bed. This resulted in a complete change in her behavior. She was clearly no longer in pain and went happily to the bathroom. This case is an example of an alternative response to 'challenging behavior' for which pain relief can be tried to see if the behavior changes. If it does so, then it may be an indication that the behavior is caused by pain. The next stage is to identify where the pain is and what is causing it, but the initial use of pain relief can begin the process of an accurate diagnosis.

Communication difficulties associated with dementia

Pain is a highly subjective experience. Many things will influence how an individual will experience pain with culture, age, ethnicity, and gender being some of the variables. The person with pain is the only person who knows how bad and enduring the pain is. Others have to ascertain the nature of the pain through observation and communication. The need to pay attention to subtle and often almost imperceptible changes is critical, and staff often talk about recognizing something as small as 'worried eyes' as the key to pain recognition. Although it is true that staff will already be attending to these changes in the people they support, what is important is that when the person has dementia, the same attention should be given to these observations. One useful definition of pain is that "pain is whatever the patient says it is and occurs whenever the patient says it does" (34). Clearly, this view presents problems for pain identification in relation to people with dementia where communication can be an increasing difficulty.

Many people with a learning disability will have experienced communication problems before the onset of dementia. Often strategies have been developed to maxi-mize the person's ability to communicate. With the onset of dementia, such strategies begin to fail and communication deteriorates from the previously achieved level. People will start to lose the words they might have had to describe pain. Damage to the parietal lobes results in a number of significant problems for pain communication (35). Amongst other things, the left side parietal lobe is responsible for our understanding of patterns, essential for the use of language in which the patterning of words is critical to communication. The left side lobe is also responsible for our understanding of the patterns and geography of the body, telling us which is our right and which is our left side. Once the part of the brain that tells the person where the head is, and where the foot and the left and right sides are becomes damaged, then they can no longer physically indicate where the pain is located. The person with a toothache may not only fail to find the word 'toothache' but also may not be able to locate the place where the pain is and not be able to put his/her hand there.

Sometimes the person will use a phrase as a substitute for the correct word, for example, 'Oh dear oh dear' will indicate distress but carers may fail to recognize this as an expression of physical rather than emotional pain. People will sometimes use a general phase such as 'My head hurts' because they cannot find the word 'toothache' but they are communicating a feeling of pain. This can lead to problems for assessment. If a person persistently says his/her leg hurts and yet is walking well, one is tempted to think that no pain exists and that the person wants attention. It could be that the pain is elsewhere. People will often use phrases they used in the past as a generalized way of expressing pain. For example, people may constantly say they have a 'tummy ache' because this was a pain they would have had in their childhood and probably the one best remembered. This statement does not indicate the location of the pain but is simply the use of a well-remembered pain-related phrase. Sometimes the communication will be not through words but through actions. The need to understand such actions is illustrated well by the following example given to the researchers on this project.

CASE STUDY 2

Geoffrey was a man with Down's syndrome and dementia. He had lost all his teeth many years ago and had ever since worn dentures successfully without any complaint. After the onset of dementia he started to take the dentures out and would try to hide them. Staff kept giving them back and, with instructions from the most senior worker, insisted that Geoffrey wear them. He would again take them out and try to hide them. This went on for some time with Geoffrey becoming more and more distressed at meal times when there was insistence on him wearing the dentures. No attempt was made to investigate his gums or to find out the meaning behind the changed behavior until finally an investigation of his mouth revealed painful gum disease.

Clearly Geoffrey had been trying to communicate. It is possible that another interpretation of Geoffrey's behavior might be that because of the dementia, his reality is that he is younger and at a time in his life when he did not wear dentures. He takes them out because he does not understand why they are there. The possibility of multiple explanations serves to underline the need to avoid automatically looking for an explanation related to the dementia rather than carrying out a differential diagnosis that would include a consideration of pain.

The influence of the person's previous history on current assessments

Of some significance can be the influence of previously known behavior on new assessments. If someone has in the past presented with certain behaviors, it is possible that the new behaviors will be seen as a regression to prior patterns. Nevertheless, it is important to consider that the present behavior, whilst similar to previous behaviors, now has a different meaning. An example of this would be Bob, who was always considered a bit cantankerous and uncooperative. Such behavior was just his personality and way of coping. After his diagnosis of dementia, the onset of gum disease made him extremely bad tempered but this irritability was inititally interpreted by the staff as Bob 'him up to his old ways.'

It is important to remember that if we do not understand what is motivating a certain behavior, then our assessment may well be inaccurate. The motivation and meaning will change often with the onset of dementia, and this might mask the fact that pain is now the underlying motivation for behaviors that previously would have been triggered by something else.

Beliefs about pain thresholds

There is a belief, which still persists, that people with a learning disability have a high pain threshold.

CASE STUDY 3

Keith is a man with Down's syndrome and a diagnosis of dementia. He is in his early fifties. Keith has a severe back problem. He is often seen shaking and unable to walk because he is in so much pain from spasms. However, when asked 'Keith is your back hurting? he replies 'no I'm alright' even though he is unable to walk. He is also reported as sometimes having diarrhoea and sickness. He 'would be vomiting into a bucket' whilst also telling staff that he is fine and there is nothing wrong with him. This man was described as 'having a high pain threshold'

It is important to recognize that past experiences may lead people to deny the existence of pain. Certain older people with a learning disability may have the experience of living in large institutions. Their experiences of past staff responses to their pain will not necessarily be positive. Throughout this study we found examples of people whose previous experience of others' responses to their pain ensured that they would never complain again. Less dramatically, but still a determinant of people's reaction to pain, is the recognition that in large institutions people did not necessarily get the attention they needed. If someone has learned not to complain early in their life, then this is the behavior to which they are likely to return when they develop dementia. People with a learning disability, like their non-disabled peers, will have individual and differing responses to pain. If some of these differences are exaggerated and generalized into a belief about pain thresholds, then the danger is that amongst staff, the sensitivity to the possibility that someone might be in pain will be reduced.

Professional awareness of the impact of older age on people with a learning disability

People with a learning disability in previous generations did not live into old age. The concentration in the education and training of the professionals who work with people with a learning disability tended to focus on the issues of young and middle-aged individuals. This means that people are often ill equipped with the necessary knowledge skills and experiences to give informed responses to older people, and we will now use the illustrations of the experiences of GPs and other health professionals interviewed in this study.

Despite the knowledge that "general practitioners are the health professionals most commonly consulted by people with intellectual disability" (36), most medical practices will have only a limited experience of people with a learning disability because any GPs list comprises only a small proportion of such individuals. Additionally, most GPs will have limited experience of people with dementia even within the general population. "A GP with 1,500 to 2,000 patients can expect to include 12-20 people with dementia, depending on the age profile of the list" (37). Consequently, the amount of experience that any one GP will have of people with a learning disability and dementia is going to be fairly limited.

The present study found highly varied experience, knowledge, skills, and attitude among the GPs in relation to supporting people with a learning disability and dementia. Clearly, such differences also led to significant variations in the knowledge, skills, and attitudes toward the pain manage-ment needs of this group. Where GPs were recognized as providing a high level of good support, these examples tended to reinforce the thinking of Lennox and Eastgate (36) on the importance of people with a learning disability having one doctor who consistently meets their health care needs.

This low experience rate of many GPs is compounded by the observation that direct care and support staff who are often well aware of the needs of younger people are often unaware of the possible painful conditions of older age. The lack of experience and knowledge amongst professionals has an impact on the detection and management of pain in older people and people with dementia. It is important to emphasize that people will also experience painful conditions that have nothing to do with age but are particular to individuals as a result of their lifestyles, life events, and individual health. It is significant then that even conditions that people have had for many years can be overlooked in old age. The diagnostic overshadowing referred to in relation to dementia can also be seen in relation to older age. The acceptance of pain as an inevitable part of old age should be challenged.

The use of 'as required' (PRN) medication

Pain relief is often prescribed 'as required.' This policy is problematic in relation to people with dementia. If, as indicated above, people supporting the person with dementia find it difficult to recognize when the person is in pain, then they are not going to use medication appropriately as 'required'. Evidence within the general population shows not only that less prescribing of analgesia occurs for people with dementia than amongst an age-matched population without dementia but also that even when analgesia is prescribed to a person with dementia, 83% do not receive it (38).

For these reasons, 'as required' medication of analgesia is not recommended for people with dementia. The World Health Organisation (WHO) guidelines on prescribing analgesia to people with dementia are clear (39). 'As required' should not be the primary approach to pain management for people with dementia. There should be regular administration; the treatment should be adjusted from one step to the next, according to increasing or decreasing pain severity, history of response, and side effect profile.

It is important that once analgesia is given, a monitoring process should begin. Because of the nature of the support that people with a learning disability receive, a number of people may be involved in their care. Often a member of staff, a carer, or a support worker may give pain relief and then by the time the effects have worn off, someone else may be with the person. It is critical that all involved know about the pain relief given and that this be constantly evaluated. There may be a tendency amongst some people who have a reluctance to use drugs to under treat. This approach is not an option if the pain relief is going to be properly administered and monitored.

Non-pharmacologic interventions to relieve pain

The use of non-pharmaceutical interventions to prevent, reduce, and relieve pain is to be encouraged, and the study observed several positive examples of where non pharmacologic interventions were highly effective. For chronic musculoskeletal pain that is associated with increased age, the "application of heat and massage or positioning can sometimes be all that is needed" (18). Chronic degenerative joint disease causes pain in the back and limbs, and osteoporotic spinal deformity causes back pain. The need to support people's bodies with appropriate seating, the use of aromatherapy, massage, and music to relax people, and the slowing down of activities and interventions will all contribute to pain reduction. People in pain will tense up and stiffen their bodies. The significance of almost all the above interventions is that they are directly or indirectly relaxing. They do not necessarily take the pain away but may make the secondary impact less and so may make pain more tolerable. The use of some of these interventions at night, especially aromatherapy, could help people to sleep better. The use of individually adapted chairs is important. These may well serve to reduce the occurrence of pain, as well as giving support and comfort to parts of the body that are painful

A number of these interventions involve touch. People with dementia need touching, both as a form of communication and as a source of comfort (40). People in pain are, as evidenced above, relieved of pain or at least enabled to cope with it through the appropriate use of touch. Many of these interventions will already be part of the repertoire of support and help that are used with people with a learning disability. The important thing to note is that these interventions must be extended consciously to the use of pain prevention, reduction and relief.

CONCLUSIONS

This chapter has highlighted some of the findings from a research study exploring the pain needs of people with a learning disability and dementia and from these findings has raised concerns that older people with a learning disability and dementia may, like the general population with dementia, be experiencing high levels of unrecognized and untreated pain. There are several reasons for this and also several lessons to be drawn from these findings. The reasons may link to the findings around the effects of 'diagnostic overshadowing', the focus within the service on 'challenging behavior', and the problems with communication that develop with the onset of dementia. The effects of these are compounded by a low level but still persistent belief that people with a learning disability have higher pain thresholds than other people. The detection of pain is further inhibited by the reduced awareness amongst staff of the painful conditions of older age. Crucially, the use of 'as required' analgesia is unsatisfactory as a response to pain relief for people with a learning disability and dementia. In responding to pain, a battery of effective nonpharmacologic interventions could be usefully explored.

Key lessons to be drawn include the following, based on the recommendations from the research (1):

- All staff require training on the impact of dementia. Such training must include a recognition of how communication difficulties may have an impact on the expression of and recognition of pain.
- A need exists for everyone involved in supporting older people with a learning disability to be aware of the potentially painful conditions of older age.
- Training on 'challenging behavior' must include recognition of the impact of dementia on pain behavior and recognition.
- 'As required' analgesia should not be the primary approach to the management of pain in people with a learning disability and dementia. Treatment must follow World Health Organisation Guidelines (39).
- The use of non pharmaceutical interventions should be integrated into pain prevention and management.

ACKNOWLEDGEMENTS

This chapter is an updated version of an earlier published paper (Kerr D, Wilkinson H. Responding to pain needs of people with learning disability/intellectual disability an dementia: What are the key lessons? Int J Disabil Hum Dev 2006;5(1): 69-75).

REFERENCES

1. Kerr D, Cunningham C, Wilkinson H. Responding to the pain needs of people with a learning disability and dementia. York, North Yorkshire, UK: Joseph Rowntree Foundation, 2006.
2. Mulvany F, Barron S. National intellectual disability database: Annual report 2002. Dublin, Ireland: Health Res Board, 2002.
3. Janicki MP Dalton AJ Henderson M and Davidson PW Mortality and morbidity among older adults with intellectual disabilities: health services consideration. Disabil Rehabil 1999;21:284-94.
4. Wilkinson H, Janicki M The Edinburgh Principles. J Intellect Disabil Res 2002;46(3):279-84.
5. Wilkinson H, Kerr D, Cunningham C, Rae C. 'Home for Good?' Models of good practice for supporting people with a learning disability and dementia. Brighton, UK: Brighton Pavilion Press, 2002.
6. Department of Health. Valuing People. London, UK: HMSO, 2001.
7. Scottish Executive. The Same as You? A review of Service for People with a Learning Disability. Edinburgh, Scotland: HMSO, 2000.
8. Cooper SA. High prevalence of dementia amongst people with learning disabilities not attributed to Down's syndrome. Psychol Med 1997;27:609-16.
9. Holland AJ, Hon J, Huppert FA, Stevens F, Watson P. Population based study of prevalence and presentation of dementia in adults with Down's syndrome. Br J Psychiatr 1998;172:493-8.
10. Lai F, Williams RS. A prospective study of Alzheimer's disease in Down's Syndrome. Arch Neurol 1989;46:849-53.
11. Prasher VP. 'End-stage Dementia in adults with Down's syndrome. Int J Geriatr Psychiatr 1995;75:607.
12. Thompson D, Wright S. Misplaced and forgotten: people with learning disabilities in residential services for older people. London, UK: Ment Health Foundation, 2001
13. NHS Health Scotland. Health needs assessment report people with learning disabilities in Scotland. Glasgow, Scotland: NHS Health Scotland, 2004.
14. Breau LM, Camfield CS, McGrath PJ, Finley A. The incidence of pain in children with severe cognitive impairments. Arch Paediatr Adolesc Med 2003;157: 1219-26.
15. Jansen R, Villien L, Aamodt G, Stanghelle JK, Holm I. Musculoskeletal pain in adults with cerebral palsy compared with the general population. J Rehabil Med 2004;36:78–84.
16. Defrin R, Pick CG, Peretz C, Carmeli E. A quantitative somatosensory testing of pain threshold in individuals with mental retardation. Pain 2004; 108:58-66.
17. Tsai P, Chang J. Assessment of pain in elders with dementia. Med Surg Nurs 2004;13(6):364-90.

18.   McClean W. Practise guide for pain management for people with dementia in institutional care. Stirling: Dementia Services Dev Centre, 2000

19.   Marzinski LR. The tragedy of dementia. Clinically assessing pain in the confused non verbal elderly. J Gerontol Nurs 1991;17(6):25-8.

20.   Breau LM, Camfield CS, McGrath PJ, Rosmus C, Finley GA. Measuring pain accurately in children with cognitive impairments: Refinement of a caregiver scale. J Paediatrics 2001;38(5):721-7.

21.   Donovan J. Learning disability nurses' experiences of being with clients who may be in pain. J Adv Nurs 2002;38(5):458-66.

22.   Craig K, Hadjistavropoulos T Different behavioral observation methods serve different purposes. Pain 2004;110:762-9.

23.   Malviya S Voepel-Lewis T Tait A Merkel S Lauer A Munro H Farley F. Pain management in children with and without cognitive impairment following spinal fusion surgery. Paediatr Anaesthesia 2001;11:453-8.

24.   Breau LM, MacLaren J, McGrath PJ, Camfield CS, Finley GA. Caregivers' beliefs regarding pain in children with cognitive impairment: Relation between pain sensation and reaction increases with severity of impairment. Clin J Pain 2003;19:335-44.

25.   Regnard C, Mathews D, Gibson L, Clarke C. Difficulties in identifying distress and its causes in people with severe communication problems. Int J Palliat Nurs 2003; 9(4):173-6.

26.   Lofland J, Lofland LH. Analyzing social settings: A guide to qualitative observation and analysis. Belmont, CA, USA: Wadsworth, 1995.

27.   Ng J, Li S. Survey exploring the educational needs of care practitioners in learning disability in relation to death, dying and people with learning disabilities. Eur J Cancer Care 2003;12(1):12-9.

28.   Mason J, Scior K. Diagnostic overshadowing amongst clinicians working with people with intellectual dis-abilities in the UK. J Intellect Disabil Res 2004;47(Suppl 1): 16-25.

29.   Stokes G, Goudie F. Working with dementia. Bicester, Oxfordshire, UK: Winslow Press, 1990.

30.   Jacques A, Jackson GA. Understand dementia. Oxford, UK: Churchill Livingstone, 2000.

31.   Meyer LH, Evans IM. Nonaversive interventions for behavioral problems. Baltimore, MD, USA: Paul H Brookes, 1994.

32.   Cohen-Mansfield J, Werner P, Marx M. Screaming in nursing home residents. J Am Geriatr Soc 1990;38: 785-92.

33.   Balfour J, O'Rouke N. Older adults with Alzheimer disease, co-morbid arthritis and prescription of psychotropic medication. Pain Resident Manage 2003; 8(4):198-204.

34.   McCaffery MS. Nursing theories related to cognition, bodily pain, and man. Environment interactions. Los Angeles, CA, USA: UCLA Students Store, 1968.

35.   Kerr D. Down's syndrome and dementia: Practitioner's guide. Birmingham, UK: Venture Press, 1997.

36.   Lennox N, Eastgate G. Adults with intellectual disability and the GP. Aust Fam Physician 2004;33(8): 601–6.

37.   Alzheimer's Disease Society. Dementia in the com-munity, management strategies for general practice. Stirling, Scotland, UK: Dementia Services Dev Centre, Univ Stirling, 1995.

38.   Dawson P. Cognitively impaired residents receive less pain medication than non-cognitively impaired residents. Perspectives 1998;22(4):16-7.

39.   World Health Organization. Guidelines. Cancer pain relief, 2nd ed. Geneva, Switzerland: WHO, 1996.

40.   Goldsmith M. Hearing the voice of people with dementia. Opportunities and obstacles. London, UK: Jessica Kingsley, 1996.

PART FIVE:

SPECIFIC HEALTH PROBLEMS

CHAPTER 14
Persons with intellectual disability and B12 deficiency

Mohammed Morad, Isack kandel and Joav Merrick

T he goal of this chapter was to determine the prevalence of vitamin B12 deficiency among intellectually disabled in a vegetarian remedial community in Israel. In this community 47 individuals with intellectual disability lived in seven enlarged families in a kibbutz style agricultural setting. These 47 individuals and 17 of their caregivers were screened for vitamin B12 deficiency. 25.5% of the disabled versus 11.8% of the caregivers were found to have levels of vitamin B12 lower than 157 pg/ml. It is concluded that persons with intellectual disability in this vegetarian residential care community seemed to be at a higher risk for vitamin B12 deficiency.

INTRODUCTION

The prevalence of vitamin B12 (cobalamin) deficiency can range from 3-29% (1) in the general population, whereas in vegetarians it can reach up to 40% (2). The daily intake of vitamin B12 in the Western diet is 5-15 mcg/day (3) and the intake in individuals with intellectual disability (ID) has been measured to be 10.8 microgram daily (4). The minimum daily requirement for cobalamin is 2.5 mcg according to Harrison's Principles of Internal Medicine (5).

Since persons with ID also live in households, communities or residential care with a vegetarian nutritional way of life the literature was surveyed to find information on vitamin B 12 deficiency, but the prevalence of vitamin B12 deficiency in this population has not been studied before. The purpose of the present chapter was to present a study to determine the prevalence of vitamin B12 or cobalamin deficiency in persons with ID and their caregivers in a vegetarian remedial community.

OUR PILOT STUDY

The Division for Mental Retardation in Israel provides service to about 25,000 persons with ID and among them 6,500 individuals in close to 60 residential care centers around the country. One center in the south of Israel was selected for this pilot study. This center has been arranged like a kibbutz with seven housing units, each with a family, their own children and seven persons with ID, who share living quarters, kitchen and dining room. During the day the family members, other staff , volunteers and the people with ID work together in the fields, a bread factory, olive oil press, wax candle factory and weaving factory.

The inspiration for this therapeutic approach has come from the German-Austrian philosopher, Rudolf Steiner (1861-1925), and there are today about 300 therapeutic communities around the world working with persons with ID at all ages. In all these communities an effort is made to harmonize the different elements of life, because the basic problems is considered to be a "dissonance" within the "symphony of life" and the healing process is trying to find a a suitable "consonant" solution. Work, social and cultural life serve as therapeutic activities together with individual treatment. The more harmonious the development of the person, the more independent the person becomes in achieving harmony in the environment. A vegetarian life style is part of the therapeutic philosophy.

As part of the yearly rutine blood examination of the residents with ID a specimen was drawn for vitamin B12 levels and examined at the Clalit Health Service Laboratory (normal range 157-1059 pg/ml). Seventeen vegetarian caregivers were also examined. Statistical analysis was not found to be relevant in this small study.

OUR FINDINGS

The residential care center studied had 47 adults (22 females and 25 males), 42 persons aged 19-45 years, 4 aged 46-60 years and 1 above 61 years. 11 had mild, 26 moderate and 10 severe intellectual disability (ID).

Of the 47 persons with ID screened 12/47 (25.5%) were found to have vitamin B12 levels lower than 157 pg/ml, while 2/17 (11.8%) of the caregivers group had vitamin B12 lower than 157 pg/ml.

Looking at the vitamin B12 levels in persons with ID from various etiologies, persons with ID and cerebral palsy had the lowest average level (200 pg/ml), followed by fragile X (206.7 pg/ml), while persons with Down syndrome had the highest average (272 pg/ml). Persons with epilepsy had lower vitamin B12 deficiency (average at 180.72 pg/ml) than persons without epilepsy (average at 260.02 pg/ml).

DISCUSSION

There are very few studies on vitamin B12 deficiency in the population of persons with intellectual disability. Cunningham and co-workers from Stewarts Hospital in Ireland (4) studied the dietary intake of 115 male and 217 female persons with mental handicap (aged 15-64 years) in five longterm institutions and found the vitamin B12 intake to be 10.8 microgram per day.

Hanley et al (6) from the Hospital for Sick Children in Toronto described a case of an 18 year old female with phenylketonuria (PKU), who presented at follow-up after years of absence with various symptoms such as spastic paraparesis, tremor, disorientation, slurred speech, distractibility, deteriorating mental function and megaloblastic anaemia. During the investigation vitamin B12 deficiency was found and after treatment most of her symptoms disappeared. The case story resulted in further investigation of 37 adolescent at that clinic with PKU and it was found that six (16%) had subnormal serum B12 levels and another six had borderline low values. Another case story (7) of an adult with PKU and vitamin B 12 deficiency has been reported.

We have not been able to find studies of vitamin B12 deficiency in the population of vegetarians with intellectual disability, but Pongstaporn and Bunyaratavej (2) studied 179 vegetarians and 58 controls without ID in Thailand. They found that hemoglobin, hematocrit, mean corpuscular hemoglobin, mean corpuscular hemoglobin concentration, white blood cells, neutrophils, serum ferritin and serum vitamin B12 in vegetarians were significantly lower than controls (P<0.05). Vitamin B12 deficiency was found in 40% of the vegetarians.

Our small sample showed that a large number (25.5%) of the person with ID living on a vegetarian diet and 11.8% of their caregivers living in the same environment and eating the same food had vitamin B12 deficiency. Since the dietary source of cobalamin is animal products, such as meat and dairy foods, it is no wonder that vegetarians are prone to deficiency.

CONCLUSION

It seems that persons with intellectual disability in this residential care center were at a higher risk for vitamin B12 deficiency. We therefore recommend rutine investigations for vitamin B12 levels in this population.

REFERENCES

1.   Lesco EP, Hyder A. Prevalence of subtle cobalamin deficiency. Arch Internal Med 1999;159(4):407.
2.   Pongstaporn W, Bunyaratavej A. Hematological parameters, ferritin and vitamin B12 in vegetarians. J Med Ass Thailand 1999;82(3):304-11.
3.   Snow CF. Laboratory diagnosis of vitamin B13 and folate deficiency: A guide for the primary care physician. Arch Internal Med 1999;159(12):1289-98.
4.   Cunningham K, Gibney MJ, Kelly A, Kevany J, Mulcahy M. Nutrient intakes in long-stay mentally handicapped persons. Br J Nutrition 1990;64(1):3-11.
5.   Babior BM, Bunn HF. Megaloblastic anemiac. In: Fauci AS et al, eds. Harrison's Principles of Internal Medicine. McGraw-Hill, New York, 1998:653-9.

6.   Hanley WB, Feigenbaum AS, Clarke JT, Schoonheyt WE, Austin VJ. Vitamin B12 deficiency in adolescents and young adults with phenylketonuria. Eur J Pediatrics 1996;155(Suppl 1):S145-7.

7.   Aung TT, Klied A, McGinn J, McGinn T. Vitamin B12 deficiency in an adult phenylketonuric patient. J Inherited Metabol. Diseases 1997;20(4):603-4.

CHAPTER 15
Hepatitis and persons with intellectual disability in residential care

Joav Merrick, Efrat Merrick and Mohammed Morad

The purpose of this chapter was to convey the issue of hepatitis in residential care and describe a study looking at the prevalence of antibodies to hepatitis A, B and C in persons with intellectual disability in residential care in Israel and especially determine the need for immunization against hepatitis A. The pilot study was conduted in four out of 53 residential care centers, where a total of 251 persons were tested and the prevalence of anti-HAV was found to be 91%, HbsAg 5.2%, anti-HBs 57% and anti-HCV 0.8%. After we conducted the pilot study we concluded to continue active immunization against hepatitis B in this population, but only to vaccinate each new person that enters the institutions from home against hepatitis A.

INTRODUCTION

Infectious diseases have been one of the leading causes of morbidity and mortality throughout the ages, with different diseases prevalent at different times. In the last century tuberculosis, polio, diphtheria and whooping cough were prevalent and caused a high morbidity and mortality. Today the medical student will rarely see such patients, which were common features for the physician just 50 years ago, but instead encounter present day public health problems, such as meningitis, gastrointestinal infections, HIV/AIDS and hepatitis.

Hepatitis A virus (HAV) infection is transmitted by the fecal-oral route (1) by person-to-person contact, or ingestion of contaminated food or water. HAV infection, once endemic in children worldwide, is now declining and as a result more adults are becoming susceptible to HAV infection. In children the infection is usually mild and asymptomatic, whereas in adults symptomatic and disabling. In the past 50 years serum immunoglobulins has been used as passive immunization, but in recent years active immunization has become a reality.

In Israel over the years there has been a reduction in the prevalence of antibodies to HAV (2-4), especially in the Jewish population, due to reduced exposure and there has been a concern that a larger percentage of the population will now be in danger of infection later in life. This was the case in Shanghai in 1988, when over 300,000 persons became infected (5). Several researchers have therefore recommended to start active immunization of the Israeli population (1,4), which was implemented in July 1999 as a universal program for immunization against hepatitis A for all children aged 18 months.

In the population of persons with intellectual or developmental disability (ID) the prevalence of viral hepatitis has been studied in Spain (6), Australia (7,8), Yugoslavia (9), California (10) and also from Belgium (11).

In order to determine the need for vaccination in the population of persons with intellectual disability in residential care centers in Israel we conducted several pilot studies (12,13).

EXPERIENCE FROM OUR RESEARCH

The Division for Mental Retardation under the Ministry of Social Affairs provide medical, social, educational and residential services for persons with intellectual disability (ID) in 60 residential centers (size 50-400 persons) and community related programs (hostels, protected apartments etc.).

We selected four residential centers in the central part of Israel for pilot study (12,13) and had send blood specimen for serologic markers of hepatitis together with the routine yearly bloodtests. These four centers were representative of the total residential care population concerning size of institution, ethnic group, level of ID and associated medical problems. It was decided to only involve residential care centers, because of the presence of a medical clinic, since persons living in community related programs receive service from individual family physicians. Routine blood tests and medical examinations are performed annually on each resident or when indicated. In connection with routine blood examination a specimen was drawn for serologic markers of hepatitis A (IgG anti-HAV) and hepatitis B (HbsAg and anti-HBs) detected by conventional radioimmunoassay (Abbott Laboratories, Chicago, Il, USA) and serologic markers for hepatitis C [anti-hepatitis C virus(HCV)] detected by microparticle enzyme immunoassay (Abbott Laboratories). Operational procedures indicated by the manufacturer were followed. Gardian consent was obtained to these procedures.

Of the 251 persons from the four centers in this study, 56% were male and 44% female. Ten percent had mild, 30% moderate, 29% severe and 31% profound mental retardation. Four percent were between the age of 11-18 years, 61% between 19-45 years, 30% between 46-60 years and five percent over 61 years of age. 16% of the population was Arab residents and in that residential center with a total Arab population we found a 100% prevalence of anti-HAV consistent with findings for the general population, where since 1988 the rates in the Arab population have exceeded those in the Jewish general population (3).

Tables 1-3 show the prevalence of anti-hepatitis A antibodies, hepatitis B viral markers and anti-hepatitis C antibodies.

Table 1. Prevalence of anti-hepatitis A antibodies in 250 persons with intellectual disability in four residential care centers in Israel

Institution	Number tested	No. positive (%)
1.	99	91(92)
2.	40	40(100)
3.	64	57(89)
4.	47	39(83)
Total	250*	227(91)

*one sample unable to test

Table 2. Prevalence of hepatitis B viral markers in 249 persons with intellectual disability in four residential care centers in Israel

Institution	HbsAg	HbsAg	Anti-HBs *	Anti-HBs *
	Tested	Positive No. (%)	Tested	Positive No. (%)
1.	99	9 (9.1)	91	63 (69)
2.	39	1 (2.6)	39	18 (46)
3.	64	1 (1.6)	63	35 (56)
4.	47	2 (4.2)	45	20 (44)
TOTAL	249**	13 (5.2)	238	136 (57)

HbsAg, hepatitis B surface antigen and HBs its corresponding antibody. *Only participants negative for HbsAg were tested. **Two samples unable to test.

Table 3. Prevalence of anti-hepatitis C antibodies in 251 persons with intellectual disability in four residential care centres in Israel

Institution	No. tested	No. positive (%)
1.	100	1(1)
2.	40	0
3.	64	0
4.	47	1(2)
Total	251	2(0.8)

The prevalence of anti-HAV was high in this population (91 %) with all four institutions having a prevalence over 80%. The prevalence of anti-HAV in Israel compared to Spain, Australia and Yugoslavia is shown in table 4.

The prevalence of antibodies to HCV was found to be 0.8%, thereby suggesting that hepatitis C infection is a minor problem in this population.

Table 4. Prevalence of anti-hepatitis A virus (anti-HAV) in the current study compared with studies from Australia, Yugoslavia and Spain

Country	Year	Anti-HAV (%)	Reference
Israel	1995	90.8	(12,13)
Australia	1978	77.4	(7)
Yugoslavia	1981	90.0	(9)
Australia	1982	74.8	(8)
Spain	1998	55.6	(6)

DISCUSSION

The decline in prevalence of hepatitis A virus (HAV) in Israel was studied by Gdalevich et al (4) by comparing data from studies in 1977, 1984, 1987 and 1996. In this sample of 578 male and female recruits inducted into the Israel Defence Force the researchers found the anti-HAV antibody prevalence at 38.4 %. This was a significant (P<0.001) decline compared to 1977 (64 %).

Another study (14) examined a sample of 987 males and 195 females reporting to military recruitment offices in 1991-92. The sample consisted of persons (males aged 17-49, females aged 17-19 years), who had arrived in Israel since 1989 from the former USSR. They found the prevalence of anti-HAV antibodies to be 37 %, anti-HBV 12.8 %, HbsAg 3.0 % and anti-HCV 1.3 %. The prevalence of anti-HAV antibodies in this population of former immigrants was the same as the Israeli population, but the prevalence of HbsAg and anti-HCV antibodies was higher and raised concern about future chronic liver pathology.

A review (3) of the changing epidemiology of hepatitis A in Israel showed an increase in the incidence for 1970-79, stabilization until 1982, decline until 1992 with a small increase and the recent data from 1998 is at the 1992 level again. Until 1987 the rates were higher in the Jewish population, but has since been higher in the Arab population. There was also observed a shift in the peak age-specific incidence from the 1-4 to the 5-9 year old age group, which occurred in the Jewish population in 1970, but only 20 years later in the Arab population. Today by age 18 years only 30-40% of the Jewish population have anti-hepatitis A antibodies (3).

Hepatitis C virus infection was studied in Southern Israel and compared with the Gaza Strip and Egypt by Shemer-Avni et al (15, who found the prevalence of antibodies to HCV in Israel at 0.5 %, Gaza at 2.2 % and Egypt at 10 %.

Studies of viral hepatitis in the population of persons with intellectual disbility have not been previously performed in Israel, but in an occupational center for the mentally handicapped in Spain (6), the prevalence of IgG anti-HAV was found to be 55.6 % (pop. 60 persons), anti-HBV 18.5 %, HbsAg 3.3 % and no cases of anti-HCV. Prevalence of antibodies to HAV was studied in Australia in 1978 (7) in a large institution (population 854 persons) and found to be 74.4 % with a higher prevalence among persons with Down syndrome (84.1 %). Another study from

Australia (8) found 74.8 % with anti-HAV and 81.2 % showed serologic evidence of current or past hepatitis B infection.

In Yugoslavia (9) researchers studied the spread of hepatitis A viral infection in a small boarding school for children with mild and moderate intellectual disability, ending with an anti-HAV prevalence of 90 % and a prevalence of 32 % seropositivity for markers of past or chronic HBV.

Our pilot study (12,13) found a higher anti-HAV prevalence (91%) than the general Israeli population (38.4% in 1996), but a prevalence comparable, albeit higher, to studies from populations of persons with intellectual disability around the world (see table 4). It should be noted that 96% of our subjects were over 19 years of age and past their childhood, where the prevalence of HAV usually is much higher. The same trend was found for hepatitis B, whereas anti-HCV was the same as the Israeli population in general. The prevalence of hepatitis B surface antigen (HbsAg) was high in institution number one (9%), whereas the levels of anti-HBs, the protective antibody, was low (57%) in spite of the whole population in all 53 institutions (total 6,022 persons) receiving the recommended dose of hepatitis B (Engerix B, three doses) active immunization two years before the study. Hepatitis B vaccine was introduced routinely in Israel in 1992 to every new born child. Vellinga et al (11) in their recent review presented data from several countries and described anti-HBs as low as 0.1% in non-institutionalized persons with Down syndrome(DS) in United States and as high as 84.2% in persosn with ID in Italy.

This low response to hepatitis B vaccine has also been observed by others (11) with a marked difference between persons with Down syndrome and others with ID. The anti-HBs response after vaccination was 75% for controls, while only 16.6% for persons with DS (16). This phenomenon does not indicate lower protection levels, since both DS and other persons with ID obtain protective levels of antibodies after vaccination (11).

The licensing of active hepatitis A vaccines (1,17) in Israel has raised the question of whom should be the candidates for vaccination. The Israeli Pediatric Society started a nationwide campaign in 1999 urging parents to vaccinate their children and since July 1999 hepatitis A vaccine has be part of the routine vaccination of all children at the age of 18 months in Israel provided by the Ministry of Health.

CONCLUSION

Our pilot study could not support the need for active vaccination against HAV in the present population of persons with intellectual disability in residential care, but rather to vaccine every new person, who enters the institutions from home (a more protected environment with lower prevalence). It will be interesting to follow the trends in hepatitis A prevalence in the future for this population.

Each new person, who enters a residential care center, has already for several years routinely received vaccine against HBV. The study also raised the question, if there is a need for repeated hepatitis B vaccination, because of the low serum response in the population after vaccination (two years prior to our study). Hepatitis C is present in the population of persons with intellectual disability in Israel, but does not seem to differ from the prevalence in the general population.

REFERENCES

1.   Adler R, Shouval D. Hepatitis A prophylaxis. Vaccine or immunoglobulin ? Clin Immunother 1996;6(4):261-72.
2.   Green MS, Block C, Slater PE. Rise in the incidence of viral hepatitis despite improved socioeconomic conditions. Rev Infect Disease 1989;11(3):464-8.
3.   Green MS, Aharonowitz G, Shohat T, Levine R, Anis E, Slater PE. The changing Epidemiology of viral hepatitis A in Israel. Isr Med Assoc J 2001;3(5):347-51.
4.   Gdalevich M, Grotto I, Mandel Y, Mimouni D, Shemer J, Ashkenazi I. Hepatitis A antibody prevalence among young adults in Israel – the decline continues. Epidemiol Infect 1998;121(2):477-9.
5.   Yao BG. Clinical spectrum and natural history of hepatitis A in an epidemic in Shanghai 1988. Int Symposium viral hepatitis liver disease. Houston, TX, Abstract 1990:28, 45.
6.   Arnedo A, Latorre MD, Pac MR, Safont L, Guillen F, Aquinaga I. Hepatitis A, B, and C in an occupational center for the mentally handicapped. Enferm Infecc Microbiol Clin 1998;16(8):370-3 [Spanish]
7.   Lehmann NI, Sharma DL, Gust ID. Prevalence of antibody to the hepatitis A virus in a large institution for the mentally retarded. J Med Virology 1978;2(4):335-9.
8.   Williamson HG, Lehmann NI, Dimitrakakis M, Sharma DL, Gust ID. A longitudinal study of hepatitis infection in an institution for the mentally retarded. Aust NZ JMed 1982;12(1):30-4.
9.   Nikolic P, Nikoloc S, Debeljkovic N, Rakela J, Edwards VM, Mosley JW. A virologically studied epidemic of type A hepatitis in a school for the mentally retarded. Am J Epidemiol 1981;114(2):260-6.
10.   Rakela J, Nugent E, Mosley JW. Viral hepatitis: enzyme assays and serologic procedures in the study of an epidemic. Am J Epidemiol 1977;106(6):493-501.
11.   Vellinga A, Van Damme P, Meheus A. Hepatitis B and C in institutions for individuals with intellectual disability. J Intellect Disabil Res 1999;43:445-53.
12.   Merrick J. Hepatitis C prevalence in persons with mental retardation. Public Health Rev 1998;26:311-6.
13.   Merrick J, Morad M, Ben Porath E. Prevalence of anti-hepatitis A antibodies, hepatitis B viral markers and anti-hepatitis C antibodies among persons with intellectual disability in institutions in Israel. J Intellect Dev Disabil 2002;27(2):85-91.

14. Almog R, Low M, Cohen D, Robin G, Ashkenazi S, Bercovier H, Gdalevich M, Samuels Y, Ashkenazi I, Shemer J, Eldad A, Green MS. Prevalence of anti-hepatitis A antibodies, hepatitis B viral markers and anti-hepatitis C antibodies among immigrants from the former USSR, who arrived in Israel during 1990-1991. Infection 1999;27(3): 212-7.

15. Shemer-Avni Y, el Astal Z, Kemper O, el Najjar KJ, Yaari A, Hanuka N, Margalith M, Sikuler E. Hepatitis C virus infection and genotypes in Southern Israel and the Gaza Strip. J Med Virology 1998;56(3):230-3.

16. Avanzini MA, Monafo V, De Amici M, Maccario R, Burgio GR. Humoral immunodeficiencies in Down syndrome: Serum IgG subclass and antibody response to hepatitis B vaccine. Am J Med Genetics 1990;7(suppl):231-3.

17. Lerman Y, Chodik G, Aloni H, Ribak J, Ashkenazi S. Occupations at increased risk of hepatitis A: A 2-year nationwide historical prospective study. Am J Epidemiol 1999;150(3):312-20.

CHAPTER 16
Helicobacter pylori infection in persons with intellectual disability in residential care

Joav Merrick, Efrat Merrick and Mohammed Morad

Helicobacter pylori (formerly Campylobacter pylori) was identified in 1982 by researchers from Australia as a pathogenic factor in peptic ulcer disease (and in 2005 they received the Nobel Prize in medicine for their discovery). Due to the few studies on Helicobacter pylori infection conducted in the population of persons with intellectual disability it was decided to conduct several prevalence studies in Israel. In one pilot study we looked at the occurrence of Helicobacter pylori infection in persons, who presented with severe dyspeptic symptoms and afterwards to monitor clinically the effect of treatment. In another center we looked at the total prevalence of all residents. From these studies we conclude that persons with developmental disability, intellectual disability or mental retardation in residential have a high incidence of Helicobacter pylori infection.

INTRODUCTION

Peptic ulcer disease, defined as a chronic inflammation of the stomach and duodenum was thought of as a disorder associated with stress and dietary factors, which resulted in bed rest treatment and special diets. Later the concept of gastric acid secretions was introduced and antacids became a standard therapy. In 1971, Sir James Black identified a subtype of the histamine receptor (H2 receptor) that appeared to be the principal mediator of gastric acid secretion and antagonists of this receptor were introduced (1).

Inhibitors of the proton pump in the gastric parietal cells, bismuth compounds and prostaglandins have also been developed as anti-ulcer drugs, but the problem is still a high recurrence rate of peptic ulcers, even after complete healing of the ulcer (1).

In 1982 another important pathogenic factor in peptic ulcer disease was identified, when J Robin Warren and Barry J Marshall (2) from Royal Perth Hospital in Australia discovered a spiral gram-negative, flagellate and microaerophilic bacteria in the narrow interface between the gastic epithelial cell surface and the overlying mucus gel in biopsies from patients with active chronic gastritis, duodenal ulcer or gastric ulcer. For a long period of time the medical establishment was sceptic about this discovery, but over time verified, accepted and in 2005 they received the Nobel Prize in Medicine for their work. This bacteria was named Campylobacter pylori, but in 1989 renamed Helicobacter pylori (3).

Helicobacter pylori (HP) causes gastritis and ulcer and it is thought to be associated with the development of gastric atrophy, intestinal metaplasia and carcinoma (1,4), but the mechanism is not fully understood and the long-term effect of medical eradication not yet proven. One study (5) has shown that Helicobacter pylori has N-acetyltransferase activity and the researchers speculated that the bioactivation of food borne heterocyclic aromatic amines into genotoxic and carcinogenic products in the stomach can be a promoter in the pathogenesis of gastric cancer.

In order to investigate the occurrence of Helicobacter pylori in the population of persons with intellectual disability (ID) we conducted two studies from different points of entry. One study (6) in order to determine the occurrence of Helicobacter pylori infection in persons with intellectual disability (ID) in residential care, who presented with severe dyspeptic symptoms and then to monitor clinically the effect of treatment, if Helicobacter pylori was found. The other study (7) in order to determine the total prevalence in another residential care center.

STUDY ON SEVERE DYSPEPTIC PRESENTING SYMPTOMS

This pilot study (6) was initiated in January 1999 and it was decided to investigate every person for Helicobacter pylori, who was presented to the medical clinic of the center (a government residential care center located in the central part of Israel) with severe dyspeptic symptoms. This method was used, instead of an examination of all residents, due to economic restrains by the Sick Fund (HMO) Laboratory on examinations. Each person was examined clinically by the physician of the center, decisions made on further investigations or referrals and a blood specimen drawn for IgG antibodies to Helicobacter pylori (examined at the Sick Fund Laboratory by ELISA, Pharmatop Millenia). In the case of positive serology for Helicobactor pylori (IgG antibody level over 40 International Units) treatment was initiated, either as amoxicillin trihydrate 1,000 mg twice daily, metronidazole 1,000 mg twice daily and pantoprazole 40 mg twice daily (type 1) or omeprazole 20 mg twice daily (type 2) for one week. Medication in the center is given individually to each patient and the patient observed by the nurse, while the medicine fully swallowed.

If symptoms persisted, omeprazole was continued for one month. Each patient was followed by the clinic for symptoms after the end of treatment and some patients followed by the gastroenterologist at the local specialist clinic.

The center studied had 224 adult persons (63 females and 161 males), 100 persons between the age of 19-45 years, 100 persons between 46-60 years and 24 persons above 61 years. 70 persons with mild and 154 with moderate mental retardation. From January 1999 to May 2001 a total of 43 persons presented with severe dyspeptic symptoms and 42 persons (98%) were found to have Helicobacter pylori infection. Of these 42 persons (26 males, 16 females) the age range was (29-64 years) with a mean of 45 years and the mean years of institutionalization was 20 years (range 6-39 years). 13 had mild and 29 moderate mental retardation. In the 21-30 year age agroup 100% were postive for HP. In the 31-50 year age group 97% were positive and in the over 51 years 100% positive. In the persons with mild mental retardation 93% were positive and 100% in the group with moderate mental retardation.

Thirty two patients were treated with type 1 treatment, ten with type 2 and six patients were also treated with omeprazole for an extra month due to persistent symptoms. At follow-up clinically all patients had improvement and only six patients had still minor complains. Only eight were re-tested for IgG antibody level after treatment, six with over 50% reduction in HP antibody titre and two without change, but with less clinical symptoms. A screening of all 42 persons after treatment was not possible due to restrictions by the Sick Fund (HMO) laboratory.

OUR PREVALENCE STUDY

This study (7) was performed at a center in the south of Israel run by a non-for-profit organization and arranged like a kibbutz with seven housing units. Each house is one family, mother, father and their own children and living with them seven persons with ID, who shares living quarters, kitchen and dining room. During the day the family members, other staff , volunteers and the people with ID work together in the fields, a bread factory, olive oil press, wax candle factory and weaving factory. Informed consent was received from the families of the person with ID. As part of the yearly routine medical examination of the residents a blood sample for IgG antibodies to HP was collected and examined at the local Sick Fund Laboratory (by ELISA, Pharmatop Mellenia).

The residential center studied had 47 adults (22 females and 25 males), one person aged 0-20 years, ten aged 21-30 years, 32 aged 31-50 years and four above 51 years. 11 had mild, 26 moderate and 10 severe mental retardation. Of the 47 persons screened, 36 (75%) were sero-positive for Helicobacter pylori with a range of 57-86% for the seven houses. One was positive in the 0-20 year age group (100% of that group), seven (70%) in the 21-30 years, 25 (78%) in the 31-50 years and three (75%) in the 51 years and above group. Eight (73%) were positive in the group with mild, 23 (89%) in the moderate and five (50%) in the group with severe mental retardation. Twenty males (80%) and 15 females (68%) were positive. Only two of the 36 positive displayed symptoms from the gastro-intestinal tract. Both were treated with eradication (triple) treatment without change in their symptoms. One was later found to have gallbladder stones and the other with chronic diarrhea had still unchanged positive HP titer after six months.

DISCUSSION

Twenty five years ago nobody had ever heard about Helicobacter pylori and after an initially rejection by a skeptical scientific community it has now been recognized as a major public health problem and one of the world's most common pathogens with a colonization of about 60% of the general population (8,9). The mode of transmission of this pathogen is still not known, but the prevalence increases with age, disadvantaged socioeconomic conditions and poor living standards although most individuals never develop clinical disease.

A review (10) of the prevalence of Helicobacter pylori in asymptomatic populations from Algeria, Israel, Saudi Arabia and Turkey revealed a prevalence is similar to findings from developing countries with a high level of infection in childhood (40-70%) and an age increase reaching 85-90%. Israel had a low prevalence among children (10%), but a rapid increase in the second decade of life to 39% and reaching 79% in persons over 60 years of age. An interesting finding was the higher prevalence rate in communal settlements (72%) compared to persons in urban dwellings (65%) (10,11). The prevalence of Helicobacter pylori in patients with gastrointestinal symptoms and endoscopy performed was also reported from Egypt, Iran, Israel, Oman, Saudi Arabia, the United Arab Emirates and Yemen (10). Patients suffering from gastritis and peptic ulcer disease showed similar rates of infection as reported from Europe, the United States and Africa, namely 71-92 %. Our studies revealed a high rate of 98% in the group of symptomatic patients (6) and 75% in the prevalence study (7).

Another study from Israel (12) investigated the prevalence of Helicobacter pylori in elderly nursing patients (aged 70 years or more) admitted to a medical center and found that the length of stay in the nursing home had a strong correlation. Patients with a short stay had a 63% prevalence, whereas patients more that 15 months in the nursing home had an 84 % prevalence. The patients in our study had a mean institutionalized stay of 20 years, but since we were unable to test all individuals, such a comparison could not be made in our case.

Studies of Helicobacter pylori infection in the population of persons with mental retardation, developmental disability or intellectual disability have not been performed before in Israel, but a few case stories and a few larger scale studies performed around the world.

Lubani et al (13) from Kuwait described two siblings with developmental disability, cystic fibrosis and Helicobacter gastritis, Mauk (14) from Philadelphia described a 6 year old boy with severe mental retardation, rumination and several other behavioral disorders. Helicobacter infection was found on examination, treated and clinical improvement found as decreased frequency of rumination and gain of weight. Researchers from Italy (15) described a 14 year old patient with microcephaly, ptosis, micrognathia, tetralogy of Fallot, mental retardation, Helicobacter infection and deletion of chromosome 18, who developed gastric carcinoma.

In a study from Delaware (16) five children with profound neurologic impairment undergoing evaluation for gastrointestinal symptoms and subsequently in seven out of 61 children (prevalence of 11%) evaluated for Helicobacter pylori infection was identified as the cause of antral gastritis.

A study in 1995 from United Kingdom (17) analyzed stored sera from 424 hospital residents with severe learning disabilities and compared with 267 age and sex matched controls from the local non-residential population. The hospital residents under 40 years of age had a 87% prevalence of Helicobacter pylori compared with 24 % for controls, whereas the overall prevalence for all ages was 87% for residents and 43% for controls.

Another larger study (338 intellectually disabled and 254 controls) from Holland (18) found a prevalence of 5% in children and 50% in the elderly in the general population, whereas 83% of the disabled and 27% of the healthy employees were infected. The presence of Helicobacter was significantly associated with male gender, longer duration of institutionalization, an IQ below 50, rumination and a history of upper abdominal symptoms. For the employees the association was a higher level of physical contact with the disabled, longer duration of employment and upper abdominal symptoms.

The mode of transmission of HP infection is not clear. The bacteria can be cultured from feces, so fecal spread is one mode, but oral spread is also a possibility. A recent study from Switzerland among 92 gastroenterologists and 168 healthy controls revealed that gastroenterologist have a higher risk of aquiring HP and would suggest oral infection via microscopic droplets of gastric juice produced by manipulating endoscopic instruments (19). The studies of HP infection in the population of persons with intellectual disability in residential care or elderly people living in nusing homes (20) is another opportunity to consider the mode of transmission. These two populations are known to live in a confined space, to take objects in the mouth and share food, to inflict injuries to self or others, to dribble or spit, to scratch and bite, to self-mutilate and to have unhygienic toilet habits, so therefore several modes of transmission could be suggested. The study from Holland (18) suggested a high incidence in this population and also trasmission to care staff.

The rate of treatment success in our study (83%) was higher than the Delaware study (16), where only 50% of the patients had complete resolution of symptoms after treatment. The longterm treatment success should be studied in order to also see the effect on the development of gastrrointestinal cancer.

CONCLUSIONS

It seems from several studies (17,18) that persons with mental retardation, developmental disability, or intellectual disability in residential care are at a higher risk for Helicobacter pylori infection, especially after some years in the institution. A study from Holland (18) also showed that staff exposed over time are prone to infection. On the basis of these studies and our study we recommend investigations for Helicobacter pylori in this population (by serology and not urea breath test, since that method is difficult in our population), when the patient develop decreased appetite, nausea, epigastric abdominal pain or dyspepsia and in case of positive serology anti-Helicobacter triple drug treatment of one week duration should be implemented.

REFERENCES

1.   NIH Consensus Statement. Helicobacter Pylori in peptic ulcer disease. Bethesda, MD: National Institutes of Health, 1994; 12(1):1-23.
2.   Warren JR, Marshall BJ. Unidentified curved bacilli on gastric epithelium in active chronic gastrititis. Lancet 1983;1:1273-5.
3.   Goodwin CS, Armstong JA, Chilvers T et al. Transfer of Campylobacter pylori and Campylobacter mustelae to Helicobacter gen. nov as Helicobacter pylori comb. nov. and Helicobacter mustalae comb. nov., respectively. Int J Syst Bacreriol 1989;39:397-405.
4.   Forbes GM, Warren JR, Glaser ME et al. Long-term follow-up of gastric histology after helicobacter pylori eradication. J Gastroenterol Hepatol 1996;11(7):670-3.
5.   Hung CF, Chung JG, Liu SI, Hung H. Arylamine -acetyltransferase: A possible promoter in Helicobacter pylori-related gastric carcinogenesis. Chung Hua I Hsueh Tsa Chih (Taipei) 1999;62(4): 203-8. [English abstract]
6.   Merrick J, Aspler S, Dubman I. Helicobacter pylori infection in persons with intellectual disability in residential care in Israel.ScientificWorldJournal 2002;1:264-8.
7.   Morad M, Merrick J, Nasri Y. Prevalence of Helicobacter in persons with intellectual disability in residential care. J Intellect Disabil Res 2002;46(2):141-3.
8.   Cave DR. How is Helicobacter pylori transmitted ? Gastroenterol 1997;113(6Suppl):S9-14.
9.   Cilley RE, Brighton VK. The significance of Helicobacter pylori colonization of the stomach. Semin Pediatrc Surg 1995;4(4):221-7.
10.   Novis BH, Gabay G, Naftali T. Helicobacter pylori: The Middle East scenario. Yale J Biol Med 1998;71(2):135-41.
11.   Gilboa S, Gabay G, Zamir D, Zeev A, Novis B. Helicobacter pyloriinfection in rural settlements (Kibbutzim) in Israel. Int J Epidemiol 1995;24(1):232-7.
12.   Regev A, Fraser GM, Braun M, Maoz E, Leibovici L, Niv Y. Seroprevalence of Helicobacter pylori and length of stay in a nursing home. Helicobacter 1999;4(2):89-93.
13.   Lubani MM, al-Saleh QA, Teebi AS, Moosa A, Kalaoui MH. Cystic fibrosis and Helicobacter pylori gastritis, megaloblastic anaemia, subnormal mentality and minor anomalies in two siblings: A new syndrome ? Eur J Pediatr 1991;150(4):253-5.

14.   Mauk JE. Helicobacter pylori infection in neurologically impaired children. J Pediatric 1995;126(5Pt1):849.

15.   Dellavecchia C, Guala A, Olivieri C et al. Early onset of gastric carcinoma and constitutional deletion of 18p. Cancer Genet Cytogenet 1999:113(1):96-9.

16.   Projansky R, Shaffer SE, Vinton NE, Bachrach SJ. Symptomatic Helicobacter pylori infection in young patients with severe neurologic impairment. J Pediatr 1994;125 (5Pt1):750-2.

17.   Harris AW, Douds A, Meurisse EV, Dennis M, Chambers S, Gould SR. Seroprevalence of Helicobacter pylori in residents of a hospital for people with severe learning difficulties. Eur J Gastroenterol Hepatol 1995;7(1):21-3.

18.   Bohmer CJ, Klinkenberg-Knol EC, Kuipers EJ et al. The prevalence of Helicobacter infection among inhabitants and healthy employees of institutes for the intellectually disabled.Am J Gastroenterol 1997;92(6):1000-4.

19.   Hildebrand P, Meyer-Wyss BM, Mossi S, Beglinger C. Risk among gastroenterologists of aquiring Helicobacter pylori infection: Case-control study. BMJ 2000;321:149.

20.   Pilotto A, Mario F, Franceschi M. Treatment of Helicobacter pylori infection in elderly subjects. Age Aging 2000;29:103-9.

CHAPTER 17
Life long diet for persons with phenylketonuria

Joav Merrick, Shoshana Aspler and Gerard Schwarz

Life long treatment with phenylalanine restricted diet to persons with phenylketonuria is in our opinion the policy that should govern national guidelines. We present a case of an older person with moderate intellectual disability, severe challenging behaviour, self-injurious behaviour, sleeping disorder, hyperactivity and masturbation, who in the last year before reassessment displayed loss of weight, muscle weakness resulting in wheelchair placement, upper respiratory infections and fungal skin infections. After reassessment the patient was started on phenylalanine restricted diet supplemented with vitamin B12, iron and folic acid. At follow-up one year later the patient had gained his weight back, walked around freely, the challenging behaviour, self-injurious behaviour and masturbation had stopped and he participated in social activities, which he had not been able to participate in before. At follow-up four years later he still remained at this level of accomplishment. All in all the quality of life for this patient had increased. We therefore recommend a policy of life long treatment with phenylalanine restricted diet and also for treatment of adults with previously untreated phenylketonuria.

INTRODUCTION

Phenylketonuria (PKU) was discovered in 1934, when a Norwegian mother brought her intellectually disabled son and daughter to professor Asbjorn Folling at the University of Oslo School of Medicine for a consultation (1). In 1947, Jervis (2) showed that the administration of phenylalanine to normal humans led to a promt rise in blood tyrosine, whereas no increase in blood tyrosine could be detected in patients with PKU, indicating both the normal pathway of phenylalanine metabolism and the metabolic error in PKU. Several years later this inborn error of the amino acid metabolism, caused by the deficiency of the liver enzyme phenylalanine hydroxylase (PAH), changed to become a preventable form of intellectual disability, when Bickel et al (3) published the results of dietary treatment. The work of Jervis (2) and Bickel et al (3) was the incentive that led to the large field of investigations into the inborn errors of metabolism that became the basis for the understanding of a range of causes of mental retardation, developmental disability or intellectual disability, the possibility for treatment and prevention.

Several further studies stressed the importance of diet for these patients and a drive started in order to develop a diagnostic method to measure phenylalanine in the blood. Guthrie (4) developed a bacterial "inhibition assay" that facilitated a sensitive, specific, inexpensive and fast method for the determination of blood phenylalanine in large number of samples.

From 1964-73 (1) different types of PKU were found and worldwide neonatal screening started resulting in early treatment and prevention of intellectual disability. Whereas everyone can agree that treatment with phenylalanine (PHE) restricted diet must start as soon as possible (first two weeks of life), there is no agreement on when to stop or even to continue a "diet for life".

In Israel neonatal screening started in 1963 and the incidence of PKU today 14.0 per 100,000 live births. The National PKU register at Chaim Sheba Medical Center in Tel Hashomer has several hundred cases registered and 150 persons are followed regularly at that clinic.

The Division for Mental Retardation, Ministry of Social Affairs provides residential care service to about 7,000 persons in close to 60 centers (government, private and public, sized from 50-400 persons) and our recent survey in these centers showed 18 known persons with PKU (5). In   this chapter we would like to present a case of a person with previously untreated PKU, where PHE-restricted diet was initiated in late adulthood.

CASE REPORT

Born in 1938 in Marokko, this male arrived in Israel in adolescence and was placed in a residential care center with 224 adult persons (63 females and 161 males). He has moderate mental retardation, no history of convulsive disorder, but in the last 30 years displayed severe challenging behaviour, self-injurious behaviour, sleeping disorder, hyperactivity and masturbation. Medically he was operated for an ingvinal hernia and developed a peptic ulcer. Shortly after arriving to Israel he was tested and diagnosed as PKU, but never received treatment.

In the year, before his reassessment (August 1998), he started to display general malaise with a weight loss of 10 kilograms, muscle weakness resulting in severe falls requiring three emergency room visits for stitching and one hospitalization for brain concussion, upper respiratory infections and fungal skin infections. His blood screening showed vitamin B 12 at 236 pg/ml (normal range 180-914), iron 48 microgram/dl (59-158) and folic acid 3.93 ngr/ml (3-17).

At the reassessment examination it was decided to refer to the National PKU Clinic for retesting and the phenylalanine level was found to be 20,9 mg/dl. After intense debate it was decided to start a PHE-restricted diet, which was started in September 1998. Together with the diet he was started on multivitamin, B 12 and iron treatment for three months.

After three months the person had gained back the ten kilograms, walked around freely, the challenging behaviour, self-injurious behaviour and masturbation had stopped, his mental health better participating in music lessons, trips and drawing activities, his B 12, iron and folic acid levels increased to the upper normal range and he did not experience upper respiratory or skin infections in spite of a cold winter. His phenylalanine level in June 1999 was 20,0 mg/dl. At last follow-up in August 2002 he had still kept his initial gains and his quality of lige much better. In September 2003 he died due to a bleeding ulcer.

DISCUSSION

The policy for treatment in many countries has been to keep children, found to have phenylketonuria at neonatal screening, on a PHE-restricted diet until their PHE level is no longer likely to affect brain development. Several studies have found a deterioration in intellect once the diet is discontinued (6,7,8) and some centers around the world are recommending a "diet for life" (9).

Koch et al (8) from Children's Hospital in Los Angeles followed a group of 43 persons, identified by neonatal screening, at an average age of 22 years. Nineteen had remained on dietary treatment (group 1) after being diagnosed at a mean age of 2.6 weeks and 24 had discontinued the diet at an average age of 7.8 years (group 2). The individuals in group 1 turned out substantially better on social and academic achievements. Their mean IQ was 104 (WAIS-R, range 74-123), 78 % attended collage, two were married (one had a child), none were on Social Security, general relief and none had been arrested. In group 2, the mean IQ was 92 (range 69-116), 28 % attended college, 15 were employed, five on welfare, one mentally ill, sex married and five in relationships (they had a total of nine children). a third group of 19 individuals from that center was diagnosed at an average age of 2.7 years and at follow-up their mean IQ was 83 (range 55-108), 10 % attended college, one married and three in relationships (total of ten children), five on welfare and one arrested for pedophilia. These findings, with the limitations of the small number studied, seem to support the conclusion to continue diet into adulthood.

Positive effects have also been reported in late diagnosed individuals with PKU (10,11) resulting in marked progress in mental capacity. Providing a PHE-restricted diet, even to these cases, can benefit the individual, but also society, because the diet prevents the need for residential care or make residential care less burdensome for the caretakers.

Very few reports (12,13) deals with the PHE-restricted diet treatment of patients with PKU born before the introduction of neonatal screening and neonatal institution of the diet, in spite of an increased life expectancy of people with untreated phenylketonuria (14) and the economical benefits to society (15).

Our older patient with untreated phenylketonuria had a marked increase in his quality of life, the ability to participate in social activities he otherwise had not been able to perform, behaviour and motor skills, even when PHE-restricted diet was started at age 60 years. It can be argued that the change in his condition could be due to the multivitamin, B 12 and folate treatment, but his pre-treatment values were within the normal range, albeit in the lower end of the normal range. We believe that the diet made the difference, even though the phenylalanine level only decreased from 20.9 to 20.0 mg/dl after treatment was initiated. We do not believe in treating according to the blood level only, but instead according to the clinical improvement in the patient.

Our findings are in accordance with a recently published study (16) from England presenting five case stories of PHE-restricted diet in previously untreated adults. Four out of five had considerable benefits in concentration, alertless, mood, irritability and adaptive behavior.

We have reviewed our policy in Israel for this population and are now recommending diet for life, because we believe that this treatment will increase the quality of live even for previously untreated individuals.

REFERENCES

1.   Guttler F. Phenylketonuria: 50 years since Folling's discovery and still expanding our clinical and biochemical knowledge. Acta Paediatr Scand1984;73:705-16.
2.   Jervis GA. Studies on phenylpyruvic oligophrenia. The position of the metabolic error. J Biol Chemistry 1947;169:651-6.
3.   Bickel H, Gerrard J, Hickmans EM. The influence of phenylalanine intake on the chemestry and behavior of a phenylketonuria child. Acta Paediatr Scand 1954;43:64-77.
4.   Guthrie R, Susi A. A simple phenylalanine method for detecting phenylketonuria in large populations of newborn infants. Pediatrics 1963;32:338-43.
5.   Merrick J. Survey of medical clinics in residential care centers, 2005. Jerusalem: Office of the Medical Director, Division for Mental Retardation, 2006.
6.   Potocnik U, Widhalm K. Long-term follow-up of children with classical phenylketonuria after diet discontinuation: A review. J Am Coll Nutrition 1994;13(3):232-6.
7.   Levy HL, Waisbren SE. PKU in adolescents: Rationale and psychosocial factors in diet continuation. Acta Paediatr Scand 1994;Suppl 407:92-7.
8.   Koch R, Azen C, Friedman EG, Fishler K, Baumann-Frischling C, Lin T. Care of the adult with phenulketonuria. Eur J Pediatrics 1996;155 suppl:S90-2.
9.   British Guidelines. Medical Research Council Working Party on phenylketonuria. Arch Dis Childhood 1993;68:426-7.
10.   Holmgren G, Blomquist HK, Samuelson G. Positive effect of a late introduced modifies diet in a 8-year old PKU child. Neuropadiatrie 1980;11(1):76-9.

11. Koch R, Moseley K, Ning J, Romstad A, Guldberg P, Guttler F. Long-term beneficial effects of the phenylalanine-restricted diet in late-diagnosed individuals with phenylketonutia. Mol Genet Metab 1999;67(2):148-55.

12. Harper M, Reid AH. Use of a restricted protein diet in the treatment of behaviour disorder in a severely mentally retarded adult female phenylketonuric patient. J Ment Defic Res 1987;31(Pt 2):209-12.

13. Williams K. Benefits of normalizing plasma phenylalanine: Impact on behaviour and health. A case report. J Inh Metab Disease 1998;21:785-90.

14. Jancar J. Increased life expectancy in people with untreated phenylketonuria. J Intellect Disabil Res 1998;42(1):97-9.

15. Brown MCJ, Guest JF. Economic impact of feeding a phenylalanine-restricted diet to adults with previously untreated phenylketonuria. J Intellect Disabil Res 1999;43(1):30-7.

16. Fitzgerald B, Morgan J, Keene N, Rollinson R, Hodgson A, Dalrymple-Smith, J. An investigation into diet treatment for adults with previously untreated phenylketonuria and severe intellectual disability. J Intellect Disabil Res 2000;44(1):53-9.

PART SIX:

LOSS AND END OF LIFE ISSUES

CHAPTER 18
Coping wih loss for persons with intellectual disability

Shlomo Kessel and Joav Merrick

Increase in life expectancy of persons with intellectual disability has brought with it the challenges of aging, including the need to cope with the reality of increasing morbidity and mortality. People with intellectual disabilities may experience age-related losses as major stressors, producing changes in the way they think, feel or act. It is therefore important to develop methods and tools to help individuals with intellectual disabilities prepare for and adjust to their losses. In recent years we have observed that several individuals with intellectual disability displayed psychological symptoms resulting from loss of physical abilities as a consequence of the aging process or morbidity and it was decided to initiate a group intervention program to support these individuals. We observed a positive change of attitudes, improvement of self-esteem and less extreme behavioral reactions in the period after the intervention. We saw many positive advantages and would therefore recommend further studies of group intervention programs in this population.

INTRODUCTION

Increase in life expectancy of persons with intellectual disability (ID) has brought with it the challenges of aging, including the need to cope with the reality of increasing morbidity and mortality. Facing and coping with major life changes and their accompanying losses is a common experience in the lives of older adults (1). For many people, with or without disabilities, approaching or experiencing the transitions of aging may invoke a psychological crisis and produce stress or confusion, while for others, it may be a time of growth and psychological development (2).

Much of the research in the field of ID has been with children and the results sometimes generalized to all ages, which in our opinion has led to little being done to create methods for the provision of adequate physical, psychological preparation and support for these individuals in midlife (3). Originally the emphasis was on what people could not do rather than to identify areas of competence (4).

The gradual diminishment of physical and sometimes mental capabilities constitutes a significant loss experienced by older adults (1). Reactions to such changes are affected by personality and life experiences. People with ID are likely to be just as troubled by the deterioration of their physical and mental abilities as older adults without disabilities, and they may experience similar threats to their identity and self-esteem (1). Family, caregivers, service providers and even professionals may fail to recognize or to acknowledge the appearance of the typical signs of loss, such as feelings of sadness, hopelessness or atypical rebellious behavior (5). Emotional problems and signs of emotional stress are attributed to the underlying intellectual disability, causing a form of diagnostic overshadowing. However, it should be realized that, similar to all aging individuals, this population has mental health and psychological needs, resulting from normal life crises and transitions, and are in need of support (6).

It is also important to emphasize that unlike individuals without disabilities, people with ID often lack the natural support sources that are readily available to other aging persons, such as family members, and in particular a spouse or children.

Group counseling is not widely employed in Israel for individuals with ID, but others have found it an extremely appropriate and effective technique in this population (7). In a group setting over time people have the opportunity to address issues of concern. Feelings, attitudes, common problems and experiences can be discussed and support offered by peers and professionals. Role playing and situational analysis may be used in the group to model and develop skills needed by members. It was felt that greater attention should be given to the group process. To begin with, using group counseling for people with ID makes good clinical and economic sense. More people can be served in group counseling than an individual setting. Specific topics may target selected groups for particular problems. In this way people with similar issues may gain support in ways not possible in individual counseling (7).

In one residential care center for people with ID in Israel the professional staff providing services to the residents realized that certain individuals were displaying signs of loss of physical abilities as the result of aging processes. In particular, older adults were experiencing sensory deterioration and a substantial decline in their mobility skills. When a number of these individuals began to demonstrate behavioral symptoms similar to those characteristic of bereavement and mourning (aggression, clinical depression, hyperactivity, detachment, etc.), it was decided to initiate a group intervention program in order to support our residents. This chapter will describe the intervention that took place (8).

OUR PROJECT

The Neve Natoa Residential Center in central Israel is home to 166 older adults with ID. The average age of the residents is 49 years and many of them have been living at Neve Natoa for more than three decades. The initial group chosen consisted of nine older adults (five males and four females), aged 39-56 years (mean age 49) (8). The participants were diagnosed as having moderate intellectual disabilities (subjects IQ's ranged from 48-70 + 5). Intelligence Quotients were determined using the Stanford-Binet Scale. All were in need of support in performing day-to-day living functions, as a result of their intellectual disabilities, a need that has been compounded and increased substantially because of their emerging physical disabilities. For example, Golda, one of the female participants (46 years old), who in the past was mobile and independent experienced a serious fall and became a quadriplegic, and as a result has become totally dependent on the support and assistance of staff members and peers. Tammy, another female group member, who works in the center's laundry, has been experiencing a significant deterioration of her sight and as a result has been finding it more and more difficult to perform her work and task of daily living. In the pregroup interview Tammy expressed her extreme frustration at not being able perform functions that were previously easy for her.

Two of the female subjects had Down's syndrome (trisomy 21). All of the participants displayed moderate mental retardation functional levels. Five of the participants (two women and three men) displayed severe difficulties in their mobility skills, two participants (one man and one woman) had seriously deteriorating sight and one man displayed disorientation and lack of stamina, manifested in the form of restlessness, exhaustion and reduced productivity at work. The remaining female showed signs of dementia and worsening cognitive detachment. As she has Down syndrome the possibility of Alzheimer disease is being examined. Indeed, her condition did not allow for her to complete the program and she left the group after three sessions.

As the program was based on verbal discussion, it was decided to include in the pilot project (8) only individuals that had fairly well developed verbal communication skills and ability to express themselves in this manner.

It was decided that the program would consist of 10 sessions, each dealing with a different issue relevant to the group participants. The topics were decided in advance, however the preferences and concerns of the group members were taken into account and adapted into the general framework. The group co-leaders endeavored to take advantage of the life experiences of the group members during the therapeutic process. Amongst the topics and issues that were dealt with in this program were:

1. Body perception and understanding physical disabilities, how they happen and what their implications are. Group members were asked to describe their parents or other older adults familiar to them and how their aging was expressed (fatigue, walking stick, white hair). The participants were encouraged to discuss the life process changes that their parents have undergone and how it has affected them. The facilitator should endeavor to show how aging is a natural phenomenon, part of normative development and in this way allay some of the fears felt by the participants.

2.   Should a person be ashamed of his disabilities? Group members
        were asked to describe their bodies - their positive features, as well
        as their disabilities. Some of the participants related how they felt
        when referred to by derogatory terms (retard, crippled) and the
        group discussed ways of responding. Others showed a great deal of
        insight and spoke of a need to accept oneself "as I am".

3.   Am I defenseless? Individuals spoke of their vulnerability and their
        dependency on external protection. The group then discussed ways
        to support each other and what the center's staff could do to assist
        them in maintaining their autonomy. People were encouraged to
        describe which daily tasks they were still able to perform without
        assistance.

4.   Mourning and bereavement. During the course of the group process
        the participants, also introduced the issue of the loss of parents and
        other loved ones. Many of the participants' parents had died or were
        very old and unable to maintain regular contact.

Pre- and post standard evaluation of the participants was not used in this
pilot study (8), but review of their charts before and after the intervention
together with an evaluation discussion between the professionals was
performed. In addition, all participants were interviewed by the facilitators,
prior to the commencement of the program. The residents expressed their
oral informed consent to participate.

EXPERIENCE FROM THE PROJECT

Of the nine participants, seven completed the whole process. One female
was excluded due to increased dementia. Another female expressed a lack of
interest and decided to withdraw after a couple of meetings. All remaining
group members participated enthusiastically and actively, taking part in all
the sessions. The primary value of this intervention was a change of attitude
and improvement of the self-image by participants. Many were no longer
ashamed of their physical disabilities and able to freely discuss their need for
assistance and support. A definite sense of reciprocity was created in the
group setting, where members allowed others to discuss difficult issues and
even direct criticism towards them.

         No formal research process was initiated before the start of this pilot
group, and therefore it is difficult to determine the immediate effects of this
intervention. Participants clearly expressed their anxieties in the early stages
of the program. Many asked, "What has happened to me?" and were
concerned with "How will I manage now?" Others were concerned with "
Am I dying?" and "What do my friends and family think of me?"

         As the group progressed it was possible to discern a pronounced
improvement in the state of mind of a number of the group members. In
particular, some of the participants seemed less dejected than they had done
prior to the program, their behavior was more temperate and their reactions
less extreme. The verbalizations of the participants during the course of the
meetings   mirrored   these   phenomena   and   illustrated   the   progress

experienced by many of the group members during the course of the meetings. In the early stages of the process participants voiced their anxieties and spoke of their difficulties, whilst later on the discussions became more solution-focused and supportive.

It is possible to identify these changes when examining and comparing the central themes of statements made by the participants before and after the group intervention process. In the initial intake interviews participants spoke of past capabilities and skills. Many expressed feelings of frustration and anger stemming from these emerging disabilities and the resulting changes in their lives. A significant number of interviewees spoke of the lack of acceptance and responsiveness to their changes and increased needs by the environment in general, and family and staff members, in particular. When asked of their greatest difficulty, the participants responded that they felt abandoned by their families, since many of could no longer be taken to the family home, due to their increasing physical disabilities.

In comparison, during the final meetings of the group it was clear that many participants had undergone a significant change in their outlook. They could now not only speak freely of their physical limitations and their need for assistance, but also were now also aware that certain functions and capabilities remained intact. With the support of the other group members, participants realized new way in which they could assist themselves and maintain their dignity and independence. For example, one group member suggested that a glass of water be placed at his bedside every evening so that when he is thirsty in the middle of the night he would no longer have to wake up his roommate, a situation that had created anger between them. Another participant, a man that had become completely blind, was finally able to accept the need to be accompanied by a friend so as to facilitate mobility around the campus. As a result this group member discuss how he was not able to get to and participate in many additional activities in the center.

Although, the pre-group interviews and content of the sessions were not methodically recorded, this anecdotal evidence may serve the basis for qualitative research in future.

DISCUSSION

The definition of "old age " in people with intellectual disability continues to be debated. Most gerontologists define aging in terms the person's years, whilst other use functionally based definitions of old age, relating to an evaluation of the person's capabilities and skills and the gradual or sudden changes therein over the years. This second approach does not see the chronological factor as the exclusive element when determining the individual's status as "old aged" (9). Many individuals with ID have developed coping skills through previous life experiences and many have come to terms with the nature of their disabilities. However, with advancing age, disabilities may have compounded or worsened, and as a result their coping mechanisms may have diminished. Age related physical, mental and emotional changes might result in the deterioration of a person's hard-won skills. There is also evidence to suggest that some people with ID, especially persons with Down syndrome, are subject to earlier aging than their peers (10). An individual, who functions independently and successfully in a residential environment, may undergo a serious crisis, if for example he suddenly begins to suffer from arthritis resulting in limited mobility. The individual may become distressed, even depressed, and the caregiver may have difficulty in assisting the individual in maintaining the quality of life through supportive services or with assistive technology. Other individuals, especially those institutionalized, are characterized by a "learned helplessness", as they have not been encouraged to function independently. These people may feel extreme distress as a result of their growing deterioration and may develop behavioral changes. Transient depressive states are common in grieving adults, but these behaviors in individuals with developmental disabilities are too often overlooked or attributed to other factors, such as noncompliance (11).

In our experience here in Israel, counseling as one of the primary tools used in providing professional support may often be overlooked by professionals in the field of ID. The reasons for this are varied and range from a lack of basic recognition that emotional problems exist in this population, to difficulties resulting from communication disabilities and diagnostic overshadowing. Part of the problem is derived from the stereotypical image of persons with intellectual disabilities as "sweet and happy" (4). Language problems may discourage intervention and may lead to communication through aggression and angry outbursts. It is therefore important to select an intervention strategy that is suitable for the population requiring service, without waiting for the person to display challenging or destructive behavior (12). Older adults with ID grieve developmental losses in the same way as everyone else. Grief counseling and anticipatory grieving activities also have been recommended to help individuals prepare for and adjust to their losses (13).

People with ID can experience age-related losses as major stressors, producing changes in the way they think, feel or act. Depression, a common human response to stress associated with loss, is typically expressed by feelings of sadness, hopelessness and withdrawal behaviors, but may also be manifested as acting out behaviors that express anger and denial, reactions commonly seen in people with ID (14). Different intervention strategies are used in the support of aging persons with ID, who are undergoing a process of losing physical skills and abilities. Therapists may choose to treat clients using psychoanalysis or non-directive counseling. They may adopt a behavioral approach; the most widely used technique for individuals with ID, or attempt to improve the client's functioning through the use of pharmacological methods.

The common ground of sharing feelings and grief helps the participants cope with their experiences and emotions. After a group experience for people with ID in a group home who had suffered the loss of a loved one, the staff reported that they felt the group process helped the clients deal with the issues of loss and grief in appropriate ways. The group program provided the group members with a positive and protected laboratory in which to learn and experiment with their social skills and attitudes towards loss, as a result of death and dying (15).

Working with adults with ID in a group setting, requires a treatment model, which is both flexible and diversified. Enhancement of each individual's potential through the group process suggest that methodology be adaptable to individual learning pace and interest, while at the same time remaining congruent with overall group work process (16).

Records of the group sessions in our study (8) showed that the group participants, older individuals with significant intellectual disabilities were indeed troubled by the physical and psychological changes in mind and body they were undergoing. Most of the participating residents demonstrated the understanding that these changes have and will have a considerable effect on their day-to-day lives. However, many were not able to formulate ways of action they could adopt in order to support themselves and improve their quality of life. This includes the acceptance of their disabilities. The group process showed to be instrumental in increasing knowledge and self-support skills of the individual participants.

In addition, and perhaps no less important, was the social support the participants received from their peers in the group setting, as well as from the facilitators. Indeed, the sharing of their feelings and distress helped the participants cope with their experiences and emotions. These results could not have been achieved in individual therapy, where the person may remain with the misconception that he is alone in his "struggle" to go on.

The residential care setting in which the participants live, does not sufficiently encourage the participants of the support group to function independently. Certain residents negated the possibility that they will be able to change anything in their lives, and seem to be totally dependent on the staff of the center. This is an important question, which was not taken into consideration initially, and later proved to be a very significant planning issue. The group treatment setting may be instrumental in providing the participants with some of the confidence they require to influence their lives in the institutionalized environment.

With all the potential advantages mentioned it would appear that group therapy should be given a more central role in the treatment planning. While this is slowly beginning to happen here in Israel there are still a few obstacles, which may be inhibiting the use of group counseling. One of these is the difficulties practitioners face with the question of scientific validation of process and outcomes. In using group therapy for people with ID the question of validity become more critical to demonstrate, yet more difficult to design. In this field groups were generally employed as a method of engineering the acquisition of a particular skill or behavior change. Only if the skill was learned, was the group successful. This almost exclusive focus on skill development often neglects the rich potential inherent in the group process, to provide generalized support (not limited to specific skill acquisition), on-going encouragement, a sense of belongingness, hope and other habilitative and rehabilitative elements that accompany a positive group process (7). The program described in this chapter was indeed operated in the spirit of these important sentiments.

CONCLUSIONS

The program described in this chapter was a unique and innovative group intervention intended for older adults with significant intellectual disabilities in Israel (8). These individuals were most certainly able to comprehend the changes they are undergoing and are in need of support and assistance. Although this group intervention was not able to improve the physical situation of its participants, it has certainly been instrumental in improving the attitudes of people with progressive physical disabilities and assists them in confronting these changes in their lives.

People are not their disability, but rather their disability (or disabilities) is only one of their attributes (4). Older people with ID have proved to be "very good at being old" (17). Indeed, older adults with ID often achieve their greatest sense of well-being late in life, despite its being a life period with a high risk of physical illness and disability (18). It is however, important to create suitable physical and psychological structures to support these older adults in difficult periods of changes and worsening physical abilities.

An additional conclusion of this initial experience is that is important to include staff members in the group process, in particular, in order that they may continue to support the initiatives and independence of the participants, both between sessions and also after the group has ceased to meet. Parents and other family members should also be informed of the group process and the possible changes their relative may undergo. For older parents and siblings, accustomed to relate to their relative with ID as a child in an adult body, this may come as a revelation and may require professional involvement and support.

It is our experience from the study (8) that a group setting has many advantages in attaining greater acceptance and improving the self-image of aging individuals with ID and progressing physical disabilities. The positive results of this pilot group will certainly serve as a springboard to the establishment of additional programs in the future.

ACKNOWLEDGEMENTS

This chapter is an adapted version of an earlier published paper (Kessel S, Merrick J, Kedem A, Borovsky L, Carmeli E. Use of group counseling to support aging-related losses in older adults with intellectual disabilities. J Gerontol Soc Work 2002;38(1/2):241-51).

REFERENCES

1.   Ludlow BL. Life after loss: Legal, ethical and practical issues. In: Herr SS, Weber G, eds.. Aging, rights and quality of life. Baltimore: Paul H Brookes, 1999:189-221.

2.   Seltzer GB. (1993). Psychological adjustment in midlife for persons
        with mental retardation. In: Sutton E, Factor AR, Hawkins BA,
        Heller T, Seltzer GB. Older adults with developmental disabilities.
        Optimizing choice and change. Baltimore: Paul H Brookes, 1993:157-
        84.

3.   Carmeli E, Merrick J, Kessel S, Mashrawi Y, Carmeli V. Elderly
        persons with intellectual disability: A study of clinical
        characteristics, functional status and sensory capacity.
        ScientificWorldJournal 2003;3:298-307.

4.   Lavin C, Doka KJ. Older adults with developmental disabilities.
        New York: Baywood, 1999.

5.   Harper DC, Wadsworth JS. Grief in adults with mental retardation:
        Preliminary findings. Res Dev Disabil 1993;14:313-30.

6.   Seltzer GB. Selected psychological processes and aging among older
        developmentally disabled persons. In: Janicki MP, Wisniewski HM,
        eds. Aging in developmental disabilities: Issues and approaches.
        Baltimore: Paul H Brookes, 1985:211-28.

7.   Tomasulo DJ, Keller E, Pfadt A. The healing crowd: Process, content
        and technique issues in group therapy for people with mental
        retardation. Habilitative Ment Healthcare Newsletter 1995;14(3):19-
        28.

8.   Kessel S, Merrick J, Kedem A, Borovsky L, Carmeli E. Use of group
        counseling to support aging-related losses in older adults with
        intellectual disabilities. J Gerontol Soc Work 2002;38(1/2):241-51.

9.   MacNellis CA. Mental retardation and aging: Mental health issues.
        Gerontol Geriatr Educ 1997;17(3):13-5.

10.   Walz T, Harper D, Wilson J. The aging developmentally disabled
        person: A review. Gerontologist 1986;26:622-9.

11.   Kloeppel DA, Hollins S. Double handicap: Mental retardation and
        death in the family. Death Stud 1989;13:31-8.

12.   Menolascino FJ, Potter JF. Mental illness in the elderly mentally
        retarded. J Appl Gerontol 1989;8(3):192-202.

13.   Yanock J, Beifus JA. Communicating about loss and mourning:
        Death education for individuals with mental retardation. Ment
        Retard 1993;33:144-7.

14.   LeBlanc EA, Matson JL. Aging in the developmentally disabled:
        Assessment and treatment. J Clin Geropsychol 1997;3(1): 37-50.

15.   McDaniel B. A group work experience with mentally retarded
        adults in the issues of death and dying. J Gerontol Soc Work
        1989;13(3/4):187-91.

16.   Laterza P. An eclectic approach to group work with the mentally
        retarded. In: Turner FJ, ed. Differential diagnosis and treatment in
        social work. New York: Free Press, 1983.

17.   Edgarton B. Quality of life issues: Some people know how to be old.
        In: Seltzer MM, Krauss MW, Janicki MP, eds. Life course
        perspectives on adulthood and old age. Washington, DC: Am Assoc
        Ment Retard, 1994:53-66.

18.   Herr SS, Weber G. Aging and developmental disabilities. Concepts
          and global perspectives. In: Herr SS, Weber G, eds. Aging, rights
          and quality of life. Baltimore: Paul H Brookes, 1999:1-16.

CHAPTER 19
What is a good death?

Søren Ventegodt and Joav Merrick

Taking responsibility is quite literally moving the barriers in our lives inside ourselves. Taking responsibility for life means that you are willing to see that the real barriers are not all these external ones, but something that can be found within yourself. Of course there is an outside world, which we cannot easily shape according to your dreams. But a responsible point of view is that although it is difficult the problem is not impossible; it is your real challenge and task. If there is something you really want, you can achieve it, but whether it happens depends on your wholehearted, goal-oriented and continuous attempts.

INTRODUCTION

Death can be seen as the real enemy (1). Death puts life in perspective as we finally see it as the very fragile, easily lost and infinitely valuable thing that it is. When you do not sense that death is after you, you relax and think yourself out of danger. But you have no guarantee that you are alive in five minutes. It is already later than you think. In a little while we are gone. In a moment we have all turned to dust.

To live with the awareness of death – death is around somewhere, waiting for our final slip in order to sweep us away – is a sinister but also wonderful situation. When we are aware of death and know that we have too little time left and that time is the only thing we do not have, then we really do our best. When we acknowledge the unique opportunity we have to become aware, straighten our lives to get a better life while there is still a chance, then we can live the way that makes each day better than the previous and the next year better than this. We can live in such a way that we are on our way up.

Ask yourself: "Am I on my way up or on my way down?" Do you have to admit that you are on your way down, even though of course it is a slow descent? The only thing that can make most of us change our course, so that we live in a manner that leads us upwards is the distinct awareness of death. When we see death threatening us all the time and coming at us in many various forms like loneliness, illness or hopelessness and when we realize that we constantly feed death with great chunks of our own flesh, because we do not make the right choices and thus unconsciously take one step further towards the grave, then we are motivated to correct these systematic faults.

Only death has the power to really make us want to change our course in life. All lesser problems and crises throughout life may be unpleasant, but not really unpleasant enough to make us want to succeed in changing ourselves. The reason for this extreme conservatism is that we already have dedicated most of our decisions to survive, i.e. to avoid dying. Therefore, the death that threatens us now is computed in our minds as more important than the death threatening us in the past. But awareness of death does not come to us easily when we are only slowly decaying. We can see people die in front of us without understanding that we, too, consist of fragile flesh and that we have to depart soon. No force in life can change this: In a little while we are gone. We have to live here and now. This moment is all we have got (2).

WHEN YOU HAVE 700 DAYS LEFT

When "terminal" cancer patients (the quotation marks are because maybe the patients are not as terminal as we usually think) visit their physician some time after they have received the diagnosis and the verdict, that according to the statistics they only have about two years left to live, they often say strange things like: "I am grateful that I got cancer." The physician thinks that this is strange and asks why. "I have never felt so well," the patient says. Most physicians tend to think that is peculiar, because here we have Mrs Larsen, who lost 35 kilogram, lost all her hair because of chemotherapy and her cancer has metastasized throughout the body. Also she looks like something the cat dragged in and then she insists that…". "But it is true, doctor," she insists. "My life has never had so much meaning, my life is more intense than it has ever been now that I know that I have only 700 days left. Now I have let go on all my worries and idiosyncrasies. I have turned simple. I see the sun rise, I feel the wind on my skin, I talk honestly with my friends and I have stopped arguing with my husband. And best of all I have started to say no in order to only do the things I really like".

However absurd it may seem, people with their back against the wall and knowing their days are numbered often live much more intensely than the rest of us, who imagine that we will live forever. Face to face with death we suddenly appear to remember that this is what life is all about, to feel good within ourselves and with each other and to do something we really like. "What a fool I have been" people often say and think. Time possesses the strange capacity to expand enormously, when we live intensely. A moment can feel like eternity or a year can appear to pass within a minute (have you ever experienced a New Year's Eve, where you feel that the past year has been uneventful, so totally empty of anything essential ?). If you know that you only have a short while left before death, then even such a moment may be enough to change the course, that fate had in store for you.

We may call this very strange power that steps in when you are facing death "the will to live." We really do possess enormous potentials for growth and change, but only rarely do these potentials come into use. Our reason and our total naiveté towards the tough and wonderful conditions that apply to us prevent us from changing. You can reclaim the meaning of life. You can break through to the experience of being totally and fully alive, to your life having meaning and your existence making a real difference to the world you live in and yourself. Patients who become well again, drug addicts who become clean, prostitutes who succeed in love, all the miracles people talk about, but do not believe in. All this happens during this process. But, of course, up to this day it has been rare. If our culture held more insight into these things they would probably be much more common, the way they appear to have been in other cultures at other times. A holistic physician often has the great fortune to live in a world, where these miracles are almost normal. In our "quality of life as medicine" projects they occur surprisingly often (3,4).

TO PULL YOURSELF BY THE HAIR

A force stronger than reason is needed, when the course of your life is to be altered. Let us call it the will to a better life. If this will is present people will possess real humility, making them open and willing to learn and change. The strange thing about this will is that it is an irrational, nonverbal force that pulls up your existence.

When the will influences your view of the world it becomes altered in a strange way. This happens because the will to live supplies a fixed point, namely what you have to believe in when you really love life, beyond all reason, beyond everything you have learnt and experienced in life. This fixed point can serve as a new foundation for your personal philosophy of life. From this moment on you will feel that deep down life is good and valuable, the world is full of opportunities, people are trustworthy, you are able to solve the problems in life on your own and through this battle you can make everything cohere.

The experience of pulling yourself up by the roots of your hair literally means that you raise or lift your own existence. You correct your faults and close up all the holes that drain your vital energy. You remove all the good reasons for not having any self-respect and start a new life on a totally new foundation. You take responsibility for your own life.

The essential part of the will is that it is able to cut through all the confusion and doubt that normally characterize human life. In reality, there is no rational way of determining the truth value of statements or philosophies of life. You cannot guess the truth about life and the world. Reason cannot distinguish very well between personal philosophies of life, because they all basically rest on principles that are irrational, ethical or even emotional. However, the will to live a good life cuts cleanly through doubt and mental fog and points out clearly and directly what is right and wrong in relation to our love of life.

Some decisions and choices are in harmony with life, others bring ruin and destruction. Some decisions lead towards the top, others towards the bottom. Some views of the world can sustain life, others weigh it down. Only the will to live a good life can make a person rise above the immaterial, the meaningless, doubt and nonsense. You rarely discover that the will is the real resource for improving life, until you are facing death. When that happens, the will to live is often the only reason why you survive.

The experience of pulling yourself up by the roots of your hair is quite amusing. But really, if we are to live fully and completely for just a moment this is what is needed, the ability to lift ourselves and take wings, despite the thousands of weights that are dragging us down. Taking responsibility for our own lives is really a process during which we elevate our own existence, in spite of all barriers and difficulties. The will to live a good life is the only thing that can create this effect.

TO FIND THE QUALITY OF LIFE

We are free to choose our values, the things we think are important and good. Some people's lives are centered on collecting stamps, while others collect good friends. Some chose expensive clothes or fast cars as values, while others grow ecological vegetables and wear only clothes made of recycled material. Some people collect dirty videos, while others are into bible studies. In our minds we are free to chose our own personal values, just as we have an enormous freedom to describe the world whatever way we want.

One thing is values, another thing is how we feel or what state we are in. Something makes one person happy, something else makes another person happy. But what about the happiness we feel: is it the same kind of happiness or are there different kinds of happiness? And what about satisfaction with life? Do we all possess the same sense of satisfaction or do we experience satisfaction in different ways? What about the meaning of life itself? When we feel deep within ourselves, in our very souls and hearts (if we are able to find it), do we then feel the same meaningfulness in life, when it is meaningful and the same senselessness, when it is not? Do two people experience the same kind of love, the same feeling of hate or sexual desire?

It is obvious that each experience carries its own qualities and intensity. But is the actual quality of the experience connected to the individual, to our egos and learned descriptions of the world? Or is the actual quality of happiness, satisfaction or the meaning of life something that is given by human nature? As it appears from this paper, we believe very strongly in nature and that life within us never has let go of its habitat in nature, because we possess our common description of the world not just as a possibility, but as a necessity. This is a given, because we are constructed the way we are and have to live together.

The decisive factor for being able to change yourself is that you are able to regain your belief, that fundamentally life is good. When we here use the word 'belief' it is because from a rational point of view, such an attitude will always be a question of belief. Subjectively, of course, it can also be experienced as certain knowledge. And it is this inner certain conviction that makes the difference.

You can believe nature as being the essential thing. Not, as is often suggested, in a primitive way, with coarse instincts and pre-programmed behavior parallel to animal behavior, but more refined. The idea is that deep down in our biological matter we possess a nature as humans. This nature is in the shape of an abstract recipe for being a human, and life is about expressing this recipe to the full, unfolding and manifesting its potential for a good life.

In this light, our nature holds the potential for all the dimensions of our lives. It is in our nature to feel good or bad, to be satisfied or dissatisfied, to have sexual feelings, to be happy and feel there is a meaning in life or to work for our innermost visions and longings. Our nature is such, that we have a heart that we need to discern and obey so that we may lead the good life.

TO SEIZE THE MEANING OF LIFE

When we finally acknowledge that the world extends beyond our reason or that there are forces at large that matter more than our impulses then we can proceed. When we realize that there are values on Earth that far surpass the value of our small life, then we will be humble enough to accept the gift (and task) that is life. Then we can put our faith in authority and our loyal, but out-of-date and limited description of the world behind us.

To rediscover the meaning of life means finding yourself and the values that you can always, and without faltering, use as foundation for your own life. To regain the meaning of life means that you acknowledge that you are a human being, subject to the conditions and laws applicable to humans. We am not talking about the highway code, but more profound laws that apply to all living beings. To take responsibility, to see yourself as active and not as a victim, to work at correcting your personal faults and repair the bumps in your inner map of the world.

To regain the meaning of life does not mean to be forever happy. It means that you find your fundamental challenge as a human being and take up the challenge. You become a person with a mission. There are things to be corrected both on the inside and the outside, things within yourself and things in the world around you. If you are really clever you will see that in reality there is often little difference between the two. The flaws in the world are evident to you, because you also sense and work on similar weaknesses and flaws within yourself. The great struggle for a better world, that all people become involved in, when they acknowledge that the meaning of life is about coherence. They cannot escape this world, however much they want to, because of all its superficiality, materialism, abuse of power and false values, then their realize that this struggle is very much about improving that part of the world that is you. To clean the place you occupy, to cultivate your own spirit.

Everything starts with yourself. Because all the barriers you see are actually within you, in your own personal view of the world. Becoming free means first and foremost becoming free of the constraints imposed by your own rational description of reality. It does not actually mean that you must get rid of this description or the framework it puts around your self-expression, but you can loosen the constraints so much that they no longer limits life, but support life. You need to get rid of the negativity in the description and the old pains that hold your limiting decisions in their place.

WHAT IS THE PURPOSE OF LIFE?

Imagine that you really wish to know the meaning of your life. You rent a small cabin in the mountains, where nobody can disturb you for the next three or four weeks. You buy provisions for the whole stay. You go alone and you spend your time on only one thing, namely answering the question: 'What is the meaning of my life'? Of course you have to find a wording that is all your own, which exactly fits you and your life. But it must be deep enough to penetrate all the way into your soul.

What is the purpose of life for you? Why are you on the surface of the Earth for a short while? In what way do you make a difference in the world? What are your dreams in life, love, real friendship, a good job or harmony with nature ?

When you compare the life you lead with your dreams, how do you measure up ? Is your personal relationship the love of your life or is it boring routine in bed and arguments at breakfast and before the evening news? Do you actually have one single friend with whom you can and do talk about everything and who does not begrudge you real progress ? A friend who can meet you right where you are and just wish you all the best and therefore ask you all the questions you should already have asked yourself, but did not dare to out of fear of meeting yourself ? Questions like what is it you want, what are your opportunities and what is needed for you to obtain what you want with the opportunities you have ?

What about your work? Do you really exert yourself and improve anything? Do you gain the expertise necessary to express yourself creatively and spontaneously? Do you solve your tasks to your own personal satisfaction? Do you have enough influence on your own work? Do you actually accept what your company produces or should you be doing something quite different in order to be of use in the world?

What about your time off? Do your holidays fulfill your dreams or do you just end up in some bar in Mallorca wasting your time on casual pursuits, before returning home to your boring routine? Do you burn for your life, your work and your love? Does you or your life contain any nerve at all? In the final analysis, how do you feel, if you are really and totally honest? Are you OK? Do you get out of life, what it can give you? Do you exploit all your opportunities? Have you accepted the challenge that is yours and is your life in balance? Are you at peace with yourself, because you have acknowledged your own personal mission in life?

We suspect that after a couple of days you are having no more fun at the cabin. After all, to study the meaning of life is rather unpleasant. The really sad truth is that we have no wish to know the truth about ourselves or the deeper meaning of life, because it is painful to learn something decidedly new and we only do this if it is absolutely necessary.

Actually, what began as a straightaway philosophical experiment now appears to be a dramatic process, where you have to confront and process the pains of a lifetime! All the bad things you have done since early childhood will come to you and ask you for a clean-up! This is not our favorite perspective, but the only perspective that will make us change into better, more innocent and more loving persons.

THE PAIN OF KNOWING THE MEANING OF YOUR LIFE

Our problem is that deep down we do not really want to know the meaning of our lives, because if we do we have to acknowledge that the life we actually live is a pale shadow of the opportunities we hold, no matter how good life is, when compared to that of other people.

We are not at all interested in realizing that we almost live in an existential gutter, when we compare our life with what we were actually created for. Our life is not first-class and maybe it is not even second-class, which we thought, but actually third-class, because our life is more or less without love to life, to other people or even to ourselves.

We are also not the decent folks we thought we were, but rather harbor fairly violent and destructive tendencies. Not a fun perspective at all. Let us assure you that one of us was surprised when, one sunny day some years ago, he finally came to the realization that his basic intentions toward other people were basically mean, while he himself thought he was such a well-meaning fellow. A close examination showed otherwise. There is a reason why we do not want to know ourselves: It hurts. This realization that our life does not have the meaning it could have or that our life is far poorer than it needs to be does not give us a nice feeling. That we are actually at fault for wasting our life and perhaps about to lose something precious, our actual existence, this realization is actually very unpleasant.

The unpleasantness lies in the realization of the magnitude of the problem, because it obliges us to do something about it for our own sake. We must take responsibility and see ourselves as the cause of our own personal mess. We must learn to associate with others and change our attitudes towards all kinds of things. We need to let go of all out-dated points of view for which we have fought and battled forever, ever since we learned them from our parents.

It is important that you can face yourself in the mirror every morning. One reason this may be difficult is the painful feeling that you are not faithful to yourself. When you know deep down what life is about and what your real purpose and meaning of life are, it hurts inside if you just continue living as always and not true to your own intuitions.

When you are conscious of your big dream, but shy away from working to make it come true, you suppress yourself. This works fine only as long as you are not too aware of it, but with the growing awareness the suppression of your own life becomes still harder to bear. The more you understand the game of life, the more you are obliged to engage in it. Knowing what you like, makes it much more difficult not to be good to yourself. When you face yourself in the mirror, you will know how much work you have to do to bring your life in better accord with the innermost wishes of your soul.

Everybody, who engages totally in the challenge of improving his or her relationship with the self will find that this game can be won. It takes a real effort, though. For most of us it is hard work every day for many years. Frankly, because our state of being is so lousy, when we start out. We are rather far from being happy, cheerful and easygoing.

One of us with the experience of this process felt a strong and almost unbearable sensation of unworthiness. When you develop an excellent inner standard of existence, you are likely to feel less proud of yourself. When you realize the brilliant standard that all mankind inhabits deep down in his soul(5) – all that we are meant to be, our real potential – then our present existence often seems pretty pale, insignificant, sometimes close to a total failure. As long as you compare yourself with your next-door neighbor you can always claim success. But when your start comparing your present state of being with that of a person at his full peek – like Moses, Buddha, Jesus, Leonardo da Vinci or and maybe spiritual masters like the Dalai Lama, Sai Baba or Baal Shem Tov– it is difficult not to feel gray.

Now, humility and humor will always be helpful. It is quite funny to be an action hero, when you compare yourself to your friends and be an existential midget, when you compare yourself to your own potentials. You might find that what nature or God intended you to be is amazingly different from whatever you thought at first. The gift of knowing the meaning of life is energy. When we see our true potential it is tempting to reach for the power and glory, the creativity and the divinity that lie within. When we do this we will immediately get all kinds of problems with the outer world and we will get an immense amount of energy. An unsurpassed energy kick.

People who know their hidden potentials and dig into them without hesitation or second thoughts will always blossom. They will soon be transformed into original beings, colorful, intelligent, troublesome, creative, lovely and often annoying like hell. These people will normally get everything they want. If they are sick they will get healed, if they are artists they will get fame, if they are scientists they will get a unique understanding of their field of research. Eventually, as their personal growth continues they might be recognized as the geniuses of this world.

The secret of these success stories is lots and lots of energy drawn from the source of existence combined with other amazing qualities like intuitive competence and emotional intelligence. These qualities pour from one single source: life. More precisely, the abundant source of energy and motivation is "the joy of life". Joyfulness seems to be the most basic and most mysterious quality of all living beings. The nature of joy is by the way still completely unexplained by science.

THE NO MAN'S LAND BETWEEN YOUR OLD AND NEW LIFE

Knowing what life is about does not necessarily mean that life becomes any easier. It is often quite the opposite: life turns even more difficult, when you wake up. But a conscious life has a peculiar quality. A person who experiences the deepest meaning in his or her life discovers that life now has touch of bliss and fragrance (6). No matter how chaotic, no matter how painful, deep down the new life is sweet.

This fine sweetness makes it possible for a human being to endure almost incredible pain and sorrow. When you strive to realize yourself and your utopian dreams many people will react as if you have the plaque. You will often turn into an incomprehensible and disturbing element of other people's worlds. To be sure, after some years of hard work you will come back as a beautiful, peaceful and happy person, but often the first thing that happens is that you turn annoying, selfish, difficult or even angry.

The fine, inner sweetness gives these people an unstoppable quality. They turn into fighters. They have seen the light and they follow it. New jobs, divorces, new friends, new habits and values, new sexual and professional interests... we are talking about major transformations here. People are not the same and will never be the same again. They are forever lost for you, if you do not follow them by developing yourself.

If you get a metastasized cancer and you heal yourself by letting go of the negative beliefs and self-suppressing decisions of a lifetime, you will be changed. You now have dramatically improved your quality of life and inner coherence. But you might also be in the situation, where you find yourself as reborn to the degree that not even your old clothing fits you any more. The price to be paid for personal growth is, unfortunately, chaos. As most people are very conservative they will try to oppose your growth the best they can. So, people who supported you, when you were down suddenly do their best to suppress you. It is sometimes difficult to believe that your relatives can jump on your back trying to hold you back. It is sometimes grotesque that you will have to escape from your whole family.

Between your new blossoming life and the old normal, boring life of habits and routines is a no man's land of very difficult nature. You discover that nothing is as your thought is was – it might be that your beloved does not really love you or that what you thought was the essence of your life is simply a substitution for a sound and healthy interest. Often people going through this transformation will at some point in time feel that they are going crazy. But relax: your are not going crazy. You have been crazy for half a lifetime living with values that did not make you happy. And now your are waking up. You are in the middle of a speedy, but unpleasant recovery. Loneliness of the most painful kind is normal at this stage. You are alone with your thoughts, and you are confused, unhappy, not seen, not loved and not understood. You cannot continue to live your old life, but you have not yet found your new ways. The fine order of your life has been broken and now chaos prevails both on the surface and in the debts of our soul.

We are healing, but first we must acknowledge that we really are sick. The pain of a whole lifetime is often overwhelming us and survival becomes dependent on our ability to be good to ourselves. Nobody but yourself is there now to show you love and concern. The miracle is that it is enough: when we love ourselves we do not really depend on other people's concern for us. But before we can enjoy the luxury of relying fully on ourselves, living in perfect inner balance, we must heal a lot of old painful wounds. This is why loneliness bites us at this stage.

Most people live lives that are not truly a life. They sense this intuitively, but they do not want to look at it at all. There are plenty of symptoms telling you that everything is not as it is supposed to be. The terrible headache or low back pain that returns still more often, problems sleeping at night, the growing sexual problems that are taking the fun out of this part of life, problems with your skin, the slips of memory, maybe the arthritis making every step you take even more painful. Enough is enough. Some day you realize that this is not how you want to life. Enough of lies and politeness and pretension. Air! You need fresh air, renewal, new inspiration. The way you live brings you slow death and this is not how life was meant to be. It takes a lot of courage to break the well-known order of daily life.

Sometimes we are lucky enough to be forced to make the move and wake up: the physician gives you the malignant diagnosis, the boss says he is sorry he has to let you go, because of your still poorer performance. This is the end. You have reached the end of the road. You only have one chance now: renewal from within. Your whole life needs repair. It is time to clean up the mess. Now a hard time usually follows. It is difficult not to feel that a lot of time is wasted living your old life. Realizing the distance to the existence you have been living, you are often overwhelmed with sorrow and bitter regrets. But eventually you will find mercy and realize that life is never wasted, you have learned your lesson, you suffered for as long as you had to. As time goes by you will appreciate a still deeper pattern of order and inherent logic in the universe.

CONCLUSIONS

We have a nature as human beings. It is this nature that makes it possible for us to be happy, cheerful, wise and lovely. When we turn natural and innocent, the extraordinary freedom that characterizes life at its fullest will return to us. All the life we hold as living organisms will now blossom and grow. Our love and passion will come back, a burning interest for our work will unexpectedly catch us, deep friendships will form and this divine creativity and humor will mark our new personality. All of us have the possibility do make a difference. The quality of our own life can be drastically improved and so can our use to people around us. We can be of real value to ourselves and to the world around us. Instead of being one more of these human beings tearing down the global ecosystem you will understand the web of life in all its forms and shadows and do what is needed to make mankind and our beautiful culture survive.

As we see it, mankind is a highly endangered species, and only by transforming our old materialistic culture into a new spiritual culture with honesty, truthfulness and contributing people can humanity survive. The right place for all of us to begin is by saving ourselves. All it takes is that we decide to seize the meaning of life. But this must be one whole-hearted move: you must give it everything you have got if you want to succeed. You can change a poor life to an excellent life (5,6-11), but you must risk your life to win. One day you will find the courage. Maybe the day is today. The wise Jewish Rabbis have a few good sayings: "Live todays as if tomorrow is your last day" or "in order to perfect yourself, one must renew oneself day by day".

Let us conclude by telling the story of Sol Gordon, professor emeritus of Child and Family Studies at Syracuse University: "Growing up as an idealistic youth, I was determined to save the world and even the more I tried, the world became worse and worse. Then I decided I had taken on too much. I thought I would just try to save the United States. The more I tried -- conditions in the US got worse and worse. So again I thought I had taken on too much. So I decided I would just try to save my neighborhood. My neighbors told me to mind my own business. But just as I was about to give up in despair, I read in the Talmud (Jewish teachings) that if you can save one life, it is as though you have saved the world. That is now my mission -- one person at a time (12). What you start there, then you will have a good death.

ACKNOWLEDGEMENTS

This chapter is an adapted version of an earlier published paper (Merrick J, Ventegodt S. What is a good death ? To use death as a mirror and find the quality of life. BMJ 2003 October 31 online at http://bmj.com/cgi/eletters/327/7406/66#39303)

REFERENCES

1. What is a good death? Join in our online discussions. BMJ 2003;327: 66.
2. Ventegodt S, Andersen NJ, Merrick J. Quality of life philosophy V: Seizing the meaning of life and becoming well again. ScientificWorldJournal 2003;3:1210-29.
3. Ventegodt S, Merrick J, Andersen NJ. Quality of life as medicine: A pilot study of patients with chronic illness and pain. ScientificWorldJournal 2003;3:520-532.
4. Ventegodt S, Merrick J, Andersen NJ. Quality of life as medicine II: A pilot study of a five day "Quality of Life and Health" cure for patients with alcoholism. ScientificWorldJournal 2003;3:842-852.
5. Ventegodt S. The life mission theory: A theory for a conciousness based medicine. Int J Adolesc Med Health 2003;15(1):89-91.

6. Huxley A. The perennial philosophy. New York, NY: Harper Collins, 1972.
7. Antonovsky A. Unravelling the mystery of health. How people manage stress and stay well. Jossey-Bass, San Franscisco, 1987.
8. Maslow A. Toward a psychology of being. Princeston, NJ: Van Nostrand Princeston, 1962.
9. Ventegodt S. Quality of life: Seizing the meaning of life and becoming well again. Copenhagen: Forskningcentrets Forlag, Copenhagen, 1995. [Danish]
10. Saint-Exupéry AMR. The little prince. New York: Harcourt Brace, 1943.
11. Castaneda C. The art of dreaming. New York: Harper-Collins, 1993.
12. Gordon S. When living hurts. New York: UAHC Press, 1994.

CHAPTER 20
Death and Jewish mourning rituals for persons with intellectual disability

Shlomo Kessel and Joav Merrick

Death in any familiy is a traumatic event that disturbs the regular course of life. The present population of persons with intellectual disability is most probably the first generation of aging people with intellectual disabilities ever living. The increase in their life expectancy makes the possibility of experiences with separation, death and mourning a new reality for this population. Parents or sibling are passing away and the person with intellectual disability continues to live. This presentation is a review of the literature of mourning with special focus on Jewish mourning rituals related to persons with intellectual disability drawn from our experiences with this population in residential care in Israel.

INTRODUCTION

The encounter and the need to deal with life transitions and their accompanying losses and grief, are common phenomena in the lives of aging people (1). As life expectancy in the western world rapidly increases, individuals are undergoing many more experiences that include bereavement. Death in the family is a traumatic event that disturbs the regular course of life. Aging should therefore be seen as an internal developmental process that set demands on the person to cope with distress caused by the loss of significant others. Bereavement includes the process of coping and the various reactions experienced by the individual who has lost a loved one. We refer to behavioral, cognitive and emotional changes. Often the bereavement is expressed in the form of behaviors that demonstrate the person's grief as the result of his having been separated from a loved one, a treasured possession or his familiar environment (2).

Older individuals experience bereavement from various sources. The death of parents, family members and other loved ones, while being the best recognized source, is only one of the reasons. The aging person may feel grief and sorrow as the result of a gradual decline of his or her physical or cognitive abilities. Functional decline is a well-known and normative phenomenon of the aging process, however it is still difficult for the individual to accept the loss of his abilities (3).

AGING ADULTS WITH INTELLECTUAL DISABILITIES

One of the important consequences of the progress of medical technology and improved social awareness in the twentieth century, is the increasing life span of people with intellectual and other developmental disabilities. In the past the majority of individuals with intellectual disability died at a young age and therefore, never underwent the aging process. Indeed, the present population is most probably the first generation of aging people with intellectual disabilities ever living. When compared to people without disabilities, the aging process creates many unique and complex tensions for aging individuals with mental retardation, mainly as a result of often being dependent on others for daily support. In addition, they may demonstrate cognitive difficulties and deficient communicative skills. The situation may be worsened as the result of discriminatory social attitudes that impede and limit the access of aging individuals with intellectual disabilities to information and support (3).

The increase in the life expectancy of people with intellectual disabilities is a "two edged sword". These individuals enjoy the blessing of a long and healthy life, however they also experience the pain and sorrow that often, accompany the aging process. More people now have contact with separation, death and mourning. Today, we witness an emerging phenomenon where traditional care providers, such as parents or siblings, are passing away, whilst their aging relatives with intellectual disabilities whom they supported, are still living, sometimes with nobody left to care for them.

The issues of loss and bereavement are familiar ones to those who are involved with adults who have developmental disabilities. Unfortunately, there is little recognition of the impact of loss on this population.

BEREAVEMENT AND PERSONS WITH INTELLECTUAL DiSABILITIES

Usually with this group, the defintion of loss tends to be a traditional one (i.e. death) rather than inclusive of the whole range of losses rather than the whole range of losses that an individual with developmental disabilities may experience. Individuals with intellectual and other developmental disabilities experience losses stemming from different sources. In addition to the "traditional" parting from a loved one whom has passed on, they experience loss resulting from the replacement of a principal caregiver, from being arbitrarily transferred from one service or residential program to another and, similar to all aging individuals, from the loss of physical and cognitive functioning (4).

Even when there is recognition of the impact of losses on the induvidual, people who make up the person;s support system may be unsure how to address losses. The loss of a significant relationship has an overpowering and often devastating effect on the lives of the individuals with intellectual disabilities, their families and the services supporting them (4).

In many cases, when the passing of a close relative of an individual with intellectual disabilities occurs, he is prevented from participating in the funeral. Often, the individual with disabilities is not told of the death for weeks or months after it has happened, or even not told at all. Thus the basic rights of these individuals are seriously violated and as professionals we should be profoundly disturbed by this phenomenon and search for appropriate solutions.

Harper and Wadworth (2) stressed the tendency to see both mental retardation (intellectual disabilities) and death as taboo subjects in western society. For many death is seen as "distant and unexplored territory". For most of our lives we lives under the illusion that life is endless and that death is something that happens to others (5). For this reason, many families and professionals are unprepared to handle death and feel unqualified to deal with the task of breaking the tragic news to the person with intellectual disabilities. They may mistakenly believe that these individuals do not possess the capacity to understand the implications of death (that it is final, that it is not their fault), that they are unable to form or experience significant relationships, or that they are unable to feel sorrow or grief for the loved person who has died (4). Moreover, there are those who believe that it is better to divert the person's attention from the memory of the person who has passed away and thus, help him to forget. Many erroneously feel that the person with intellectual disabilities has had a difficult and distressful life and should be protected from further pain and sorrow.

While the intentions of the family members and others may be noble, it is our opinion that this form of over-protectiveness is misplaced and indeed, violates the basic human rights of the person involved. Many professionals claim that excluding the person with intellectual disabilities from the bereavement process, is the cause of irreparable psychological harm and injury to his spiritual wellbeing (6). The lack of an appropriate opportunity to express his previous losses, may trigger a delayed and exaggerated grief response in the person with intellectual disabilities who has not yet successfully completed an earlier grieving process (4).

MOURNING CUSTOMS AND RITUAL

Grief responses involve accepting the loss, experiencing grief, ajusting to an environment without the deceased, withdrawing emotional energy from their relationship, and reinvesting it in new relationships. Some indicators of an individual going through this process may include: behavioral changes, mood changes, isolation, difficulties in realtionships, decreased activity, fluctuations in eating and sleeping patterns and difficulties concentrating. These indices are experienced in people with and without developmental disabilities (4).

It is well acknowledged by psychologists and professionals in the field of death research, that mourning customs and rituals, particularly participation in the funeral, are powerful and significant means of assisting the bereft person to overcome and handle his grief. Over the ages, different cultures and religions have developed rites and customs that help the mourner express his feelings and get through this critical period as peacefully as possible, while rearranging his life according to the altered reality (7).

Luchterhand and Murphy (8) in their book "Helping Adults With Mental Retardation Grieve a Death Loss", stress the special importance of the mourning rituals to the bereaving individual with intellectual disabilities. Why is that so? It must be emphasized that the cognitive processes of persons with intellectual and other developmental disabilities are generally concrete and they often require tangible and practical expression of a concept or a notion in order to understand its meaning. Given that opportunity and perhaps, some additional time, we believe that the person with disabilities will be able to sufficiently comprehend most of his life experiences, including the death of a loved one. It is therefore, of paramount importance that the bereft person with intellectual disabilities be allowed to participate fully in the mourning rituals and practices that are the custom of his family or the culture in which he lives (1). These rituals may be divided into three categories:

- Rituals performed with the departed, such as sitting with body, saying prayers, wake
- Rituals performed to mark the passing, such as obituary columns
- Prescribed Social Behavior, such as wearing black or not wearing make-up.

JEWISH MOURNING RITUALS

Jewish law and tradition are not different from other religions in this regard. Many diverse and detailed customs govern the behavior of the Jewish mourner and those in contact with him or her at this difficult time. An examination of Jewish mourning rituals shows that many of these practices are indeed suitable for the inclusion of individuals with intellectual disabilities and will serve the purpose of assisting them in confronting their loss and grief and grasping the reality of death (9). This will be illustrated with a number of examples from our experiences with the study population:

The funeral
The Jewish traditional funeral is generally attended by many friends and relatives who accompany the deceased on his final journey. Indeed, the Hebrew word for funeral is Levayah – which literally means to escort or to accompany. The law (Halacha) requires that the deceased be eulogized and then carried to the grave by participants of the funeral, where he is placed for eternal rest. The person with intellectual disabilities should be encouraged to participate in the funeral and take his place with the other

bereaved family members. A brief explanation should help him to understand that he is an active participant in bringing his loved one to his or her resting place and that the deceased feels no pain or suffering. Active participation will increase the probability that the person with intellectual disabilities will paint a realistic picture of the burial process, minimizing misconceptions and anxieties. Two additional rituals, part of the funeral service, emphasize to the individual with disabilities his "mourner status".

First, the kriyah – the ritual tearing of the garments – an expression of pain, which is done at a point of extreme grief and distress. This is an especially tangible expression of mourning.

Second, the Shurah, - after the burial the participants form two parallel lines and as the mourners pass between them, they are comforted. In this manner the person with intellectual disabilities is shown to be part of the family, his grief is recognized and legitimate and he too is comforted.

HaShiva – the seven days of mourning

Perhaps the best known Jewish mourning custom, sitting Shiva involves numerous and detailed manifestations of the mourner's bereavement and hardship. The customs are practical and designed to emphasize and encourage expressions of grief and sorrow. Examples are:

- Sitting on a low seat
- Restrictions of washing oneself
- Refraining from having one's hair cut or shaving
- Refraining from changing into clean clothes or wearing leather shoes
- Refraining from joyous activity

The person with intellectual disabilities will benefit greatly from his participation in the shiva for as long as it is possible. The different manifestations of mourning will allow the person the opportunity to express his personal grief in a fitting manner, while in a sympathetic and supportive environment. Indeed, the Jewish sages have said that crying is the natural way of expressing grief and that the first three days of mourning are the appropriate time for cying.

A further aspect of sitting shiva is the comforting of the mourners by visitors. Sitting shiva creates a unique opportunity for friends (who may also have intellectual disabilities) and professionals to visit and console the bereft individual. Professionals may, for example, remark: "I fully understand how you feel" or "I know how hard it is for you", thereby, helping the person with disabilities understand what is happening to him, and know that it is all right to feel that way.

The final example is the obituary

In many countries it is customary to publicize a person's passing by placing an obituary in the newspaper. In Israel this is done uniquely by putting up the obituary in the form of a notice, posted at the entrance to the deceased or the mourners' homes, in the neighborhood, and at places of work. In many of our residential settings when a resident suffers the loss of a loved one, the staff will prepare an obituary notice and put it up. In this way the entire resident and staff community may offer their condolences to the bereft individual.

CONCLUSION

Contact with dying and bereavement, unfortunate as it may be, is a critical part of one's formulation of the concept of death. Individuals with intellectual disabilities who during their lifetime experience loss and separation, will be better equipped to handle additional incidents of death and bereavement It is therefore of extreme importance that these individuals are allowed to take part in ritual practices and customs when experiencing the death of a loved one. Jewish mourning rituals, as a result of their practical and structured nature are seemingly beneficial to bereft individuals with intellectual disabilities, assisting them in confronting their loss and grief and grasping the reality of death.

ACKNOWLEDGEMENTS

This chapter is an adapted version of an earlier published paper (Kessel S, Merrick J. The benefits of Jewish mourning rituals for the grieving individual with intellectual disability. J Religion Disabil Health 2001;5(2/3):147-56)

REFERENCES

1. Kloeppel DA, Hollins S. Double handicap: Mental retardation and death in the family. Death Stud 1989;13:31-8.
2. Harper DC, Wadsworth JS. Grief in adults with mental retardation: Preliminary findings. Res Dev Disabil 1993;14:313-30.
3. Ludlow BL. Life after loss: Legal, ethical and practical issues. In: Herr SS, Weber G, eds.. Aging, rights and quality of life. Baltimore: Paul H Brookes, 1999:189-221.
4. Stoddart K, McDonnell J. Addressing grief and loss in adults with developmental disabilities. J Dev Disabil 1999;6(2): 51-65.
5. Moise LE. In sickness and in death. Ment Retard 1978;16:397-8.
6. Seltzer MM. Informal supports for aging mentally retarded persons. Am J Ment Defic 1985;73:259-65.
7. Raphael B. The anatomy of bereavement. Northvale, NJ: Jason Aronson, 1994.
8. Luchterhand C, Murphy N. Helping adults with mental retardation grieve a death loss. Philadelphia, PA: Taylor Francis, 1998.
9. Wagschal S. Halochos of aveilus. Laws for the mourner. Nanuet, NY: Feldheim, 1999.

CHAPTER 21
Suicide in holistic medicine

Søren Ventegodt and Joav Merrick

Suicide has been honoured and respected in the eastern culture, especially in Japan with the famous tradition of Hara-kiri or seppuku, while in most western societies suicide has been seen negatively and many contemporary physicians tend to consider suicide the most self-destructive and evil thing a human being can do and something that should be avoided at all cost. Religions also have different viewpoints on suicide, but from a philosophical point of view we believe that considering the choice of life and dead to be extremely relevant for a good living. The choice of life and dead is real, since responsibility for life is necessary in order to live life and even the best physician cannot keep a patient alive, who deep inside wants to die. In this chapter we present parts of a story of a young girl who had experienced child sexual abuse. In holistic existential therapy it is our experience, when the patient is well supported in the confrontation of the fundamental questions related to assuming responsibility for the coherence, that this confrontation will almost always lead to a big YES to life. Without confronting the fundamental question of "to be or not to be" life can never be chosen 100% and thus never be lived fully.

INTRODUCTION

Suicide (from latin sui caedere, self killing) is the act of ending your own life, which has been considered a sin and crime in many religions and societies, but some cultures have viewed it as an honorable way to exit certain shameful or hopeless situations. Parasuicide is the term for "attempted suicide".

Suicide has been honoured and respected in the eastern cultures with the famous tradition of Hara-kiri (called seppuku) as a well-known example. Hara-kiri is a ritual and honorable suicide with Japanese origins. Traditionally, it is done in a spiritually clean temple by cutting open your abdomen with a wakizashi (traditional Japanese sword with a shoto blade between 30 and 60 cm, with an average of 50 cm), thereby releasing the soul. The traditional form is one deep cut down and one across, while a slightly less honorable version (and much less painful) is that at the same time, a friend severs the head for an instant death. Hara-kiri was traditionally used as the ultimate protest, when your own morals stood in the way of executing an order from the master. It was also permissible as a form of repentance when one had committed an unforgivable sin, either by accident or on purpose.

HISTORY AND RELIGION

Many famous people through history have committed suicide, such as Cleopatra VII of Egypt, Hannibal, Nero, Adolf Hitler, Ernest Hemingway or Vincent van Gogh.

In Buddhism, the past influence our present and what an individual does in the present influence his or her future, in this life or the next. This is cause and effect, as taught by Gautama Buddha. Known as karma, intentional action by mind, body or speech has a reaction and its repercussion is the reason behind the conditions and differences we come across in the world. Suffering primarily originates from past negative deeds or just from being in samsara (the cycle of birth and death). Another reason for the prelvalent suffering we experience is due to impermanence. Since everything is in a constant state of flux, we experience unsatisfactoriness with the fleeting events of life. To break out of samsara, one simply must realize their true nature, by Enlightenment in the present moment; this is Nirvana. For Buddhists, since the first precept is to refrain from the destruction of life (including oneself), suicide is clearly considered a negative form of action. But despite this view, an ancient Asian ideology similar to Hara-kiri persists to influence Buddhists by, when under oppression, commiting the act of "honorable" suicide.

Christianity is traditionally opposed to suicide, and assisted suicide and especially in Catholicism, suicide has been considered a grave and sometimes mortal sin. The chief Catholic argument is that your life is the property of God and to destroy your own life is to assert dominion over what belongs to God. Many Christians believe in the sanctity of human life, a principle which, broadly speaking, says that all human life is sacred - a wonderful, even miraculous creation of the divine God - and every effort must be made to save and preserve it whenever possible.

In Islam, God is creator, he is the giver of life, and he alone has the right to end it. Suicide is forbidden in Islam and listed as a sin among the "enormities" in Reliance of the Traveller, a manual of Sharia in the tradition of Imam Shafi'i. Those who commit suicide should be roasted in a fire (do not kill yourselves, for Allah is compassionate towards you. Whoever does so, in transgression and wrongfully, We shall roast in a fire, and that is an easy matter for Allah. (an-Nisaa 4:29-30)), forbidden Paradise (the Prophet said, "Whoever intentionally swears falsely by a religion other than Islam, then he is what he has said, (e.g. if he says, 'If such thing is not true then I am a Jew,' he is really a Jew). And whoever commits suicide with piece of iron will be punished with the same piece of iron in the Hell Fire." Narrated Jundab the Prophet said, "A man was inflicted with wounds and he committed suicide, and so Allah said: My slave has caused death on himself hurriedly, so I forbid Paradise for him." (Sahih Bukhari 2.445) and will be punished in hell by whatever used for suicide (the Prophet said, "He who commits suicide by throttling shall keep on throttling himself in the Hell Fire (forever) and he who commits suicide by stabbing himself shall keep on stabbing himself in the Hell-Fire." (Sahih Bukhari 2.446, 2.445)).

Judaism views suicide as one of the most serious of sins. Suicide has always been forbidden by Jewish law, except for three specific cases: if one is being forced by someone to commit murder, forced to commit an act of idolatry, or forced to commit adultery or incest. However, outside those cases, suicide is forbidden, and this includes taking part in assisted suicide. One may not ask someone to assist in killing themselves for two separate reasons: (a) killing oneself is forbidden, and (b) one is then making someone else accomplice to a sin.

WESTERN SOCIETY

In most western societies suicide has mostly been seen negatively, and many contemporary physicians tend to consider suicide the most self-destructive and evil thing a human being can do and something that should be avoided at all cost. Even the patient's contemplation of suicide is often considers harmful and treated as a disease in itself.

From a philosophical point of view considering the choice of life and dead is extremely relevant to good living and very sound considerations. The choice of life and dead is real, since responsibility for life is necessary in order to live life and even the best physician cannot keep a patient alive, who deep inside wants to die.

The reason for the western suicide is normally bad thriving as the tendency to have suicidal thoughts are closely connected to poor quality of life or a feeling of having no value or even harmful to the surrounding world. One in 20 of the Danish population is at a given point in time considering suicide (1).

HOLISTIC MEDICINE

In the process of holistic medical treatment the physician or therapist must some times use a deep existential rehabilitation process (2), which can include a crisis where the patient will consider committing suicide (3) and this danger must be considered as real. On the other hand, the deep contemplation of suicide and the following unconditional choice of life seem to be extremely beneficial for the patient deeply involved with personal development. This turns our view of suicide upside down and forces us to analyse the phenomenon of urge for suicide (or urge for dead as described by Freud (4)) in the existential perspective of healing the "soul" or core of existence. Freud stated that the subconscious of man contains two fundamental forces: a life force (or sexual force) and a death force. The life mission theory states that to annulate a painful life purpose, one must intent destruction of self and other (5). The logic is that we deepest down in existence wants to do good, but when this is to difficult it turns so

Fig 1

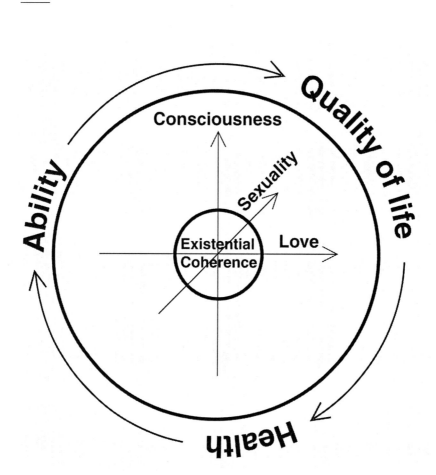

Figure 1. The human existence consist of three layers: 1) the layer of global quality of life (QOL), mental/physical health and ability, 2) the layer of love, power/consciousness and sexuality, and 3) the layer of existential coherence, where life inside the human being cohere with the outside world. When the patient or spiritually seeking person go still deeper towards the innermost core of existence (s)he will one day confront the most fundamental question in life: To be or not to be. This is the birth of the suicidal crises, which can only be definitely terminated by the patient deciding unconditionally to live. This decision must be taken autonomously, that is without any kind of pressure of external motivation

emotionally painful that we want to get out of this purpose and the only way to do so is to repress is by intending the opposite of the original purpose. This dynamic seems to be highly active in early childhood.

To understand the process of healing, the concept of "peeling the onion" is relevant (6). In therapy the patient digs deeper and deeper down the historical layers of traumas, and deeper and deeper into the heart of being. Three layers of existence can be identified, as they reveal themselves during holistic existential therapy (see figure 1):

- the layer of global quality of life (QOL), mental/physical health and ability
- the layer of love, power/consciousness and sexuality
- the layer of existential coherence, where life inside the human being cohere with the outside world

Normally what brings the patient to the clinic is a problem with one of the major issues of the first layer: quality of life – the patient is unhappy, stressed or in a crisis; health – the patient is sick, in pain or mentally disturbed or depressed or ability – the patient is poor functioning and of little value to self or others. Searching for the causes of the problems in this layer normally will bring the patient to the second, inner layer of existence, where often the disturbances in the dimensions of love, understanding and gender/character can be seen as the diseases causing the problems of health, QOL and ability. The problems of love, consciousness and sexuality are often emotionally overwhelmingly painful, and only with great support and intense "holding" will the roots of the existential imbalances be healed in the holistic medical clinic.

As the therapy goes still deeper, one day a third layer of existence is revealed. This layer seems to contain the core of existential responsibility. We call this innermost layer "coherence", or existential coherence (7) or Antonovsky coherence after the researcher naming it first (Aaron Antonovsky, 1923-1994) (8,9). The problem of this layer is that it cannot really be processed in therapy as the question is: Do I want to be connected to the world? Do I want to be a part of this world? Do I want to live or do I want to die? So we are back at the famous core question of existence, so beautifully worded by William Sheakspeare (1564-1616)(10): "To be or not to be".

The value of our autonomy is our free will, the prize of it is our loneliness. Only I can say if I want to live. So in the course of personal development, people who seek all the way to the basis of existence will face this question: when it comes down to it, do you want to live of do you want to die? The urge to die is very logical at this level: to be connected is to painful, to reach for the meaning of life is too much for me, to be is connected with to unbearable feelings and emotions for me to be acceptable. The urge to live is as logical: I am here as a gifted person, and the meaning of my life is to share my gift with other people and to the world in order to create value, as I was meant to.

The internal struggle on life and death that follows from these contradictory and opposing forces in the root of every individual human soul is from this perspective what causes the suicidal crises of man. Interestingly, therefore, the suicidal crisis becomes extremely important in the process of healing with the understanding and wise handling of the suicidal patient guiding the patient towards confronting the fundamental existential question "To be or not to be". This question is what brings growth, learning and personal progress to the troubled patient.

A CASE HISTORY

Anna was a student aged 22 years, who had completely repressed over 100 episodes of sexual abuse, incest and rape throughout her early childhood. She now seems to have recovered completely, including regaining her full emotional range, though holistic existential therapy, individually and in a group. The therapy took 18 month and more than one hundred hours of intensive therapy. In the beginning of the therapy, the issues were her physical and mental health, in the middle of the therapy the central issue was about her purpose of life and her love life. In the end of the therapy the issue was gender and sexuality. The strategy was building up her strength for several months, mobilising all her hidden resources and motivation for living, before the painful old traumas were confronted and integrated.

The following is from her own case diary, just before she ends her therapy, the suicidal crisis came and choosing life in the end of this crisis was what gave her the final breakthrough to life (3).

Saturday
After a nice bath I dressed and got ready to go out enjoying the nature. To begin with I must say that the sun had been shining on me the whole day; so beautiful and fine it was that I couldn't help saying hallo, while warming me on the outside and on the inside. This grew into many greetings. I was down near the Marienlyst Castle and was sitting at the end of the avenue, of course with the sun on my chins. The place was really beautiful and minimalistic. I proceeded a bit towards Helsingoer, but it wasn't the right way; too many cars, houses and first and foremost, too much noise. Therefore I went back to Hellebaek and followed the beach with my recently purchased goods in the bag: chips and white bread, uhmmm. How great an outing it had been! I could sense how I got calmed and at the same time boosted from listening to the roar of the waves. I sat down on a big stone, on the cushion I had brought along, enjoyed the sound of the water and shuddered slightly at the warm sunbeams. While sitting there I thought of it once again: that I am an unwritten leaf and that right now I am exceptionally lucky, because I have got the chance of shaping my life and myself like I want it most. Now I can cultivate the capacities, skills and qualities I greatly prefer to possess, and this without the usual, rotten wreckage in tow, which could prevent me from doing it. There is a huge opportunity right now! I was also thinking

this means that now I will actually be capable of getting/achieving ANYTHING I want. I just have to set about getting/achieving it. I walked to Hellebaek, about 6 km, along the beach and walked back via the woods. I thought of the song "The woods around the country are turning yellow now" and changed the title into "The woods around the country are glowing now" because I found that was what they actually did. The woods were unbelievably beautiful right now, in fact got my eyes filled with tears. It's indeed a huge gift for me to be up here in the beautiful nature. It was, no doubt, the completely right impulse to follow! As I returned here I began to paint/colour a bit in the colouring book. However, it didn't really mean anything to me though, so I didn't finish the drawing. It was so boring ... Then I laid down to rest. I dreamed a little, but as I didn't manage to maintain the dream, I forgot it again. Now I have been taking a bath thus, and I want to read a little before going to sleep again. Tomorrow I shall check out at 9:30 a.m. I am curious to know whether I'll wake up, having got no watch. What I have been experiencing has been right: To stay in the pleasure: going for a walk today, giving myself fully into the pleasure; not holding back at all and being able to stay in it. To give myself for: the anger. The same principle as for the pleasure: not holding back, being one hundred percent in it. - This is to be alive!

Saturday night

I twist about miserably in my bed, sweat as if I had got a very high temperature. The anger is huge and while lying here I am full of it. I beat the mattress, swear, snub them, and then begin projecting anger onto Søren (the therapist/physician). I get angry with him at the way he treated me this week; the rough way mixed with an apparent indifference as to the way he had been reflecting me. Then the suicide thoughts appeared:

- pistol: too much mess and too traumatic for those who find me
- cut my throat: same thing as with the pistol
- cut the wrists: then I shall suffer too long
- liquidation: I could pay someone to do it; this one is the best I immediately find until I am thinking of:
- overdose: which would be much better. A second later I think that I would probably not hit the correct dose, but would brain-damage myself and end as a vegetable, dribbling and not even being able to communicate to people that they must kill me. Then Søren would call on me, hold me close, and this would be the ultimate hell; me not being able to communicate, only dribble.

Now I cry and am totally miserable. I still sweat fever. I think then: Stop – just be quiet. One day at the time. I say aloud: "I bring life and joy. I bring life. I bring life" quite a lot of times and this calms me; this slowly makes me to relax. [Anna is here assuming responsibility for her own existence at the most deep level; she is facing the need of choosing to live or to die, accepting life on its own conditions or not accepting it. This is really the deepest level of existential choice for any human being: do you want to live or do you want to die? And it is a strictly personal question; nobody can really help you out here, you need to solve this for yourself, as Anna instinctively did.]

Monday

At long last I had a decent conversation with Søren. I had hurt his feelings, made him sad. He said I did it to create a distance between us. I told him that I was fond of him. He thanked and finished the conversation saying he was fond of me too. Subjects: detachment, independence. I slept very bad tonight, Søren and our understanding dialogue about "what did happen" the last few days being constantly in my thoughts. I even wrote a poem while shifting about restlessly.

Tuesday

I was at my gestalt therapist today. Further I am thinking that if I play my cards well I can end as something big. With my story, my intuitive intelligence and my courage I think I can become an entirely tough therapist. Watch me! Later I talked with Søren; he was making fun and said I would soon be able to take my gestalt therapist in therapy. It was funny said, and I must admit that later I will be forgetting her face while telling her how I had been experiencing my therapy. Not only was she gaping, she also realized that she was facing a very intelligent girl who had just discovered how intelligent she was. An educational experience, indeed! Let me finish here by mentioning that my personal development will no doubt carry on. I have been releasing so amazingly much insecurity. Never before have I been feeling so confident that everything will turn out all right. I find I keep on getting ever more gorgeous, and I am sure I shall get the best boyfriend in the whole world. I am in the process of being quite happy; I am not miserable any more. I am convinced I shall become entirely happy.

DISCUSSION

Fear of letting the patient confront the deep existential pain of loneliness and low coherence often makes the physician use force to save the patient's life. Often the physician use strong antipsychotic drugs and conversational therapy of a cognitive type to turn the patient's attention outwards against the outer world and away from the existential problems, thus avoiding the patient's confrontation of the emotional pain and the temptation of the suicidal perspective.

From a holistic perspective this approach is only dealing with the symptoms of the real disease, which is lack of existential coherence, and can thus not be recommended as the problem stays with the patient and can surface anytime again leaving the patient in tremendous danger of actually committing the suicide, the physician so eagerly tries to prevent. There is always a risk that the patient during the process of confronting the original painful causes of the existential disconnection can waste his or her own life, if not sufficiently supported. In holistic existential therapy it is our experience, when the patient is well supported in the confrontation of the fundamental questions related to assuming responsibility for the coherence, that this confrontation will almost always lead to a big YES to life. Without confronting the fundamental question of "to be or not to be" life can never be chosen 100% and thus never be lived fully.

CONCLUSION

The dynamics of suicide, wanting to die so much that self-destruction of the body becomes an issue, is the most painful a human being can go through. On the other hand it seems that solving the existential problems at the deepest level is the most beneficial achievement of all and the most important thing a person can be supported in doing. The taboo of dead in most western cultures has turned an existentially sound quest for meaning and search for healing of the soul and reconnection to the world into something shameful and bad, something that are often condemned. With a more profound, honest and brave understanding of life and personal growth, the reflection on suicide can be changed from being something we in our society and medical facilities try to avoid at all cost, to something natural and beautiful, we as holistic physicians and health professionals must support and guide our patients through.

The intense suffering connected to the dynamics of suicide is something we cannot spare the patient, but we can give him the benefit of his hard work, which only becomes obvious when the choice of life and dead is real, and life is finally chosen unconditionally. With a lot of "holding" and caring support even the most painful feelings of being completely worthless and unwanted on this planet is easier to deal with, contain and finally integrate for the patient.

ACKNOWLEDGEMENTS

This chapter is an adapted version of an earlier published paper (Ventegodt S, Merrick J. Suicide from a holistic point of view. ScientificWorldJournal 2005;5:759-66).

REFERENCES

1.   Ventegodt S. Quality of life in Denmark. Results from a population survey. Copenhagen: Forskningscentrets Forlag, 1995. [Danish]
2.   Ventegodt S, Gringols M, Merrick J. Clinical holistic medicine: Holistic rehabilitation. ScientificWorldJournal 2005;5:280-7.
3.   Ventegodt S, Clausen B, Merrick J. Clinical holistic medicine: The case story of Anna. II Patient diary with the holistic process of healing seen from within the patient. TSW-Holistic Health Med 2006;1:42-70.
4.   Freud S, Brill AA, ed. The basic writings of Sigmund Freud. New York: Modern Library, 1938
5.   Ventegodt S. The life mission theory: A theory for a consciousness-based medicine. Int J Adolesc Med Health 2003;15(1):89-91.

6.   Perls F, Hefferline R, Goodman P. Gestalt therapy. New York: Julian
        Press, 1951.
7.   Ventegodt S, Flensborg-Madsen T, Andersen NJ, Merrick J. Life
        Mission Theory VII: Theory of existential (Antonovsky) coherence: a
        theory of quality of life, health and ability for use in holistic
        medicine. ScientificWorldJournal 2005;5:377-89.
8.   Antonovsky A. Health, stress and coping. London: Jossey-Bass,
        1985.
9.   Antonovsky A. Unravelling the mystery of health. How people
        manage stress and stay well. San Franscisco: Jossey-Bass, 1987.
10.   Alexander P. William Sheakspeare: The complete works. London:
        Collins, 1991.

CHAPTER 22
Suicide and persons with intellectual disability

Joav Merrick, Efrat Merrick and Isack Kandel

S ome researchers have believed that impaired intellectual capacity could act as a buffer to suicidality, but later studies contest this assumption and it was found that the characteristics of suicidality in the population of persons with intellectual disability were very similar to that in persons without intellectual disability. In this chapter we review the studies conducted, describe the symptomatology in this population, risk factors, screening and intervention. Professionals working with this population should therefore be aware of and assess for this behavior in their clients. There is limited research on intervention for suicidal behavior in the ID population, but professionals should consider risk factors for suicide in this population and intervene, when suicidal risk/behavior is found.

INTRODUCTION

Suicide is today a leading cause of death (1) with an estimate that about one third of all people have suicidal ideation at some time during their life time (2). With this in mind, it is interesting to find little attention in the scientific literature to suicidal behavior in persons with intellectual disability (ID), since children, adolescents and adults with ID are at high risk for developing mental health problems with a prevalence of psychopathology approximately four times higher than that found in the general population (3-5). There still seems to be a tendency to underdiagnose psychiatric disorders in this population, which could be due to diagnostic overshadowing, lack of appropriate diagnostic criteria or appropriate assessment measures. Since people with ID have a higher incidence of depression (6,7), we have found it interesting that the issue of suicide in this population has received very little interest by researchers (7). Prevalence rates of suicide and suicide attempts in this population seems much lower, but it does occur (6,7). This chapter will review research on suicidal behavior in the population of persons with intellectual disability.

ADULTS WITH INTELLECTUAL DISABILITY

Suicide in adults with intellectual disability (ID) has been reported (6,8,14-18), but very few in-depths studies undertaken. A retrospective out-patient study of the first psychiatric diagnostic evaluation for 100 adults with mild ID, 100 patients with moderate, severe or profound ID compared with 100 matching patients without ID (N-ID) showed that N-ID were significantly more likely to present with mood complaints, anxiety complaints and suicidality (14 patients) (6). When mild ID was compared with moderate, severe and profound ID it was found that mild ID was significantly more likely to present with anxiety complaints and suicidality (6 cases with mild ID and none with moderate, severe or profound ID).

A study from Toronto (7), included 98 adults with borderline to moderate ID from several community (eight service agencies for persons with ID in Southern Ontario) and one out-patient clinical setting (University of Toronto Centre for Addiction and Mental Health), showed that 26 reported that they thought that life was not worth living "sometimes" (three with borderline, 18 with mild and five with moderate ID), while seven reported that they thought about that "most of the time" (six with mild and one with moderate ID). Of this total of 33 persons (34% of the sample), 23 told the interviewer that they thought about killing themselves and 11 said that they knew how they would do it (three with an overdose of pills, three slashing wrists, four with a jump, one with knife and one shooting). A total of eleven reported earlier suicide attempts. An interesting finding was that 16 of the persons, who had self-reported feeling suicidal, were not rated as so by the informants meaning that for 23% of the cases family/staff were unaware of the presence of these thoughts.

When the different groups were compared the suicidal adults were more likely to be unemployed, have dual diagnosis, under greater stress, lonely, depressed and with increased anxiety. They also reported less family support, less reciprocity in relationships and less overall social support. A review of the clinical charts revealed that the death of a relative or abuse history were common precursors to suicidal behavior (18,19).

PERSONS WITH DOWN SYNDROME

A study of 164 adults with Down syndrome found nine cases of depression with one who had suicidal ideation, a 23 year old female with moderate intellectual disability (ID), who lived with her recently divorced, depressed and hostile mother (20).

Another study (16) includes two case reports of suicide attempts, both of which occurred during major depressive periods. One was a 26 year old male, who from adolescence had approached females without disability for dates, but mostly rejected. With these rejections he started suicidal ideation, burning himself with lighter and finally jumped form a second story building, but was only slightly injured. The second case was a 25 year old female, who ran away from home in a depressive state and attempted to throw herself in front of a car, which missed her.

COMPLETED SUICIDE

One study from the United Kingdom (21) of 204 sudden deaths in residential care for persons with ID over a 50 year period found one case of suicide (jumping off a bridge). Another study of mortality over 60 years from a large US residential care center in California (22) did not report any case of suicide.

A 35 year follow-up study from Finland (9) based on a national cohort of 2,369 people with ID reported 10 cases of suicide with most of them (six) residing in mental hospitals. Social support were lacking in all cases and one case of sexual abuse. The overall suicide rate was 16.2 per 100,000 persons in this population, which was less than one third of the rate in the general Finnish population.

A study of mortality and morbidity among older adults with ID from the 1984-1993 period in New York (2,752 deaths of adults 40 years and older) showed a 9.5 per 100,000 rate for accidents, suicides and homicides (23).

In Israel the Division for Mental Retardation (DMR) of the Ministry of Social Affairs provides service to about 25,000 persons with intellectual disability in Israel (24). About 6,500 are provided service in residential care centers, about 2,000 in community living (hostels, protected apartments), while the rest are provided service, but living with their family (23). The Office of the Medical Director reviews every case of death in residential or community care and for the 1991-2005 period there has been no case of suicide in this population (25,26).

RISK FACTORS

In order to prevent suicide in this population, it is important to identify relevant risk factors for such behaviour. Clinical studies describing samples of individuals with ID, who were suicidal have identified sexual abuse, family instability, stress, and lack of social support as risk factors. In the general population, gender has been identified as a risk factor, with women being more likely to attempt suicide, but less likely to succeed, while men less likely to attempt, but more likely to succeed (19). The majority of case studies of attempted and completed suicide in ID tend to focus on men, but further research is warranted (19).

Only two studies have systematically examined differences between suicidal and non-suicidal individuals with ID with regard to risk factors. Benson and Laman (14) reported that suicidal individuals were more likely to be higher functioning, to have a history of hospitalization, and to have comorbid physical disabilities. The two groups did not differ in terms of where they lived or worked, family involvement, family history of psychiatric issues, or comorbid substance abuse. Lunsky (7,19) reported, based on a larger sample, that suicidal individuals with ID were more likely (than non-suicidal individuals with ID) to be unemployed, have a psychiatric diagnosis, and endorse greater stress, loneliness, depression and anxiety. They also reported less family support, less reciprocity in their relationships and less overall social support compared to individuals with ID, who were not suicidal. A review of the clinical charts revealed that the death of a relative and abuse history were common precursors to suicidal behavior. Similar reports of abuse history have been found in studies with adolescents (10).

INTERVENTION

There is limited research on intervention for suicidal behaviour in the ID population. Treatments for depression include medication, cognitive behavior therapy, behavioral and psychodynamic approaches, but no large scale studies have targeted suicidality specifically.

Two recent case reports on combined approaches for individuals with parasuicidal behaviours and borderline personality disorder reported significant reductions in parasuicidal behaviours in individuals with ID (27,28). It is possible that some of these strategies have utility with individuals, who have made several suicide attempts, but who do not have a borderline personality disorder diagnosis. Again, further research on treatment is warranted.

Intervention should consider risk factors for suicide and intervene in relation to such factors. If the person is very stressed for example, intervention could focus on reducing such stress. If the person is isolated, intervention could target increasing that person's social support. For any client with suicidal issues, a crisis plan should be developed that is agreed upon by the client, his or her caregivers, and all service providers. Consistency is very important in this area. With regard to behavioral strategies, understanding the function of the suicidal behaviour is critical (28). When these behaviours have an attention seeking component, it is important to reward alternative strategies to gaining attention rather than providing attention to such behaviours (see Esbensen and Benson (28) for a clear example). When the function of the behaviour is to escape from the current demands of life, the person may benefit from medical intervention to treat the underlying depression. If it is possible to help that person escape certain stressful demands without trying to end their life, such efforts should be made (29).

DISCUSSION

Suicidal behavior in persons with intellectual disability (ID) is a topic barely studied by professionals working with this population and therefore thought to be a rare phenomenon. The two studies discussed above (10,13) from two psychiatric settings in the United States catering for the population of children/adolescents with intellectual disability from the 1995-1999 period showed a frequency of 20-21% with suicidal behavior (thoughts, threats and behaviors, but rare attempts). These studies also showed that this behavior was more frequent in the inpatient setting, as a consequence of the worst cases getting hospitalized or maybe learned behavior during hospitalization.

In both studies (10,13) the characteristics, sex distribution and methods of suicide ideation and attempts were similar to that of adolescents without intellectual disability, but both studies had no case of completed suicide. The first study (10) had a high number of adolescents abused prior to admission, while the second study did not report on abuse, but this information (as in the general adolescent population) should alert every professional to investigate every case of attempetd suicide in an adolescent for possible prior abuse (physical or sexual).

In adults with ID, from a community and out-patient sample in Canada , 34% reported that "life was not worth living" sometimes, 23% were thinking about killing themselves and 11% reported that they had attempted to kill themselves in the past (7), while an out-patient psychiatric sample from the US (6) reported a finding of 6%. It seems that suicidal thoughts, threats and behaviors) are common in persons with mild-moderate ID, while extremely rare in persons with severe-profound ID (6,7).

Most of the studies described a life event (family member death, abuse, rejection), dual diagnosis or depression as important risk factors. It therefore seems important to be able to diagnose depression in this population, a separate problem in this population (19,30). For those with mild-moderate ID there is consensus that standardized diagnostic criteria be used, but for persons with severe-profound ID there is still doubt concerning the method of diagnosis (30).

CONCLUSIONS

It is our impression that suicidal ideation and attempts do occur among persons with intellectual disability and professionals should therefore be aware of and assess for this behavior. Sadness or depression are symptoms that could indicate later suicidal behavior and should be recognized, and subsequently diagnosed and treated accordingly. Hurley and Sovner (31) published recommendations for the assessment and treatment of suicidal behaviour in individuals with ID, where they outlined several essential questions related to risk of suicide (e.g., history in individual or family member of suicide attempts of mental illness, increase in stressors, impulsivity, substance abuse, precautions taken against discovering suicidal behaviour, suicide note, lethality of past attempts, hopelessness in future) and key events associated with suicide (recent dramatic loss of relationship or home, recent event considered shameful, diagnosis or experience of extreme medical condition, and expectation of death from medical condition.)

The assessment of suicidality in those with ID covers similar content to what is assessed in the general population. What complicates such an assessment is that the person with ID often has communication impairments that make obtaining such information difficult. The individual may be hesitant to disclose such information, because of their fear of being punished for such feelings or because they are eager to please and give the "right answer" to the clinician. Suggestions on how to facilitate this type of interview has been published (32) and they suggested for example, finding a comfortable place for the assessment, using visual aids, comfort objects, explaining procedures clearly, involving caregivers as much as possible. A clinician may opt to avoid potential reporting biases by asking a caregiver about suicidality, but such a strategy will also have bias, since many caregivers are unaware of suicidality in their clients (7). Speaking with caregivers is an important part of the assessment, and identifying discrepancies important, however information from one informant cannot replace the perspective of another.

ACKNOWLEDGEMENTS

This chapter is an adapter version of an earlier published paper (Merrick J, Merric E, Lunsky Y, Kandel I. A review of suicidality in persons with intellectual disability. Isr j Psychiatr Relat Sci 2006;43(4):258-64.

REFERENCES

1.   CDC/NCHS, National Vital Statistics System. Website: http://www.cdc.gov/nchs/data/dvs/LCWK9_2002.pdf
2.   Bongar BM. The suicidal aptient: Clinical and legal standards of care, 2nd Ed. Washington, DC: Am Psychol Ass, 2002.
3.   Rush KS, Bowman LG, Eidman SL, Toole LM, Mortenson BP. Assessing psychopathology in individuals with developmental disabilities. Behav Modif 2004;28(5):621-37.
4.   Gustafsson C, Sonnander K. Occurrence of mental health problems in Swedish samples of adults with intellectual disabilities. Soc Psychiatry Psychiatr Epidemiol 2004;39(6):448-56.
5.   Richards M, Maughan B, Hardy R, Hall I, Strydom A, Wadsworth M. Long-term affective disorder in people with mild learning disability. Br J Psychiatry 2001;179:523-7.
6.   Hurley AD, Folstein M, Lam N. Patients with and without intellectual disability seeking outpatient psychiatric services: diagnoses and prescribing pattern. J Intellect Disabil Res 2003;47(Pt 1):39-50.
7.   Lunsky Y. Suicidality in a clinical and community sample of adults with mental retardation. Res Dev Disabil 2004;25:231-43.
8.   Menolascino FJ, Lazer J, Stark JA. Diagnosis and management of depression and suicidal behavior in persons with severe mental retardation. J Multihandicap Pers 1989;2:89-103.
9.   Patja K, Iivanainen M, Raitasuo S, Lonnqvist J. Suicide mortality in mental retardation: A 35-year follow-up study. Acta Psychiatr Scand 2001;103:307-11.
10.   Walters AS, Barrett RP, Knapp LG, Boden MC. Suicidal behavior in children and adolescents with mental retardation. Res Dev Disabil 1995;16(2):85-96.

11.   Tiet QQ, Finney JW, Moos RH.Recent sexual abuse, physical abuse, and suicide attempts among male veterans seeking psychiatric treatment.Psychiatr Serv 2006:57(1):107-13.

12.   Ammerman RT, VanHasselt VB, Hersen M, McGonigle JJ, Lubetsky MJ. Abuse and neglect in psychiatrically hospitalized multihandicapped children. Chil Abuse Neglect 1989;13:335-43.

13.   Hardan A, Sahl R. Suicidal behavior in children and adolescents with developmental disorders. Res Dev Disabil 1999;20(4):287-96.

14.   Benson BA, Laman DS. Suicidal tendencies of mentally retarded adults in community settings. Aust NZ J Dev Disabil 1988;14:49-54.

15.   Grossi V, Brown RI. Suicide attempts among mentally handicapped individuals. A pilot study. Alberta Psychol 1985;14:12-3.

16.   Hurley AD. Two cases of suicide attempt by patients with Down's syndrome. Psychiatr Service 1998;49:1618-9.

17.   Walters RM. Suicidal behaviour in severely mentally handicapped patients. Br J Psychiatry 1990;151:444-6.

18.   Hurley AD. Potentially lethal suicide attempts in persons with developmental disabilities: Review and three new case reports. Ment Health Aspects Dev Disabil 2002;5(3):90-5.

19.   Lunsky Y, Canrinus M. Gender issues, mental retardation and depression. In: Sturmey P, ed. Mood disorders in people with mental retardation. Kingston, NY: NADD Press, 2005:113-29.

20.   Myers BA, Pueschel SM. Major depression in a small group of adults with Down syndrome. Res Dev Disabil 1995;16(4):285-99.

21.   Carter G, Jancer J. Mortality in the mentally handicapped: A 50 year survey at the Stoke Park Group of Hospitals. J Ment Defic Res 1983;27:143-56.

22.   Chaney RH, Eyman RK. Patterns in mortality over 60 years among persons with mental retardation in a residential facility. Ment Retard 2000;38(3):289-93.

23.   Janicki MP, Dalton AJ, Henderson CM, Davidson PW. Mortality and morbidity among older adults with intellectual disability: Health services considerations. Disabil Rehab 1999;21(5-6):284-94.

24.   Merrick J. Trends in the population served by the Divison for Mental Retardation, 1985-2003. Jerusalem: Office Med Dir, Min Labour Soc Affairs, 2004.

25.   Merrick J. Mortality of persons with intellectual disability in residential care in Israel, 1991-1997. J Intell Dev Disabil 2002;27(4):265-72.

26.   Merrick J. Trends in cause of death for persons with intellectual disability in residential care in Israel 1991-2005. Jerusalem: Office Med Director, Min Soc Affairs, 2006.

27.   Wilson SR, A four-stage model for management of borderline personality disorder in people with mental retardation. Ment Health Aspects Dev Disabil 2001;4:68-76.

28.   Esbensen AJ, Benson BA. Cognitive variables and depressed mood in adults with intellectual disability. J Intellect Disabil Res 2005;49(Pt7):481-9.

29.   Sturmey P. Suicidal threats and behavior in a person with developmental disabilities: Effective psychiatric monitoring based on a fundamental assessment. Behav Intervent 1994;9:235-45.

30.   McBrien JA. Assessment and diagnosis of depression in people with intellectual disability. J Intellect Disabil Res 2003;47(1):1-13.

31.   Hurley AD, Sovner S. Suicidal behavior in mentally retarded persons. Psychiatr Aspects Ment Retard 1998;1:35-8.

32.   Bradley E, Lofchy J. Learning disability in the accident and emergency department. Adv Psychiatr Treatment 2005;11(1):45-57.

CHAPTER 23
A good and easy death - euthanasia

Isack Kandel and Joav Merrick

This chapter reviews the historical aspects of euthanasia and the right of a person to decide what will happen to his body, honoring the wishes in his last moments, when there is no hope of recovery and death is only a question of time. Euthanasia means "good or easy death", and if we give this term a different meaning, "merciful death", then euthanasia means the killing of a person by others, causing intentional death as a result of feelings of mercy toward a suffering person. Mercy killing is a contradiction to criminal law in most countries and considered an act of murder, which is the source of most of the ethical dilemmas concerning euthanasia. Religious aspects, legal aspects, and the experience in different regions of the world are discussed here, with a focus on the medical model implemented in the Netherlands.

INTRODUCTION

The term euthanasia stems from two Greek words–eu (good or easy) and thanotos (death) or in other words, a good and easy death (1,2). The term itself, nice or easy death, is not problematic and even expresses respect toward humankind. People live nicely and should die similarly. The question is whether it is morally and legally imperative to endeavor to help them leave this world nicely. The term euthanasia includes the word death and does not mention release. The term explicitly mentions the wish that death should be easy, good, and not difficult. In modern terminology, the customary term for euthanasia is 'mercy killing'.

If we analyze the term, we see that it presents the merciful deed that is performed by killing. In other words, euthanasia is seen as a positive act performed because of the kindness of its enactor, perhaps a type of gift to the person killed. When we discuss the need to ease the process of death, it is important to clarify that we are dealing with an incurable patient who is dying and has no chance of recovery (3). In fact, the idea of reducing suffering motivates those who demand legal recognition of euthanasia. We may ask, "Whose suffering? Merciful toward whom? By whom?"

The medical profession perceives death as a process, in contrast to the legal profession, which perceives death as occurring at a specific moment, a transient, one-time event. The conventional image of death in society determines the prevalent concept of health. Society's image of death indicates the level of independence of its members. The image of a natural death—death with medical supervision, with good health and reason—is completely new. Following the development of technology in the eighteenth century and the increase in life expectancy, the economic status of the elderly, as well as their physical functioning, has improved. A new concept has evolved, one that can be aspired to in old age. In the late nineteenth and early twentieth centuries, the term 'clinical death' replaced the term 'natural death'. Clinical death determines that a person has died or will die in a few minutes, unless heart activity is renewed by external intervention.

HISTORICAL BACKGROUND

Sacks (4) wrote that euthanasia was usual among primitive tribes and nations. It was customary to take an ill or elderly person wishing to die out of the settlement or to allow the individual to die peacefully instead of continuing to sustain his life through means considered artificial.

One of the first persons to defend euthanasia and to support it as a method was Plato, who claimed that the invalid should not be kept alive. This did not stem from compassion toward the disabled but rather from concern about their becoming a burden on society. The custom of euthanasia is also alluded to in the Hippocratic Oath: "I will give no deadly medicine to any one if asked, nor suggest any such counsel."

Russell (5) stated that euthanasia was apparently customary, but Hippocrates (460-377 BCE) objected (as can be understood from the Oath). During the Middle Ages, Sir Thomas More (1478-1535) in his book Utopia (1516) suggested that the state enact a law in favor of merciful murder on behalf of mortally ill patients, which should be supervised by the state and the church. More was one of the first to coin the term euthanasia in its present interpretation.

In the United Kingdom (UK) in 1798, the economist Thomas Malthus published his theory on poverty and called for population control; and in the 1850s the philosopher Herbert Spencer published Social Statics, in which he coined the term survival of the fittest; in 1859 Charles Darwin published Origin of Species, all of which were a prelude to bringing the English statistician Francis J Galton on the scene, who introduced the term Eugenics (Greek for well-born) (6). Galton's ideas were exported to the United States (US), where Charles B Davenport and Harry H Laughlin, with funding from the Carnegie Institution of Washington, established the Station for Experimental Evolution at Cold Spring Harbor in 1904. The grounds for eugenicide were laid and partly carried out in the US but were later adopted by Nazi Germany in the 1940s on a much larger scale (6). In fact, the idea of a lethal chamber for mass murder came from British eugenicists, like George Bernard Shaw, who in 1910 lectured on the subject to the Eugenics Education Society. This view also featured in the landmark book Textbook on Mental Deficiency by Arthur F Tredgold (7), first published in 1908 but later published in several editions, where he concluded that for about 80,000 persons in Britain with intellectual disability "In my opinion it would be an economical and humane procedure were their existence to be painlessly terminated... the time has come when euthanasia should be permitted..." (6).

The book Permitting the Destruction of Life not Worthy of Life was published in Germany in 1920 by Karl Binding, a professor of law from the University of Leipzig, and Alfred Hoche, MD, a professor of psychiatry at the University of Freiburg, where they argued that patients who asked for 'death assistance' should, under very carefully controlled conditions, be able to obtain it from a physician. This book, together with the work by British and American eugenicists, eventually helped support the involuntary euthanasia and mass murder implemented by Nazi Germany (4,6). In 1998, the state of Oregon legalized assisted suicide, and in 1999, Jack Kevorkian, MD, was sentenced to a 10-25 year prison term for giving a lethal injection to Thomas Youk, whose death was shown on the 60 Minutes television program. In 2001, the Netherlands legalized euthanasia and in 2002, Belgium legalized euthanasia (2,3).

RELIGION AND EUTHANASIA

Most Christian dominations are against euthanasia because of the belief that life is given by God and that human beings are made in God's image. Some churches also emphasize the importance of not interfering with the natural process of death. Life is seen as a gift from God, with birth and death as part of the life processes that God has created and we should respect these processes; therefore, no human being has the authority to take the life of any innocent person, even if that person wants to die. The process of dying is spiritually important and should not be disrupted, with many churches believing that the period just before death is a profoundly spiritual time. Christians believe that the intrinsic dignity and value of human lives means that the value of each human life is identical. Believers do not think that human dignity and value are measured by mobility, intelligence, or any achievements in life. Patients who are in a persistent vegetative state, although seriously damaged, remain living human beings, and so their intrinsic value remains the same, so it would be wrong to treat their lives as worthless. Patients who are old or sick and near the end and people who have mental or physical handicaps have the same value as any other human being. Therefore, the Christian church objects to euthanasia (5).

The basic Jewish law directly related to this subject is the Sixth Commandment: Thou shalt not kill. The Jewish tradition regards the preservation of human life as one of its supreme moral values and forbids doing anything that might shorten life; yet, Jewish law does not require physicians to make dying last longer than it naturally would. Jewish law and tradition regard human life as sacred and find it wrong for anyone to shorten a human life because our lives are not ours to dispose of as we wish. All life is of infinite value, regardless of its duration or quality because all human beings are made in the image of God. Saving an individual from pain is not a reason to kill a person, nor is it lawful to kill oneself to save oneself from pain, but there is a limit to the duty to keep people alive. If a life is ending and there is serious pain, then the physician has no duty to make that person suffer more by artificially extending their dying moments. Jewish law forbids active euthanasia and regards this as murder. There are no exceptions to this rule and it makes no difference if the person wants to die. To shorten a life even if it would end very soon is wrong because every moment of human life is considered equal in value to many years of life. So even if a person is a 'goses' (someone who has started to die and will die within 72 hours), any action that might hasten their death—for example closing the eyes or moving a limb—is prohibited.

On the other hand, if the person is kept alive only by a ventilator, for example, a physician is allowed to switch it off because the ventilator is impeding the natural process of death (8). This ruling has been made by several great rabbis and if the patient is in pain, giving medicine is allowed even though this medicine will hasten death, as long as the dosage is intended only to relieve pain. From the above, we understand that Jewish law is unequivocally opposed to the active facilitation of a patient's death, while permitting the removal of obstacles that prevent easy death, thus enabling passive euthanasia in certain cases.

Muslims believe that human life is sacred, given by Allah, and are therefore against euthanasia. Suicide and euthanasia are explicitly forbidden in the Quran (Koran), the sacred text of Islam. In Buddhism and Hinduism, the situation is less clear, but suicide was a significant part of the Japanese samurai tradition; Sikhs, on the other hand, are against euthanasia.

EUTHANASIA TODAY

With the assistance of innovative medical technology, modern medicine can today revive sick persons who were once considered as good as dead. Although technology has developed and continues to do so, the ethical world has not advanced at the same pace. Complex treatments sometimes cause pain and suffering. Postponing death prolongs life, but does not always improve its quality (9). Pharmacologic developments enable various treatments of difficult diseases. In addition, analgesic medications have been developed that help patients to cope with suffering but at the same time destroy body cells and sometimes hasten the patient's end. The question is, therefore, whether to use painkilling medication when it is known to hasten the end (9).

Modern medicine has almost doubled human life expectancy. Because of this increase, the number of elderly adults has also risen, some of whom create an economic/ social/sociological burden worldwide. This reality will constitute a problem when these individuals reach complete senility and exist only from a biological point of view. Then we will have to decide whether to do all possible to prolong their lives or to find other ways, such as organ transplants. Transplants require the extraction of body parts from those who have recently died or those defined as brain dead and whose body parts are operated by various machines. Here is the double bind—are we entitled to keep a person alive artificially only to use his body for trying to save another human being? Can we interrupt the operation of life-sustaining machines and at what stage may this be done? Enormous financial resources have been invested in the maintenance of instruments for terminally ill patients, and a large staff is required for their operation. Thus, sustaining a terminally ill person with the help of technology can be seen as economically problematic (9).

FORMS OF EUTHANASIA

Customarily, the concept of euthanasia can be divided into four main types (1):

- Active euthanasia (performance of a direct act leading to the termination of life)
- Passive euthanasia (death caused by avoiding life-prolonging activity, such as not giving food, fluid, or not providing medical care)
- Voluntary euthanasia (the patient himself performs the act, requests or agrees that it be performed, after his health condition has been explained to him and he makes the decision while fully conscious)
- Involuntary euthanasia (the patient does not express his opinion or cannot express his opinion because he is unconscious, or when the patient is a baby and those surrounding him wish to make the decision in his place based on various considerations).

Active euthanasia means taking specific steps to cause death—for example, injecting an overdose of pain-killers or sleeping pills or other drugs to induce death. Passive euthanasia is defined as allowing a person to die by withholding medical treatment. For example, disconnecting a kidney dialysis machine from a patient who requires one for survival will lead to an earlier death. Active differs from passive euthanasia in that something is done to end life in the former, whereas something is not done that might have preserved life in the latter. Voluntary euthanasia means when the patient requests that his life be ended or that life-saving treatment be stopped, with full knowledge that death will soon follow. Involuntary euthanasia is taking a patient's life without the patient's knowledge or consent, usually because the patient is unconscious, unable to communicate, or too sick and weak.

LEGAL ASPECTS

Euthanasia is not recognized by Israeli law. According to the Criminal Code Ordinance of 1936, which is based on English law, the motivation for performing an act of killing or murder is irrelevant. Even when a person is killed according to his own wish or request and even if his motives were mercy killing, this law is still upheld. Many sections deal with euthanasia, but section 214 states that any person who has caused the death of another is guilty of murder. According to section 216 of the Penal Code, euthanasia fits the category of "premeditated murder", because the following conditions exist: (a) there was no provocation by the other side; (b) it was preceded by planning; (c) it was performed in cold blood. A person accused of premeditated murder is liable to be sentenced to life imprisonment without pardon. Section 231 places professional responsibility on the physician, who must be properly trained and behave with reasonable responsibility, while engaged in his work.

In December 2005 a new government bill was passed by the Israel Knesset (parliament) after six years of discussions and deliberations, which will allow the terminally ill to die in dignity without being forced to be kept alive by artificial means. A delayed response timer build into the respirator (ventilator) will be the solution to the problem of how to let terminally ill patients end their lives, if they have so indicated in a living will and are over the age of 17 years (10).

United States and Canada

Over many years, both a professional and lay debate has been going on over the issue of what actively causes death and what is the process of natural death. A precedent was set for turning off life-support equipment in terminal illnesses following a decision by the Missouri Supreme Court in Cruzan v. Director (11), Missouri Department of Health. In 1983, a near-fatal automobile accident left Nancy

Beth Cruzan in a persistent vegetative state and she was rendered incompetent. For several weeks, she was fed through a tube. When her parents wanted to terminate the life-support system, state hospital officials would not do so without court approval. The Supreme Court of Missouri held that because no clear and convincing evidence was available regarding Nancy's desire to have life-sustaining treatment withdrawn under such circumstances, her parents lacked authority to effect such a request. In a 5-to-4 decision, the Court held that while individuals enjoyed the right to refuse medical treatment under the Due Process Clause, incompetent persons are not able to exercise such rights (11). The US Supreme court affirmed.

Therefore, living wills became a practical solution, and California was the first to pass a law to this effect in 1977, known as the California Natural Death Act or "Death-With-Dignity Statute". In Florida, the lack of a written will to determine what her wishes would have been regarding life-prolonging procedures complicated the case of Terri Schiavo (12). Following cardiac arrest, Schiavo lingered in a persistent vegetative state from 1990 until she died after her feeding tube was removed in 2005. In 2000, Schiavo's husband (and legal guardian) received the legal authori-zation to remove her feeding tube, based on what he claimed were her orally expressed wishes that she would not want to be kept on a machine with no hope for recovery. Nevertheless, because oral feeding is not considered a life-prolonging procedure under Florida law, her parents challenged the decision and succeeded in delaying the removal of the tube for 5 years through legal channels (12).

Several groups and societies, in both England and the US (6), have pressed for right-to-die legislation. The pro-euthanasia movement in the US gained momentum, when in 1975, a 21-year-old woman named Karen Ann Quinlan suffered respiratory arrest requiring a respirator to assist her breathing. Severe and irreversible brain damage left her in a state of coma, eventually diagnosed as being in being in a chronic persistent vegetative state. Karen's family did not want to take extraordinary means to keep her alive, but hospital officials refused their request. In 1976, the parents obtained a court order from the New Jersey Supreme Court allowing them to remove the artificial respirator. After the respirator was unplugged, Karen began to breathe on her own but remained in a coma for almost 10 years without ever regaining consciousness until her death in 1985 (13).

In the 1990s, Jack Kevorkian, a physician who had gained public interest by assisting a number of people to commit suicide was tried and acquitted repeatedly in the assisted deaths of seriously ill people. In 1997, the Supreme Court upheld state laws banning assisted suicide (in most US states assisting in a suicide is a crime). Voters in Oregon in 1994 approved physician-assisted suicide for the terminal ill and the law went into effect in 1997 after a long court challenge. In 1999, Kevorkian was convicted of murder in Michigan for an assisted suicide that was seen on national television (3). In 2001, Oregon sued to prohibit the enforcement of a directive issued under the federal Controlled Substances Act by the Bush Administration in an attempt to undermine the law. The Supreme Court ruled that the federal government had exceeded its authority (14).

Public awareness of the issues surrounding euthanasia was aroused by the decision of Nancy B. v. Hotel-Dieu de Quebec in Canada in January 1992. In this case, a Québec superior court judge authorized the physician to disconnect a respirator from a young woman, paralyzed as a result of Guillain-Barré syndrome (incurable neurological disease), who requested that the respirator be removed (15).

In both the United States and Canada, a legal distinction between passive and active euthanasia prevails, based on public acceptance of the right of patients to refuse treatment. Despite a prohibition against active euthanasia, courts in both countries have ruled that physicians should not be legally punished for withholding or withdrawing life-sustaining treatment at a patient's request or by the request of an authorized representative.

Australia

On 25 May 1995, The Rights of the Terminally Ill Bill was passed by the Legislative Assembly of the Northern Territory of Australia (16), the only authority in the world to enact both legally assisted suicide and euthanasia. The law went into effect in July 1996 but the following amendment, passed by the national parliament (Commonwealth) in 1997, made the law ineffective:

> "8A. ASSISTANCE NOT TO BE PROVIDED AT PUBLIC HOSPITALS AND HEALTH CLINICS. A substance shall not be administered to a patient for the purpose her life under this Act at premises

declared under section 6 (2)(a) managed, and from which medical services,
within the meaning Territory."

The repeal was possible because the Commonwealth can review and repeal a Northern Territory Act if the Act can be shown to be in conflict with national views.

Philip Nitschke was listed as the physician in all four deaths that occurred as assisted-suicide while the law was in effect. The method used has been described as "death-by-laptop". Nitschke came to the house carrying a laptop computer, plastic tubing, and a pump-driven syringe filled with barbiturates. The computer was equipped with an interactive suicide software program, in which the patient had to answer three questions after being hooked up to an intravenous line connected to the computer. The three questions had to be answered as yes/no:

1.   Are you aware that if you go ahead to the last screen and press the 'yes' button, you will be given a lethal dose of medicine and die?
2.   Are you certain you understand that if you proceed and press the 'yes' button on the next screen, you will die?
3.   In 15 seconds you will be given a lethal injection.

Activation of the syringe and was triggered by a "yes" reply to each question, resulting in a sequential delivery of the drug. The method supported the notion that the patient and not the physician administered the fatal dose (17).

Japan
In Japan, the term anraku-shi (euthanasia) means peaceful (anraku) death (shi). In 1962, in a landmark case in which a son helped to kill his terminally ill father, the High Court in Nagoya first outlined the guidelines for euthanasia by laying down six conditions for legal euthanasia:

1.   the inevitability of death despite all medical attempts
2.   the suffering of those close to the patient
3.   the need to attempt to save the patient from suffering
4.   a clear expression to die from the patient
5.   the method of killing should be appropriate
6.   the procedure must be performed by a physician.

In 1995, the 1962 precedent was reiterated by the Yokohama District Court, which set out the following four conditions that must be met before euthanasia can be performed (18):

1.   a patient must be suffering unbearable pain
2.   death is unavoidable
3.   there is no alternative to relieve suffering
4.   the patient's will is clear.

Europe

Since 1937, the Swiss penal code states,

> *"Whoever, from selfish motives, induces another to commit suicide or assists him therein shall be punished, if the suicide was successful or attempted, by confinement in a penitentiary for not more than five years or by imprisonment."*

Although assisted suicide is not legal in Switzerland, the above statement is de facto legalization. No prosecution can take place if the person assisting the suicide denies having self-seeking intentions. Therefore, the act is unpunishable in the absence of a proven selfish motive (17).

In 1936, the Voluntary Euthanasia Act was proposed in England, but it was rejected by a majority of 35 to 14. In England, euthanasia is considered a criminal act, however there is an alternative via hospices commonly found in England, who support relief of pain and suffering with respect and attention toward the dying person. The patient participates in choosing proper care, but there is no legislation supporting the use of a living will or the cessation of life-sustaining care of vegetative patients (19).   Until   2002 in the Netherlands, euthanasia and assisted suicide were against the law, despite being widely practiced since 1973. Between 1973 and 2002, several court decisions and medical association guidelines influenced the Dutch situation. In 1973, Geertruida Postma, a physician, ended the life of her seriously ill mother and was subsequently convicted in a District Court case accusing her of the crime of euthanasia. After finding her guilty of mercy killing, the court imposed a one-week suspended sentence and probation rather than imprisonment for a maximum of 12 years. The court was influenced by expert testimony from the district medical inspector stating that the average physician thought that euthanasia should be considered acceptable under certain conditions, which formed the basis for the acceptance of euthanasia and assisted suicide in the Netherlands (2,17). Although euthanasia and assisted suicide remained punishable, they were not prosecuted if these guidelines were followed.

In 1991, a new procedure for reporting physician-assisted deaths was introduced in the Netherlands, which led to a tripling in the number of reported cases. In 1995, a nationwide study of euthanasia and other medical practices concerning the end of life began, which was identical to a study conducted in 1990. This study involved interviews with 405 physicians (general practitioners, nursing home physicians, and clinical specialists) and questionnaires mailed to physicians, who attended to 6,060 deaths identified from death certificates (20). 2.3% of those in the interview study and 2.4% of those in the death-certificate study were estimated to have resulted from euthanasia and 0.4% and 0.2% resulted from physician-assisted suicide. In 0.7% of cases, life was ended without the explicit, concurrent request of the patient. Pain and symptoms were alleviated with opioids that may have shortened life in 14.7 to 19.1% of cases, while decisions to withdraw life-prolonging treatment were made in 20.2%.

In the Netherlands, the "Termination of Life on Request and Assisted Suicide (Review Procedures) Act", passed by the Dutch Parliament in 2001, amended certain sections of the criminal code regarding euthanasia and assisted suicide. The Act specifically states that such 'offenses' are not punishable if (a) such acts were "committed by a physician who has met the requirements of due care" as described in the act and (b) those assisting such acts have informed the municipal "autopsist" as sated in the Burial and Cremation Act (17). Hence, such 'crimes' were transformed into medical treatments by the "due care" requirements, as physicians had advocated. Under the new law, minors between sixteen and eighteen years of age can request that their lives be terminated. Parents or guardians must be consulted but have no authority to prevent the requested death. Although children between the ages of twelve and sixteen years of age can request euthanasia or assisted suicide, a parent or guardian must agree with the decision (17). Based on a written advance request for death of a currently incapacitated patient who is 16 years old or older, the physician has the legal right to carry out euthanasia. Later, the University Medical Center in Groningen acknowledged that it had been euthanizing infants, not only in the case of terminally ill newborns, but also in cases of children who had spina bifida and other disabilities (21).

Belgium followed suit in 2002 with an act legalizing euthanasia, which limits euthanasia to competent adults and emancipated minors. In 2005, a pharmaceutical company announced that home "euthanasia kits" would be available soon in Belgian pharmacies. Reports indicated that the kits will contain a barbiturate, a paralyzing agent, an anesthetic and instructions for use costing 45 Euro (17).

DISCUSSION

In response to advances in medical technology, physicians and lawmakers are slowly developing new professional and legal definitions of death. Additionally, experts are formulating rules to implement these definitions in clinical situations, as for example when procuring organs for transplantation. The majority of countries have accepted a definition of brain death, the point when there is a complete and irreversible cessation of brain activity, as the time when it is legal to turn off life-support system with permission from the family.

Europe and especially the Netherlands seems to be the front runners, when in 2001 the Netherlands became the first country to legalize active euthanasia and assisted suicide and this way formalize a medical practice that the government had tolerated for many years. Under the Dutch law, euthanasia is justified, if the physician follows strict guidelines, which include: 1) the patient makes a voluntary, informed and stable request; 2) the patient is suffering unbearably with no prospect of improvement; 3) the physician consults with another physician, who in turn concurs with the decision to help the patient die and 4) the physician performing the euthanasia procedure carefully reviews the patient's condition. Today it is estimated that about 2% of all deaths in he Netherlands each year occur as a result of euthanasia.

In 2002, the parliament of Belgium also legalized active euthanasia, permitting physicians to perform euthanasia only for patients who are suffering unbearably with no hope of improvement. The patient must make a voluntary, well-considered and repeated request to die in writing. Other physicians must be consulted to confirm the condition of the patient and each act of euthanasia must be reported to a government commission for review.

A discussion of euthanasia concerns questions from the medical, social and ethical fields and it is no wonder that the approach to the subject differs from society to society and from country to country. When the view of passive euthanasia was examined, most of the studies leaned toward consent and acceptance. If, however, we discuss the clear definition of active euthanasia, then most countries prohibit it absolutely. The studies quoted also discussed the effect of religion on these views.

The accelerated medical development in our generation enables us to prolong life artificially. This tendency will increase, and therefore the question presented in this paper will become more acute and require a clearer answer. The world around us is becoming more scientific and sophisticated, we, as human beings, must maintain the connection to our moral values, and when we try to answer the question of euthanasia, we must discern the true motive of our acts. When are we directed by the needs of the suffering individual? Do we distinguish between the interests of the individual, the family, and society? Courageous answers to these questions, and to many others, are a necessary precondition when deciding on the weighty issue of euthanasia.

A critical review of the euthanasia system in the Netherlands has been published by an Israeli researcher (2), who before visiting that country was a supporter of the way euthanasia was practiced there, but came back with reservations about the practicality of its implementation. It is worth listening to his proposed guidelines:

- The physician should not suggest assisted suicide to his patient, but instead the patient should have the option to ask for such assistance
- The request for physician assisted suicide of an adult and competent patient who suffers from an intractable, incurable and irreversible disease must by voluntary
- Palliative care must be implemented so the patient will not ask or be influenced by severe pain
- The patient must be informed of the situation and the prognosis for recovery or escalation of the disease and the suffering it may involve
- It must be ensured that the decision is not the result of familial or environmental pressures
- The decision-making process must include a second opinion to verify diagnosis
- A consultant must review requests for physician-assisted suicide

- Prior to the performance of physician-assisted suicide, a physician and a psychiatrist must visit and examine the patient
- The patient can rescind at any time
- Physician-assisted suicide must be performed only by a physician with another present
- Physician-assisted suicide must be conducted by one of three options: oral medication, self-administered lethal intravenous infusion, or self-administered lethal injection
- Physicians must not demand a special fee for physician-assisted suicide
- There must be extensive documentation in the patient's medical file
- Pharmacists must be required to report all prescriptions for lethal medications
- Physicians must not be coerced into actions against their conscience
- A legal medical association must monitor physician assisted suicide
- Sanctions must be in effect if physicians fail to follow these guidelines.

ACKNOWLEDGEMENTS

This chapter is an adapted versison of an earlier published paper (Kandel I, Merrick J. Euthanasia: A review. Int J Disabil Hum dev 2006;5(1):27-33).

REFERENCES

1. Darbyshire P. Euthanasia. Whose life, whose decision. Nurs Times 1987;83(45):26-9.
2. Cohen-Almagor R. Euthanasia in the Netherlands. The policy and practice of mercy killing. Dordrecht, the Netherlands: Kluwer, 2004.
3. Cohen-Almagor R. The right to die with dignity. An argument in ethics, medicine and law. New Brunswick, NJ, USA: Rutgers Univ Press, 2001.
4. Sacks S. Aktion T 4: Annihilation of disabled in the Third Reich. Tel-Aviv: Papyrus, 1985. [Hebrew]
5. Russell O. Freedom to die. Moral and legal aspects of euthanasia. New York, NY, USA: Human Sci, 1977.
6. Black E. War against the weak. Eugenics and America's campaign to create a master race. New York, NY, USA: Thunder's Mouth Press, 2003.
7. Tredgold AF. Textbook on mental deficiency (Amentia). New York, NY, USA: William Wood, 1908.
8. Jakobovits I. Jewish medical ethics. A comparative and historical study of the Jewish religious attitude to medicine and its practice. New York, NY, USA: Bloch, 1967.
9. Turton P. The death debate. Nurs Times 1987;83(45):31.
10. Siegel-Itzkovich J. Israelis turn to timer device to facilitate passive euthanasia. BMJ 2005;331:1357.

11. Cruzan V. Director. Missouri Dept. of Health. 497 US 261, Docket Number 88-1503, 1990.
12. Wikipedia. Terry Schiavo. http://en.wikipedia.org/wiki/Terri_Schiavo
13. Wikipedia. Karen Ann Quinlan. http://en.wikipedia.org/wiki/Karen_Ann_Quinlan
14. Lavi SJ. Euthanasia. The modern art of dying: A history of euthanasia in the United States. Princeton, NJ, USA: Princeton Univ Press, 2005.
15. Canada Quebec Superior Court. Nancy B. v. Hotel-Dieu de Quebec. Dominion Law Reports 86, 1992; 385-395.
16. Northern Territory Government. Rights of the Termi-nally Ill Act 1995. Northern Territory of Australia, Darwin, Australia: Government Publisher, 1995.
17. International Task Force. http://www.internationaltaskforce.org/rpt2005_3.htm#236
18. Hoshino K. Four newly established legal requisites for active euthanasia in Japan. Med Law 1996;15(2):291-4.
19. Keown J. Euthanasia in England: courts, committees and consistency. Med Law 1997;16(4):805-11.
20. van der Maas, P.J., van der Wal, G., Haverkate, I., de Graaff, C.L., Kester JG, Onwuteaka-Philipsen BD, van der Heide A, Bosma JM, Willems DL. Euthanasia, physician-assisted suicide, and other medical practices involving the end of life in the Netherlands, 1990-1995. New Engl J Med 1996;335(22):1699-1705.
21. Sheldon T. Killing or caring? BMJ 2005;330:560.

CHAPTER 24
The role of carer in chronic disease and end of life care

Rose Wiles, Paula Smith, Christine Davey and Ann Ashburn

Informal caregiving has traditionally been constructed as a burden, which is viewed as having a detrimental effect on carers' quality of life. However, more recently researchers have identified caregiving as a source of satisfaction. This chapter draws on two qualitative studies that have explored carers' experiences of caring in Parkinson's Disease (PD) and end-stage cancer in order to compare how family carers experience and describe their role and to consider the extent to which notions of satisfactions and difficulties emerge from their accounts. A comparison of the findings from these two studies has indicated that in end of life cancer care, carers tend to make greater reference to the satisfactions of caregiving compared with carers of relatives with PD. In the end-stage cancer study, carers made reference to notions of reciprocity and the ways in which caregiving tasks demonstrated their love and support for the person they 'cared for' and 'cared about'. In contrast, in the PD study, carers made little reference to such notions and their descriptions of their role and their response to it were couched in language that denoted high levels of burden and strain. There are a number of factors that might explain the differences in carers' descriptions. The obvious differences relate to duration of illness, the stage of carer career and level of support. Deteriorating conditions of a long duration, such as PD, may have a negative impact on the relationship and the experience of caring. Notions of reciprocity are challenged in such conditions because of the loss of the person and the relationship and the inevitable imbalance in patterns of give and take that occur. Such situations may encourage a sense of burden and obligation rather than reciprocity and satisfaction to thrive.

INTRODUCTION

An aging population and improving treatment regimes for a range of conditions has resulted in an increasing reliance on family members to provide the majority of daily care and management of the physical, emotional and psychological consequences of chronic and terminal conditions (1,2). International Governmental policy aims to encourage and support informal carers to provide care in the community (3). In the United Kingdom (UK), the Department of Health emphasises the importance of incorporating care for carers into service provision (4-8). However despite this, improvements in services are slow and many carers continue to bear the main responsibility for care and receive only limited support due to lack of resources and the varying views of agencies and practitioners about the roles and status of carers (8,9).

The informal caregiving role has traditionally been constructed in the literature as one of burden, which is viewed as having a detrimental effect on carers' quality of life (10,11). However, more recently researchers such as Nolan et al (11-13) have identified caregiving as a source of satisfaction and have noted that, for the majority of carers, caregiving can be a source of both difficulty and satisfaction. A sense of satisfaction has been linked with feelings of reciprocity and being able to return care received in the past, or as a way of demonstrating love for the ill person (14,15). For others there may be social or moral obligations to participation in caregiving that offset the difficulties encountered (14).

This chapter draws on two studies that have explored carers' experiences of caring in the context of two different conditions: Parkinson's Disease and end-stage cancer. The aim is to compare how family carers experience and describe their role in providing care in these two different conditions and the extent to which notions of satisfactions and difficulties emerge from their accounts.

Parkinson's Disease (PD) is a progressive degenerative disease characterised by slow and decreased movement, muscular rigidity, tremor and postural instability. It has a varying prevalence of 3-30 per 10,000 of the population (16). The disease progresses slowly and people with PD are generally managed at home with regular out patient checks until increased frailty or inability of carers to manage the patient prevents this.

Whilst cancer is often viewed and feared as an immediate and life threatening illness, with early diagnosis and improved treatment regimes it can often have an extended and lengthy disease trajectory, including periods of recurrence, active treatment and remission (17). In end-stage cancer, general and Specialist Palliative Care Services (SPCS) often become involved in order to provide additional support and services to both the patient and the family carer.

The impact on carers' physical, social and psychological well being are widely reported. In relation to caring for someone who has PD, chronic illness amongst carers (18) especially among carers who are spouses (19) has been identified. Raised levels of psychological distress have also been reported (20) with some carers experiencing depression (21) and others sadness and tiredness (22). Carergivers who are caring for someone with end-of-life needs have been identified as having extremely high levels of unmet need and distress. Family carers have been noted as having higher rates of GP visits (23) and higher levels of anxiety (24). Long term carers may be at particular risk, especially if they live in a rural location (25).

The effects of being a carer, especially a spouse carer, on social life have also been reported. In PD, spouse carers in particular have been found to have only limited contact outside the home (19,26), especially as the spouse's need for care increases (19). Within end of life cancer care similar difficulties are often experienced, particularly if care is seen to extend beyond that originally anticipated at diagnosis (27, 28).

The formal support available to patients with PD compared to end stage cancer appears to differ. In PD, the support provided appears to be varied but there is a general view that support is limited with carers bearing the responsibility of everyday care with limited support from primary and secondary care services (29). Contact with a PD nurse advisor has been identified as helpful (18,30). However, the costs associated with PD nurse specialists means that the number of PD nurse advisors and the amount of support they can provide is limited (31,32). There is increasing Government recognition of the need to improve services in the UK for people with a range of chronic neurological conditions and their carers (7) and a strategy for improving services has been introduced. However, the ten year implementation period for improvements in care indicate both the extent of need and the likelihood that change is likely to occur only very slowly.

In end stage cancer care, access to additional services is generally perceived to be better, and 95 % of SPCS are provided to cancer patients (33). SPCS have been developed extensively in the last 40 years (34) and there is increasing government recognition of the need to improve such services (5,6). The recently published (35) guidelines on supportive and palliative care make explicit recognition of the support needs of carers in end-stage cancer and palliative care. Within palliative care, family carers have always been considered integral to the patient's care and additional support services for this particular group are now being developed in a number of areas (36,37). However, whilst services for family carers in end stage cancer care may be greater, not everyone with end of life needs receives the level and type of support they require (27,38).

This chapter will compare the findings of two studies relating to caring in PD and end stage cancer. Although the studies have different methodological designs there are some striking differences within the accounts of the carers in their understanding of the role and sources of support. The aim is to explore carers' accounts of the difficulties and satisfactions inherent in their experience of caring for a relative with PD or end stage cancer, and to consider these in the light of current literature, policy and service provision.

STUDY OF PARKINSON'S DISEASE

The PD study was conducted in 2001. The aim of the study was to explore the views and experiences of informal carers of people with PD who had experienced repeated falls (39). Falls are a particular issue for people with PD and their carers because they are a frequent occurrence (40) and have been identified as a contributory factor to decreasing quality of life for people with PD (41).

A qualitative approach was used comprising semi-structured interviews with a sample of 14 carers. It was intended that the interviews would focus primarily on falls and how the carer coped with these. However interviewees were keen to talk about their experience of being a carer for someone with PD and a large amount of data were generated on their experiences of the caring role. Interviews were audio-taped and took place in carers' own homes. They lasted an average of 45 minutes (range 30-90 minutes). The study participants (n=14) were recruited from two sources; from two PD support groups in one UK County (n=8) and from a list of people with PD who had participated in a previous study on PD (n=6). All of the participants were the marital partners of a person with PD. Eleven carers were female and three were male and their ages ranged from 44-79 years (average 69.9 years). Their partners had been diagnosed with PD between 6-29 years ago (average 16.7 years). All participants identified themselves as the main carer for the person with PD. Twelve of these participants said that their spouse needed some level of care with ten people noting the amount of care needed was moderate or substantial.

The audio-taped interviews were fully transcribed. A grounded theory approach was used in which the findings emerging from the first few interviews were used to inform the topics explored in subsequent interviews with the sample. Transcripts of the first five interviews were coded independently by members of the research team who then met and agreed the emergent themes. Subsequent transcripts were coded by the researcher and were used to clarify and develop the emergent themes. This process resulted in the identification of new themes as well as the merging of existing themes. Six major themes emerged. Within each of these six themes a number of sub-themes were identified. While the focus of the study was on falls, a significant amount of data were generated relating to the experience of caring for someone with PD. This issue comprised one of the themes identified from this study and is the focus of this paper.

END-STAGE CANCER STUDY

The end-stage cancer study was conducted between 1997-2000 to explore family carers' perception of their role and sources of support as a carer within a palliative care setting. A prospective case study methodology was employed. In addition to a range of standardised measures relating to carer activities such as stress, anxiety and perceived social support, each family carer participated in a semi-structured interview about their role and sources of support. Information presented here is taken from the semi-structured interviews.

A purposive sample of sixteen family carers from two areas in the south of England who were willing to participate in the study were recruited via SPCS. All the family carers were closely related to the ill person. Fourteen were spouses (6 female and 8 male) and two were the patients' daughters. The mean age of the family carers was 56.8 years (range 37-77). Family carers had been involved in caring for a variable amount of time from a few weeks to two years. All were carers for a relative with end stage cancer.

Family carers were interviewed up to four times over a four month period. Each interview was audio-taped and took place in the carers' own home. The first interview generally took approximately one hour (range 1-2 hours), however, subsequent interviews were often shorter. Wherever possible the family carers were interviewed separately from the ill person to ensure privacy and the opportunity to respond openly to the questions.

The audio-taped interviews were fully transcribed. Analysis of the interview data was based on an Interpretative Phenomenological Approach (IPA) (42,43). IPA combines both phenomenology and symbolic interaction. The aim of IPA is to explore the participant's view of the world and to adopt, as far as is possible, an 'insider's perspective' of the phenomenon under study. Thus, the approach is phenomenological in that it attempts to capture the individuals' account of an object or event rather than an objective statement about the event itself (43). Furthermore IPA attempts to make explicit the cognitions or beliefs behind an individuals statement about an event. That is working from a social cognitive paradigm there would be an assumption that what someone says reflect an underlying cognition or belief about an event. At the same time IPA acknowledges the dynamic nature of the research process, and the interpretative activity through which the researcher attempts to understand the perceptions of the participant.

Initial interviews were read and re-read and notable themes and summary interpretations were made. As analysis continued with subsequent transcripts, new and emerging themes were added and checked against previously coded transcripts. This resulted in a final list of five major themes: the patient's story; perception of role; the family carer story; relationship with health professionals; and, other sources of support. Each major theme was comprised of a number of sub-themes that helped to explain and define the major theme. This chapter focuses on data from two of these themes: perception of role and sources of support. Verbatim quotes have been used to highlight the issues being described. All names have been changed to protect anonymity of the participants.

FINDINGS
Descriptions of the carer role

The overwhelming expression of the carers' role in caring for their partner with PD for the majority of participants was one of burden, albeit one which participants bore with varying degrees of stoicism. Only a minority of participants (n=4) viewed their partners as in need of little support and as able to be left alone for longer than short periods of time. These carers viewed the impact of PD, as yet, to be relatively minor but were aware that their partners' condition was likely to deteriorate in the future and that their caring role would become more demanding. These carers did not describe their role in terms of burden in the way that the other study participants did and made reference to notions of managing and coping, for example:

"Yes because funnily enough, we were talking at lunchtime and we were saying what has it been, six years. He's done well up to now and he said "yes but I am deteriorating", you see. So obviously um, it will happen I suppose. ... you've got to live with it, you can't do anything more and there you are" (Mary Downer)

" well yes it does because um I do far more of the general domestic and garden work than I ever did before um though I always did a certain amount um but we manage very well, hardly call it managing really" (Gordon Jones)

For the other participants in the PD study, their role as carer was one which had developed into 'a full time job' with which people felt, to some degree, 'trapped'. This sense of feeling trapped related to the perceived long-term nature of their partner's condition and the sense that their role as carer was one that stretched on long into the future with no clearly defined endpoint. These carers had been involved in caring for their spouse with PD for a long period of time (ranging from 10-29 years for these 10 carers). While their caring activities in the initial years following diagnosis were described as minor and their impact slight, these had increased over the years to become significant so that they comprised their main role and a significant responsibility. At this stage, these carers did not make reference to their caring role as a source of any satisfaction or describe caring tasks as ones that they were glad to provide for their spouse or as part of reciprocity in their relationship. Rather the role was identified as one of burden which had a significant negative impact on their quality of life. When asked to describe what it was like caring for someone with PD, the following quotes were commonplace:

"sheer frustration ... well I just think why am I doing this, why am I bothering, I want a life, I'm entitled to a life" (Clare Chalmers)

"I feel a bit, if I say trapped it sounds awful because I want to be, you know, I wouldn't want to leave him ... [but] um I'm not free ... it's awful really but I try to think to myself this is my job now, this is what I have to do you know, this is not just for now this is forever sort of thing" (Sarah Gaylor)

The PD study participants reported that their role as carer resulted in having to cope with physically and mentally difficult day-to-day caring tasks. This was coupled with feelings of loss of their previously valued relationship with their partner and their social roles within their relationship as well as loss of the social activities they engaged with as a couple. These losses were sources of great regret. Additionally, some carers the demands of their caring role resulted in the loss of their own social activities and indeed limited their ability to go out at all. This varied according to the amount of formal and informal support they could call on to assist them. The demanding tasks of caring coupled with the various losses they experienced contributed to the view of caring as a burden. The following quotes illustrate this:

> "We've been married 51 years and up to these last two or three years he's always been a rock to lean on and that, and once he cries, that's it, I'm finished .. he's always supported me you see and now, I don't know, there's not that closeness" (Sarah Gaylor)

> "I won't go out and leave him and we've got no social life now really, not at all" (Janet Bryant)

> "I mean, you know, we had a very nice normal family life, lots of lovely friends and, you know, you went out for meals or whatever, a normal life, and then because David's got Parkinson's it completely, as the years have gone when we first had it or he had it, it didn't matter too much but now it's got that he, you know, it restricts so much what he does it restricts my life completely" (Pauline New)

The pressures experienced by these carers were frequently reported as resulting in PD study participants shouting or losing their temper or crying. Participants generally noted that they felt 'guilty' for feeling frustrated and for expressing this frustration because it was not their partner's fault that they had PD and they felt they should be able to be more sympathetic. However, they noted that at times the pressure was so great that they could not help giving vent to their feelings. This was not always the case and some participants felt that their partners were intentionally difficult and set out to make the carer's life hard. The following quotes illustrate these points:

> "Sometimes it's not his fault but I might blow at him which is totally unfair but you can't help it you know" (Pauline New)

> "take a few deep breaths and try and control yourself, it's not always easy I can assure you" (Martin Pearce)

> "I mean sometimes you can get very irritable with him because it's hard helping someone who won't take advice" (Joan Gower)

In contrast, the family carers in the end-stage cancer study did not always strongly associate with the role of 'carer' at all and saw their position as strongly aligned to their relationship and obligations towards the ill person prior to the illness developing.

> "Cos when you're actually married to someone you're there through thick and thin any way aren't you? If I was ill she'd look after me, and if she was ill I'd look after her. Um, I remember when I was in hospital, I had two bad injuries playing rugby where I was put in hospital and I had an operation. When I came out I couldn't, I was on crutches. She always looked after me

then. I mean it's just this is, I don't know, a bit longer that's all." (Mr Lloyd)

The additional activities carers undertook, such as increasing household chores, were considered to be 'nothing special'. Indeed even activities that were new and required specialised skills to be developed were engaged in without apparent dissent or worry.

"I mean it's been a gradual process, it's not been an overnight thing. I suppose that's what's pushing a lot of it, it's just an extension really." (Mr Andrews)

"I've always worked outside, I've always been outside, but um, I've got to alter at the moment for a while so I've got to put up with it." (Mr Bradley)

This apparent acceptance of changing circumstance and roles required in the situation may have been the result of the perceived short-term nature of caring within the palliative care setting. Whilst this was rarely explicitly stated it was implicitly demonstrated in the importance placed on the patient's needs and wishes being attended to. The openness regarding the prognosis of the individuals receiving palliative care often increased the desire to accommodate the ill person's desires and wishes as much as possible. The overall sense from the majority of these carers was that they were pleased to be able to undertake and demonstrate their love and support for the ill person through their caring activities.

"Well my part obviously is to support (husband) as much as I can, and um, help keep him in the same mood." (Mrs Davis)

"Well I used to work. Um, when Mum found out about her illness um, she said would you be there at home with me in case I need you? And I said yes." (Mrs Nash)

However, some of the family carers in this study had in fact been involved in caring for considerable periods of time sometimes extending to years. This did appear to impact on their perception of their role within the situation, and it was possible to detect a sense of burden and strain developing.

"You sort of run out of momentum sometimes. ... Because you begin to wonder yourself sometimes which is only, you know, understandable is there going to be an end." (Mrs Foster)

When the caregiving situation was extended beyond that originally anticipated, a detrimental effect on relationships with other family members and restrictions to social activities were observed. This effect was particularly noticeable with younger carers who reported difficulties in juggling numerous roles such as partner, parent and worker. For one of the daughter carers this led to tension in dividing her time between her mother and her husband who had had to take early retirement himself due to ill-health.

> *"You can't split yourself in two, you know.   You can't be over the road there and over here as well. .. If you please one, you upset the other, and I know lately I have got very, more often than not upset my husband rather than upset my mother." (Mrs Page)*

Despite these difficulties the family carers rarely demonstrated a sense of anger or frustration with the ill person due to the restrictions in their lifestyle. Rather they mourned with them the loss of expectations about the future, particularly if they demonstrated a very enmeshed relationship.

> *"I feel cheated. …. Because of all the things that we were going to do, and we can't do. For (husband) more than myself I think." (Mrs White)*

Formal and informal support

The amount of formal or informal support carers in both these studies could draw on to mediate these difficulties varied. In the PD study, the amount of formal support from health and social care services appeared to be minimal and sporadic and most of these carers bore the brunt of day-to-day caring responsibilities themselves. The support provided to the spouses with PD on a regular basis comprised attendance at day hospitals one or two days a week (in two cases) or a formal carer coming into the house for some periods during the week (in a further two cases). Some carers had been able to arrange for their spouse to have occasional respite care to give them a break but this was not a regular occurrence. The types of support made available appeared to be largely dependent on the willingness of carers to ask for help from their general practitioners (GPs) or on GPs' goodwill and interest in the patient, carer or in PD more generally. All spouses attended PD out-patient clinics at regular intervals, generally six monthly. These were viewed as being for the purpose of monitoring the patient's condition but were also a time when referral for other services had occurred. Hospital doctors and GPs also appeared to be the gatekeeper to a range of other services, such as occupational therapy and physiotherapy. The support that could be provided by these professions was valued but participants reported receiving services from these professions as a one-off with the onus left on carers to contact them if they needed more assistance. The following quotes illustrate the carers' experiences in relation to formal support:

> *"I tried to get physio for him at home … but they're rare creatures physios, there aren't many of them I've discovered" (Claire Chalmers)*

> *"I'd like a bit more support from the hospital unit … I feel we've got to a stage now where they can't be bothered to do anything else, you know … I mean we go every six months and [we] just come away thinking well what have we sat there and gone through that for, we've got nowhere, [he's] done*

nothing, he's asked him nothing, he hasn't looked at him, physically looked
at him for a few years" (Pauline New)

The amount of informal support carers could call on was also varied. Most
support, where it existed, came from other family members, generally
daughters. This was often in the form of sitting with the person with PD to
enable the carer to 'have a break' or taking them shopping while the person
with PD was looked after by another formal or informal carer. There were no
cases in this sample where significant caring tasks were taken on by other
family members. Some people had neighbours or friends who helped them
with going out or any emergency that arose, such as a fall. However, it was
noted that the long-term nature of PD frequently caused a breakdown in
'normal' friendships that existed prior to diagnosis.

In the end-stage cancer study, carers noted varying levels of formal
and informal support. In addition they appeared to rely on formal and
informal support for different things. In most cases family carers tended to
rely on one or two health professionals for informational support or access
into other services that they might require. This appeared to be based on the
group that they had most contact with rather than on particular roles or
qualifications. Thus, Mr Bradley tended to rely on the District nurses who
visited daily to care for his wife, whereas Mrs Vaughan relied more heavily
on the visiting Macmillan nurses.

> *"They (district nurses) are the people that are dealing with this sort of*
> *thing all the time aren't they? And you know you've got to take their*
> *advice" (Mr Bradley)*

> *"Because she's (hospice nurse) what you call my tie line between the*
> *hospice and home". (Mrs Vaughan)*

Provision of social care was made available to younger carers if the patient's
condition deteriorated and it was clear that the family carer could no longer
sustain the situation without more practical support. Referral into this type
of support service was by no means automatic and not all the family carers
were able to access this very practical level of support.

> *"That was organised because when (husband) was very bad, just before*
> *then it was suggested that we needed some form of home help. ... They do*
> *the hoovering, and she washes the kitchen floor and bathroom floor, and the*
> *downstairs loo." (Mrs White)*

Close family and friends, despite changing demographic and work related
patterns, were generally identified as providing informal support to the
family carer. Half the family carers reported having at least one member of
the extended family available to assist with both practical and emotional
support, such as transport to hospital appointments and help with shopping,
or just being available for a chat on the phone. For family carers who did not
have a close family network to provide practical support, friends and

neighbours became more significant. However, the expectation of help from this group was generally lower than that expected from a family network.

> *"And usually people have volunteered, and to start with we didn't take it up because we didn't think it was going to be, but after two years you've got to take help from somebody." (Mrs Foster)*

DISCUSSION

A comparison of the findings from these two studies on carers' descriptions of their caring role has indicated that in end of life cancer care, carers tend to make greater reference to the satisfactions of caregiving compared with carers for relatives with PD. In the end-stage cancer study reported here, carers made reference to notions of reciprocity and the ways in which caregiving tasks demonstrated their love and support for the person they cared for and cared about. In contrast, in the PD study, carers made little reference to such notions and their descriptions of their role and their response to it were couched in language that denoted high levels of burden and strain. What factors might account for this?

There are a number of limitations that need to be considered before drawing any conclusions from the data presented here. This paper reports on research conducted by different researchers, using different approaches and with different study aims. It may be the case that these differences account, to some degree, for the different descriptions of caregiving reported by carers in these two studies. Clearly, as Payne and Ellis-Hill (2) noted, the methodological approach as well as the type of questions and the way that they were asked are important factors influencing study participants' responses and subsequently a research study's 'findings'. Both the PD and end-stage cancer study were conducted from the notion of caring as burden but both were conducted in ways that aimed to enable participants to express their thoughts and feelings on their experiences. We recognise the potential limitations of comparisons between the two sets of data but nevertheless view the similarities in our approaches as justification of the appropriateness of using these data in this way. Methodologically, while we agree that interviews produce data that are, to some degree, socially constructed, the approach to data collection and analysis in both studies is one of subtle realism (44). This approach views in-depth interviews as a means to discover people's experiences of a phenomenon, provided that data are collected and analysed in a reflexive and rigorous fashion. We have used a range of ways to establish rigour in the two studies through the use of negative cases, peer reviewing of transcripts and the use of reflexive diaries (45,46). Thus our underpinning methodological approaches were very similar, albeit that different approaches to analysis were used. A further justification for using the two sets of data in this way is that we view a comparison of the similarities and differences between the experiences of the two sets of carers as having a potentially important contribution to make to the debates within the caring literature. Thus the data are presented here as making a contribution to those debates.

There are a number of factors that might explain the differences in carers' descriptions of their experiences of their caring role in PD and end-stage cancer. The obvious differences relate to duration of illness, the stage of carer career and level of support. These differences are drawn out in the data presented above but can usefully be elaborated on further.

The importance of temporal issues in caring has been identified by a number of authors (11,12,14,28). Caregiving is not a role that exists in a vacuum and the way that it is experienced and managed changes over time. At diagnosis, family carers are often willing and eager to provide high levels of care, and notions of reciprocity, love and support provide explanations for this response (14). While it is clearly hard to distinguish between love, affection, duty, obligation and reciprocity (47) it has been noted that family carers, particularly spouses and adult children view providing care in the face of an impending crisis as a means of displaying the love and care they have for their relative and to 'pay back' what that person has done for them in the past and may do again in the future (45,48,49). They derive feelings of satisfaction from providing care in such contexts. However, where conditions have a very long duration and are deteriorating these notions are severely tested. Deteriorating illnesses with a long duration challenge the notion of specific reciprocity (i.e., reciprocity within a specific relationship rather than more general reciprocity within a kinship network). Notions of reciprocity between two individuals, especially between spouses, is not generally quantified. Rather, individuals operate within notions of 'give and take' in which there may be inequities in what is 'given' or 'taken' by particular individuals or at particular stages in the lifecourse (50). Nevertheless, an illness that makes great demands on a carer over a very prolonged period of time may reach a point where the carer perceives the scale of reciprocity tilts so far that the imbalance in notions of 'give and take' mean that the relationship can no longer be considered reciprocal. Perceived inequities in the 'give and take' of the relationship in the past may hasten this point (51) as may the perceived loss of the person they once knew and the relationship they once had. Chronic conditions, particularly neurological conditions, frequently result in changes in the individual so that the person they loved may appear 'lost' to the carer and it may seem that there is little left of the person that they knew. In these circumstances maintaining notions of love and support may be difficult and satisfactions may be lost. This is unlikely to mean that carers stop providing care but that notions of burden and obligation rather than satisfaction and reciprocity may become more dominant (14). Nolan (11) has noted that it is the nature and quality of the relationship between the carer and the cared-for rather than the level of care provided that denotes the extent to which caring is experienced as a burden. We do not dispute this but note that deteriorating illnesses of a long duration may impact on the relationship and therefore challenge notions of reciprocity and contribute to feelings of burden.

In the data presented here, most of the PD carers described their roles as an experience of what Twigg and Atkin (10) have termed 'engulfment' where carers' needs are subordinated to the needs of the person they care for. This contrasts with the descriptions given by most of the carers in the end-stage cancer study whose descriptions were closer to those that Twigg and Atkin (10) have termed 'symbiosis' in which carers identify gains from their caring role. We argue here that it is the deteriorating nature of certain conditions in conjunction with a long duration that tests notions of reciprocity, love and support and that these influence the accounts that carers give of their roles. The same may not be true in conditions that have a long duration but are more stable (11). The PD carers were older and many had been providing high levels of care for a spouse with a deteriorating condition for a much longer period of time than the carers of people with end-stage cancer. Furthermore, in contrast with the carers of people with end-stage cancer, they could see no end in prospect to their role as carer. It is interesting to note that in the end-stage cancer study, in cases where the duration of the illness was longer than the carer had envisaged, notions of burden appeared to become dominant in carers' descriptions of their role. Carers in both studies could be seen to be at the 'enduring' or 'total care' stage of the carer career in that both sets of participants were, in the main, providing high levels of care (14). However, the major difference between the two experiences was that while the carers in the end-stage cancer study could see a time and the circumstances that would enable them to exit from their role, the PD carers could not.

The experience of caring as a source of satisfaction or burden may also be mediated by the amount of support from formal services and informal support networks. More health and social care services are available to patients and carers in the context of end stage cancer than PD although this should improve over the next decade (7). However, even with the presence of adequate services, individuals with end-stage cancer may not always receive the amount of support they feel they need (27). The lack of support from statutory services to patients and carers in the context of PD has been noted (29) and may be accounted for by the limited funding of services, charitable giving and agencies available for neurological conditions in contrast to cancer. The long-term nature of chronic conditions may also account for the lack of support from informal networks that carers in the PD study identified. In acute conditions, which are perceived as immediately life-threatening, extended family, friends and neighbours appear willing to 'pull the stops out' to provide support (45). This support tends not to be sustained over the longer period and as the shock and perceived urgency of the situation recedes the everyday demands on individuals begin to take precedence (52, 53).

CONCLUSIONS

The studies explored here indicate that deteriorating conditions of a long duration, such as PD, may have a negative impact on the relationship and the experience of caring. Notions of reciprocity are challenged in such conditions because of the loss of the person and the relationship and the inevitable imbalance in patterns of give and take that occur. Such situations may encourage a sense of burden and obligation rather than reciprocity and satisfaction to thrive. By understanding the potential sense of burden in both PD and end stage cancer carers' health professionals are better placed to offer appropriate and timely support. The guidelines on supportive and palliative care (35) and the National Service Framework for Long Term Conditions (6) recognises the impact caring has on carers and calls for appropriate service provision and support to be provided.

ACKNOWLEDGEMENTS

The authors would like to acknowledge the contribution of the participants in sharing their during this study.

REFERENCES

1.   Hirst M. Trends in informal care in Great Britain during the 1990s. Health Soc Care Community 2001;9(6):348-57.
2.   Payne S, Ellis-Hill C. Chronic and terminal illness: New perspectives on caring and carers. Oxford: Oxford Univ Press, 2001.
3.   Wiles J. Informal caregivers' experiences of formal support in a changing context. Health Soc Care Community 2003;11(3): 189-207.
4.   Department of Health. Caring About arers: A national strategy for carers. London: Dept Health, 1999.
5.   Department of Health. The cancer plan. London: Dept Health, 1999.
6.   Department of Health. NICE guidance on supportive and palliative care. London: Dept Health, 2004.
7.   Department of Health. The national service framework for long term conditions. London: Dept Health, 2005.
8.   Seddon D, Robinson C. Carers of older people with dementia: Assessment and the carers act. Health Soc Care Community 2001;9(3):151-8.
9.   Guberman N, Nicholas E, Nolan M, Rembicki D, Lundh U, Keefe J. Impacts on practitioners of using research-based carer assessment tools: experiences from the UK, Canada and Sweden, with insights from Australia. Health Soc Care Community 2003;11(4):345-55.
10.   Twigg J, Atkin K. Carers perceived: Policy and practice in informal care. Buckingham: Open Univ Press, 1994.
11.   Nolan M. Positive aspects of caring. In: Payne S, Ellis-Hill C, eds. chronic and terminal illness: New perspectives on caring and carers. Oxford: Oxford Univ Press, 2001:22-43.
12.   Nolan M, Grant G, Keady J. Understanding family care: A multidisciplinary model of caring and coping. Buckingham: Open Univ Press, 1996.
13.   Nolan M, Lundh U, Grant G, Keady J. Partnerships in family care: Understanding the caregiving career. Buckingham: Open Univ Press, 2003
14.   Boeije H, Duijnstee M, Grypdonck M. Continuation of caregiving among partners who gave total care to spouses with multiple sclerosis. Health Soc Care Community 2003;11(3):242-52.

15.   Grbich C, Parker D, Maddocks I. The emotions and coping strategies of caregivers of family members with a terminal cancer. J Palliat Care 2001;17(1):30-6.

16.   Perkin G. Mosby's color atlas and text of neurology. London: Mosby, 1998.

17.   Thomas C, Morris S, Harman J. Companions through cancer: The care given by informal carers in cancer contexts. Soc Sci Med 2002;54(4):529-44.

18.   Clarke C, Zobkiw R, Gullaksen E . Quality of life and care in Parkinson's disease. Br J Clin Pract 1995;49(6):288-93.

19.   O'Reilly F, Finnan F, Allwright S, Smith G, Ben-Shlomo Y. The effects of caring for a spouse with Parkinson's disease on social, psychological and physical well-being. Br J Gen Pract 1996;46:507-12.

20.   Miller E, Berrios G, Politynska B. Caring for someone with Parkinson's disease: Factors that contribute to distress. Int J Geriatr Psychiatr 1996;11(3):263-8.

21.   Meara J, Mitchelmore E, Hobson P. Use of the GDS-15 geriatric depression scale as a screening instrument for depressive symptomatology in patients with Parkinson's disease and their carers in the community. Age Ageing 1999;28(1):35-8.

22.   Aarsland D, Larsen J, Karlsen K, Lim N, Tandberg E. Mental symptoms in Parkinson's disease are important contributors to caregiver distress. Int J Geriatr Psychiatr 1994;14(10):866-74.

23.   Mor V, McHorney C, Sherwood S. Secondary morbidity among the recently bereaved. Am J Psychiatr 1986;143(2):158-62.

24.   Hinton J. Can home care maintain an acceptable quality of life for patients with terminal cancer and their relatives? Palliat Med 1994;8:183-96.

25.   Meyers J, Gray L. The relationships between family primary caregiver characteristics and satisfaction with hospice care, quality of life, and burden. Oncol Nurs Forum 2001;28(1):73-82.

26.   Lee K, Merriman A, Owen A, Chew B, Tan T. The medical, social and functional profile of Parkinson's disease patients. Singapore Med J 1994;35(3):265-8.

27.   Rhodes P, Shaw S. Informal care and terminal illness. Health Soc Care Community 1999;7(1):39-50.

28.   Smith P. Working with family caregivers in a palliative care setting. In: Payne S, Seymour J, Ingleton C, eds. Palliative care nursing: Principles and evidence for practice. Buckingham: Open Univ Press, 2004:312-8.

29.   Peto V, Fitzpatrick R, Jenkinson C. Self-reported health status and access to health services in a community sample with Parkinson's Disease. Disabil Rehabil 1997;19(3):97-103.

30.   MacMahon D. Parkinson's Disease nurse specialists: An important role in disease management. Neurology 1999;52(suppl 3):S21-5.

31.   Reynolds H, Wilson-Barnett J, Richardson G. Evaluation of the role of the Parkinson's Disease Nurse specialist. Int J Nurs Stud 2000;37(4):337-49.

32. Noble C. Access is denied: Many people with Parkinson's Disease are discriminated against on grounds of age. Nurs Stand 2001;15(47):16-7.

33. Payne S, Seymour J. Introduction. In: Payne S, Seymour J, Ingleton C, eds. Palliative care nursing: Principles and evidence for practice. Berkshire: Open Univ Press, 2004:1-12.

34. National Council for Hospice and Specialist Palliative Care Services (NCHSPCS). Dilemmas and directions: The future of specialist palliative care: A discussion paper. London: NCHSPCS, Occasional paper 11, 1997. London

35. National Cancer Research Institute. Supportive and palliative care research in the UK. Report of the NCRI strategic planning group on supportive and palliative care. London: NCRI, 2004 (www.ncri.org.uk)

36. Clark D, Ferguson C, Nelson C. Macmillan carers schemes in England: Results of a multicentre evaluation. Palliat Med 2000;14:129-39.

37. Harding R, Higginson IH, Leam C, Donaldson N, Pearce A, George R, Robinson V, Taylor L. Evaluation of a short-term group intervention for informal carers of patients attending a home palliative care service. J Pain Symptom Manage 2004;27:396-408

38. Ingleton C, Morgan J, Hughes P, Noble B, Evans A. Carer satisfaction with end-of-life care in Powys, Wales: a cross-sectional survey. Health Soc Care Community 2004;12(1):43-52.

39. Davey C, Wiles R, Ashburn A, Murphy C. Falling in Parkinson's disease: The impact on informal caregivers. Disabil Rehabil 2004;26(23):1360-6.

40. Ashburn A, Stack E, Pickering R, Ward C. A community dwelling sample of people with Parkinson's Disease: characteristics of fallers and non-fallers. Age Ageing 2001;30:47-52.

41. Martinez-Martin P. Quality of life in Parkinson's Disease at the Pan-European Symposium, Marbella, May 24, 1997: An introduction to the concept of 'quality of life' in Parkinson's Disease. J Neurology 1998;245 (Suppl 1):S2-6.

42. Smith JA. Beyond the divide between cognition and discourse: using interpretative phenomenological analysis in health psychology. Psychol Health 1996;11:261-71.

43. Smith JA, Jarman M, Osborn M. Doing interpretative phenomenological analysis. In: Murry M, Chamberlain K, eds. Qualitative health psychology: Theories and methods. London: Sage, 1999:218-40.

44. Mays N, Pope C. Assessing quality in qualitative research. BMJ 2000;320:50-2.

45. Smith P. Family caregivers in palliative care: perception of their role and sources of support. Unpublished PhD Thesis. Southhampton: Univ Southampton, 2000.

46.   Davey C, Wiles R, Ashburn A, Murphy C, Large S. Falls in Parkinson's Disease: The caregivers' perspective. Final Report for the Parkinson's Disease Society, 2001.

47.   Roberts E. Women and families. Oxford: Blackwell, 1995.

48.   Lewis J, Meredith B. Daughters who care. London: Routledge, 1988.

49.   Finch J. Responsibilities, obligations and commitments. In: Allen I, Perkins E, eds. The future of family care for older people. London: HMSO, 1995:51-64.

50.   Brannen J, Wilson G, eds. Give and take in families: Studies in resource distribution. London: Unwin Hyman, 1987.

51.   Qureshi H, Simons K. Resources within families: Caring for elderly people. In: Brannen J, Wilson G, eds. Give and take in Families: Studies in resource distribution. London: Unwin Hyman, 1987:171-35.

52.   Bulmer M. The social basis of community care. London: Unwin Hyman, 1987.

53.   Ingleton C, Payne S, Nolan M, Carey I. Respite in palliative care: a review and discussion of the literature. Palliat Med 2003;17(7):567-75.

PART SEVEN:
AGING IN SPECIFIC POPULATIONS

CHAPTER 25
Trends in the aging of people with intellectual disability

Joav Merrick, Efrat Merrick and Isack Kandel

Increased lifespan in persons with intellectual disability (ID) has been observed worldwide due to progress in medical technology and improved social awareness and pressure for better treatment. This chapter describe a study conducted to monitor the trends in aging in persons with ID in residential care centers in Israel. The aging population is about 25% of the total population of persons known with ID in Israel. Since 1998-1999, an annual survey of medical-clinic activity for all residential care centers for people with ID has been conducted, and data from these surveys were used to investigate the trend in aging. The residential care center population today comprises about 6,500 persons of all ages. From 1999 to 2005, the population of 40-49 year olds remained stable, but the 50-59 year olds increased by 5.4 %, while the 60 years and older group increased by 2.6%. Older people with ID have the same needs as other older people do and are subject to the same age-related impairments and illnesses, albeit at an earlier pace than the general population. Recommendations for service for this population are discussed.

INTRODUCTION

In recent years, an increase in the number of aging adults with intellectual disability (ID) has been observed world-wide, together with increased life expectancy. In the 1930s, the mean age at death for people with ID was about 19 years, in the 1970s about 59 years, and in the 1990s 66 years, whereas for Down syndrome, the mean age at death was 9 years in the 1920s and is 56 years now (1). Such an increase in lifespan can be seen as the consequence of progress in medical technology and improved social awareness in the twentieth century. In the past, most individuals with intellectual disability died at a young age and therefore, never underwent the aging process. Indeed, the present population is probably the first generation of aging people with ID ever. When compared with people without disabilities, the aging process creates many unique and complex tensions for aging individuals with ID, mainly because of often being dependent on others for their daily support. In addition, such individuals may demonstrate cognitive difficulties and deficient communicative skills. The situation may become worse because of discriminatory social attitudes that impede and limit the access of aging individuals with ID to information, support, and service.

The increase in the life expectancy of people with ID is a two edged sword. Such individuals enjoy the blessing of a longer and healthier life, yet they also have to experience the pain and sorrow that often accompany the aging process. More people with ID now have contact with separation, death, and mourning. Today, we are witness to an emerging phenomenon, in which traditional care providers, such as parents or siblings, are passing away, whilst their aging relatives with ID, whom they supported, are still living, sometimes with nobody left to care for them.

The issues of loss and bereavement are familiar to those, who are involved with adults with developmental disabilities. Unfortunately, there is little recognition of the impact of loss on this population and together with this, are emerging health problems of aging that have never been seen in this population before.

RESIDENTIAL CARE FOR PERSONS WITH ID IN ISRAEL

From 1948, when the modern State of Israel was established, until 1962, the Ministry of Welfare was responsible for the care of persons with ID. In 1962 the Division for Mental Retardation (DMR) was established under the Ministry of Labour and Social Affairs (MOLSA) with the responsibility for the assessment, treatment, and rehabilitation of persons with ID. By the end of 2005 the total population in Israel was 6,987,000 persons (2); the DMR in 2005 was in contact with close to 24,000 persons of all ages. Residential care is provided to about 6,700 persons in 59 residential centers all over the country; in about another 50 locations, residential care is provided to an additional 2,000 persons in hostels or in group homes in the community, whereas the remainder are served with day-care kindergarten, day-treatment centers, sheltered workshops, or integrated care in the community while living at home with their families (3).

In 1997/1998, a questionnaire was developed for annual survey of medical clinic activity for all residential care centers for people with ID in Israel (4). The questionnaire or survey instrument has the following sections: information on the age, gender and level of intellectual disability of persons served at the residential care center in question, status of the population served (educational, treatment, rehabilitation, nursing and challenging behavior), profile (various aspects of the nursing load like number of persons with gastric tubes, catheters, gastrostomy, dialysis, oncology, epilepsy, diabetes, hypertension, blindness etc), nursing, medical and allied professional staff, number of annual examinations, preventive medicine aspects, medications, number of annual cases of infectious disease, annual unintentional injury, number of deaths, number of hospitali-zations, internal residential center hospitalization, ambulatory out-patient utilization, utilization of outside laboratory examinations and dental care.

DATA FROM OUR LAST SURVEY

The most recent data available are from the 2005 National survey (5). The age distribution of 6,749 persons with ID in residential centers from 2005 is presented in table 1 and the level of ID is presented in table 2. Nine government, 37 private, and 12 public centers had a mean of 116.36 persons in each residential center (range 23-366). It is worth to note that the total expenditure is provided by the government, which also runs the government residential centers, whereas the private and public centers are under their own admini-stration, but the government provides the budget, clients, and supervision.

Table 1. Population of persons with intellectual disability in residential care centers in Israel 2005

Age in years	Males	Females	Total	Percent
0-9	101	58	159	2.36
10-19	428	359	787	11.66
20-39	1,660	1,164	2,824	41.84
40-49	746	624	1,370	20.30
50-59	575	569	1,144	16.95
> 60	241	224	465	6.89
Total	3,751	2,998	6,749	100.00
%	55.58	44.42	100.00	

The trend toward longer living can be seen from tables 3 and 4, in which the data have been extracted from the 1999-2005 national surveys.

DISCUSSION

Because of a decline in fertility and a 20-year increase in the average life span during the second half of the twentieth century, the median age of the population of the world is increasing (6). This phenomenon, combined with the 'Baby Boom', will result in increased numbers of persons over 65 years from 2010 to 2030. This larger number of older people worldwide will require a better and more effective health and social service, because many will have chronic diseases in need of service and surveillance. This load will increase health, social, and long-term care expenses, but also make public health interventions important in order to sustain good health and a good quality in life even in the face of chronic disease.

Table 2. Level of intellectual disability (ID) in the population of persons with intellectual disability in residential care in Israel 2005

Age (years)	Mild	Moderate	Severe	Profound	Other	Total	Percent
0-9	10	21	81	47	0	159	2,36
10-19	94	256	311	123	3	787	11.66
20-39	250	1,121	932	503	18	2,824	41.84
40-49	191	613	436	130	0	1,370	20.30
50-59	166	520	355	103	0	1,144	16.95
>60	58	256	112	39	0	465	6.89
Total	769	2,787	2,227	945	21	6,749	100,00
Percent	11.39	41.30	33.00	14.00	0.31	100.00	

Legend: Mild MR: IQ 55-70, moderate: IQ 35-54, severe: IQ 20-34 and profound: IQ < 20. Other are 10 persons, who historically were placed in institutions for other reasons and prefered to stay on, because they regarded the institution as their home or persons under observation.

Table 3. The population of persons with intellectual disability in residential care centers in Israel aged 40 years and older 1999-2005 in percent of total population

Age in years	1999	2000	2001	2002	2003	2004	2005
40–49	21.69	21.81	21.73	22.23	21.32	20.49	20.30
50–59	11.52	12.36	13.22	14.15	15.32	16.05	16.95
>60	4.26	4.46	4.88	5.64	5.72	6.38	6.89
40 and older	37.47	39.63	39.83	42.02	42.36	42.92	44.14

Table 4. The population of persons with intellectual disability in residential care centers in Israel aged 40 years and older 1999-2004 in numbers

Age in years	1999	2000	2001	2002	2003	2004	2005
40–49	1328	1355	1384	1412	1386	1354	1,370
50–59	705	768	842	899	996	1061	1,144
>60	261	277	311	358	372	422	465
40 and older	2294	2400	2537	2669	2754	2837	2,979

The increase in the number of older people in the general population is also reflected in the population of persons with intellectual disability (ID), and today the average life expectancy of older adults with ID is 66.1 years and growing (7). This population will present increasing challenges to the clinician and to the public health system (7,8), characterized by increased rates of hearing and visual impairments, obesity, osteoporosis, dementia, and other chronic diseases (8).

With this data, we showed that the data collected from annual national surveys in Israel since 1999 of medical clinic activities in all residential care centers also revealed a trend of aging in this population. From 1999 to 2005, the population of 40-49 year olds remained stable, but the number of 50-59 year olds increased by 5.4 %, and those 60 years and older increased by 2.6%.

Older people with ID have the same needs as other older people do, and they are subject to the same age-related impairments and illnesses (8). Moreover, because many disabled individuals live together with their families, the burden is double because the family members are also aging and with time, will not be able to continue their care-giving. The International Association for the Scientific Study of Intellectual Disabilities (URL: www.iassid.org) at a meeting in 2002 in Madrid, Spain already had the following recommendations related to services or supports for older people with intellectual disabilities:

- Social needs for many adults can be met by the elimination of stigmatization and discrimination in general community services and through the promotion of equal access and use. People with intellectual disabilities should be able to attend, use, and benefit from the social, recreational, and leisure resources and amenities that communities develop and operate for their elderly citizens.
- Housing needs can met by supporting families when they are the primary carer or by providing financial resources for rentals or ownership of property. Housing can also be providing by brokering co-living arrange-ments with other people or by providing for small group homes or self-catered apartments.
- Medical needs can be met by enrollment in universal health schemes or programs. Periodic health assess-ments and routing health care should be normalized and provided as an overall system of supports, when needed or as assistance provided for the adequate self-directed use of general or specialty health services. Risk assessments and routinized health reviews should be part of the individual's life-plan and be provided to catch diseases and conditions that could compromise longevity.
- Activity or work is a normal part of life and is no less needed by aging adults with ID. With research supporting continued activation as a preventative for old-age associated depression and other emotional problems, involvement in social and community activities should be the norm. Personal circumstances and abilities will dictate level of need and desire for involvement.

- Special care needs for age-associated conditions, such as Alzheimer's disease and related dementias, increasing fragility, or conditions or diseases compromising independent functioning, should be addressed with the focus on care in community or family settings. Insti-tutionalization of persons with ID can never be justified or rationalized simply based on old age alone.

In Israel, most people with ID are living at home, but even persons in need of long-term nursing facilities should be able to benefit from the above recommendations.

ACKNOWLEDGEMENTS

This chapter is an adapted version of an earlier published paper (Merrick J, Merrick E, Kandel I. Trends in aging. Persons with intellectual disability in residential care centers in Israel. Int J Disabil Hum Dev 2006;5(1):91-4).

REFERENCES
1. Janicki MP, Dalton AJ, Henderson CM, Davidson PW. Mortality and morbidity among older adults with intellectual disability: Health services considerations. Disabil Rehabil 1999;21:284-94.
2. Israel Central Bureau Statistics. http://www.cbs.gov.il/population/new_2006/table1.pdf
3. Merrick J. Community based services for persons with intellectual disability in Israel, 1985-2004. Jerusalem, Israel: Office Med Dir, Min Soc Affairs, 2005.
4. Merrick J. National survey 1998 on medical services for persons with intellectual disability in residential care in Israel. Int J Disabil Hum Dev 2005;4(2):139-46.
5. Merrick J. Survey of medical clinics, 2005. Jerusalem: Office Med Dir, Min Soc Affairs, 2006.
6. Centers for Disease Control and Prevention (CDC). Trends in aging—United States and worldwide. MMWR Morb Mortal Wkly Rep 2003;52(6):101-6.
7. Fisher K, Kettl P. Aging with mental retardation: increasing population of older adults with MR require health interventions and prevention strategies. Geriatrics 2005;60(4):26-9.
8. Merrick J, Davidson PW, Morad M, Janicki MP, Wexler O, Henderson CM. Older adults with intellectual disability in residential care centers in Israel: health status and service utilization. Am J Ment Retard 2004;109(5):413-20.

CHAPTER 26
Aging in people with autism

Joav Merrick, Ditza Zachor and Isack Kandel

L eo Kanner (1894-1981) and Hans Asperger (1906-1980) were the first to diagnose autism in 1943-1944. Diagnostic criteria have since been changed and expanded resulting in an increase in diagnosed cases. Most of the research so far has been with children and adolescents and very few studies have been concerned with the long-term or natural outcome results of autism. Such studies are important for families, but also for administrators, planners and service providers as well as clinicians in order to provide the best available service for this aging population. A literature review revealed basically three centers (St George's Hospital Medical School in London, Queen Silvia Children's Hospital in Gottenburg and Waisman Center at the University of Wisconsin-Madison), which have conducted long-term follow-up studies. Outcome data showed that intellectual level measured in childhood was a predictive factor for later outcome as to level of independence in adulthood. A majority of the people followed showed dependence upon family and care staff into adulthood and health problems usually related to associated medical conditions with a higher mortality in the group with many associated disorders. Epilepsy was found in 15-38% of the persons at follow-up, which was a much higher prevalence that in the general population. More research is needed to describe the health problems in this population in order to provide information for both families and service providers as this population age.

INTRODUCTION

Leo Kanner (1894-1981) was born in Austria, but moved to the United States in 1924 to become professor of child psychiatry at Johns Hopkins University. He was the first to describe this specific syndrome of autism in 1943 (1), using the Greek word autos (or self) to what he termed early infantile autism (Kanner's syndrome), characterized by: the inability to relate to and interact with other human beings from the beginning of life, the inability to communicate with others through language, an obsession with maintaining sameness and resisting change, a preoccupation with objects rather than people, and the occasional evidence of good potential for intelligence.

One year later, Hans Asperger (1906-1980), an Austrian pediatrician described (2) a neurobiological disorder with a pattern of behaviors in several young boys, who had normal intelligence and language development but who also exhibited autistic-like behaviors and marked deficiencies in social and communication skills. Despite the publication of his paper in 1944, it was not until 1994 that Asperger syndrome (AS) was added to the DSM IV and only in the past few years has AS been recognized by professionals and parents.

The term Pervasive Developmental Disorders (PDD) was first used in the 1980s to describe a class of disorders having in common the following characteristics: impairment in social interaction, imaginative activity, verbal and non-verbal communication skills, and a limited number of interests and activities that tend to be repetitive. In the Diagnostic and Statistical Manual of Mental Disorders (DSM) used by physicians and mental health professionals as a guide to diagnosing disorders, five disorders are identified under the category of Pervasive Developmental Disorder: (1) Autistic disorder, (2) Rett disorder or syndrome, (3) Childhood Disintegrative Disorder, (4) Asperger's disorder or syndrome, and (5) Pervasive Developmental Disorder Not Otherwise Specified, or PDD-NOS.

Autism and PDD-NOS are developmental disabilities that share many of the same characteristics. Usually evident by age three, autism and PDD-NOS are neurological disorders that affect a child's ability to communicate, understand language, play, and relate to others. Due to the similarity of behaviors associated with autism and PDD, use of the term pervasive developmental disorder has caused some confusion among parents and professionals. However, the treatment and educational needs are similar for both diagnoses. The causes of autism and PDD are unknown, except for Rett syndrome, which is an X-linked dominant mutation.

PREVALENCE OF AUTISM

Surveys conducted in the 1960s and 1970s examined the prevalence of autism as defined by Kanner (1), which today is looked upon as a narrow definition. Autism prevalence studies published before 1985 showed prevalence rates of 4 to 5 per 10,000 children for the broader autism spectrum (Autistic disorder, Asperger syndrome, and PDD-NOS) and about 2 per 10,000 for the classic autism definition (3).

In the United Kingdom in 1979, Lorna Wing and Judith Gould (4) studied the prevalence in the Camberwell area of London and found a prevalence of 5 per 10,000 for those with an IQ under 70 and 15 per 10,000 for those with an impairment of social interaction, communication, and imagination—a total prevalence of 20 per 10,000. In Japan (5), a survey of children under 18 years of age showed that 2.33 per 10,000 had early infantile autism (1). The average prevalence rate of autistic children born between 1968 and 1974 was 4.96 per 10,000 children, with a boy-to-girl ratio of 9:1. A Swedish study from Gothenburg (6) of children born during 1962-76 found in 1980 that 2.0 per 10,000 had infantile autism.

Since 1985, higher rates of autism have been reported from several countries, partly because of a broader definition and partly as a true increase in the number of cases (7). A study from the United Kingdom in 2001 (8) reported a prevalence rate of 16.8 per 10,000 children for specific autistic disorder and 62.6 per 10,000 for the entire autistic spectrum disorder. A recent study from South Thames, United Kingdom in a total population cohort of 56 946 children aged 9-10 years found the prevalence of childhood autism at 38.9 per 10,000 (95% CI 29.9-47.8) and that of other ASD at 77.2 per 10,000 (52.1-102.3) or in other words a total prevalence of all ASD at 116.1 per 10,000 (90.4-141.8). A narrower definition of childhood autism, which combined clinical consensus with instrument criteria for past and current presentation, provided a prevalence of 24.8 per 10,000 (17.6-32.0) (9). In Sweden, a study of Asperger syn-drome found a prevalence of 36 per 10,000 for Asperger and 35 per 10,000 for social impairment, or a total prevalence of 71 per 10,000 for suspected and possible cases (10).

Studies in the United States have also found higher prevalence rates in recent years. One study from 1998 in Brick Township, New Jersey found 40 per 10,000 children aged 3-10 years for autistic disorder and 67 per 10,000 children for the entire autism spectrum (11). The data from California can show the dramatic increase in autism prevalence (12): in 1970, the prevalence rate for autism was 4 per 10,000; in 1997, 31 per 10,000; and in 2002, 31.2 per 10,000. The last published study was from five counties in Atlanta, Georgia (3) with a prevalence rate of 34 per 10,000 children aged 3-10 years.

AUTISM IN ISRAEL

To our knowledge, only one study has been reported on the incidence of autism in Israel, which was conducted in the northern region for children born in the Haifa area between 1989 and 1993 (13). This study was conducted through three service providers, where children with autism would have been registered. Twenty-six children were found (twenty one males and five females), resulting in an incidence rate of 10 per 10,000. Again as in other studies, the male-to-female ratio was 4.2 male:1 female. The age at initial assessment and diagnosis was 32 months. No study on the prevalence of the entire autistic spectrum disorder has been reported to date. Data are available on the total number of children and adolescents treated by ALUT (Israel Society for Autistic Children), showing 361 in 1993, 422 in 1995, 591 in 1998, and 641 in 1999 (14), so here an increase can also be seen.

In recent years there has been a lot of concern about the possible increase in the prevalence of autistic spectrum disorders (15). Studies have shown an increase, but during the last 20 years the diagnostic criteria and definition have also changed, so many factors are at play, but nevertheless, the increase is evident.

AUTISM AND AGING

As autism was first diagnosed in 1943, now persons 60 years and older should have autism, but there is a striking lack of data concerning the long-term effects, care, and health aspects of this disorder (16). We see today that persons with autism and other developmental disability now have a life expectancy close to that of the general popu-lation. Yet, a search of the Medline/PubMed database revealed that most studies are concerned with children with autism, very few on adults, and almost none on the health aspects of autism in later life.

More information and data are needed not only for parents and professionals working with this population, but also for planners and service providers to give optimal service in the future for this growing population.

St George's Hospital Medical School in London has conducted a few studies with adults with autism (17,18). Sixty-eight individuals who had fulfilled the criteria for autism with a performance IQ of 50 or above in childhood were followed up as adults. When first seen by the team, the mean age was 7 years (range 3-15 years), whereas at follow-up, the average age was 29 years (range 21-48 years). A few of these adults had achieved relatively high levels of independence, but most remained very dependent on their families/support services. A few lived alone, had close friends or permanent employment, but their communica-tion was generally impaired, with poor reading and spelling abilities. Stereotyped behaviors or interests frequently persisted into adulthood. Ten individuals (14.7%) had developed epilepsy. Overall, only 12% were rated as having a "very good" outcome, 10% rated as "good", and 19% as "fair", whereas 46% had a "poor" and 12% a "very poor" outcome. Although persons with a performance IQ of at least 70 in childhood had a significantly better outcome, within the normal IQ range, the outcome was extremely variable and, on an individual level, neither verbal nor performance IQ proved to be consistent prognostic indicators.

The same center looked at the outcome of a supported employment service for adults with autism or Asperger syndrome (IQ 60 plus) over an 8-year period (17), where about 68 percent found employment. Of the 192 jobs, most were permanent contracts and involved administrative, technical, or computing work.

The Queen Silvia Children's Hospital in Gottenburg has also recently published follow-up studies of 120 persons diagnosed with autism in childhood (19,20). The 120 persons were followed for 13-22 years and reevaluated at age 17-40 years. Six (5%) had died at follow-up (one unknown cause, two status epilepticus, accidental fire, complications after major heart surgery, and brain tumor), and the overall out-come was poor for 78%, with only four persons being independent but living isolated lives. The overall outcome was very poor for 57%, poor for 21%, 13% restricted, 9% fair, and none had a good outcome. The childhood IQ level was positively correlated with a better adult outcome (18). As adults, most subjects had intellectual disability, autistic disorder, or an autistic-like condition, with 38% having epilepsy at follow-up. About half of this cohort had a medical problem that required regular medical attention (19).

A study from Australia and New Zealand (21) of 12 women with autism (eight with autism, four with Asperger syndrome, aged 15-27 years) compared with 12 women with Down syndrome (15-25 years) found that

62.5% of the women with autism, 75% with Down syndrome, and 100% with Asperger syndrome had period pain. 75% of women with Down syndrome and 75% of women with autism and Asperger syndrome had symptoms of premenstrual syndrome, with the Asperger syndrome women being the most affected (21).

A study from Finland (22) recently reported on neurological abnormalities in 20 young adults with Asperger syndrome compared with 10 healthy control subjects. The investigators found that the neurological abnormalities of Asperger syndrome persist into adulthood and were higher than in normal controls.

UNIVERSITY OF WISCONSIN-MADISON STUDY

The Waisman Center at the University of Wisconsin-Madison together with Brandeis University in 1998 started a study of family caregiving in adults and adolescents with autism with a cohort of 400 families (200 in Wisconsin and 200 in Massachusetts) studied over a 5-year period. This investigation was undertaken to describe, understand, and convey the nature of the lives of adults with autism and their families during the later decades of their life (see http://www.waisman.wisc.edu/family/autism-study-info.html).
Three questions were addressed in this study:

1.   What are the challenges and rewards of the caregiving experienced by aging parents and adult siblings of persons with autism?
2.   What factors are associated with a favorable quality of life of the adult with autism?
3.   How do the challenges and rewards of caregiving and the quality of life change over time, and what factors contribute to these changes.

This is a longitudinal study of adults with autism with their aging parents and adult siblings. Mothers, fathers, and siblings were the sources of data in three waves of data collection. The families must meet two recruitment criteria: 1) the adult with autism will also have the diagnosis of intellectual disability (ID), and 2) the mother will be between the age of 55-85. About half the adults lived at home with their parents, while the other half lived in a variety of types of residential programs.

Families were recruited through a collaboration with the Massachusetts and Wisconsin chapters of the Autism Society of America (via mailings, announcements placed in newsletters and at parent meetings), public and private schools serving persons with autism (using alumni informa-tion), community psychiatrists, area offices of the Department of Mental Retardation (in Massachusetts) and county Developmental Disability Coordinators (in Wisconsin), professional staff at the Waisman Center and other clinical sites in Wisconsin, and professional staff at the Shriver Center in Waltham, Massachusetts.

Mothers were interviewed in their homes by a trained interviewer (about one hour) and following the interview, mothers were asked to complete a brief self-administered questionnaire that contained standardized and validated measures on such issues as parenting stress, sense of competence as a parent, psychological well-being, coping strategies, and concerns about the future. A separate phone interview was conducted with fathers within two weeks after the mother interview. The phone interview was conducted by a different interviewer than the one who interviewed the mother (to ensure confidentiality). The questions focused on the father's personal experiences as a parent of a person with autism, his expectations for the future, and the advice he would offer to other parents and to service providers. The fathers also completed self-admini-stered measures and returned them by mail. One adult sibling was contacted and asked to complete a mailed survey. The sibling who was be surveyed was the brother or sister having the closest relationship with the individual with autism, as identified by the mother. The questions in the survey asked the sibling to describe his or her relationship with the brother or sister with autism during childhood, adolescence, and now in adulthood. Also, the degree of knowledge about the brother or sister's service needs was assessed, various aspects of life (e.g., career, where to live, friends), and expectations for the future care or supervision of her brother or sister with autism. They were also asked what advice they would offer to parents of persons with autism, other siblings, and service professionals.

In the present chapter, we will not go into all the findings from this extensive family project (the reports and publication list can be found on the website mentioned above) but rather focus on the findings from report number seven on the health-related aspects (the report can be found on the website also). The health report is based on data collection from the fourth round of visits with data from 286 families.

Among the parents, 29% rated their son's or daughter's physical health as excellent, 55% as good, 15% as fair, and 1% as poor, with 74% of parents reporting that the health had not changed since last interview/visit. Of the 26% who reported change, 15% reported worse health and 11% better health. Sleep difficulty (70%) and gastrointestinal problems (58%) were the most reported problems, followed by anxiety (34%), respiratory problems (32%), depression (25%), and convulsive disorders (25%). The frequency of health problems varied greatly from daily to less than once a month.

Concerning healthcare service utilization, 94% had visited a physician during the past 12 months (also great variation here with some reporting many visits), 89% had been to a dentist, 85% had undergone a complete health or physical examination, 12% had been to the emergency room, and 9% had been hospitalized.

More than 80% were on a daily medication with the top 10 prescription medications: 41% on anti-depressants, 35% on anti-convulsants, 33% on psychotropics, 15% on hypo-tensive, 14% on anti-anxiety, 10% on respiratory agents, 7% on CNS stimulants, 6% on gastrointestinal, 5% on laxatives, and 5% on hormones. On average, each person received three medications (range 1-12).

Parental health was also investigated and most parents were in good health, but about half experienced some kind of chronic medical condition or disability. The type of condition varied by gender; for example, the most common medical condition was pain in mothers and hypertension in fathers. Mothers of a child with autism reported more frequently health problems than did mothers of the same age in the general population.

DISCUSSION

Autism is coming of age, but we lack information and research about the long-term effects, because only now we are seeing people with autism entering the third age. What is the life course of autism for the person him/herself, the parents, the siblings, and the family? But it is not important only for the family, because the care staff and other professionals also lack information.

When we searched the literature, very few studies were available with even fewer dealing with long-term health aspects or natural outcome of autism. In our search, we found basically three centers that have conducted long-term follow-up studies, and each has a different approach or focus in their research.

St George's Hospital Medical School in London (17,18) reported on 68 persons with autism and a non-verbal IQ of at least 50 and found that some made progress in adulthood. Of these, 20% had managed to obtain some academic qualifications at school and five of these had gone on to college or university, with two studying at the postgraduate level. About one-third was employed, but only a total of eight individuals could be rated as having achieved a high level of independence (12%). The majority remained very dependent upon their families or care staff. Outcome was correlated to the level of intellectual functioning in childhood. An IQ level of >50 was associated with more positive outcome, and those with an IQ >70 were doing even better.

The study from the Queen Silvia Children's Hospital in Gottenburg (19,20) found that poor and very poor outcome affected more persons than originally predicted, and epilepsy was found more common than expected at follow-up. Female gender was not associated with a worse outcome, and the outcome of atypical autism was as restricted as that of classic autistic disorder. Mortality (5%) was also described in this study, mainly due to associated medical disorders. Concerning epilepsy, new cases appeared in post-adolescence but seemed rare after 20 years of age. The overall prevalence of epilepsy was the highest (38%) in the three center studies. Other major problems were self-injury (50%) and violent behavior (19% showed extreme violent behaviors and 23% less but still violent behavior that concerned their environment) that concerned the family and care staff. All in all, half of the population studied showed medical problems in need of regular care.

The University of Wisconsin-Madison and Brandeis University study of family caregiving in adults and adolescents with autism is so far the biggest follow-up study, with 400 families being monitored. In this paper, we looked only at the health-related data from this family focused study, which showed that the majority of adolescent and adults were in good health and that their health remained stable over time. The major health problems found were sleep difficulty and gastrointestinal problems, whereas epilepsy was found in 25%.

CONCLUSIONS

The review presented here revealed that we have very little information today about the natural long-term outcome of autism. A literature search revealed three major studies from centers in London, Gottenburg, and Madison. The outcome data showed that the intellectual level achieved in childhood was a predictive factor for later outcome as to level of independence reached in adulthood.

Long-term follow-up studies found that most persons with autism showed dependence upon family and care staff into adulthood, and that their health problems usually related to associated medical conditions, with a higher mortality in the group having many associated disorders.
Epilepsy was found in 15% to 38% of the persons at follow-up, which is a much higher prevalence than found in the general population.

ACKNOWLEDGEMENTS

This chapter is an adapted version of an earlier published paper (Merrick J, Zachor D, Kandel I. Aging with autism. Int J Disabil Hum Dev 2006;5(1):17-21).

REFERENCES
1.   Kanner L. Autistic disturbances of affectice contact. Nervous Child 1943;2:217-50.
2.   Asperger H. [Die autistischen psychopathen im kindersalter]. Arch Psychiatrie Nervenkrankheit 1944; 117:76-136. [German].
3.   Yeargin-Allsopp M, Rice C, Karapurkar T, Doernberg N, Boyle C, Murphy C. Prevalence of autism in a US Metropolitamn area. JAMA 2003;289(1):49-55.
4.   Wing L, Gould J. Severe impairments of social interaction and associated abnormalities in children: Epidemiology and classification. J Autism Dev Disord 1979;9(1):11-29.
5.   Hoshino Y, Kumashiro H, Yashima Y, Tachibana R, Watanabe M. The epidemiological study of autism in Fukushima-ken. Folia Psychiatr Neurol Jpn 1982; 36(2):115-24.
6.   Gillberg C. Infantile autism and other childhood psychoses in a Swedish urban region. Epidemiological aspects. J Child Psychol Psychiatry 1984;25(1):35-43.
7.   Fombonne E. The prevalence of autism. JAMA 2003; 289(1):87-9.
8.   Chakrabarti S, Fombonne E. Pervasive developmental disorders in preschool children. JAMA 2001;285:3093-9.

9.   Baird G, Simonoff E, Pickles A, Chandler S, Loucas T, Meldrum D, Charman T. Prevalence of disorders of the autism spectrum in a population cohort of children in South Thames: the Special Needs and Autism Project (SNAP). Lancet 2006;368(9531):210-5.

10.   Ehlers S, Gillberg C. The epidemiology of Asperger syndrome. A total population study. J Child Psychol Psychiatry 1993;34(8):1327-50.

11.   Bertrand J, Mars A, Boyle C, Bove F, Yeargin-Allsopp M, Decoufle P. Prevalence of autism in a United States population. Pediatrics 2001;108:1155-61.

12.   California Dept Dev Services. Autistic spectrum disorders. Changes in the California caseload. An update: 1999 through 2002. Sacramento, California, USA: California Health and Human Services, 2003 (www.dds.ca.gov)

13.   Davidovitch M, Holtzman G, Tirosh E. Autism in the Haifa area. An epidemiological perspective. Isr Med Ass J 2001;3:188-9.

14.   Ben-Arieh A, Tzionit Y, Beenstock-Rivlin Z, eds. The state of the child in Israel. A statistical abstract 2000. Jerusalem: Isr Nat Council Child, 2001.

15.   Hyman SL, Rodier PM, Davidson P. Pervasive devel-opmental disorders in young children. JAMA 2001; 285(24):3141-2.

16.   Hemsoth T. Autism and aging. A crisis of reliable data and informed care options. Assoc Conten 2006. http://www.associatedcontent.com/article/16952/autism_and_agi ng.html

17.   Howlin P, Goode S, Hutton J, Rutter M. Adult out-come for children with autism. J Child Psychol Psychiatry 2004;45(2):212-29.

18.   Howlin P, Alcock J, Burkin C. An 8 year follow-up of a specialist supported employment service for high-ability adults with autism or Asperger syndrome. Autism 2005;9(5):533-49.

19.   Billstedt E, Gillberg C, Gillberg C. Autism after adolescence: Population based 13- to 22-year follow-up study of 120 individuals with autism diagnosed in childhood. J Autism Dev Disord 2005;35(30:351-60.

20.   Danielsson S, Gillberg IC, Billstedt E, Gillberg C, Olsson I. Epilepsy in young adults with autism: A prospective population based follow-up study of 120 individuals diagnosed in childhood. Epilepsia 2005; 46(6):918-23.

21.   Kyrkou M. Health issues and quality of life in women with intellectual disability. J Intellect Disabil Res 2005;49(10):770-2.

22.   Tani P, Lindberg N, Appelberg B, Nieminen-von Wendt T, von Mendt L, Porkka-Heiskanen T. Clinical neurological abnormalities in young adults with Asperger syndrome. Psychiatry Clin Neurosci 2006; 60(2):253-5.

CHAPTER 27
Aging in persons with Rett syndrome

Joav Merrick, Meir Lotan, Mohammed Morad and Isack Kandel

R ett syndrome (RS) is a neurological disease characterized by an arrest of brain development caused by an X chromosome mutation affecting mainly females. Rett syndrome is the first human disease found to be caused by defects in a protein involved in regulating gene expression through its interaction with methylated DNA. The disease has been traced to a defective gene called MECP2 on the X chromosome. This review of aging with RS revealed very few studies, but the published case stories showed that females with RS can live even to age 79 years, but larger studies are needed to bring more light into the natural and long-term consequences of this syndrome. Clinical knowledge suggests that individuals with RS present the therapist/physician with specific clinical challenges that require proper intervention programs to be tailored for this population.

INTRODUCTION

The original study, by Andreas Rett (1924-1997) from Austria, of six girls with a peculiar disease was published in German in 1966 (1), but this syndrome only gained international attention when Bengt Hagberg from Sweden and colleagues (2) published their findings on 35 cases in 1983. This author had in fact already observed his first patient in 1960 (3).

Rett syndrome (RS) is a neurological disease characterized by arrest of brain development (4) caused by an X chromosome mutation affecting mainly females (5). RS is the first human disease found to be caused by defects in a protein involved in regulating gene expression through its interaction with methylated DNA (6) and has been traced to a defective gene on the X chromosome, called MECP2 (pronounced meck-pea-two). This discovery was made by Huda Zoghbi, a neuro-geneticist at Baylor College of Medicine in Texas, working together with the Israeli physician Ruthie Amir, who also found the first mutations (6,7). RS typically presents after the first year of life (6-18 months of age) and is one of the most common causes for multiple-disability among females. The disease incidence is one in 10-15,000, with a gradual reduction of speech and purposeful hand use, seizures, autistic like behavior, ataxia, intermittent hyperventilation, and stereotypic hand movements. After initial regression, the condition stabilizes and patients usually survive into adulthood (3).

Although 50% to 75% of patients achieve independent mobility at early childhood, about 75% lose the ability to walk at later years and become wheelchair bound (8). Some professionals recommend walking or other physical fitness programs as a preventive intervention that might hold back or diminish secondary regression (8-11). One of the most debilitating disabilities is scoliosis, appearing in up to 85% of affected individuals (9). A poor prognosis for scoliosis has been linked with lack of walking and an inability to ascend and descend stairs. Additional characteristic factors are constipation and osteoporosis at a young age, with both situations known to be positively affected by physical activity.

RETT SYNDROME STAGES

The stages of RS have been described as: Onset or pre-regression (or stage 1), destructive, motor deterioration or regression (or stage 2), essentially stable or plateau (or stage 3), and in some cases the term fourth stage (late motor deterioration) has been used in circumstances, when an individual becomes very handicapped and loses ambulation (12,13). Childhood development in females with RS proceeds in an apparently normal fashion in-utero and during the first 6-18 months of life, at which point their development comes to a halt with regression and loss of many of their acquired skills (14). Thereafter, a rapid deterioration with loss of acquired speech and purposeful hand use ensues. A deceleration of head growth and jerky body movements of the trunk and limbs accompany the developmental deterioration in individuals with RS. Typically, they present with a broad-base gait and swaying movements of the shoulders when walking (15). Other physical problems, such as seizures, scoliosis, and breathing abnormalities may appear (16), which require constant care for the rest of the person's life (17). The scoliosis is a prominent feature in females with RS, but can vary from mild to severe (18). Apraxia (dyspraxia), the inability to program the body to perform motor movements, is the most fundamental and severely handicapping aspect of the syndrome. Apraxia can interfere with all body movement, including eye gaze and speech, making it difficult for individuals with RS to execute what they want to do. To sum things up, the child and adolescent with RS is in need of an intensive and comprehensive management program across their life span (estimated life expectancy at 50 years) (19).

CLINICAL CHARACTERISTICS

The person with RS presents some clinical manifestations that are common for this syndrome and therefore require specific acknowledgement, proper evaluation and specific intervention.

- Scoliosis – 80-85% of individuals with RS (20,21) are diagnosed with scoliosis. It was found that intensive therapeutic intervention that gave adequate sensory (16) and physical (10) support could regress the deterioration of the scoliosis (10) and might even prevent the need for corrective surgery (16).

- Epilepsy – according to different studies 30-90% of individuals with RS will be diagnosed with epilepsy (20,22-25). Individuals with RS show acute reactions to anti-epileptic medication and therefore the diagnostic procedure, as well as medication prescription should be performed by physicians acquainted with this specific disorder (20). Moreover, since many individuals with RS tend to present irregular night sleep (26) and excessive amount of day sleeping (27) anti-epileptic medication should be introduced only if the seizures disturb the child daily routine or function. Since it was found that 82% of individuals with RS present breathing abnormalities that might sometime appear as epileptic-like attacks, telemetry Electro-Encephalogram (video-EEG) should be performed to discourage anti-epileptic over-medication. Another aspect of epilepsy typical of this population is the fact that many of them show reduction in the severity and frequency of epileptic attacks in adulthood. Therefore a slow reduction of anti-convulsive medication should be performed with adults with RS under the supervision of a neurologist (20). Phenobarbitone and to a lesser extent benzodiazepines display a severe effect on the level of alertness and responsiveness of the client with RS to a point of sudden pseudo-motor deterioration, therefore their use should be avoided as much as possible (28).

- Cranitine - is a biological enhancer needed for cell fat metabolism. Reduction in cranitine level might cause: muscle weakness, liver-insufficiency, neurological problems and hypotonia. All these behaviors might damage the functional ability of the individual with RS yet they are masked by the fluctuating nature of the RS manifestation. Since individuals with RS have been found to show low levels of cranitine in the past, and since the supply of cranitine was found to positively contribute to the height, weight and motor function of these individuals (29,30), cranitine level should be evaluated and supplemented in case of deficiency. Moreover, the combination of anti-convulsive medication, especially Depakot, with cranitine was found beneficial for this population.

- Constipation - is common in individuals with RS (25). It is estimated that 85% of individuals with RS will experience severe constipation at least once in their life (31). Constipation in this population is derived from lack of physical activity, low muscle tone, improper diet, medication, scoliosis and reduced liquid intake (32). Since all the these contributing factors are treatable, treatment for these factors should be examined prior to the use of laxatives and enemas (33).

- Nutrition - intestinal problems are present in 74% of individuals with RS (25) and a significant component in this syndrome. There is evidence that these symptoms worsened with age in connection with their functional/orthopedic situation (18,34), so constant and proper evaluation should be a part of the follow-up procedure of the adult person with RS. Moreover, moderate to severe malnutrition is present in 85% of individuals with RS (35) and aggravated with age (24,32). Yet many of the nutritional problems of this population are treatable (33), when properly diagnosed.

- Osteoporosis - occurs frequently in females with RS and has been reported in very young girls (36-38). Patients with RS have been found with decreased bone mineral density compared to controls (39). These findings supports the need for routine checking of bone density of individuals with RS from childhood, and to commence physical (such as intensive standing and walking programs (11,40), nutritional (33) and medical intervention (36) as preventive intervention (28).

- Dental treatment – specific dental disorder related problems have been identified in individuals with RS (41,42). These problems include: gum problems, teeth closure (42), bruxism, high risk of falling and facial trauma (34), teeth damage due to prolonged use of anti-convulsive medication and reflux (16). These problems require dental attention and care (43,44).

- Functional improvements – few studies have demonstrated that proper intervention can improve function of children (11) as well as adults with RS, up to a point were walking was restored for a woman with RS who stopped walking 20 years earlier (45). Due to longevity of individuals with RS, it is suggested that proper and intensive care should be provided at all ages with the hope of preventing or at least reducing the age-related deterioration typical for this population (46).

All the above mentioned symptoms are typical of individuals with RS and can be treated with conventional intervention, therby contributing to longevity and better quality of life in this population. We therefore recommend longitudinal follow-up with proper evaluational procedures and intervention as needed for this population when aging.

LONGITUDINAL FOLLOW-UP OF ADULTS WITH RETT SYNDROME

Research on aging and RS are scarce with only a few case studies. The present paragraph describes longitudinal follow-up of adults with RS thereby emphasizing the importance of such documentation. One case study described (45) a woman from Norway with RS, who lived to the age of 60 years. That paper provides no information about any genetic test, only a clinical diagnosis. The study was based on medical records, older and more recent videotapes, and interviews with her sister and care staff. After 21 years without walking, following intensive physiotherapy, the woman regained the ability to walk without support. She also showed improvement in hand use a few years before she died. During the early regression, she appeared to lose social interest. The interest improved after some time, but she remained wary of people she did not know.

Another case study was published from Denmark of a 77-year-old woman (47), born in 1923 after a normal pregnancy and delivery, who walked unsupported at the age of about one year. She deviated from normal development at age two years. At age 38 years, she had lost all purposeful hand use and swung them constantly. She developed severe kyphosis and at age 41 years ambulation was lost. At age 66, she was diagnosed as RS with the following mutation in her MECP2 alleles: a C to P transition in exon 4 leading to a substitution of threonine by methionine at position 158, T158M in the conserved methyl binding domain (MBD), of the corresponding gene product. The XCI showed a non-random pattern with an inactivation ratio of 10:90. This T158 mutation is a common mutation in RS, and her skewed XCI may have resulted in her long survival. She died at age 79 years from peritonitis, caused by an abscess after the removal of a large spleen.

Hagberg (48) has recently described three cases to illustrate the long-term clinical follow-up in RS. The first case story was a girl born in 1957, who had developmental delay and referred at age 3.5 years, but not diagnosed with RS until age 19 years. At that time, the main problems were her apraxia, her general developmental retardation, and her aggressive behavior. In addition, she was considerably growth retarded, had developed a severe kyphosis, and a more modest left convex C scoliosis. Her epileptiform symptomatology, which started at age 6 months, was under full control and no longer a problem. At the last follow-up (age 47 years), she was a very small woman, 134 cm tall, weighing 50 kg, with an occipitofrontal head circumference (OFC) of 54 cm. She had short, thin, slightly distorted feet (only 34 cm long). She was still able to walk unsupported, but showed some balance problems. She was less active in motor terms and had signs of excessively early gross motor muscle aging of the legs. She had hand-finger stereotypes more or less continuously, but a more subtle form of the regular hand stereotypic wringing and twisting performed by females with RS. Her neurology was characterized by a complex gross motor dysfunction of the RS type, not only a complete grasp apraxia but also some sort of dyspraxia in her whole-body movement pattern. She had a complex MECP2 rearrangement with deletions both of exon 3 and exon 4.

The second case story was a female born in 1960, second of three siblings in a healthy family. Her pre- and perinatal history was uneventful with birth at full term (weight 3,720 g, length 50 cm, OFC 34.5 cm). Her first 1.25 years of life were reported to have been uneventful. At that age, she was able to walk with support, pincer-grasp, and manipulated toys as expected. She had, however, never learned to crawl on all fours. At this point a general stagnation occurred, followed rapidly by marked developmental regression. At the age of 1.75 years, she had stopped walking completely, had lost contact with her parents, had developed intense "hand-clapping" stereotypes (movie documented), and showed autistic traits. In parallel, her head growth curve indicated a marked deceleration. At age 23 years, she was diagnosed as a classic Rett syndrome. At last visit (age 44 years), she was an extremely handicapped, very small and thin, with a small head (height 130 cm, weight 24 kg, OFC 48.5 cm). She had a complex S-curved RS kyphoscoliosis and a markedly distended abdomen of the RS bloating type. Her feet were cold and sweaty, bluish in color, and extremely thin and small (length only 22 cm). Her examination was characterized by a dystonic-rigid syndrome of the advanced RS type with a right-sided dominance. She was reported to have repeated, unmotivated, long laughing attacks, as well as paroxysmal night screaming. She has never had any epileptic seizures. She has a commonly found MECP2 mutation in axon 4 (R270X).

The third case, born in 1965, was one of two siblings in a healthy family. Her peri- and neonatal histories were uneventful, as were her developmental abilities when she was born at full term (weight 3,590 g, length 50 cm, OFC 34 cm). She developed normally, but at health check-up at age one year, she was considered to be "late", but able to creep on her knees and sit up and walk with support and play with toys. She could say many single words. After 1.5 years of age, she slowly regressed, did not use her hands as before, no longer had any contact with her parents, and was more or less in her "own world". At the same time, she stopped crawling and talking and repeatedly had unmotivated screaming attacks. At the age of 2.5 years, her skull growth had stagnated significantly. She was slightly hypotonic and had some sort of ataxic movement patterns of the truncal ataxia type, as well as intention tremor in her hands and stereotypic movement patterns. She did not develop seizures. Through the following three decades, she successively deteriorated neurologically into a generalized most severe dystonic-atrophic syndrome with side-asym-metric secondary deformities, contractures, and a collapse scoliosis. This was in contrast to good contact with and recognition of family members and her personal assistants. She died at the age of 36 years in a deformed, growth-retarded, emaciated stage.

ADULTS WITH RETT SYNDROME

Due to the fact that RS has been acknowledged only in the last 25 years after the publication of the first English article regarding RS by Hagberg and his colleagues (2), the majority of adults with RS is not diagnosed and might therefore lack proper intervention.

In the attached figure the prevalence of RS in Israel is presented. It is clear from the graph that not all adults over the age of 15 have been located and diagnosed and older adults (25 years and up) have been scarcely detected.

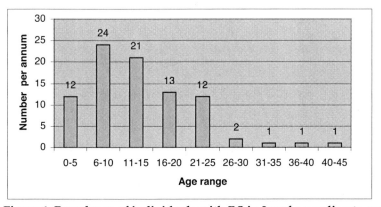

Figure 1. Prevalence of individuals with RS in Israel according to age

Due to the specific challenges presented by adults with RS, the authors call for wide spread organized search for this population, to detect, diagnose and implement proper intervention programs adapted for the specific needs of individuals with RS.

MORTALITY IN RETT SYNDROME

Persons with RS can survive into middle and old age, but life expectancy is reduced and the occurrence of sudden death is greater than in the general population. Longitudinal records of persons with RS began in the United Kingdom in 1982 and developed into the British Survey in 1993. From this British Survey, the mortality rate for RS has been estimated at 1.2% per annum (49), with 48% of deaths occurring in debilitated people, 13% from natural causes, 13% with prior severe seizures and 26% sudden and unexpected (49-52). Respiratory dysrhythmias were usually present. Neuropathological studies confirmed reductions in cortical dendrites and in one case, immaturity of cardiac conducting tissues (49). The possible causes of sudden death can include brain-stem autonomic failure (respiratory failure, apnoea, cardiac arrhythmias) (49-52).

DISCUSSION

This review of aging individuals with Rett syndrome (RS) revealed very few studies, and we have still to wait for additional, larger follow-up studies in the future.

The five case stories from Norway, Denmark, and Sweden showed deceleration of head growth appearing at an early stage that was associated with increased motor disability and with the appearance of intractable epilepsy (48). The hand stereotypes so obvious from early childhood usually change in adult middle age toward frozen and stiff mal-positions. From childhood to young adulthood, some gross motor functions appear to improve slightly with a temporary recovery and compensation in contrast to the loss of fine motor abilities. In the long term, middle-aged women with RS lose a great deal of muscle volume, strength, and power and present with general premature neuromuscular aging. The early general growth deceleration not only affects body and skull growth but also involves the overly thin, small, cold, and sweaty feet and the insufficient, compressed, and curved spine (10,48).

Epilepsy occurs in more than 90% of cases with onset of clinical seizures at around 3-5 years of age, with a peak frequency in adolescence into young adulthood and successively decreases in early middle age, with only rare and minor problems occurring after the age of 40 years (48,53). After 40 years of age, an attempt should be made to withdraw antiepileptic drugs completely (48,53).

Many common characteristics of adults with RS are known. These include: constipation, osteoporosis, functional abilities, dental problems, nutritional needs, orthopedic problems as well as medical needs. This makes special evaluation a must, which should then lead to improved and more focused intervention for this population. Nevertheless the novelty of this syndrome requires a search for undiagnosed adults with RS in order to enable the implementation of proper care.

The case stories presented here showed that females with RS can live even to age 79 years, but larger studies are needed to bring more light to the natural and long-term consequences of this syndrome. Due to the observed longevity of individuals with RS, it is suggested that proper and intensive care should be provided at all ages with the hope of preventing or at least reducing the age-related deterioration that is typical of this population.

ACKNOWLEDGEMENTS

This chapter is an adapted version of an earlier published paper (Merrick J, Lotan M, Morad M,, Kandel I. Rett syndrome and aging. Int J Disabil Hum Dev 2006;5(1):23-6).

REFERENCES

1. Rett A. Uber ein eigenartiges hirnatrophisches Syndrom bei Hyperammonamie im Kindesalter. Wiener Medi-zinische Wochenschrift 1966;116:723-38. [German]

2. Hagberg B, Aicardi J, Dias K, Ramos O. A progres-sive syndrome of autism, dementia, ataxia and loss of purposeful hand use in girls: Rett's syndrome. Report of 35 cases. Ann Neurol 1983;14:471-9.

3. Hagberg B. Rett syndrome: Swedish approach to analysis of prevalence and cause. Brain Dev 1985;7: 277-80.

4. Armstrong DD. The neuropathology of Rett Syndrome overview 1994. Neuropediatrics 1995;26,100-4.

5. Amir RE, Van den Veyver IB, Schultz R, Malicki DM, Tran CQ, Dahle EJ, Philippi A, Timar L, Percy AK, Motil KJ, Lichtarge O, Smith EO, Glaze DG, Zoghbi HY. Influence of mutation type and X chrom-osome inactivation on Rett syndrome phenotypes. Ann Neurol 2000;47:670-9.

6. Amir RE, Van den Veyer IB, Wan M, Tran CQ, Francke U, Zoghbi HY. Rett syndrome is caused by mutations in X-linked MECP2, encoding methyl-CpG-binding protein 2. Nature Genetics 1999;23:185-8.

7. Amir RE, Zoghbi HY. Rett syndrome: Methyl-CpG-binding protein 2 mutations and phenotype-genotype correlations. Am J Med Genetics 2000;97:147-52.

8. Lotan M, Hadar-Frumer M. Hydrotherapy for Rett syndrome. Physiother Bull 2002;4:23-8. [Hebrew]

9. McClure MK, Battaglia C, McClure RJ. The relation-ship of cumulative motor asymmetries to scoliosis in Rett syndrome. Am J Occup Ther 1998;52(3):488-93.

10. Lotan M, Merrick J, Carmeli E. Managing scoliosis in a young child with Rett syndrome: a case study. ScientificWorldJournal 2005;5:264-73.

11. Lotan M, Isakov E, Merrick J. Improving functional skills and physical fitness in children with Rett syndrome. J Intellect Disabil Res 2004;48(8):730-5.

12. Kerr AM. Annotation: Rett syndrome: recent progress and implications for research and clinical practice. J Child Psychol Child Psychiatry 2002;43(3): 277-87.

13. Lotan M, Merrick J. Rett syndrome management with Snoezelen or controlled multi-sensory stimulation. A review. Int J Adolesc Med Health 2004;16(1):5-12.

14. Graham JM. Rett syndrome. Information packet. Los Angeles, California, USA: Cedars-Sinai Medical Center, 1995.

15. Kerr AM, Stephenson JBP. Rett syndrome in the west of Scotland. BMJ 1985;291(6495): 579-82.

16. Budden SS. Management of Rett Syndrome: A ten years experience. Neuropediatrics 1995;26(2):75-7.

17.   Leonard H, Fyfe S, Leonard S, Msall M. Functional status, medical impairments, and rehabilitation re-sources in 84 females with Rett syndrome: a snapshot across the world from the parental perspective. Disabil Rehabil 2001;23(3-4):107-17.

18.   Sponseller P. Orthopedic update in Rett Syndrome. IRSA-Int Rett Syndr Ass Inf Resources. www. rettsyndrome.org/main/ orthopaedic-update.htm

19.   Percy AK. International research review. IRSA-Int Rett Syndr Ass 12th Ann Conf. Boston, Massachusetts, USA: 24-27 May,1996.

20.   Hagberg B. Rett syndrome: Clinical and biological aspects. London: Mac Keith, 1993.

21.   Rossin L. Effectiveness of therapeutic and surgical intervention in the treatment of scoliosis in Rett syndrome. A seminar work, Duquesne: Univ Duquesne, 1997:1-19.

22.   Nieto MA, Candau RS, Prieto P. Contribution to studies of seizures in Rett Syndrome analysis of critical forms of four cases. Rev Neurol 1995; 23: 1185-9.

23.   Glaze D. Epilepsy. Paper presented at the IRSA 12th Annual Conference, Boston, MA, tape 622-18, 1996.

24.   Ellaway C, Christodoulou J. Rett syndrome: Clinical characteristics and recent genetic advances. Disabil Rehabil 2001;23:98-106.

25.   Leonard S. The Australian Rett syndrome study inaugural report. Westrern Australia: Telethon Inst Child Health Res, 2002.

26.   Nomura Y. Early behavior characteristics and sleep disturbance in Rett syndrome. Brain Dev 2005;Suppl 1:S35-S42.

27.   Piazza CC, Fisher W, Kiesewetter BS, Bowman L, Moser H. Aberrant sleep patterns in children with Rett Syndrome. Brain Dev 1990;2: 488-93.

28.   Lotan M, Ben-Zeev B. Rett Syndrome. A review with emphasis on clinical characteristics and intervention. ScientificWorldJournal 2006; 6,1517–41.

29.   Plioplys AV, Kasnicka I. L-Carnitine as treatment for Rett Syndrome. South Afr Med J 1993;86:1411-2.

30.   Glaze D. Research updates from Baylor College. IRSA annual conference, Las Vegas May 18-21, 2000, tape RS 10.

31.   Saavedra JM. Gastrointestinal crises in Rett Syndrome. Int Rett Syndr Assoc Newsletter 1997; 4:3-5.

32.   Reilly S, Cass H. Growth and nutrition in Rett syndrome. Disabil Rehabil 2001;23:118-28.

33.   Lotan M, Zysman L. The digestive system and nutritional considerations for individuals with Rett Syndrome. A review. ScientificWorldJournal 2006;6:1737–49.

34.   Lotan M. Angels of silence: Caring for Rett syndrome. Sheba, Tel Hashomer: Rotem publ, Rett Syndr Center, 2006. [Hebrew]

35.   Hunter K. The Rett Syndrome handbook, Washington, DC: Int Rett Syndr Assoc, 1999.

36.   Zysman L, Lotan M, Ben-Zeev B. Osteoporosis in Rett syndrome: A study on normal values. ScientificWorldJournal 2006;6:1619–30.

37.   Budden SS, Gunness ME. Possible mechanisms of osteopenia in Rett syndrome: Bone histomorphometric studies. J Child Neurol 2003;18(10):698-702.

38.   Leonard H, Thomson M, Glasson E, Fyfe S, Leonard S, Ellaway C, Christodouloon J, Bower C. Metacarpophalangeal pattern profile and bone age in Rett Syndrome: Further radiological clues to the diagnosis. Am J Med Genetics 1999;12(83):88-95.

39.   Haas RH, Dixon SD, Sartoris DJ, Hennessy MJ. Osteopenia in Rett syndrome. J Pediatr 1997;131(5):771-4.

40.   Weeks L. Rett Syndrome. A lecture. Sydney, Aust, 1997.

41.   Tesini DA, Fenton-Sanford J. Oral health needs of persons with physical or mental disabilities. Dent Clin North Am 1994;38:483-98.

42.   Ribeiro RA, Romano AR, Birman-Goldenberg E, Mayer MP. Oral manifestations in Rett Syndrome: A study of 17 cases. Pediatr Dent 1997;19:349-52.

43.   Tenisi DA. Developing dental health education programs for persons with special needs. A training guide and reference text. Amherst, MA: Massachusetts Res Inst and Massachusetts Dept Dental Health, 1988.

44.   Tenisi DA. Providing dental services for citizens with handicaps: a prototype community program. Ment Retard 1987;25:219-22.

45.   Jacobsen K, Viken A, von Tetzchner S. Rett syndrome and ageing: A case study. Disabil Rehabil 2001; 23(3-4):160-6.

46.   Ben Zeev B. Lessons from Rett syndrome and the MECP2 gene as a model for a neurodevelopemental disorder. Sheba, Tel Hashomer: Annual Conf Rare Dis, 2004.

47.   Nielsen JB, Ravn K, Schwartz M. A 77-year-old woman and a preserved speech variant among Danish Rett patients with mutations in MECP2. Brain Dev 2001;23:S230-2.

48.   Hagberg B. Rett syndrome. Long-term clinical follow- up experiences over four decades. J Child Neurol 2005;20(9):722-6.

49.   Kerr AM, Armstrong DD, Prescott RJ, Doyle D, Kearney DL. Rett syndrome: analysis of deaths in the British survey. Eur Child Adolesc Psychiatry 1997; 6(Suppl 1):71-4.

50.   Acampa M, Guideri. Cardiac disease and Rett syndrome. Arch Dis Child 2006;91:440-3.

51.   Ohya T, Yamashita Y, Matsuishi T. [Sudden death in Rett syndrome]. Nippon Rinsho 2005;63(7):1178-82. [Japanese]

52.   Byard RW. Forensic issues and possible mechanisms of sudden death in Rett syndrome. J Clin Forensic Med 2006;13(2):96-9.

53.   Steffenburg U, Hagberg G, Hagberg B. Epilepsy in a representative series of Rett syndrome. Acta Paediatr 200;89:198-202.

PART EIGHT:
OLDER PEOPLE WITH DEMENTIA

CHAPTER 28
Housing and persons with dementia

Simon Evans and Robin Means

This chapter discusses the findings from a qualitative, longitudinal study into the suitability of extra care housing for people with dementia. Particular attention is paid to the perceptions and responses of care professionals to risk management in relation to the specific needs of people with dementia. Extra care housing is widely promoted as a popular option for older people with dementia, largely because it can maximize independence and offer a homely alternative to other forms of housing with care. At the same time, older people with dementia are often perceived as one of society's most vulnerable and 'at risk' groups who are in particular need of protection. We explore the potential paradox between managing risk and at the same time supporting independence in the extra care housing setting. Conclusions drawn suggest that care staff adopt a guarded approach to managing risk, shaped by social and organizational preoccupations and policies that overemphasize risk elimination. This leads to the undermining of attempts to support independence and choice for tenants with dementia. We recommend the development of comprehensive risk-assessment processes and strategies for supporting behaviors that staff experience as anxiety provoking and difficult to manage. These developments should be based on a person-centered approach to identifying the needs, preferences, and values of individuals to maintain safety while promoting independence.

INTRODUCTION

Whereas the term 'risk' had been with us for hundreds of years, modern society has become increasingly focused on how to avoid the negative aspects of risk-related behavior. In the United Kingdom (UK), this emphasis on risk reduction is reflected in a range policy initiatives, such as the establishment by New Labour of the National Patient Safety Agency, which aims to learn from prior mistakes and protect patients from future harm, and the development of a myriad of new posts, such as 'clinical risk manager'. It has also led to a new health-promotion agenda focusing on re-ducing behaviors that are seen to cause a risk to health. This agenda incorporates the concepts of 'surveillance medicine' and 'health surveillance', which recognize a move toward health systems that calculate and communicate the prob-ability of illness for individuals or groups by identifying and measuring risk factors (1). This shift is reflected in a rapid increase in the use of the term 'risk' in medical journal articles (2). Joyce (3) goes further in describing a new two-way form of health agency, whereby the role of health agencies is limited to providing individuals with resources to combat risks that they cannot reasonably be expected to avoid through self-governed aspects of lifestyle. This is part of what Beck (4) and others refer to as 'reflexive modernization', the creation of a new social order based on the monitoring of self and others through the burgeoning availability of information.

This chapter explores the potential conflict between such professional perceptions and practices in relation to risk and the strong desire of older people to remain independent. This aim is achieved through an exploration of the views of professionals about older people with dementia in extra care housing in the UK.

THE ISSUE OF RISK

With an increased social awareness of risk comes a new emphasis on blame, which is particularly evident in the delivery of health and social care services. For example, nurses experience risk as an ever-present factor in their daily practice, leading to fear of mistakes, blame, and litigation (5). This is particularly true for patients who are considered to be frail, and the Royal College of Nursing has recognized that in order to protect themselves, nurses might be tempted to discourage older people from taking risks (6). The issue of conflicting pressures on health and social care professionals when making decisions about risk for their clients is evident in media portrayals of social workers as unable to assess and manage risk properly, leading either to the death of children under their care or to the removal of children from their parents without justification.

Some argue that what is now called 'risk management' is merely a new name for what professionals have always done to reduce negative outcomes (7). Others have cautioned against placing too much emphasis on risk (8,9) or have even suggested that the word 'risk' is unhelpful because it leads to decisions that take insufficient account of individual values and preferences (10). The UK government itself has emphasized the desirability of allowing older people to monitor their own behavior in terms of risk (11,12), but little evidence has emerged of this approach leading to changes in service delivery. Matthews and Pitts (13) suggest that in terms of health and social care services delivery, 'needs-led' assessment has now become 'risk-led' assessment. Douglas (14) believes that risk is constructed through institutional rather than individual frameworks, leading to assumptions and weightings that are culturally learned and maintained within organizations and agencies. Logically then, the definitions of and attitudes toward risk differ according to the service environment in which they occur. For example, the dominant model of risk in contemporary health agencies focuses on hazards and their potential to cause harm (15). Nevertheless, the supported housing sector has not developed its own risk culture but rather has tended to adopt the attitudes to risk of its staff, most of whom come from nursing and social care back-grounds. For example, recent studies of risk in residential care have focused on verbal and behavioral aggression, non-compliance with medication, falls, and burns (16-18). Some evidence, however, has shown that the needs and preferences of older people routinely take second place to the consider-ations of risk in terms of both nursing practices (19) and building design (20).

Certain subpopulations within society have been identified as more 'at risk' than others and therefore in need of more intensive surveillance to reduce the risk they pose to themselves and others. Older people are widely viewed as being one of these 'vulnerable' groups, both because of the potential harm leading from the physical changes of aging and because of their perceived susceptibility to criminal fraud, violence, and deception.

People with dementia are widely viewed as one of the most 'at risk' groups, as illustrated by the National Service Framework for Mental Health in England and Wales (21). This view is partly because dementia is commonly associated with extreme old age but also because of two other issues: cognitive function and mental capacity. Over one hundred different dementias exist with a wide range of symptoms, but cognitive impairment is commonly experienced. Cognitive impairment can lead to memory loss and dis-orientation, with a corresponding increased risk in physical injury like that from falling (22). Another issue in relation to people with dementia is that of competency and the frequent assumption that such individuals lack the capacity to make decisions, including those about their own health (23). The logical consequences of this assumption are that people with cognitive impairment are unable to make an informed assessment of risk in relation to their own behavior and therefore require a greater level of protection from risks than do other people of a similar age. Although scientific evidence has shown that lack of capacity is associated with dementia (24), the Mental Capacity Act is clear in that the capacity to make informed decisions should be assumed unless there is evidence to the contrary. A diagnosis of dementia is not seen as evidence on its own but rather has to be independently assessed.

SHELTERED OR EXTRA CARE HOUSING

Extra care housing, sometimes called very sheltered housing, is increasingly considered a solution to the unpopularity of some traditional sheltered housing and a viable alternative to certain models of residential care. Although a number of different types of extra care housing exist, some basic principles distinguish extra care housing as a unique form of provision.

- Firstly, extra care housing gives people with relatively high care needs the opportunity to live an independent life in their own homes through renting what is usually a small flat. Maximizing independence is widely promoted by government and providers as one of the main advantages of extra are housing over other forms of housing with care; extra care is also rated as one of the most important features by both tenants and their relatives (25). The concept of independence is very much a matter of individual interpretation, but the evidence shows that for people with dementia, the opportunity to come and go alone contributes toward a sense of independence and self respect (26).

- Secondly, extra care housing schemes have an on-site care team providing day and night cover. Care is delivered to people within their own homes.
- Thirdly, extra care housing developments are generally designed to a high specification incorporating features which enable barrier-free living, and are accessible for people with high levels of disability.

All these factors, along with general population aging, mean that extra care housing is likely to accommodate growing numbers of people with dementia; both those who have dementia when they move into the scheme and those who develop dementia whilst living there. United Kingdom Government policy places considerable emphasis on the importance of enabling older people to avoid residential and nursing home care (27), which has led to growing interest in the potential role of extra care housing to provide a more 'homely' alternative to the traditional forms of institutional care (28,29).

A LONGITUDINAL STUDY

The rest of this chapter draws on a study that explored the suitability of extra care housing for people with dementia in the UK (25). A longitudinal design was chosen to identify changes in user perspectives of extra care housing by tenants whose dementia was likely to increase in severity during the three-year course of the project. The project was jointly funded by Housing 21, a large, not-for-profit housing association that specializes in provision for older people, and the Housing Corporation, the government agency that is responsible for overseeing the housing sector in England. A mixed methodology approach was employed. The quantitative data-monitoring element tracked approximately 60 people with dementia or significant memory problems in all of Housing 21's extra care housing courts nationally over a period of 3 years. A parallel qualitative component focused on six extra care housing courts as case study sites. In each court, periodic interviews were carried out with people with dementia, other tenants, relatives, court managers, and carers, as well as local health, social care and housing managers, to explore complex issues in more depth. The benefits of a mixed methods approach have been well documented and include triangulation, complementarity, and expansion (30,31).

In this chapter we focus on the findings from interviews with care professionals and their perceptions of risk in relation to tenants with dementia.

EXPERIENCE FROM OUR STUDY

Overall, the study found that extra care housing can support people with early-stage dementia successfully, as long as an appropriate level of flexible, person-centered care is provided by a well-trained and supported team of care staff. Independence emerged as a major attraction of extra care housing, both for tenants with dementia and their relatives. This view is summed up by the following quote in which a relative describes why they chose extra care housing:

> *"They've got a bit of their own independence you know their own room, they can make their breakfast and their tea and their cups of tea when they want it and they can come down to the lounge for stimulation or they can go upstairs and just be themselves." (relative 3; scheme 4)*

For tenants independence meant doing as much as possible for themselves. For example, one tenant explained,

> *"I do my own meals, I go out to shops, and if I want anything I'll get it" (resident 4; scheme 2).*

The opportunity to come and go as they pleased also seemed to be an important part of independence for many. For one 82-year-old man who went out walking every day, that "you're free to go in and out as you want" (tenant 3; scheme 6) appeared to be crucial to his independence and quality of life.

Although care staff also identified independence as one of the strengths of extra care housing, they felt that risk-related behaviors were a significant challenge to maintaining tenants with dementia in this setting and were the main reason for some of them having to move on to residential care. One care worker expressed this opinion in a very general way, saying, "Some people with dementia, it's not safe for them to be here" (staff 2; scheme 2). Further analysis of interview transcripts shows staff awareness of two specific types of risk in relation to tenants with dementia: risk to self and risk to others.

As in many other environments that include frail older people, those working in extra care housing were very aware of the risk of tenants falling, particularly those with dementia. Hence, communal areas and every room in each flat in the six case study schemes were equipped with social alarms to reduce the risks related with falling. This approach allowed tenants to contact staff and summon help if required, wherever the tenants may be in the complex. Some staff, however, felt that this system was not necessarily sufficient in terms of potential risk of serious harm. For example, one care worker told us about a resident with dementia who was regularly found on the floor.

> *"We find her on the floor, we don't know whether she has fallen, put it this way I don't think this place is for her. We always call an ambulance for her*

and sometimes when the ambulance man comes he says she's faking it, so we don't know and we have to call the ambulance every time." (staff 4; scheme 3)

It is interesting to note here that the concern of staff is not merely about potential risk to self but also concerns the difficulty of assessing whether the risk is real or whether, as she puts it, the resident is 'faking it'. This dilemma indicates some of the difficulties that staff experience in assessing levels of risk and the ways in which they develop strategies and routines to restrict behaviors that they perceive as 'risky' and minimize their own anxiety.

A second major concern for staff in terms of risk to self focused on 'wandering'. This term refers to a behavior which, when displayed by people with dementia, is frequently viewed as lacking in purpose and suggesting restlessness. Although staff identified a number of issues in relation to this behavior, such conduct was seen as particularly problematic because it could lead to tenants leaving the extra care building and going out on their own into the wider community. An almost unanimous view was reached among interviewed staff that this approach inevitably led to the tenants with dementia being placed in danger. For example, one care worker said:

> *"I think our biggest problem here is it is an open building so if they want to wander out then that's a concern. It is a concern if they go outside and they are determined they want to go somewhere and we do not have the right to say don't go but they will be lost and confused if they do." (staff 3; scheme 6)*

In this quote, the staff member alludes to a crucial feature of extra care housing in terms of risk. People living in extra care have legal rights as private tenants under UK law, whereas those in care homes and certain other models of supported housing do not enjoy the same level of rights.

Extra care staff also identified a range of behaviors on the part of tenants with dementia that could cause risk not only to self but also to others. Such behaviors included leaving the gas turned on an unlit cooker, a tea towel being left on a lit cooker and catching fire, and flooding being caused by a bath being left running for too long and overflowing. Further risks to others, both staff and tenants, were perceived in relation to aggressive behavior. In particular, physical aggression by tenants with dementia was described as a risk to the well-being of staff and other tenants. One scheme manager, talking about staff experiences of a male tenant with dementia who was over six foot tall said,

> *"If you're pinned to the bathroom he could threaten danger" (staff 1; scheme 5).*

Overall then, care professionals identified a wide range of risks both to self and to others that they felt were dementia-related. These risks were perceived as sufficiently significant to be a major challenge for supporting tenants with dementia and were frequently quoted as reasons for staff having to move on to other care settings. Further analysis of the interview data, however, questions these perceptions of risk in a number of ways.

How often are the potential risks identified by care professionals actually present in the behavior of tenants with dementia? This study cannot provide a definitive answer, but few concrete examples of the types of behavior quoted by staff as 'risky' were identified in practice. One court manager described how a tenant with dementia had left the building for more than 24 hours. A major search had been instigated, including the use of a police helicopter, before he was found. In another incident, a tenant collected large numbers of newspapers that he stored in a high stack in his flat. The stack had caught on fire from the heat of a light bulb, leading to extensive smoke damage to his flat. Such dramatic incidents were the exception, however, in terms of professionals being able to provide illustrative back up for their concerns. More examples of conflict involving tenants with dementia were noted, but most of these appeared likely to cause distress rather than actual risk of harm. For example, one tenant had been into other tenant's flat uninvited, whereas another was seen using someone's letter box as a rubbish bin. Only one report of conflict could be described as posing a threat of real physical risk, when a carer was pinned to the wall by a tenant with dementia. Many of the examples given seem to be based on the assumption that the risks described are only applicable to tenants with dementia. One could argue, however, that many of the behaviors quoted are also likely to be displayed by other tenants. For example, collecting large piles of newspapers may be seen as rather eccentric but it is not necessarily related to having dementia. Orientation difficulties, which appear to be at the core of perceived risks of wandering, are a common symptom of many forms of dementia but they can be experienced by anyone. In fact, members of the research team found it difficult to find their way around some of the extra care schemes being studied on several occasions.

In the light of evidence of some potential increased risk associated with dementia, for example the risk of falls (26) and of becoming lost (22), how are such risks managed in extra care housing? All extra care schemes incorporate systems for restricting access. The main stated aim of these is to protect tenants from harm by people who might enter the scheme without a genuine reason. Nevertheless, despite the recognition by staff that tenants have the legal right to come and go, such systems are not easy to operate and can therefore serve to discourage tenants with dementia from leaving the building.

The potential of electronic assistive technology to support residents in extra care housing has been widely recognized. Assistive technology can be tailored to meet an individual's needs and the potential benefits include increased independence, social inclusion, safety/security, and improved communication. A range of devices can be used in this setting, including alarms, sensors, and lifestyle monitoring equipment, either on a stand-alone basis or as part of more complex telecare systems. Certain devices have a particular role to play in reducing risk by, for example, preventing baths from overflowing, automatically turning off cookers, and monitoring wandering. Yet, the research found very few examples of assistive technology being implemented and concluded that it was an under-used resource, partly because staff had not been fully trained in how to use it (25).

Care professionals frequently perceived a range of unusual behaviors, such as restlessness and wandering, as a potential threat to the wellbeing and security of tenants with dementia. Evidence is growing, however, that person-centered care is effective in managing such behavioral symptoms (32) by exploring the reasons behind individual behaviors and developing an understanding of the needs that lead to them. For example, some people with dementia wander in a way that can appear to be lacking in purpose and, in some situations, this behavior can lead to conflict or distress. An understanding that such behavior can be triggered by a range of factors, including surplus energy, boredom, loss of memory and pain, however, can enable care staff to respond appropriately. This approach can lead to the development of 'safe' wandering, whereby staff can become more comfortable with the perceived level of risk, and crisis interventions can be avoided (33).

CONCLUSIONS

In this chapter we have seen that extra care is widely seen as a good housing choice for older people with dementia, largely because of its potential to support and maximize independence. This belief is evident from government policy in the UK, as well as from the views of tenants with dementia. For many tenants with dementia, two crucial aspects of independence are (a) choosing how to spend their time and (b) having the opportunity to do things for them-selves. These activities, however, can involve behaviors that contain an element of risk, such as using cooking equipment and going out alone. Society's attitude toward risk, particularly for the so-called vulnerable groups like older people with dementia, leads housing organizations and their care staff to take a guarded approach toward managing risk. This attitude creates a paradox between risk and independence and can lead to an overemphasis on eliminating risk, which threatens attempts to support independence.

We acknowledge the notion that specific challenges and risks are attached to supporting people with dementia in extra care housing. We suggest, however, that such risks are sometimes overstated and poorly understood. We call for the development of comprehensive risk assessment processes and strategies for supporting behaviors that cause anxiety in staff to maintain safety while also promoting independence. These developments should be based on a person-centered approach to identifying the needs, preferences, and values of individuals. Specific measures could include a better use of electronic assistive technology and more dementia-specific training for care staff.

ACKNOWLEDGEMENTS

This study was funded by the Housing Corporation and Housing 21. Thanks go to co-researchers Tina Fear and Sarah Vallelly and the research advisory group. Finally, thanks to all of the tenants, relatives, and care professionals without whose contribution the research could not have taken place. This chapter is an adapted version of an earlier published paper (Evans S, Means R. Perspectives on risk for older people with dementia in extra care housing in the United Kingdsom: Findings from a longitudinal study. Int J Disabil Hum Dev 2006;5(1):77-82).

REFERENCES

1. Armstrong D. The rise of surveillance medicine. Sociol Health Illness 1994;17(3):393-404.
2. Skolbekken A. The risk epidemic in medical journals. Soc Sci Med 1995;40(3):291-305.
3. Joyce P. Governmentality and risk: setting priorities in the new NHS. Sociol Health Illness 2001;23(5): 594-614.
4. Beck U. Risk society: Towards a New Modernity. London, UK: Sage, 1992.
5. Annaldale E. Working on the front-line: risk culture and nursing in the new NHS. Sociol Rev 1996;44(3): 416-51.
6. Royal College of Nursing Institute. The picture of a life-study guide. London, UK: Royal Coll Nurs Inst, 2004.
7. Parsloe P. Risk assessment in social care and social work. London, UK: Jessica Kingsley, 1999.
8. O'Malley P. Risk societies and the government of crime. In: Brown M, Pratt J, eds. Dangerous offenders. London, UK: Routledge, 2000.
9. Luhmann N. The reality of the mass media. Cambridge, UK: Cambridge Univ Press, 2000.
10. Dowie J. Communication for better decisions: not about 'risk'. Health Risk Soc 1999;1(1):41-53.
11. Department Health. The national service framework for older people. London, UK: HMSO, 2001.
12. Department Health. A new ambition for old age: new steps in implementing the national framework for older people. London, UK: HMSO, 2006.
13. Matthews R, Pitts J. Crime, disorder and community safety. London, UK: Routledge, 2001.
14. Douglas M. Risk and blame: Essays in cultural theory. London, UK: Routledge, 1992.
15. Alaszewski A. Managing risk in community practice: Nursing risk and decision-making. In: Godin P, ed. Risk and nursing practice. London, UK: Palgrave, 2006.

16.   Gruber-Baldini A, Boustani M, Sloane PD, Zimmerman S. Behavioral symptoms in residential care/assisted living facilities: prevalence, risk factors, and medication management. Journal of the Am Geriatr Soc 2004; 52(10):1771-3.

17.   Lundin-Olsson L, Jensen J, Nyberg L, Gustafson Y. Predicting falls in residential care by a risk assessment tool, staff judgment, and history of falls. Aging Clin Exp Res 2003;15(1):51-9.

18.   Harper RD, Dickson WA. Reducing the burn risk to elderly persons living in residential care. Burns 1995; 21(3):205-8.

19.   Bowling A, Grant K. Accidents in elderly care: a randomised controlled trial (Part 3). Nurs Standard 1992;6(31):25-7.

20.   Parker C, Barnes S, Mckee K, Morgan K, Torrington J, Tregenza P. Quality of life and building design in residential and nursing homes for older people. Aging Soc 2004;24:941-62.

21.   Department Health. National service framework for mental health: Modern standards and service models. London, UK: HMSO, 1999.

22.   Shaw FE, Bond J, Richardson DA, Dawson P, Steen IN, McKeith IG et al. Multifactorial intervention after a fall in older people with cognitive impairment and dementia presenting to the accident and emergency department: randomised controlled trial. BMJ 2003; 326: 73.

23.   Gilliard J, Means R, Beattie A, Daker White G. Dementia Care in England and the social model of disability: Lessons and issues. Dementia 2005;4(4): 571-86.

24.   Mukherjee S, Shah A. The prevalence and correlates of capacity to consent to a geriatric psychiatry admission. Aging Ment Health 2001;5(4):335-9.

25.   Vallelly S, Evans S, Fear T, Means R. Opening doors to independence. A longitudinal study exploring the contribution of extra care housing to the care and support of older people with dementia. London, UK: Housing 21, 2006.

26.   Burton E, Mitchell,L. Inclusive urban design: streets for life. Oxford, UK: Architectural Press, 2006.

27.   Department Health. The NHS Plan: The Government's response to the Royal Commission on long term care. London, UK: HMSO, 2001.

28.   Royal Commission Long Term Care. The Sutherland Report. With respect to old age: Long term care - Rights and responsibilities. London, UK: HMSO, 1999.

29.   Means R, Heywood F, Oldman J. Housing and home in later life. Buckingham, UK: Open Univ Press, 2002.

30.   Creswell JW. Research design: qualitative and quanti-tative approaches. Thousand Oaks, CA, USA: Sage Publications, 1994.

31.   Johnstone PL. Mixed methods, mixed methodology. Health services research in practice. Qual Health Res 2004; 14 (2): 259-271.

32.   Fossey J, Ballard C, Juszczak E, James I, Alder N, Jacoby R et al. Effect of enhanced psychological care on antipsychotic use in nursing home tenants with severe dementia: cluster randomised trial. BMJ 2006; 332(7544):756-61.

33.   Dewing J. Screening for wandering among older persons with dementia. Nurs Older People 2005; 17(3):20-2.

PART NINE:
COMMUNITY BASED REHABILITATION

CHAPTER 29
Rehabilitation in the community after stroke or hip fracture

Tony Ryan, Pam Enderby and Alan S Rigby

In order to compare intensive with non-intensive home based rehabilitation provision following stroke or hip fracture in old age (65 years plus) we conducted a parallel single-blind randomized control trial at home. 160 patients aged 65 or over recently discharged from hospital after suffering a stroke or hip fracture were assigned to receive six or more face-to-face contacts or three or less face-to-face contacts from members of a multi-disciplinary rehabilitation team. Patients were assessed using the Barthel Index, Therapy Outcome Measure, Euroqol, Hospital Anxiety and Depression Scale (HADS), Frenchay Activities Index (FAI) and service use at 12 months. All follow-up assessments were conducted blind to allocation. Sub-group analysis was conducted based on incident condition (stroke or hip fracture). One significant difference was detected for the stroke subgroup at 12 months (Hospital Anxiety and Depression Scale (Anxiety) (p < .05)). No significant differences were detected between the two arms of the study for the hip-fracture sub-group. Those patients receiving less-intensive rehabilitation used more services at 12 months, although the difference was nonsignificant. Following stroke, older people who receive a more intensive community-based multidisciplinary rehabilitation service may experience long-term benefit in psychological health. A more intensive service after discharge from hospital following a hip fracture is unlikely to result in similar patient benefit.

INTRODUCTION

Stroke and hip fracture remain two of the largest causes of disability for older people. Stroke incidence rises from 1 per 1,000, among those aged 45 and under, to 15 per 1,000 for those aged 85 or more (1), others suggest that self-reported stroke prevalence is much higher (2). Above 65 years of age, incidence of hip fracture doubles every five years (3). Both incident conditions are related to a poor functional outcome and a poor quality of life (4,5). In addition, stroke and hip fracture are responsible for the majority of inpatient rehabilitation bed days (6) and community rehabilitation team workload (7).

Given the huge personal and financial cost, the interest in the efficacy of rehabilitation provision for these two incident conditions has grown in recent years. Two meta-analyses have focused on the question of intensity of treatment for stroke and suggest small yet significant short term patient benefit (8, 9), other task specific studies have mirrored these findings, whilst one recent RCT evaluating early intensive, interdisciplinary rehabilitation provision indicated no patient benefit (10). Also, some evidence suggests that short-term benefits do not carry over into the longer term (11). Several observational studies endorse the notion of improved outcome following more intensive physical and occupational therapy (12-15). Intensity of inpatient rehabilitation for hip fracture has also been evaluated, although to a lesser extent, with patient benefit being less discernable within the literature (16-19).

The bias toward research in hospital-based intensity research is evident within this evidence, despite community based rehabilitation services for older people flourishing in recent years (20). Indeed, early supported discharge and other such schemes proposing some form of organized rehabilitation provision in the community have been shown to be as effective as hospital based rehabilitation programs (21-24). Prompted by these reports, the authors chose to undertake an evaluation of the efficacy of an augmented form of community rehabilitation. The study hypothesized that a more intensive regime of multi-disciplinary rehabili-tation would result in an improved patient outcome. The results from followup at three months have been reported elsewhere (25). The data suggested that providing a more intensive regime of rehabilitation resulted in minor patient benefit to the stroke subgroup, particularly in the domains of health-related quality of life and social participation. The paper also reported that a more intensive regime did not improve patient outcome for the hip fracture subgroup. This chapter describe the results of follow-up at 12 months.

OUR STUDY

North Sheffield LREC granted ethical approval for the study (3 July 2000). An internal pilot involving 25 patients was undertaken in the first weeks of the study, and the data were included in the final analysis. Two changes were made following this pilot. The responsibility for undertaking base-line assessment shifted from senior clinicians to the research team, and more specific guidance relating to changes in the medical status of participating patients was included in the trial protocol.

A Randomized Controlled Trial (RCT) was undertaken during the period from July 2000 and June 2002. During the trial, consecutive patients were referred to the research team. Patients who met inclusion criteria, aged 65 years or over, recovering from stroke or hip fracture, and not suffering from a concomitant disease (e.g. Parkinson's disease or dementia), were contacted by the research team within five working days of referral to a community rehabilitation team. Randomization was carried out using a random number table (blocks of ten) and was stratified based on the diagnosis of hip fracture or stroke and locality team. Blinded follow-up assessments were carried out at 12 months. All treatment and followup assessment was undertaken in the patient's own home.

The sample size calculation was based on a clinically relevant change of two points on the Barthel Index. This change was also used by Young and Forster (24). The standardized difference (0.4) was calculated assuming a standard deviation of five, estimated using data generated previously by local clinicians. With a 5 percent significance level (two tailed) and power of 80 percent, a sample size of 100 per arm was estimated (200 patients in total).

Measures aimed at addressing outcomes in the dimensions of impairment, activity (disability), participation (handicap) (26), well-being, and quality of life were chosen. The outcome measures used at the three-month followup were the Barthel Index (27), Frenchay Activities Index (FAI) (28), Hospital Anxiety & Depression Scale (29), Euroqol 5D (EQ-5D), and Euroqol Visual Analogue Scale (EQ-VAS) (30). EQ-5D is recorded on a scale of 0 to 1. The EQ-VAS is recorded on a scale of 1 to 100. In addition, the Therapy Outcome Measure (31) was used.

In addition to those outcomes relating to function, well-being, depression and anxiety, data concerning service utilization and family care were also collected at 12 months. Hospital admission episodes were collected using local Health Authority information. Other data were collected from patients during the final followup visit.

All data were analyzed using an intention to treat approach. For ordinal outcome measures at three months, the Mann Whitney test for difference was used. The median and the inter-quartile range for each group are also presented. The non-adjusted significance for each outcome is presented in the tables. Patient-change data were approached in a different manner. Normal distributions could be assumed for such data, and independent t-tests were therefore used. The mean difference between the two groups and the 95 percent confidence interval are presented. For some of the analysis, missing data was estimated and replaced using regression (predictor variables: gender, trial allocation, age, diagnosis), and although such data are not used for the main analysis, they are mentioned in the text.

Those consenting to take part in the study were randomly allocated to receive either routine treatment (consisting of three or less face-to-face contacts with a member of the MDT) or an augmented rehabilitation service (six or more face to face contacts with a member of the MDT). The service (both augmented and routine) was provided to both groups of patients by a local multidisciplinary team (MDT) (physiotherapist, occupational therapist, speech and language therapist or therapy assistant). The maximum length of treatment time was 12 weeks. Independent t-tests were con-ducted on the contact data. Significant differences existed between the two groups for the number of face-to-face contacts at four weeks (mean difference = 6.1 95% CI (4.7, 7.4)), eight weeks (mean difference = 7.4 95% CI (4.6, 10.3)) and 12 weeks (mean difference = 8.1 95% CI (4.7, 11.5)).

EXPERIENCE FROM OUR RESEARCH

The mean age of study participants was 78.6 (SD 6.8). The mean number of days spent in hospital before being referred to community rehabilitation services was 42 (SD 37.7). Just under half (48.8 per cent, n=78) lived with a carer and almost two-thirds were female (61.3 per cent, n=98). Table 1 shows the mean age (years), mean length of time since stroke or hip fracture (days), and median scores for each outcome measure for each group at baseline.

Table 1. Baseline data for each randomized group and diagnosis subgroup. TOM=Therapy Outcome Measure; HADS=Hospital Anxiety and Depression Scale; EQ Euroqol

Parameter	Stroke (n=89)		Hip fracture (n=71)	
	Less Intensive	Intensive	Less Intensive	Intensive
Age (mean yrs, SD)	77.3 (6.4)	76.4 (6.1)	80.9 (6.3)	80.7 (7.4)
Length of time since incident (mean days, SD)	45.8 (31.2)	45 (47.3)	35 (24.6)	40.6 (42.2)
Barthel score (median, IQR)	16 (12-18)	16 (14-18)	16 (14.75-17)	17 (15-17)
Frenchay Activities Index (median, IQR)	25 (18-31)	24 (16.5-30)	28 (22.75-31.25)	28 (19.5-32)
EQ-5D (median, IQR)	.52 (.26-.75)	.56 (.28-.72)	.62 (.32-.73)	.52 (.26-.69)
EQ VAS (median, IQR)	.70 (.50-.80)	.6 (.48-.66)	.63 (.57-.81)	.6 (.51-.71)
TOM Impairment (median, IQR)	3.5 (3-4)	4 (3-4)	3 (3-3.5)	3 (3-3.7)
TOM Disability (median, IQR)	3.25 (2.5-3.5)	3.5 (2.5-3.5)	3.5 (3.5-4)	3.5 (3-4)
TOM Handicap (median, IQR)	2.5 (2-3)	2.5 (2-3)	2.5 (2-3)	2.25 (2-3)
TOM Well Being (median, IQR)	4 (3-4)	4 (3.25-4)	4 (3.5-4.5)	4 (3-4.5)
HADS Anxiety (median, IQR)	5 (1-10)	5 (2-7)	4 (2-10.5)	5 (3-8)
HADS Depression (median, IQR)	5 (3-7)	5 (4-10)	4 (2-6.5)	4 (2-6)

Results at 12 Months

Tables 2 and 3 show the results of Mann-Whitney test for difference for each of the two subgroups (stroke and hip fracture), respectively. Table 2 shows just one significant difference at 12 months (HADS Anxiety). In all other outcome measures, the results from both augmented and routine groups are comparable. Table 3 indicates that the results for hip fracture patients at 12-

month followup for both groups within the study were almost identical with no significant differences.

Table 2. Results of Mann Whitney U Test with medians (IQR) for stroke sub-group at 12 months

Outcome Measure	Non-intensive(n=28)		Intensive(n=35)		Significance
	Median	Inter-quartile range	Median	Inter-quartile range	
1	19	15.5-20	19	16-20	0.65
2	4	3.6-4.5	4	3-4.5	0.34
3	4	3.6-4.5	4	3.5-4.5	0.84
4	4	3-4.5	3.5	3-4	0.54
5	4.5	4-5	4.5	4-5	0.74
6	5	3-8.5	3	1-6	0.02
7	6	2.5-9	5	3-8	0.9
8	0.59	0.24-0.81	0.64	0.27-0.74	0.71
9	0.75	0.42-.8	0.6	0.5-0.8	0.5
10	12	6.5-24.5	12	7-25	0.64

1=Barthel; 2=TOM Impairment; 3=TOM Disability; 4=TOM Handicap; 5=TOM Well-being; 6=HADS Anxiety; 7=HADS Depression; 8=EQ-5D; 9=EQ-VAS; 10=FAI; TOM=Therapy Outcome Measure), HADS=Hospital Anxiety and Depression Scale; EQ=Euroqol)

Table 3. Results of Mann Whitney U Test with medians (IQR) for hip fracture sub-group at 12 months

Outcome Measure	Non-intensive (n=28)		Intensive (n=30)		Significance
	Median	Inter-quartile range	Median	Inter-quartile range	
1	20	19-20	20	19-20	0.18
2	4	3.5-4	4	3-4	0.5
3	4	4-4.5	4	4.75	0.9
4	4	3.5-4.5	4	3.25-4.75	0.6
5	5	4.5-5	5	4-5	0.37
6	6	2-11	5	3-8	0.9
7	4	3-5	4	2.5-7	0.67
8	0.7	0.62-0.74	0.7	0.59-8	0.67
9	0.65	0.5-0.8	0.7	0.5-0.78	0.88
10	21	13-26	22	16.5-29.5	0.27

1=Barthel; 2=TOM Impairment; 3=TOM Disability; 4=TOM Handicap; 5=TOM Well-being; 6=HADS Anxiety; 7=HADS Depression; 8=EQ-5D; 9=EQ-VAS; 10=FAI; TOM=Therapy Outcome Measure), HADS=Hospital Anxiety and Depression Scale; EQ=Euroqol)

Tables 4 and 5 show the results of independent t-tests comparing the intensive and non-intensive treatment groups, in terms of patient change data, for the stroke and hip-fracture subgroups. Table 4 (stroke subgroup) indicates that for certain measures, the non-intensive group showed more favorable outcomes in terms of patient change (Barthel, TOM Impairment,

Table 4. Results of independent t-test for patient change at 12 months for stroke sub-group

Outcome measure	Mean change		Difference	95% CI
	Intensive	Non-intensive		
1	1.87	2.24	0.37	-1.2, 1.9
2	0.28	0.46	0.18	-0.24, 0.60
3	0.85	0.77	0.08	-0.4, 0.22
4	1.04	1.31	0.27	-0.22, 0.76
5	0.57	0.96	0.39	-0.16, 0.94
6	0-7.84	-9.61	1.77	-6.74, 3.21
7	0.01	-0.03	0.04	-0.22, 0.12
8	0.05	-0.03	0.08	-0.05, 0.22
9	-1.16	0.21	1.37	-0.16, 2.92
10	-0.7	1.03	1.73	-0.14, 3.61

1=Barthel; 2=TOM Impairment; 3=TOM Disability; 4=TOM Handicap; 5=TOM Well-being; 6=FAI; 7=EQ5D; 8=EQ-VAS; 9=HADS Anxiety; 10=HADS Depression; TOM=Therapy Outcome Measure, HADS=Hospital Anxiety and Depression Scale, EQ=Euroqol; CI = confidence interval

Table 5. Results of independent t-test for patient change at 12 months for hip-fracture sub-group

Outcome	Mean change		Difference	95% CI
	Intensive	Non-intensive		
1	3.36	3.47	0.11	-1.2, 0.99
2	0.54	0.47	0.07	-0.41, 0.53
3	0.79	0.61	0.18	-0.17, 0.54
4	1.6	1.13	0.47	-0.16, 1.11
5	0.8	0.6	0.2	-0.5, 0.9
6	-3.8	-5.8	2	-2.4, 6.5
7	0.16	0.08	0.08	-0.08,0.24
8	0.04	-0.05	0.09	-0.06, .2
9	-0.83	1.1	1.93	-4,0.18
10	0.08	1.4	1.32	-0.9, 3.5

1=Barthel; 2=TOM Impairment; 3=TOM Disability; 4=TOM Handicap; 5=TOM Well-being; 6=FAI; 7=EQ5D; 8=EQ-VAS; 9=HADS Anxiety; 10=HADS Depression; TOM=Therapy Outcome Measure, HADS=Hospital Anxiety and Depression Scale, EQ=Euroqol; CI = confidence interval

TOM Handicap, and TOM Well-being), whereas the intensive group indicated improved change over the non-intensive group in other areas (health-related quality of life, TOM Disability, FAI, HADS). In all cases, the 95 per cent confidence intervals around the means show the differences to be non-significant. Within the hip-fracture sub-group (Table 5), the intensive arm of the study showed more favorable change outcomes at 12 months in all but one outcomes measure (Barthel). Again, as with the stroke sub-group data, the 95 per cent confidence intervals around the means show the differences to be non-significant.

Service use data

Table 6 shows the data relating to service usage, hospital admission (post-trial), GP usage, and the number of hours provided by a family caregiver at 12 months. The data suggest that those patients who were allocated to the intensive treatment regime were less likely to be re-admitted to hospital, spent fewer days in hospital post-trial period to 12 months, were less likely to use home care and received fewer hours of home care and other paid care. They were also less likely to attend a day center. This group did, however, depend more on unpaid family care. All the above differences were, however, shown to be non-significant.

Table 6. Service use outcomes at 12 months. *includes only those followed up at 12 months (n=108) **includes all study patients whose hospital records were searched with the exception of those who withdrew from study (n=130)

Outcome	1	2	3
Proportion spending time in hospital**	19.7	28.1	8.4(-6.2,22.7)
Mean days in hospital at 12 months**	3.1	7.1	4 (-1,9)
Proportion using home care services*	8.9	15.2	6.3 (-6.3, 20.8)
Mean home care hours per week*	0.46	1.1	0.6 (-0.3, 1.6)
Proportion using other paid care*	23.2	33.3	10.1 (-7.2, 27.3)
Proportion attending a day centre*	5.3	13.3	8 (-3.6, 21.2)
Mean number of visits to GP in last 4 weeks*	0.6	0.52	0.08 (-.42, .24)
Mean hours care provided by relatives or friends*	33.8	26.7	7.1 (-12.4, 26.5)

1=Intensive; 2=Non-intensive; 3=Mean difference + 95% CI; TOM=Therapy Outcome Measure, HADS=Hospital Anxiety and Depression Scale, EQ= Euroqol; CI = confidence interval

DISCUSSION

Three important study weaknesses should be considered when explaining the lack of significant differences. First, the study set out to achieve a ratio of 2:1 (intensive/non-intensive). Despite protocol arrangements to ensure that such a ratio was provided, this goal was not achieved. The failure to achieve this ratio may have contributed to the lack of difference detected between the two groups in most outcomes.

Second, the power calculation indicated that a sample size of 200 (100/arm) would be required. Almost half (47.8 percent, n= 147) of suitable patients did not consent to participate. Given this high non-response and time limita-tions, it was possible to recruit only 160 patients to the study. A further 35 study participants were lost to follow-up at three months. The capacity to detect significant differences was therefore limited. This problem has been partially addressed through the method of imputation. A third weakness lies in the lack of available information regarding the nature of the intervention. Although therapists were requested to provide a more intensive service to those allocated to the intervention group, what occurred within those additional face-to-face contacts was not prescribed, neither was it known. It is not known therefore if, in addition to the quantitative difference between the two study groups, a qualitative difference also existed. Having little information about how therapists used this additional time means that the interpretation of the findings are exposed to supposition and speculation.

Follow-up assessments showed a significant relation between severe disability and anxiety and depression and also between lack of social participation and depression. Further analysis of the data gathered for this research is required to determine the nature and strength of these relations.

An earlier paper had presented results from this RCT at the three-month follow-up (25). The data from that report suggested a minor patient benefit within the stroke subgroup. Noted within the paper was that patient benefit was to be found within the areas of social participation, psychological health, and health-related quality of life. It was speculated at this stage that patient benefits may have been interrelated, due to the link between social participation and good quality of life (32). The data presented here suggests that any differences that existed at three-months were not detected at one-year followup. Again, the only difference detected was found within the stroke subgroup. Study weaknesses aside, these findings have implications for community-based service development for both incident conditions. Within stroke services, the notion of augmented rehabilitation is well established, is closely related to issues of neuroplasticity, and suggests that 'more is better' (33,34). The findings presented here suggest that although some patient benefit may be detected within the short term, those benefits are short lived, further supporting the evidence gathered from within hospital settings (11) Furthermore, this paper has again supported the idea that intensive or augmented community-based rehabilitation provision aimed at older people recovering at home from hip fracture does not result in additional patient benefit.

ACKNOWLEDGMENT

This study was funded by NHS Executive Trent, United Kingdom. This chapter is an adapted version of an earlier published paper (Ryan T, Enderby P, Rigby AS. A randomized controlled trial to evaluate intensity of community-based rehabilitation provision following stroke or hip fracture in old age: Results at 12-month follow-up. Int J Disabil Hum Dev 2006;5(1):83-9).

REFERENCES

1. Wolfe CD, Taube N, Bryan S. Variations in the incidence, management and outcome of stroke in residents under the age of 75 in two health districts in Southern England. J Public Health Med 1995;53:16-22.

2. Geddes JML, Chamberlain MA. Home-based rehabili-tation for people with stroke: a comparative study of six community services providing coordinated, multi-disciplinary treatment. Clin Rehabil 2001;15:589-99.

3. Schurch MA, Rizzoli R, Mermillod B, Vasey H, Michel JP, Bonjour JP. A prospective study on socioeconomic aspects of fracture of the proximal femur. J Bone Mineral Res. 1996;11(12):1935-42.

4. Hall SE, Williams JA, Senior JA, Goldswain PR, Criddle RA. Hip fracture outcomes: quality of life and functional status in older adults living in the community. Aust N Z J Med 2000;30(3):327-32.

5. King RB. Quality of life after stroke. Stroke 1996; 27(9):1467-72.

6. Weinrich M, Good D, Reding M, Roth EJ, Cifu DX, Silver KH, Craik RL, Magaziner J, Terrin M, Scwartz M, Gerber L. Timing, intensity and duration of rehab-ilitation for hip fracture and stroke: Report of a work-shop at the National Centre for Medical Rehabilitation Research. Am Soc Neurorehabil 2004;18(1):12-28.

7. Geddes JM, Fear J, Tennant A, Pickering A, Hillman M, Chamberlain MA. Prevalence of self reported stroke in a population in northern England. J Epidemiol Community Health 1996;50(2):140-43.

8. Kwakkel G, Wagenaar R, Koelman T, Lankhorst G, Koetsier J. Effects of intensity of rehabilitation after stroke: A research synthesis. Stroke 1997;28(8):1550-6.

9. Langhorne P, Wagenaar R, Partridge C. Physiotherapy after stroke: more is better? Physiother Res Int 1996; 1(2):75-88.

10. Rodgers H, Mackintosh J, Price C, Wood R, Mac Namee P, Fearon T, Marritt A, Curless R. Does an early increased-intensity interdisciplinary upper limb therapy programme following acute stroke improve outcome? Clin Rehabil 2003;17:579-89.

11. Kwakkel G, Kollen BJ, Wagenaar RC. Long term effects of intensity of upper and lower limb training after stroke: a randomised trial. J Neurol Neurosurg Psychiatry 2006;72:473-9.

12. Bode RK, Heinemann AW, Semick P, Mallinson T. Relative importance of rehabilitation therapy charac-teristics on functional outcomes for person with stroke. Stroke 2005;35:2537-42.

13. Chen CC, Heinemann AW, Granger CV, Linn RT. Functional gains and therapy intensity during subacute rehabilitation: a study of 20 facilities. Arch Phys Med Rehabil 2002 ;83(11):1514-23.

14. Jette DU, Warren RL, Wirtalla C. The relations between therapy intensity and outcomes of rehabili-tation in skilled nursing facilities. Arch Phys Med Rehabil 2006;86:373-9.

15.   Wade DT, Skilbeck C, Langton Hewer R, Wood V. Therapy after stroke: amounts determinants and effects. Int J Rehabil Med 1984;6(9):105-10.

16.   Hoenig H, Rubenstein LV, Sloane R, Horner R, Kahn K. What is the role of timing in the surgical and rehabilitative care of community-dwelling older persons with acute hip fracture? [see comments]. [erratum appears in Arch Intern Med 1997;157(13):1444] Arch Intern Med 1997;157(5):513-20.

17.   Karumo I. Intensive physical therapy after fractures of the femoral shaft. Ann Chir Gynaecol 1977;66(6): 278-83.

18.   Mitchell SL, Stott DJ, Martin BJ, Grant SJ. Randomized controlled trial of quadriceps training after proximal femoral fracture. Clin Rehabil 2001; 15:282-90.

19.   Swanson CE, Day GA, Yelland CE, Broome JR, Massey L, Richardson HR, Dimitri K, Marsh A. The management of elderly patients with femoral fractures. A randomised controlled trial of early inter-vention versus standard care. Med J Aust 1998; 169(10):515-8.

20.   Enderby P, Wade DT. Community rehabilitation in the United Kingdom. Clin Rehabil 2001;15:577-81.

21.   Bautz-Holtert E, Sveen U, Rygh J, Rodgers H, Wyller TB. Early supported discharge of patients with acute stroke: a randomized controlled trial. Disabil Rehabil 2002;24(7):348-55.

22.   Crotty M, Whitehead CH, Gray S, Finucane PM. Early discharge and home rehabilitation after hip fracture achieves functional improvements: a random-ized controlled trial. Clin Rehabil 2002;16(4):406-13.

23.   Rudd AG, Wolfe CD, Tilling K, Beech R. Random-ised controlled trial to evaluate early discharge scheme for patients with stroke [see comments] [published erratum appears in BMJ 1998 Feb 7;316(7129):435]. Br Med J 1997;315(7115):1039-44.

24.   Young JB, Forster A. The Bradford community stroke trial: results at six months. BMJ 1992;304(6834): 1085-9.

25.   Ryan T, Enderby P, Rigby AS. A Randomized controlled trial to evaluate intensity of community-based rehabilitation provision following stroke or hip-fracture in old age. Clin Rehabil 2006;20(2):123-31

26.   World Health Organisation. International classification of function, disability and health (ICF). Geneva, Switzerland: WHO, 2001.

27.   Wade DT, Collin C. The Barthel ADL Index: a standard measure of physical disability? Int Disabil Stud 1998;10(2):64-67.

28.   Wade DT. Measurement in neurological rehabilitation. Oxford, UK: Oxford Univ Press, 1992..

29.   Zigmond A, Snaith R. The Hospital Anxiety Depres-sion Scale. Acta Psychiatr Scand 1983;67:361-70.

30.   The EuroQol Group. EuroQol-a new facility for the measurement of health-related quality of life. Health Policy 1990;16(3):199-208.

31.   Enderby P, John A, Petheram B. Therapy outcome measures manual: Physiotherapy, occuptational therapy, rehabilitation nursing. San Diego, CA, USA: Singular Publ, 1998.

32.   Bisscop M, Kreigsman D, Deeg D, Beekman A, van Tilburg W. The longitudinal relation between chronic disease and depression in older persons in the community: the longitudinal aging study Amsterdam. J Clin Epidemiol 2004;57:187-94.

33.   Carr J, Shepherd R. Neurological rehabilitation: Opti-mizing motor performance. Oxford, UK: Butterworth, 2000.

34.   Nudo RJ, Friel KM. Cortical plasticity after stroke: implications for rehabilitation. Rev Neurol (Paris) 1999;155(9):713-7.

CHAPTER 30
Persons with intellectual disability living at home or in the community

Hefziba Lifshitz and Joav Merrick

We believe that the best place for each child is to grow up at home, even when that specific child has a disability. The role of society is to provide conditions so that the families can cope with that extra burden. With increase in age of both the child with disability and the parents this burden can result in placement out of home. In order to study aging persons with intellectual disability (ID) we conducted two studies in Jerusalem of persons living at home and in community residence. Both studies showed that health problems had appeared already by the age of 40 years among all the participants. Differences in background variables between the two types of living were associated with aging characteristics between the two settings. There were significant differences between the two residential groups regarding hypertension, psychiatric problems, and weight problems. These were found at higher rate amongst the community residence. More dental problems were seen in individuals who resided at home. Persons in community residence were less independent in ADL and leisure activity, the study showed a decline in functioning in both groups. Interestingly, the scores for social and leisure activities were better for the community residential group. Health problems among the participants with Down syndrome were significantly higher.

INTRODUCTION

The best place to grow up for every child should be at home, even in case of a disability or intellectual disability (ID). With increase in age the burden on the family will increase and families will over time find it hard to keep the child at home and will want a solution either in a community program, like a hostel or protected apartment, or maybe a residential care center. With increase in medical problems both in the person with ID and also aging and fragile parents residential care will most likely be their solution.

In recent years we have tried to look at the aging population of persons with ID living at home or in community residence in order to compare the aging process, their health status, ADL and leisure activity (1,2).

As people with ID age, they like the general population when they grow older, experinece more problems with mobility, hearing and vision with a increase in morbidity, chronic disease and early mortality (3).

COMMUNITY RESIDENCE VERSUS LIVING AT HOME

Research has been conducted on the health status of persons with ID living in different residential settings. Several researchers (4,5) found the rate of deterioration among adults with Down syndrome living in residential care centers significantly higher, compared to their counterparts in community residence and persons with Down syndrome living in the community functioned better than their control group in residential care.

The supervision in community care is often less than in residential care, which could be the reason for some findings of age-associated conditions and diseases undetected among adults with ID living in the community (6,7). This underdiagnosis seems to be due to a lack of awareness among primary physicians, a lack of suitable screening procedures or a lack of health surveillance in general for this population. Several barriers to health care for the person with ID who live in community were found, such as a lack of training pertaining to ID, a lack of training on health issues related to ID, a lack of pertinent information on the medical history of the individual and difficulties in medical assessment due to communication or behavioural problems (8).

One study (9), which compared the health status of people with ID residing in three living arrangements found that the institutional group had a lower BMI (Body Mass Index), less body fat and lower lipoprotein concentrations compared to those, who lived with their families. They attributed the results to the closer supervision and monitoring of food in institutions compared to less restrictive settings, such as living at home.

A PILOT STUDY

In a collaboration between the School of Education at Bar Ilan University, AKIM (Israel Association for Rehabilitation of Persons with Intellectual Disability), the Municipality of Jerusalem and the Ministry of Social Affairs (1) a pilot study was conduted to compare aging phenomena of people with intellectual disability (ID) aged 40 years and above living in community residence (29 persons) with those living with their families (31 persons). The goals were to compare the health status between the two types of settings, to compare the health status between this sample and the general Israeli population of the same age group and to investigate whether deterioration occured among our participants in Activity of Daily Living (ADL), cognitive ability and leisure activity.

Health

For all the participants it was found that health problems first appeared around age 40 years. The most common problem was a sensory deterioration: 33% suffered from visual impairment, 17% had cataracts and 12% suffered from hearing impairments. Regarding disease-related heath problems such as cardiac disease, raised blood pressure and diabetes, it was found that 12% suffered from hypertension and 12% from diabetes. Eight percent used psychotropic medicine, 8% had weight problems, 7% had incontinence and less than 5% suffered from the following problems: liver (3%); thyroid problems (2%); cancer (2%) or falls (1%). Dental problems were found in 30% of the sample.

When these health problems were compared with data from the general Israeli population aged 40-65 years we found no significant difference between our sample and the general population.

The mean number of health problems for those in community residence was significantly higher than that for those living at home. It is worth noting that the mean chronological age in the community residence was significantly higher compared to those living at home. Furthermore, a significant correlation was found between age and the mean number of health problems with more medical problems occurring with an increase in age. Analysis of covariance (ANCOVA) with the age variable entered as a covariate did not yield any significant difference in numbers of health problems between the two types of residence. Apparently the differences in health problems between the two types of living stemmed from differences in age.

When health problems were compared between the two residence settings we found that health problems (except for dental problems that were significantly higher in the home group) were significantly higher in residential care compared to living at home. The rate of other health indicators, such as, psychotropic medication, menopause, weight problem, incontinence, liver problems, and thyroid problems, were higher in community residence, but not significantly.

ADL, cognitive ability and leisure activity

We were interested in investigating whether deterioration in the ADL, cognitive ability and leisure activity occurred over time, whether there were differences in deterioration in relation to types of living and regarding age groups. The measurement scales showed high levels of internal consistency.

Using multivariate analysis of variance (MANOVA), no significant differences were found for ADL skills regarding type of residence, no difference was found in relation to age group and no decline was found when comparing past to present. Moreover, no significant interactions were found among these variables, meaning that no difference was found between types of residence regarding changes in function that occurred over time.

Regarding cognitive skills and leisure activity, the MANOVA analysis did not show a significant difference in relation to age group and no decline occurred between the past and the present. Also we found no significant interactions among these variables, but a significant difference was found between the two types of residence. When univariate analysis of variance (ANOVA) was conducted for each variable separately we found a significant difference between the two types of residence only for leisure activities and for social life. No significant differences in relation to types of residence were found for ADL or for cognitive ability. Results showed that in ADL and cognition, the functioning of the participants was high, meaning that the participants were independent in the areas of eating, dressing, personal hygiene and there was no decline in cognitive functioning over time.

Regarding leisure activity, results indicated a decline in functioning in both residential groups. Furthermore, the scores for social and leisure activities were higher for those in community housing than those at home.

Conclusions from this pilot study

It seemed that parents tended to keep their children with intellectual disability at home as long as there were few medical problems, but placement was seeked with increase in medical problems.

Physiological changes in health problems showed that among all the participants the health problems appeared by the age of 40 years. When compared to the general population no significant differences in health problems between the groups were found. There were significant differences between the two residential groups regarding vision and hearing problems, heart problems and diabetes, which were found at higher rate among the community based residence group. More dental problems were seen in those individuals residing at home. This finding resulted in policy changes and today dental service is made available by the Ministry of Social Affair dental clinics in residential care centers also for persons with ID living at home.

Concerning leisure time the study showed a decline in functioning in both residential groups and interestingly the scores for social and leisure activities were better for the community residential group. This finding was not related to aging, but a question of the availability of services.

A LARGER STUDY

Based on the pilot study above we used the same collaborations and investigated a total of 108 persons living in community residence (65 persons) and living with their family (43 persons) in Jerusalem (2). The trends we found in the pilot study were the same for this larger study.

Health problems

The most common health problem was sensory deterioration (33%, had visual impairment (16.7% had cataracts) and 20.4% hearing impairments). Twelve percent had hypertension, 7.4 % other cardiac disease and 10% diabetes. The frequency of psychiatric problems was 15.7%, 13.9% had weight problems, and 13.9% of the women were menopausal. In addition, 13% of the participants suffered from incontinence, 10% had digestion and intestinal tract problems, and less than 5% suffered from problems with their liver (3.3%), thyroid (6%), cancer (1.8%) or falls (0.9%). In addition 3% used a wheelchair and 3% had some physical infirmity. The frequency of dental problems was 28.7%.

In order to examine whether differences in health status would be found between participants in the two types of living, one-way ANOVA analysis was performed. The mean health problems of residents in community residence was higher compared to those who lived at home. Further analysis significant differences in hypertension, weight and psychiatric problems with more in the community residence group, but dental problems more frequent for the home group.

19% of the participants had Down syndrome (DS) and 22% had cerebral palsy (CP). An analysis of variance was performed to examine whether the differences in health problems between the participants in the two types of settings were related to etiology. No significant interaction based on type of living was noted versus etiology, while significant differences were found in relation to etiology. The mean for health problems among the Down group was significantly higher than that of persons with non-specific intellectual disability and cerebral palsy.

In order to examine which health problem were typical of each etiology analyses were performed for each problem separately, but no significant differences were found between the etiologies in any one of the health problems. Analyses performed to examine whether significant differences in health problems would be detected among the three age groups (40-49, 50-59, 60+ years) showed only significant difference in cardiac disease and hypertension. The frequency of these in the oldest group (60+ years) was significantly higher (27.3% for cardiac disease and 36.4% for hypertension) compared to the middle group (50 –59) (7.7% and 5.8%, respectively). The frequency of the above diseases in the younger group (age 40-49) was similar to the middle group (3% for cardiac disease and 10% for hypertension).

ADL, cognitive ability and leisure activity

When investigated whether differences would be found in ADL, cognition, and leisure activities in relation to type of living and etiology, we found significant differences in relation to type of residence, while no significant interaction was found. Analysis revealed significant differences between the etiology in relation to ADL with significant differences between participants with intellectual disability without specific syndrome, which were more independent compared to those with DS and CP. As to cognition (including reading, writing, comprehension) no differences were found between the etiologies. The scores of the Down group in leisure activities were significantly lower.

The mean chronological age in the community residence was significantly higher than the age of those living at home. Hierarchical regression was performed to determine to what extent each of the following background characteristics (age, gender, etiology, level of intellectual disability, type of living and health status) explained variance. Participants with mild ID were more independent and functioned higher in all the variables. Living arrangements contributed also to the explained variance regarding cognition and leisure. Persons who lived at home functioned lower in cognition and were less active concerning leisure activities. Etiology contributed to the explained variance in ADL. Participants who had Down syndrome functioned at a lower level than those with NSID.

CONCLUSIONS

Both studies (1,2) showed that health problems had appeared already by the age of 40 years among all the participants. Differences in background variables between the two types of living were associated with aging characteristics between the two settings. There were significant differences between the two residential groups regarding hypertension, psychiatric problems, and weight problems. These were found at higher rate amongst the community residence. More dental problems were seen in individuals who resided at home. Persons in community residence were less independent in ADL and leisure activity, the study showed a decline in functioning in both groups. Interestingly, the scores for social and leisure activities were better for the community residential group. Health problems among the participants with Down syndrome were significantly higher.

The data and experience from these two studies (1,2) could serve as a resource for developing geriatric services for older adults with ID living at home or in community residence.

REFERENCES

1. Lifshitz H, Merrick J. Ageing and intellectual disability in Israel: a study to compare community residence with living at home. Health Soc Care Community 2003;11(4):364-71.
2. Lifshitz H, Merrick J. Aging among persons with intellectual disability in Israel in relation to type of residence, age, and etiology. Res Dev Disabil 2004;25(2):193-205.
3. Evenhuis H, Henderson CM, Beange H, Lennoz N, Chicoine B. Healthy aging. Adults with intellectual disabilities. Physical health issues. Geneva: World Health Organization, 2000.
4. Collacott RA. The effect of age and residential placement on daptive behavior of adults with Down syndrome. Br J Psychiatry 1992;61:675-9.
5. Frasher VP, Chung MC. Cause of age-related decline in adaptive behavior of adults with Down syndrome: Differential diagnosis of dementia. Am J Ment Retard 1996;101:175-83.
6. Harper DC, Wadsworth JS. Improving health care communication for persons with mental retardation. Public Health Reports 1992;107:297-302.
7. Carlsen WR, Galliuzzi KE, Forman LF, Cavalieri TA. Comprehensive geriatric assessment: Applications for community residing, elderly people with mental retardation/developmental disabilities. Ment Retard 1994;32:334-40.

8.   Lennox NG, Diggens J, Ugon A. Health care for people with an intellectual disability: General practitioner's attitudes and provision of care. J Intellect Dev Disabil 2000;25:127-33.

9.   Rimmer JH, Braddock D, Marks B. Health characteristics and behaviors of adults with mental retardation residing in three living arrangements. Res Dev Disabil 1995;16:489-99.

PART TEN:
POLICY ISSUES

CHAPTER 31
Aging and disability. Policies for economic and social factors that create inequality and challenge dignity, independence and choice

Mary Cooke

This chapter aims to look at how factors like inequality in health outcomes may be created by social responses and economics, and the policies created to contend with these changes. These factors also present challenges to older people's dignity, independence and choice in determining their levels of adaptation to their personal health expectations. A literature review took place in response to a question that was raised in discussion following an academic seminar on older people and pain. This question asked "whether older people's socio-economic and health status had a relationship with their ability to maintain independence, dignity when accessing health services and choice when pain is a marker for loss of these factors." The review includes published papers linking socio-economic issues in understanding the debilitating effects of older age and the perception of pain in complex conditions that affects staff and older people's expectations of choice in care, dignity when receiving care, and maintenance of independence. The literature draws upon information about the older population in Britain, and reflects similar problems encountered in other cultures. The results are presented here as a discussion of the findings.

INTRODUCTION

Examining the key issues for older people in the 21st century, provides evidence which indicates that policies are linked to multicultural attitudes to old age, particularly in the United Kingdom (UK), and in other western style industrialised cultures based on economic fortunes (1, 2). If we evaluate the effectiveness of resources on attitudes to managing complex long-term conditions. Issues and policies associated with age, income and education are reviewed. Aging and the effect of increasing disability on an individual's capacity to adapt are considered, as well as the physical and mental health management of older people by diet, medication and activity. Before this, we look at aspects of economics that link to health, and issues related to health policy that directly influence older people's experiences. The relationship that longevity has with health status, socio-economics, demographic and other characteristics of elderly people can help in understanding complex interactions with genetic and environmental factors and older population adaptation to and maintenance of their quality of life (3). The aim is to answer by a review of the current literature, the questions of "whether older people's socio-economic and health status had a relationship with their ability to maintain independence, dignity when accessing health services and choice when pain is a marker for loss of these factors."

The material linking these factors in the literature is sparse. Most articles generalise around disability and older people, and health inequalities. Macro economics of national statistics cannot focus specifically on the older people in a population, neither will figures provide information that details the issues for older adults in either the UK, in the United States of America (USA), or in other countries as defined later in this chapter. The recent National Service Framework for Older People (NSF) (4) and its subsequent report by Ian Phelp (5) highlights the issues of place of care, how the older person is supported financially and in making choices about this place of care, and what this care may entail. Papers based on actuarial calculations are used in this review, but assumptions are made about their links with the focus of the question, because the evidence is sparse and most economic modelling is based on assumptions rather than actual figures.

A search of the health journals on line was conducted by using AHMED, CINAHL, MEDLINE, EMBASE and Science Citation Index, ageinfo. These databases include access to economics journals. Where policy, economic and actuarial reports were known to exist, these specific sources were hand-searched.

The chapter is made up of three main sections. In the first section we look at the expectation of economic independence in older age, and compare this with economic dependence based on the importance of control or alleviation of painful conditions as a benchmark. In the next section, in association with understanding the role of a person's economic status and control over their health, we examine the issue of dignity in old age and how assumptions are made on behalf of the older population, society and individuals. Finally, we look at how economic choices are set for older people, what these choices are based on, and whether opportunities to alter health status in old age can be selected.

SHORT GLOSSARY OF TERMS

GDP: Gross Domestic Product. This is a way of measuring the size of the total economy during a given year. This is what a country produces. It has a monetary value and the expenditure is calculated from this GDP for all public services and Government spending This would include for example; defence, health and social services, education, the legal system, Government administrative activity.

GNP: Gross National Product. This is the sum in any given year that can be calculated by Governments that it can receive from all taxation. This money is used by Government to spend on GDP.

ECONOMICS, HEALTH, AGE AND INDEPENDENCE

That health decreases with age (normally) is a fundamental fact of biology (6). Because age is frequently correlated with income, education and other variables, it is essential to control for age through age-adjustment, or analysis of age-specific data (7). Interactions between age and other variables such as income and education then become important; in particular, the correlation between health and income varies greatly over the life cycle, and not monotonically. At the close of the 20th century, the life expectancy of women exceeded that of men in every country. This is attributable to biological differences, but interactions between these differences and the physical and social environment vary. In low-income countries ($1,000 gross domestic product [GDP] per capita or less) the female–male difference in life expectancy is only about 4%. For countries with GDP per capita around $3,000 it is 8%, and at around $9,000 it averages 11%. These figures are relatively stable over time but relate to data around the turn of the 21st century.

However, the differential does not follow this path continuously. In the 30 highest income countries (GDP per capita [per person] averaging $21,000) the gender differential in life expectancy is only 8%. Over the past 30 years the differential in higher-income countries has tended to fall, reversing the previous long-term trend towards a higher ratio in the course of economic development. In the United States, for example, the downward trend occurred at the same time that the female–male education ratio was rising (8,9). Over age 65 the sex ratio has for a long time been 49% male 51% female, but this percentage is shifting to indicate that more men live longer. The needs of the elderly population will alter in response to this. Pensions and benefits are already adjusted to support people living longer on average by 10 years than they did 20 years ago in Western industrialised countries. Currently decisions are being made to raise the age of retirement for the fit elderly, so that pensions and welfare benefits are given to those who are unable to support themselves in older age, while others can contribute more towards their retirement for when they choose to cease work. The economic benefits to older people of working longer are not yet quantified. The US and the UK as well as other industrialised countries, government policy decisions are being made on an assumption that the entitlement figures for older adults predicted for the next fifty years will increase exponentially. The number of elderly eligible to receive benefits such as health and social care, (social security and Medicare the health system specifically designed for the older population who have paid insurances or worked in the US) will increase dramatically. Health care costs for the elderly will increase in line with the population numbers. What is unknown is whether the GNP will increase more than the GDP to pay for the greater cost of elderly care, because production or wages will rise. This is unlikely. But uncertainty of the situation of the future has not driven the likelihood of politicians making uncomfortable decisions in the present (10).

HEALTH ECONOMICS

Health economics is a way of expressing a personal and social value for health and health services. The unique British National Health Service (NHS) provides health care free at the point of delivery for people who need it. For people over 60 years, this also means free prescriptions, eye tests and other benefits. People who need health care decide with their GP when and where this will happen. The point at which the cost of care becomes important is when people are willing and able to pay for treatment independently of the NHS.

In the UK people may choose either to pay part or all of their care to a private provider, or have NHS care. Most interventions and treatments have an outcomes related benefit. This means that the cost related to effectiveness or benefit is calculated on various characteristics of patients and the treatment, to suggest whether an intervention is likely to be effective, beneficial or too costly. In the UK there are standardized reference costs of interventions linked to people aged under and over 70 years. These costs are calculated with reference to national average calculations of treatment costs giving, for example, various prices for the cost of a bed used per day, an expected length of stay per treatment, and the intervention. There is a clear anomaly here, between the age at which people can receive extra benefits or supported health care (age 60 years) and the related extra costs of similar treatment for older adults (at age 70 years) calculated by factors associated with recovery, outcomes and risks borne by health service resources. Socio-economic factors such as mobility, multiple pathological illness and genetic predispositions link changes in older people's health status with the need to recognise the additional and higher cost of their care to the state in the UK, or to insurance premiums for older people in other countries.

Currently, nine strategic (regional) health authorities hold the budget for treatments in the NHS and make decisions at macro-economic level. Several systems help make the decision along with the patient about what treatment is available, whether the budget will pay for the intervention, and what is likely to be a good outcome for the patient and for society generally. Sometimes people may not get the treatment they need when they need it because the resources have been spent (opportunity costs) and this relates to micro-economics at local level. This decision making system is called either rationing, resource allocation or budget management, and depends upon whether it is viewed from the perspective of the patient, the budget holders, or the Public Health Commissioners responsible for the health of the national population. Balancing available resources (staff, technology, equipment and money as income from various sources) with the needs of people in a local population is the basis of econometric science. Individuals' values for health and local health services are the criteria for decisions about health spending and health policies that control health-care delivery.

CULTURAL AND POLICY ISSUES IN OLDER AGE

Numbers of people in age bands in different countries can be proportional to a variety of characteristics associated with genetic inheritance, local and national industry and the type of health care available or taken up as a resource (paid for directly, or by subscription, or by insurance premium) by people during their working lives. The rise in the number of people over 60 years old in most western societies in recent years has important implications for western cultures and their social construct. For example, life expectancy is seven years less for black Americans than for white Americans, and possibly greater for Hispanics than for white Americans, but the reasons for this are not understood (9). The health services of many countries, including Australia, the Balkan states, Canada, Finland, Greece, Israel, Italy, Japan, Poland, Spain, Sweden, Taiwan, Turkey, the UK and the USA, are beginning to recognize the impact of the needs of older people when considering cultural aspects of illness prevention by nutrition, controlling pain and symptoms of long-term illness and disease by 'safe' analgesia, and prevention of pain through symptom recognition. Fuchs (9) suggests that few policies actually defer health care for specific cultures in western medicine. Most people's cost of care rises dramatically in the last six months of life (11), mainly because of heroic treatments and increased hospital episodes of care. Older people's genetic and ethnic differences become more pronounced for managing and controlling pain, but in the UK analgesia is not selected according to race, age (generally) or cost.

Long-term, complex chronic illness is the norm for many people over 50 in the UK and other countries. The ease of international travel means that older people from many cultures visit or live in the UK, and they may have different ways of thinking about older age. In countries such as Ukraine, for example, average life expectancy is 68 years, whereas in the UK it is 84 years (8,9).

There are cultural differences too: in Japan and other Asian countries older people are venerated and cared for in their family home until death. In Asian cultures, 'old' may mean over 45 years of age. These key culture-specific issues provide different perspectives for many British older people, and particularly those who have moved from other cultures to live here. Costs for families with ill older members differ in accordance with cultural influences. The National Service Framework (NSF) for Older People published in the UK in 2001(4), defined specific plan for care for older people to be implemented over the following ten years. A sequential document from the UK Government (5) is a report by Ian Phelp, which determines that

> "Our approach to promoting person-centred care has been about a personalised response, the treatment of older people with dignity and respect and the rooting out of age discrimination. In the next phase (of

planning service change), we want more control to pass to service users through direct payments for social care, greater choice, increased control and responsibility for self-care. This will require fair and consistent assessment of needs, with budgets devolved either as direct payments to social service users, or to front-line practitioners who can work with service users to align service response to users' priorities. Diversity of service provision will be required to increase choice for service users." (Phelp 2004:8)

Unfortunately, actuarial studies have not been calculated, that would indicate that older people (and other disabled and unable to work, who are in receipt of welfare benefits) respond positively to being able to control who or which agency does what for them and managing when this occurs and how often. Case studies and individual experiences are presented in the Phelp report that indicate the cost of this choice has proven to be higher in some instances but lower in others. The outcomes in terms of better health status for people who are in these systems of voucher rated care tend to identify situations where older people pay for different programmes of care then that provided by government commissioned services through health and social care professionals, so comparisons are infrequently made. However, in 2000-2001, 500 older people were receiving these vouchers. By 2002-2003, 2,700 older people had gained control over their social support mechanism (5). This system of benefit is especially important for older people and their carers who have been discharged home from hospital from example an episode of care that provided rehabilitation after stroke (5). UK Government policy has strongly supported the use of mechanisms to target populations, select opportunities for evidence of success, and direct services in accordance with resource control and reduction. Those who have not been able to benefit from the targeted implementation of this policy remain in service agreements for provision where health and social care is fragmented and liable to spontaneous intervention by voluntary agency or local service management interpretation of need.

Below is a diagram reproduced from the Phelp report that shows the outline of how the targets for changes to care delivery are expected to take place. It shows the numbers of people who will participate in receiving the services. The diagram makes an assumption that the numbers of people in the population targeted in the top of the triangle will be reducing rather than remain static which is likely to be the case. From this we can predict that the resources available for each person classified in this smallest category will receive even less funds and support in their old age. According to the NSF for older people (4) this population will be living longer in their home accommodation, and when analysed with the information just presented, will receive fewer services in that setting over a longer time.

HEALTH INEQUALITIES AND CHOICE

Analysis of the causes of inequalities in health has shown that variation in the utilization of medical care cannot fully explain observed health differences (12,13). Epidemiologists, sociologists and economists have indicated that lifestyle contributes to these inequalities. It is personal lifestyle that causes the greatest variation, beyond a low level of food, hygiene and basic health-care provision. McGinnis and Foege (14) estimated that the three leading external (non-degenerative or directly genetically determined) causes of mortality in the USA in 1990 were tobacco, diet and activity, and alcohol consumption. These lifestyle variables explained around 38% of premature mortality, and the researchers noted that a dramatically reduced quality of life is associated with many of the diseases related to these behaviours (7).

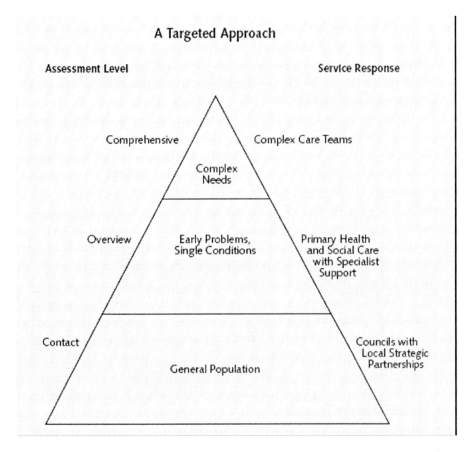

Figure 1. The framework for UK Government targets related to care for older people directed from health and social care for 2003-2010 (The Phelp Report 2004; page 10.
http://www.dh.gov.uk/assetRoot/04/09/32/15/04093215.pdf accessed March **10 2007)**

The impact of disability arising from poor pain control is the same in the UK as it is internationally. Epidemiological outcomes of interventions and planning for illness prevention in care of the elderly and their personal infirmities are based on the individuals' inherited poverty or wealth, their nutritional habits, their lifetime opportunities taken through education, their manner of resource use, and their resulting health status. This is sometimes called the social capital of a community, meaning its wealth of health and each individual's ability to maintain their personal independence.

We can conclude from the facts derived from papers cited here that, as in most western style industrialised countries, multicultural societies are the norm, that access to health services for the older adults is determined by their personal expectations and need, as well as level of capacity to pay for the services not freely available. That pain control as a marker of disability is poor in most countries and that people's health in older age is dependent upon their intrinsic health status at birth, their education, and their lifestyle during youth and midlife. Government policies attempt to redress this balance, but balancing the economy is more important.

RESOURCES LINKED WITH BEING OLDER AND DISABLED BY PAIN

While they are still young and active, few people expect or plan for the experiences of chronic pain, illness and complex diseases of old age, or for the personal costs of support required. This means that few resources are forthcoming from individuals themselves, except learned coping strategies for pain or adaptation. The effect of chronic pain on each individual's daily life will cause them to adjust their activity by adapting to the changing problems of mobility, diet, activity and an individual expectation of successful adoption of personal coping strategies tested through life experience. Relative fitness and frailty can be defined by accumulation of physical deficits until the person is unable to improve health by medical or other treatment. Mitnitski et al (15) state that 'there are maximal values of deficit accumulation beyond which survival is unlikely'. Several studies recognize that health-care staff's attitudes and methods of communication in the community setting are associated with recognizing individual's needs arising from complex conditions, and where existing personal coping and management strategies are important (16). Where they do not exist, physical or nutritional education ion older age can be a problem.

Older people cite methods of coping with pain that include spending time with friends and family, reading and watching television, rest, and favourite old folk remedies. Some of these remedies require financial resources such as funds for transport or for treatments that are not part of NHS care. Other studies show that pain in older age influences mental health status (17,18), and attitude towards food and nutrition or even access to health care (19).

Most people over 60 in the UK as in other European countries linked with the event, will have lived through the Second World War and its aftermath, when they experienced rationing of food and goods. The wartime diet was high in fibre and vegetables, but after rationing ended foods that were low in fibre and high in fat and sugar became part of the diet again. The current rise in cancer of the colon in people over 50 years, which is affected by diet, may be the cost to society of this change (although evidence now exists to indicate infection is also a cause). For most older people, medication for pain is taken as a last resort, mainly because of the attitude of health-care staff towards 'strong' medication, and also because of the side effects of continuous analgesic use (16) The variety of the coping mechanisms listed above indicates that the individual achieves something other than reduction of pain, based to an extent on culture, level of independence, maintenance of personal dignity and choices available in the use of resources (19). These resources are considered to be personal (coping methods learned through life experiences), financial (income), and interdependent decision-making with regard to access and choice of methods of pain reduction. Older people use a hierarchy of symptom control and contact with health or social care services (16) with the intention of avoiding expenditure of personal financial resources.

It is inevitable that rates of morbidity and mortality increase with age, reflecting the ongoing deterioration of health. Buckley et al (6) modelled the influences of socio-economic factors on the state of health of older Canadians. The Canadian system offers universal access to a publicly funded health-care system that covers 'essential services', which (in the late 1990s) meant about 70% of all health expenditure on services. The income–health connection has been reviewed in depth by, for example, Smith (22); Evans (23); Deaton (24, 25). One conclusion of the literature discussed here, is that the determinants of health indicate that at least among citizens of wealthy industrialised societies, any relationship between individual income level and health status has to arise from the effects of the social context within which people at different levels find themselves. Income inequality, like air pollution, is itself a health hazard. However, it is not certain that income inequality itself is a major determinant of population health . . . "[I]t is low incomes that are important, not inequality and there is no evidence that making the rich richer . . . is hazardous to the health of the poor" (6).

Lifetime income affects both men and women. Higher income means greater command over resources, including greater access to adequate nutrition. It could also affect access to health care; even in a universal system some elements of care (e.g. prescription drugs, access to health-care professionals such as physiotherapists) or the private costs of accessing the systems (such as transport costs) are not covered. The system may be too 'downstream' – concerned with health-related behaviour and health-care delivery and drugs – when the underlying 'causes of causes' of diseases and death are more 'upstream' in the social and economic structure of society. The treatments for complex conditions and pain control lie within this layered structure (24).

Evidence is published by the UK government to show that some older people access specific programmes for treatment that increase mobility and decrease disability. For stroke services, one of the UK aims for older people is for them to have treatment in specialised centres so that rehabilitation to living at home is achieved. In 1998, 45% of all people diagnosed with stroke had access to specialised stroke units, in October 2004, 90% are receiving this specialised treatment. In 2000, there were 7.4 per 1,000 in the population over 65 years who received elective hip replacement, in 2003, this had increased to 7.7 per 1,000 population aged over 65 years. In 2000 3.7 people per 1,000 had elective knee replacements compare to 4.4 per 1,000 population aged over 65 years in 2003. In 2000, 27 per 1,000 population over 65 years had cataract operation, and in 2003 it is recorded that 29.7 per 1,000 population over 65 years had elective cataract operations (5).

It may therefore be assumed that: chronic pain from illness and complex conditions in older age is often untreated, leading to greater levels of disability in association with ability adapt to situations of mobility; older people from all cultures do not always access or accept health services to treat pain or use medication, sometimes because of staff attitude to that medication; life experiences, culture-specific remedies and maintenance of independence promote an adaptation to disability in older people and that income while working is a factor influencing men's and women's health in older age.

POLICY IN HEALTH SERVICES, ECONOMICS AND OLDER PEOPLE

In the UK the National Service Framework (NSF) for Older People was published by the Labour Government in 2001 (4) as one of a series of frameworks for modernizing health services with a focus on managing people's health needs in a community setting. This NSF requires the setting up and maintenance of a network of services for older people to be purchased and managed from primary care trusts (PCTs), with links for social services to deliver social care when appropriate. A PCT in a region or area takes the lead on managing services for the elderly. Other related non disease- specific NSFs have been set up, such as the NSF for Long Term Conditions (26). Adult-focused NSFs have also been issued for specific conditions or diagnoses such as cancer, heart disease, diabetes and asthma. A successful NSF is seen as being interactive between patients, health-care staff and social services, using available resources to benefit local populations and interlinking various health-enhancing services as required by local groups representative of elderly people.

The social context of shared benefits in health is shown in a Danish study (27). In this study equity was traded off for greater health gains, and related to whether the questions in the survey were framed to elicit a social or an individual choice. If social decision-making is the issue, health gains which involve relieving patients of extreme problems are found to be valued more highly than relief of minor ailments. This is a defined value system for making decisions affecting personal health and comfort.

The practical physical and psychosocial limitations of pain confronting older people are dealt with by strategies for maintaining independence and control, and adaptation to life with chronic pain (28).

Navigating systems of access to health care is a mystery to most older people, although one third of then suffer chronic pain and live in fear of losing their independence. Many participants in Sofaer's study (28) used adaptation, acceptance or non-acceptance of their condition, but by pacing themselves, helping others, prayer, and using a 'public face' they were able to overcome the pain (28). Such strategies are anticipated to be cost free for the older people using them and for the state, but this attitude determines the value older people have for their independence.

Policies for GPs and community drug prescribers have recently been associated with reducing the costs of prescription drugs. Insufficient pain management in the community and in acute settings is a public health concern, and adequate relief depends upon a variety of treatment options including the appropriate use of controlled substances for moderate or severe pain. In the UK the use of opioids in pain management is regulated by local health authorities, and is the concern of GPs and specialist nurses who alter dose and rate in the individual's home or hospice according to need. Research in the USA (29,30) identifies concerns about older people having state controlled substances in their homes, and being vulnerable to theft or diversion and abuse of drugs by family or health-care staff. In the UK, current policies support the reduction in length of hospital stay, and rehabilitation and treatment are focused on the home setting. Future policies will concern pain management and strategies to reduce crime in the community.

DIET AND HEALTH IN OLDER AGE, RELATED TO ECONOMICS

Disease-related diet and information (for example sugar-free foods for diabetics, fresh fruit and vegetables for raising energy and reducing depression, protein and vitamin-rich foods for wound healing) may inform but not influence an individual's compliance with advice. Older people in the UK have experienced many countervailing arguments around food and food products, so confusion in popular and cultural notions of the 'right' food to eat is likely. Food interests may not be related to health interests, and information relating to pain reduction through promoting mental health may be inaccessible. Gustafsson, Ekblad and Sidenvall (20) show that within a culture members often eat foods specific to that culture (31) because the meaning of eating healthily for older people may not always be to eat a variety of foods including fresh meat and vegetables. For others, this is seen as 'proper food' (32). Hirani and Primatesta's study (33) shows significantly that older people (over 65) living in institutions and at home risk poor bone and muscle health and increased risk of fractures because of low vitamin D levels. Deficiency is more likely to be found in women than in men, is more likely in the autumn and winter, and is associated with long limiting illness, manual social class and poor general health. Vitamin D is an indicator of diet containing fresh fruit and vegetables.

Food choice is influenced by socio-economic factors, level of education and whether an individual lives independently or in an institution. Allen's study (34) indicates that based on personal resources, even the presence of an elderly individual's own teeth has a significant effect on dental treatment, because of cost, and on diet. Easily chewed food items with a low fibre and high fat content may increase their risk of cardiovascular disease and bowel cancer. Current dietary choices using similar content are based on cost rather than perceived quality (20). This provides health and social care professionals with important information about individual dietary influences on the health of the local population.

The differences in adjustment made by women in old age who will have experienced many life changes, and possibly hardship, are explored (35). She found that depression, maintaining intimacy through friends and managing change are the key influences on women's perceptions of health and pain management. Distress related to poverty, and the need for social and emotional support, become important for women in older life, who may be widowed or whose family may no longer be close enough to provide a financial or social cushion. It is becoming recognised that diet has an influence on mood, and social exchange, so mental illness may be alleviated by healthier diet and personal independence in choosing a healthier nutritional content. Family ties become important when government policy changes benefits assessments, pension rights, investments, and taxable allowances for older people's incomes. Information about pensions, welfare and benefits income, or support through voluntary and public services is not universally available, and an older person who is isolated will be disadvantaged, possibly in debt, and with a reduced standard of living.

The independence of older people is often associated with the availability and use of transport. Having no personal transport, and thus lacking access to local shops and therefore to fresh produce, is associated with low income and poor education. Older drivers will become more prevalent because of the large post-war social cohort, and it is predicted that future older drivers will drive greater distances and take more trips (36, 8). Statistically older people are safer drivers, but the presence of more older drivers will increase the morbidity and mortality of people involved in road traffic accidents (37).

Dignity associated with older age is usually linked to assessment of need for services and predictions of ageing populations. Assessment of frailty may or may not be helpful (38). To avoid allocating a person to a category from which they cannot escape may require several sequential assessments – costly, time consuming and inconvenient – to reduce the risk that expediency might override fairness.

In conclusion for this section of the chapter, we may draw on evidence that indicates firstly that successfully reducing symptoms causing pain and disability in older people is based on individual understanding and experiences of what they will 'lose' by going to the doctor, (opportunity costs of using health services) rather than what they will gain. Health policies in many parts of the world increase health inequalities of immigrants because of loss of equal access to health care by low income, poor diet and understanding of independent responsibilities. Secondly, that older people have learned habits of using few resources that are difficult to change. Thirdly, that some cultures in the world consider 'old' to be around 50 years, while others venerate older people aged 80 or more. These cultural differences are noticed more when people go without health care because they think it costs them more money. Prevention of ill health by diet and exercise into old age is not a learned behaviour. Fourthly, past events such as wars affect people's attitudes towards what they can and/or should eat, shape opinions on the cost of things and affect the older person's ability to access fresh produce.

INDEPENDENCE

The safety of older people living at home is normally ignored. In the UK this becomes important as people are expected to remain in their home situation for longer, either receiving health and social care, or paying for personal services independently. In the USA unintentional injuries that include the home situation are the ninth leading cause of death in people aged 65 and older, and for every death there are 650 non-fatal injuries (39). Two important studies indicate that costs of care increase for all reasons including accidents and disease through the last 15 years before death. The association between age and health expenditure may well be an artefact of a stronger relationship between proximity to death and health expenditure, as mentioned above (11,40). Lagergren (40) also makes the point that guidance of the provision of health services for older people requires better data to make predictions associated with need. Cost reduction in older age is linked to policy measures directed at improving the health of elderly people by promoting conditions of increased physical and mental activity and better outcomes for medical interventions (40, 68).

Choice in how to maintain a reasonable income while older and retired from mainstream work is a current debate in many countries, relating to pensions, ability to work and health. In Ukraine older people, if they live beyond the average of 67 years, will take up laborious jobs on the streets to make ends meet. Because Ukrainian health policies are weak, people turn to folk medicine and Eastern medications to treat illnesses, or emigrate to obtain western health care (41). Poor rural Chinese who have lived through the transition from Communism to private health insurance mostly have to pay directly for health care, which means that only 6.1% of them access services (42).

Poverty in old age is related to the person's ability to adapt to their reduction in income, or choose to move. Health status is associated with physical and mental health, mobility, and accrued investment during working life. Long-term benefits and state pensions form a baseline income but reduce mental health further, with a risk of early entry to the care-home setting (43, 44, 45, 46). The alternative is to accommodate health needs to health expectations. Policies assume that older people will be independent as long as possible (43), which reduces costs of health care (11). Personal dignity is lost or retained when older people can no longer choose their destiny because of personal resources, government policy, or local application of social rules that are applied to regulate the cost of illness to society (47).

People who are older and living independently have a healthier and longer life if they are not depressed (48). Physical ill-health, as well as any indication of loss of mental health, contributes to a gradual rise in dependence and loss of ability to make decisions independent of family and others upon whom the older person may depend. Physical health can be assessed in several ways: here we use temperature, fitness, safety, diet, depression and understanding of diagnosis as markers for independence. Many older people have to decide whether to leave their family home and move to live in a care home, or with younger family members. Van Houtven and Norton (49) identified factors that reduced the need for or introduction of home health care, and delayed nursing home entry significantly.

Depression is an underlying condition for many older adults, and predicts their ability to adapt to changes in health status (48) and rehabilitation after a stroke or other episodes of illness. There are few studies that clarify the effect of depression on the in-patient rehabilitation process. Once depression is apparent the functional deficits associated with its occurrence persist, even after remission of the depressive episode. If two populations of in-patients with and without stroke are compared, their clinically meaningful symptoms of depression are similar. This is because there are underlying complications of managing a chronic illness or condition. Nahcivan and Demirezen (50) have shown that more than 50% of the population of older adults living on low incomes in a rural community setting in Turkey suffer symptoms of depression. This half of the population is more likely to be women or widows, to lack health insurance and to live alone. The psycho-social aspect of pain associated with being older is partly linked with income and social standing, and closely linked with coping and resources. Older people in the UK from various cultures often assume they have to pay for services that are actually free, and this means they do not receive some aspects of care.

Informal care given by family members complements professional care or substitutes for it, but this care is not conducive to the long-term interests of the individual family member who becomes the chief carer. Muira, Ari and Yamasaki (17) show the burden of caring on spouses and the co-morbidity linked with reduction in quality of life because of mental capacity and verbal communication.

The relationship between depression and anxiety among long-term caregivers and their feelings of burden are succinctly linked here. Previous work indicated that social activity added value to quality of relationship. This requires an element of resource use, and consequent funds to accommodate this activity (17). The influence of depression when linked to independent living is applied from a physiological perspective to core body temperature and reflects the use of resources. Gomolin et al (51) used this phenomenon in a study that showed older people in a nursing home setting were colder than those living independently in the community. In fact older people were colder in all settings: nursing home, office and community.

Independence in older age assumes that a person is living in the community in their own home setting, either alone or with at least one other person. Further, it means that resources defined as financial (pension, benefits, interest on savings and investments) and personal (health, education and knowledge about their condition, ability to decide about or pay for treatments) have been accrued by the person during their life, and are now being used to their benefit in older age.

The study by Hirani and Primatesta (33) showed in a large cross-sectional sample that vitamin D is an indicator of older people's ability to access or afford fresh produce, or even appreciate the benefit of vegetables and fruit in the diet. Many older people are physically unable to prepare vegetables, or find cooking costly. Older people's inability to provide themselves with an adequate diet may affect their independence.

Cresci (39) described the use of a Cochrane systematic review to underpin assessment of elderly home safety. The home care nurse, as a key member of the team, raises awareness of extrinsic and intrinsic factors that may lead to injury in the home, and suggest strategies for injury prevention. Home safety resources (local, state and internet) and the personal injury plan are part of an education process. The lack of independence is outlined by the process of accumulated health-related problems (deficits) defined by Mitnitski et al (15), as mentioned earlier. Here the team use an index of frailty in older adults and mortality in population-based and clinical or institutional-based samples to identify a hazard rate for mortality from a level of accumulated ill health.

DIGNITY

In most western democratised societies, individual independence means being able to make decisions that affect each individual. Although the ability to do this assumes a level of education, knowledge and understanding, it also assumes the person has achieved adulthood and is socially dignified by being able to make knowledgeable choices.

Even in the UK, health care expenditure and development policy is bound by finances and a managed market. This means that for the providers in the health-care system – GPs and secondary or acute health care organizations – patients can be seen as income, or at least income generating. Managing the balance between raising income and reducing expenditure on health-enhancing treatments economically, as described above, is the reduction in resource use. A healthy older person (a consumer) has a capitation fee, and a fee for service, which raises each GP's income, whereas an ill 'patient' is costly. A study by Iversen (52) identified the active recruitment of patients by GPs if they experienced a reduction in income. This perception of the patient as income has not been explicitly expressed previously (52).

In contrast, patients can decide to use private health care. The current state of the NHS, characterized by long waits and generally poor quality, has driven many to spend savings accrued for precautionary reasons. Guariglia and Rossi (53) found a correlation between insurance coverage and saving in the UK, suggesting that private medical insurance does not generally crowd out private saving, yet preserves the dignity of having health care when and where it is important to the individual.

The study by Janlov et al (46) indicated the loss of dignity and 'walking a fine line' while balancing the feelings of guilt and need for comfort against resources when deciding on accepting 'a necessary evil' by incorporating the home help into daily life to gain a sense of continuity. The assessment of personal wealth under these circumstances has the effect of reducing control over resources, because giving information away in relation to wealth provides others – even if they are anonymous public agencies – with a means by which an individual is measured, and their capacity associated with their ability to pay rather than their willingness to pay for services.

Barnes and Bennet (54) and Roberts (55, 56) found that older people in later life who are increasingly frail because of disease and co-morbidity are vulnerable when exercising their right to participate in and influence decisions relating to their own health and social care. Older people experienced countervailing pressures by health staff either through assessments of needs before admission to an institution, or assessment of ability before discharge. This assessment is entirely professional-led, taking little account of the patient- or person centred approach favoured by current policies.

There is little attempt to understand the functioning of the NHS as an institution in a study by Campbell et al (57) describing predictors of clinical outcomes from a European collaborative group, measuring physical function, cognition, age, gender and living arrangement as a factors associated with outcome. There was little recognition that the NHS and social care system often prevents the older person from leaving the institution within the 90 day 'deadline' for institutionalization (58).

Drawing conclusions from this perspective of the literature, we can state that economics balances expenses and costs with individual as well as national income, and has little to do with the dignity of the individual, seen by some in government or private business of health care as an enhancement to fees or income. Further, that, if older people accept help at home by private care, or by informal carers, they are defined as being or becoming a burden on the family. When assessment of needs of older people is associated with costs, the process is centred on health professionals and not on the person about whom decisions will be made. This loss of dignity and consequently independence lessens the older person's chances of having control over their income and expenditure for health and social care services. Conversely, it increases the control that the state and local government have, (through the health professionals) who are likely to provide the services.

CHOICE

Understanding generations can be enhanced by avoiding defining them rigidly as chronological cohorts, but rather linking generational experiences with a historically informed political economy. The 'War generation' recognizes itself and therefore has a common identity, with values, attitudes and sense of national solidarity and mutual obligation arising from those experiences. However, the generation is divided by divergent economic interests in property, insurance protection and pension rights, based on historical experiences of life course by experienced groups. Some would identify the choices they had in developing financial opportunities, others deny they had a choice of life experience (59).

Inevitably, selecting financial gain early in life indicated better health outcomes and greater independence in older age (49). The construction of the National Insurance system in the UK is intended for the benefit of all, yet clearly older people are expected to use a greater proportion of their financial resources in accessing and using the NHS, as well as subsidizing it by the use of other methods of health maintenance for pain and symptom control or reduction and thus increasing their mobility and lessening disability (16) This raises the question whether older people choose to use the health service, or choose to put off accepting help with pain relief as long as possible. The reduction in pain can be either physical (28,48) or mental, as described by Muira, Ari and Yamasaki (18). The study by Wang et al (42) showed that across most populations the poorer/healthier populations subsidize the rich/sick in utilization of health services, which counters the findings of Buckley et al (6). This idea is upheld by Le Grand (60,61) who indicates that health policy intended to help the poor and sick cannot acknowledge the needs of that population without the rich and sick taking advantage of the health provision to the detriment of those needy poor.

Outpatient and in-patient services use by a poor rural community are modelled by Wang et al (42) based on income and health status. These authors made an assumption that if individuals consume more non-medical goods then they have capacity to pay for more health care, and this reflects people's ability to pay. The health status of any given population has been shown to have a positive relationship with the standard of education of that population, although this does not take account of the risk-taking behaviour of members of that population.

Lipsitz (41) writes of a Ukrainian population where 15% are aged over 65 years, despite the average length of life being only 67 years. The ratio of older women to men is 2:1, and the presence of elderly women is so ubiquitous that they even have a special word (babushka) to describe them. As in most other cultures, the incidence of poverty increases with age and 49% of households with two or more elderly people are considered to be poor, because the average pension is 40% below the poverty line, based on an annual household consumption of $24 per month. This is why the most vulnerable segment of the population seemingly provides much of the hard labour in Ukrainian cities. During the Soviet era health care was free as a public service, although standards were and are considered lower than in western health care. Central and eastern European countries collectively report reduction in real income and widening disparities, because of stress and stress-related behaviour (e.g. consumption of alcohol and tobacco) lax regulation of environmental and occupational risks, and breakdown in basic health services.

Preventive care is rare in the Ukraine, because of the proportion of resources allocated to community and ambulatory care. The high cost of drugs prevents older people from affording lipid-lowering medications, modern antihypertensive medication, calcium, vitamin D or even aspirin. The system is able to provide only rudimentary acute care, despite spending two thirds of health funds on secondary services which are highly specialized but poorly equipped, with minimal nursing care and little heating. Because of the high prevalence of drug abuse in the population (a result of social and psychological pressures) there is limited access to modern psychiatric care. Depression, anxiety and psychoses therefore often remain untreated in frail elderly patients unable to travel far for treatment. Opiate analgesics are strictly regulated in the Ukraine, and are generally unavailable except to patients with end-stage cancer. Most of the elderly population treat themselves with herbs, folk medicine and devices they can make themselves or purchase cheaply in local pharmacies, according to long-standing cultural practices and beliefs based on specific treatment or behaviour for every symptom.

Many families travel and migrate with their elderly relatives to countries with better-developed health services such as the UK of Germany. The description of conditions in the Ukraine is given here to indicate the similarities of belief by older people in health care and lack of preventive health care that exists between the UK and the Ukraine.

The continuing increase in the use of complementary medicines in many western countries indicates that people of all ages are making positive choices between allopathic and complementary health approaches. NHS prescriptions are free for people over 60 in the UK, so the cost of complementary therapies may not be prohibitive when culture-specific remedies are required. A specific study of older people's use of complementary medications in the USA indicated a growth in use similar to that in the UK (25% over the last 20 years). The study showed that out-of-pocket expenditure on complementary therapies by older people was more than that spent on hospitalization (62).

The use of health services is greater by older people in the population than by others, except that the proportion of people who are educated and considered to be wealthy access health care more frequently. This selective inverse use of services indulges the GDP per capita in the UK. Older people do not always choose to use health services; their attitude towards pain and seeking help appears to be laissez-faire. A decision not to access services is not always based on ability or willingness to pay for medication; rather, a choice to go without is associated with an ability to make that choice, or else the system in the UK is so complex that navigating it is too difficult. In countries where resources to pay for health care and pain relief are low, older people counteract their lack of pain relief by work. In the UK, a comprehensive approach to meeting the health-care needs of the older population comes from understanding the older person's perception of pain.

Drawing conclusions from this evidence, we can show that older people are expected to use the health services more than other sectors of the population in all societies, and those health professionals often implicitly place restrictions on older people's choice of interventions for treatment. Then older people tend to pay for complementary therapies of their choice to treat pain, when they could access these at no cost in some circumstances. It is understood that migration plays an increasingly important part in the cost and accessibility of health services. People from poorer countries tend to migrate to welfare-based health economies to gain better access to health care if they can, and consequentially better prospects of maintaining independence and mobility. A further important point to make is that health risk-taking at a younger age reflects an attitude to health in older age, but is linked to the perceived and future ability to pay for services.

CONCLUSION

The spectrum of social capital and health among older people in the UK ranges from personal investment in health by reducing their acknowledgement of disability caused by pain or enhancing life through lifestyle, to loss of independence and lack of choice about health interventions, and to depression. This continuum indicates that dignity is an important factor. Social capital may function on several levels, through individual behaviours (such as community participation) individual norms (trust in the community and perceptions of community reciprocity), through the neighbourhood environment, and is defined at the macro level by historical, social, political and economic features. Changes in abilities to participate mean that the older person or group comes to depend upon social capital at each of these points (63,64). The recognition that older people will either be living at home, or in a supported care environment, means that the quality of life in either setting will become more important. Personal expectations of each older person resonate with their health status and ability to communicate needs and choices.

Symptoms and dependency will reduce quality of life, even though 'cure' is impossible. We know that the longer independence is maintained, the greater the quality of life that will be experienced, but the need for help and the ability to pay for the support to retain independence is balanced by the income and other resources each older person has at their disposal. Income from pensions, benefits and other insurances in old age has a direct relationship with each individual's income and education in earlier life. This affects dependence, loss and depressive mental illness (65, 66).The context of each older person's habitation and accommodation plays a definitive part in health, adaptation to pain symptoms and access to health services (68).
The stereotyped views of professionals on how it is to be old, and what decisions an older person should make, often affect relationships between the older person and their family members (67).

The holistic care of an older person in pain, based on the principles of how intrinsic or extrinsic decisions affect their independence, dignity and choice, has social and economic outcomes.

REFERENCES

1.   Baggott R. Health and health care in Britain, 3rd ed. Basingstoke: Palgrave Macmillan, 2004.

2.   Ham C. Health policy in Britain, 5th ed. Basingstoke: Palgrave Macmillan, 2004.

3.   Gallucci M, Ongaro F, Bresolin F, Bernardi U, Salvato C, Minello A, et al. The Treviso Longeva (Trelong) Study: A biomedical, demographic, economic and social investigation on people 70 years and over in a typical town of North East Italy. Arch Gerontol Geriatrics 2007; 1(suppl):173-92.

4.   Department of Health. National service framework for older people. London: HMSO, 2001.

5.   Phelp I. Better health on old age. London: Dept Health, 2004.

6.   Buckley NJ, Denton FT, Robb L, Spencer BG. The transition from good to poor health: an econometric study of the older population. J Health Econ 2004;23(5):1013–34.

7.   Contoyannis P, Jones AM. Socio-economic status, health and lifestyle. J Health Econ 2004;23(5):965–95.

8.   Office of National Statistics. http://www.ons.gov.uk for UK figures and http://en.wikipedia.org/wiki/Economy_of_the_United_States for data on the US economy.

9.   Fuchs VR. Reflections on the socio-economic correlates of health. J Health Econ 2004;23(4):653–61.

10.   Stiglitz JE. Economics of the public sector, 3rd ed. London: Norton, 2000.

11.   Sheshamani M, Gray AM. A longitudinal study of the effects of age and time to death on hospital costs. J Health Econ 2004;23(2), 217–35.

12.   Auster R, Levenson I, Sarachek D. The production of health: An exploratory study. J Hum Resources 1969;4:412–36.

13.   Evans R, Barer M, Marmor T. Why are some people healthy and others not? The determinants of health of populations, 1st ed. New York: Walter de Gruyter, 1994.

14.   McGinnis J, Foege WH. Actual causes of death in the United States. JAMA 1993;270:2207–12.

15.   Mitnitski A, Song X, Skoog I, Broe GA, Cox JL, Grunfeld E, Rockwood K. Relative fitness and frailty of elderly men and women in developed countries and their relationship with mortality. J Am Geriatr Soc 2005;53(12):2184–9.

16.   Schofield P, Dunham M, Black C, Aveyard B. The management of pain in older people. Sheffield: Univ Sheffield School Nurs Midwifery, 2005.

17.   Muira H, Kariyasu M, Yamasaki K, Sumi Y. Physical, mental and social factors affecting self-rated verbal communication among elderly individuals. Geriatr Gerontol Int 2004;4:100–4

18. Muira H, Ari Y, Yamasaki K. Feelings of burden and health-related quality of life among family care-givers looking after the impaired elderly. Psychiatr Clin Neurosci 2005;59:551–5.

19. Litaker D, Love TE. Health care resource allocation and individuals' health care needs; examining the degree of fit. Health Policy 2005;73:183–93.

20. Gustafsson K, Sidenvall B. Food-related health perceptions and food habits among older women. J Adv Nurs 2002;39:164–73.

21. Schofield P, Dunham M, Clarke A, Falkner M, Ryan T, Howarth A. An annotated bibliography for the management of pain in the older adult. Sheffield: University Sheffield School Nurs Midwifery, 2005.

22. Smith JP. Healthy bodies and thick wallets: The dual relation between health and economic status. J Econ Perspect 1999;13(2):145–66.

23. Evans R. Interpreting and addressing inequalities in health: From Black to Aicheson to Blair to . . . ? Seventh OHE Ann Lecture. Office Health Econ, 2002.

24. Deaton A. Policy implications for the gradient of health and wealth. Health Affairs 2002;21(2):13–30.

25. Deaton A. Health, inequality and economic development. J Econ Lit 2003;61:113–58.

26. Department of Health. National service framework for people diagnosed with long term conditions. London: HMSO, 2005. See http://www.dh.gov.uk/

27. Gyrd-Hansen D. Investigating the social value of health changes. J Health Econ 2004;23(6):1101–16.

28. Sofaer B, Moore AP, Holloway I, Lamberty JM, Thorpe TAS, O'Dwyer J. Chronic pain as perceived by older people: A qualitative study. Age Ageing 2005;34:462–6.

29. Gilson AM, Maurer M, Joranson DE. State policy affecting pain management: recent improvements and the positive impact of regulatory health policies. Health Policy 2005;74:192–204.

30. Guglielmo WJ. Doctors: the new target in the war on drugs? Med Econ, 2006.
    http://www.memag.com/memag/article/articleDetail.jsp

31. Douglas M. Purity and danger. An analysis of the concepts of pollution and taboo. London: Routledge, 1966.

32. Dickinson A. The food choices and eating habits of older people: a grounded theory. Unpublished PhD Thesis. Buckinghamshire and Chilterns College UK: Brunel University, 1999.

33. Hirani V, Primatesta P. Vitamin D concentrations among people aged 65 years and over living in private households and institutions in England: population survey. Age Ageing 2005;34:485–91.

34. Allen PF. Association between diet, social resources and oral health related quality of life in edentulous patients. J Oral Rehabil 2005;32:623–8.

35. Traynor V. Understanding the lives of older women. Nurs Stand 2005;19(44):41–8.

36.   OECD. Aging and transport: Mobility needs and safety issues. Paris: OECD, 2001.

37.   Hakamies-Blomqvist L, Wiklund M, Henriksson P. Predicting older drivers' accident involvement – Smeed's law revisited. Accid Anal Prev 2005;37, 675–80.

38.   Duke D. Measuring frailty in geriatric patients. Can Med Assoc J 2006;174(3):352.http://www.cmaj.ca/cgi/content/full/174/3/352-c

39.   Cresci MK. Older adults living in the community: issues in home safety. Geriatr Nurs 2005;26(5):282–6.

40.   Lagergren M. Whither care of older persons in Sweden? A prospective analysis based upon simulation model calculations 1000–2030. Health Policy 2005;74: 325-34.

41.   Lipsitz LA. The elderly people of post-Soviet Ukraine: medical, social and economic challenges. J Am Geriatr Soc 2005;53(12):2216–20.

42.   Wang H, Yip W, Zhang L, Wang L, Hsiao W. Community based health insurance in poor rural China: the distribution of net benefits. Health Policy Plan 2005;10:366–74.

43.   Crist JD. The meaning for elders of receiving family care. J Adv Nurs 2005;49(5):485–93.

44.   Okoro CA, Strine TW, Young SL, Balluz LS, Mokdad AH. Access to health care among older adults and receipt of preventive services. Results from the Behavioural Risk Factor Surveillance System 2002. Prev Med 2005;40:337–43.

45.   Polansky P, Smoyak S. Independence, dignity and choice in assisted living. J Psychosoc Nurs 2005;43(3):16–9.

46.   Janlov A-C, Hallberg IR, Petersson K. Older persons' experience of being assessed for and receiving public home help: do they have any influence over it? Health Soc Care Community 2006;14(1):26–36.

47.   Byford S, Torgerson D, Raftery J. Cost of illness studies. BMJ 2000;320:1335.

48.   Cully JA, Gfeller JD, Heise RA, Ross MJ, Teal CR, Kunik ME. Geriatric depression, medical diagnosis, and functional recovery during acute rehabilitation. Arch Phys Med Rehabil 2005;86(12):2256–60.

49.   Van Hootven CH, Norton EC. Informal care and health use of older adults. J Health Econ 2004;23(6):1159–80.

50.   Nahcivan NO, Demirezen E. Depressive symptomatology among Turkish older adults with low incomes in a rural community sample. J Clin Nurs 2005;14:1232–40.

51.   Gomolin IH, Aung MM, Wolf-Klein G, Auerbach C. Older is colder: temperature range and variation in older people. J Am Geriatr Soc 2005;53(12):2170–2.

52.   Iversen T. The effects of patient shortage on a general practitioners' future income and list of patients. J Health Econ 2004;23(4):673–94.

53.   Guariglia A, Rossi M. Private medical insurance and saving: Evidence from the British Household Panel Survey. J Health Econ 2004;23(4):761–83.

54. Barnes M, Bennet G. Frail bodies, courageous voices: older peopleinfluencing community care. Health Soc Care Community 1998;6(2):102–11.

55 Roberts K. Across the health–social care divide: elderly people as active users of health care and social care. Health Soc Care Community 2001;9(2):100–7.

56 Roberts K. Issues and innovations in nursing practice. Exploring participation: Older people on discharge from hospital. J Adv Nurs 2002;40(4):413–20.

57. Campbell SE, Seymour DG, Primrose WR, Lynch JE, Dunstan E, Espallargues M, Lamura G, Lawson P, Philp I et al. A multi-centre European study of factors affecting the discharge destination of older people admitted to hospital: analysis of in-hospital data from the ACMEplus project. Age Ageing 2005;34:467–75.

58. Gray L, Martin F. Classifying patients in hospital. Age Ageing 2005;34:422–4.

59. Vincent JA. Understanding generations: political economy and culture in an ageing society. Br J Sociol 2005;56(4):579–99.

60. Le Grand J. Equity and choice. London: Harper Collins Acad, 1991.

61. Le Grand J. Motivation, agency and public policy – of knights and knaves, pawns and queens. Oxford: Oxford Univ Press, 2003.

62. Shreffler-Grant J, Weinert C, Nichols E, Ide B. Complementary therapy use among older rural adults. Public Health Nurs 2005;22(4):323–31.

63. Canniscio C, Block J, Kawachi I. Social capital and successful ageing: the role of senior housing. Ann Intern Med 2003;139:395–9.

64. Pollack CE, von dem Knesebeck O. Social capital and health among the aged: Comparisons between the United States and Germany. Health Place 2004;10:383–91.

65. Hellström Y, Persson G, Hallberg, I.R. Quality of life and symptoms among older people living at home. J Adv Nurs Pract 2003;48(6): 584–93.

66. Gustafsson K, Ekblad J, Sidenvall B. Older women and dietary advice: Occurrence, comprehension and compliance. J Hum Nutr Dietetics 2005;18:453–60.

67. Manthorpe J, Mailn N, Stubbs H. (2004) Older people's views of rural life: a study of three villages. Int J Older People Nurs J Clin Nurs 2004;13(2):97–104.

68. Lyons RA, Sanders LV, Weightman AL et al. Modifications of home environment for reduction of injuries. Cochrane Database Syst Rev 2005;2,

PART ELEVEN:
ACKNOWLEDGEMENTS

CHAPTER 32
About the authors

Ann Ashburn, MCSP, MPhil, PhD, School of Health Professions and Rehabilitation Sciences, University of Southampton, England. E-mail: a.m.ashburn@soton.ac.uk

Shoshana Aspler, RN, Kfar Nachman Residential Care Center, Raanana, Israel. E-mail: shoshia@molsa.gov.il

Carmit Cahana, BPT, MSc, Office of the Medical Director, Division for Mental Retardation, Ministry of Social Affairs, POBox 1260, IL-91012 Jerusalem, Israel. E-mail: carmit_c@netvision.net.il

Eli Carmeli, PT, PhD, Department of Physical Therapy, Sackler Faculty of Medicine, Tel Aviv University, IL-69978 Ramat Aviv, Israel. Email: elie@post.tau.ac.il

Amanda Clarke, BA(Hons), MA, PhD, RGN, University of Sheffield, Trent Research and Development Support Unit, ICOSS Building, 219 Portobello Sheffield S1 4D, United Kingdom. E-mail: a.e.clarke@sheffield.ac.uk

Raymond Coleman, PhD, Department of Anatomy and Cell Biology, Bruce Rappaport Faculty of Medicine, Technion-Israel Institute of Technology, IL-31096 Haifa, Israel, E-mail: coleman@tx.technion.ac.il

Mary Cooke, PhD, School of Nursing and Midwifery, University of Sheffield, Winter Street, Sheffield S3 7ND, United Kingdom. Email: Mary.Cooke@sheffield.ac.uk

Christine Davey, MCSP, MSc, PhD, North Yorkshire Alliance Research and Development Unit, York, United Kingdom. E-mail: christine.davey@hhc-hdft.nhs.uk

Sue Davies, PhD, RGN, RHV, University of Sheffield, School of Nursing and Midwifery, Bartolome House, Winter Street, Sheffield, S3 7ND, United Kingdom. E-mail: s.davies@sheffield.ac.uk

Pam Enderby, PhD, Institute of General Practice and Primary Care, School of Health and Related Research, University of Sheffield, United Kingdom. E-mail: p.m.enderby@sheffield.ac.uk

Simon Evans, BSc, Health Training and Research Centre, Faculty of Health and Social Care, Coldharbour Lane, University of the West of England, Bristol BS16 1QY, United Kingdom. E-mail: Simon.Evans@uwe.ac.uk

Mark Faulkner, PhD, RGN. Faculty of Health and Wellbeing, Sheffield Hallam University, 30 Collegiate Crescent, Sheffield, S10 2BP. E-mail: m.faulkner@shu.ac.uk

Amanda Howarth, RGN, BmedSci, MSc, School of Nursing and Midwifery, Humphry Davy House, Wath upon Dearne, United Kingdom. E-mail: A.L.Howarth@sheffield.ac.uk

Isack Kandel, MA, PhD, Faculty of Social Sciences, Department of Behavioral Sciences, Academic College of Judea and Samaria, Ariel, Israel. E-mail: kandelii@zahav.net.il

Diana Kerr, BA, Dip soc admin, CQSW, PGCE, Research Fellow, Centre for Research on Families and Relationships, University of Edinburgh, 23 Buccleuch Place, Edinburgh EH8 9NB, United Kingdom. E-mail: dkerr3@staffmail.ed.ac.uk; Website: www.crfr.ac.uk

Shlomo Kessel, MSW, Sarah Herzog Emunah Children's Center, Afula, Israel. E-mail: skessel@internet-zahav.net

Hefziba Lifshitz, PhD, School of Education, Bar Ilan University, IL-52900 Ramat Gan, Israel. Email: lifshih1@mail.biu.ac.il

Meir Lotan, BPT, MScPT, Therapeutic Department, Zvi Quittman Residential Center, Millie Shime Campus, Elwyn, POB 9011, IL-91090 Jerusalem. E-mail: ml_pt_rs@netvision.net.il

David T Lowenthal, MD, PhD, VA Medical Center, 1601 Archer Rd, Geriatric Research, Education and Clinical Center, GRECC (182), College of Medicine, University of Florida, Gainesville, FL, United States, E-mail: dlowen4241@bellsouth.net

Robin Means, BA, MA, PhD, Faculty of Health and Social Care, Health Training and Research Centre, University of the West of England, Bristol, United Kingdom. E-mail: Robin Means@uwe.ac.uk

Efrat Merrick, MD, National Institute of Child Health and Human Development, Office of the Medical Director, Division for Mental Retardation, Ministry of Social Affairs, POBox 1260, IL-91012 Jerusalem, Israel. E-mail: efratmerrick@gmail.com

Joav Merrick, MD, MMedSci, DMSci, Division for Mental Retardation, Ministry of Social Affairs, POBox 1260, IL-91012 Jerusalem, Israel. E-mail: jmerrick@internet-zahav.net

Mohammed Morad, MD, Division of Community Health and Center for Multidisciplinary Research in Aging, Faculty of Health Sciences, Ben Gurion University of the Negev and Clalit Health Services, Beer-Sheva, Israel. E-mail: morad62@013.net.il

Gail Mountain, DipCOT, MPhil, PhD, Sheffield Hallam University, Faculty of Health and Wellbeing, Collegiate Hall, Collegiate Crecent Campus, Sheffield, United Kingdom. E-mail: g.a.mountain@shu.ac.uk

Mike Nolan, PhD, RN,
University of Sheffield, School of Medicine and Biomedical Sciences, Samuel Fox House, Northern General Hospital, Herries Road, Sheffield S5 7AU United Kingdom. E-mail: m.r.nolan@sheffield.ac.uk

Pini Orbach, PhD, Cardiovascular Research Center, Massachusetts General Hospital, Harvard School of Medicine, Boston, MA, USA. E mail: porbach@minervabio.com

Alan S Rigby, MSc C Stat, Department of Academic Cardiology, University of Hull, United Kingdom. E-mail: asr1960@hotmail.com

Tony Ryan, PhD, MA, BSc, Faculty of Health and Wellbeing, Sheffield Hallam University, Broomhall Building, Collegiate Crescent Campus, Sheffield S10 2BP, United Kingdom . E-mail: a.w.ryan@shu.ac.uk

Patricia Schofield, RN, PhD, PGDipEd, DipN, Senior Lecturer, Centre for Advanced Studies in Nursing,Department of General Practice and Primary Care, University of Aberdeen, Foresterhill Health Centre, Westburn Road, Aberdeen AB25 2AY, United Kingdom. E-mail: p.a.schofield@abdn.ac.uk

Gerard Schwarz, MD, National PKU Center, Ministry of Health, Chaim Sheba Medical Center, Tel Hashomer, Ramat Gan, Israel. E-mail: gerard.schwarz@sheba.health.gov.il

Paula Smith, RN, BSc, MSc, PhD, Faculty of Health and Well Being, Collegiate Crescent Campus, Broomhall Building, Sheffield Hallam University, Sheffield S1 1WB, United Kingdom. E-mail: p.c.smith@shu.ac.uk

Josephine Tetley, MA, BSc (hons), PGCE, DANS, RGN, Sheffield Hallam University, Faculty of Health and Wellbeing, Mundella House, 34 Collegiate Crescent, Collegiate Campus, Sheffield S1 1WB United Kingdom. E-mail j.w.tetley@shu.ac.uk

Søren Ventegodt, MD, MMedSci, EURO-MSc, Quality-of-Life Research Center, Nordic School or Holistic Medicine and Research Clinic for Holistic Medicine, Copenhagen, Denmark. E-mail: ventegodt@livskvalitet.org

Lorna Warren, BA(Hons), MA, PhD, Department of Sociological Studies, University   of   Sheffield,   Sheffield,   United   Kingdom.   E-mail: l.warren@sheffield.ac.uk

Rose Wiles, BSc, PhD, ESRC National Centre for Research Methods, School of   Social   Sciences,   University   of   Southampton,   England.   E-mail: r.a.wiles@soton.ac.uk

Heather Wilkinson, PhD, Centre   for   Research   on   Families   and Relationships, University of Edinburgh, 23 Buccleuch Place, Edinburgh EH8 9NB, United Kingdom. E-mail: h.wilkinson@ed.ac.uk

Ditza Zachor, MD, Department of Pediatrics, Assaf HaRofeh Medical Center, IL-70300 Zerifin, Israel. E-mail: dzachor@asaf.health.gov.il

CHAPTER 33
About the editors

Isack Kandel, MA, PhD, is senior lecturer (assistant professor) at the Faculty of Social Sciences, Department of Behavioral Sciences, Academic College of Judea and Samaria, Ariel. During the period 1985-93 he served as the director of the Division for Mental Retardation, Ministry of Social Affairs, Jerusalem, Israel. Several books and numerous other publications in the areas of rehabilitation, disability, health and intellectual disability. E-mail: kandelii@zahav.net.il

Patricia Schofield, RGN, PhD, PGDipEd, DipN is senior lecturer at the Centre for Advanced Studies in Nursing, Department of General Practice and Primary Care, University of Aberdeen in the United Kingdom, who has worked in pain management since 1988. Originally as a clinical nurse specialist in Chesterfield and then as a lecturer and senior lecturer. PhD thesis on nursing interventions for the management of chronic pain and initiated the first pain management course for nurses in the UK. Completed a number of post doctoral projects around pain management in older people including talking to them about their pain experiences, a systematic review and two annotated bibliographies. Served on council for the British Pain Society and recently set up a special interest group around pain in older adults. Currently working with the British Geriatric Society setting up guidelines for pain assessment in older adults and leading a group of researchers developing a number of projects around pain assessment in care homes and pain management for older adults. Several books and publications in this area of research. E-mail: p.a.schofield@abdn.ac.uk

Joav Merrick, MD, MMedSci, DMSc, is professor of child health and human development affiliated with the Center for Multidisciplinary Research in Aging, Zusman Child Development Center, Division of Pediatrics at the Ben Gurion University, Beer-Sheva, Israel, the medical director of the Division for Mental Retardation, Ministry of Social Affairs, Jerusalem, the founder and director of the National Institute of Child Health and Human Development. Numerous publications in the field of child health and human development, rehabilitation, intellectual disability, disability, health, welfare, abuse, advocacy, quality of life and prevention. Received the Peter Sabroe Child Award for outstanding work on behalf of Danish Children in 1985 and the International LEGO-Prize ("The Children's   Nobel Prize") for an extraordinary contribution towards improvement in child welfare and well-being in 1987. E-Mail: jmerrick@internet-zahav.net. Website: www.nichd-israel.com

CHAPTER 34
About the National Institute of Child Health and Human Development in Israel

T he National Institute of Child Health and Human Development (NICHD) was established in 1998-99 in Israel under the auspices of the Medical Director, Ministry of Social Affairs in order to function as the research arm for the Office of the Medical Director. In 1998 the National Council for Child Health and Pediatrics of the Ministry of Health and in 1999 the Director General and Deputy Director General of the Ministry of Health endorsed the establishment of the NICHD.

In the year 2000 the International Journal of Adolescent Medicine and Health (Freund Publishing House, London and Tel Aviv) and in the year 2003 the Child Health and Human Development Domain of the Scientific World Journal (Newbury, UK and New York), both Medline indexed peer-reviewed journals, were affiliated with the NICHD.

During 2002 many activities became focused in the south of Israel due to an affiliation with the Division for Community Health and the School of Continuing Medical Education at the Faculty of Health Sciences (FOHS) at the Ben Gurion University of the Negev (BGU). In 2002 a full course on "Disability" was established at the Recanati School for Allied Professions in the Community, FOHS, BGU and twice a year seminars for specialists in family medicine. In 2002-3 an affiliation with the Zusman Child Development Center at the Pediatric Division of Soroka University Medical Center was established and collaboration around the Down Syndrome Clinic at that center. In 2003-4 an affiliation was established with the Saban Children's Medical Center under construction at Soroka University Medical Center and in 2005 with the Center for Multidisciplinary Research in Aging. In 2005 a course on "Aging with disability" became part of the MSc program in Gerontology.

In 2005 the International Journal on Disability and Human development published by Freund Publishing House, London and Tel Aviv was also affiliated with the National Institute of Child Health and Human Development.

The mission of a National Institute for Child Health and Human Development in Israel is to provide an academic focal point for the scholarly interdisciplinary study of child life, health, public health, welfare, disability, rehabilitation, intellectual disability and related aspects of human development.

The mission includes research, teaching, clinical work, information and public service activities in the field of child health and human development. The Institute should be the obvious resource to turn to for professionals, politicians, the general public and the media concerned with the care of children, the disabled and the intellectually disabled in our society.

Collaboration

Nationally the NICHD works in collaboration with the Faculty of Health Sciences, Ben Gurion University of the Negev and the Soroka University Medical Center in Beer-Sheva, Department of Physiotherapy, Sackler School of Medicine, Tel Aviv University, Department of Physiotherapy, Haifa University, Department of Education, Bar Ilan University, Ramat Gan and the Faculty of Social Sciences and Health Sciences, College of Judea and Samaria in Ariel.

Internationally with the Department of Disability and Human Development, College of Applied Health Sciences, University of Illinois at Chicago, Strong Center for Developmental Disabilities, Golisano Children's Hospital at Strong, University of Rochester School of Medicine and Dentistry, New York, Centre on Intellectual Disabilities, University of Albany, New York, Centre for Chronic Disease Prevention and Control, Health Canada, Ottawa, Chandler Medical Center and Children's Hospital, Section of Adolescent Medicine, University of Kentucky, Lexington, Quality of Life Research Center and Nordic School of Holistic Health, Copenhagen, Denmark, Nordic School of Public Health, Gottenburg, Sweden, Scandinavian Institute of Quality of Working Life, Oslo, Norway, School of Social Work, Chinese University, Hong Kong.

The vision

The vision of a National Institute for Child Health and Human Development in Israel is to seek to assure as far as possible that every individual is born healthy, is born wanted and has the opportunity to fulfill his or her potential for a healthy and productive life unhampered by disease or disability. The Institute should become an international leader in child health, welfare and human development and an advocate for the children, the disabled and persons with intellectual disability of our society.

Target areas of interests

The interest areas of the NICHD are child health, disability and human development. The NICHD will alone or in collaboration have local, national, regional and international responsibilities in research, academics, model clinical service and policy.

Contact address

E-mail: jmerrick@internet-zahav.net
Website: www.nichd-israel.com

PART TWELFE:

PUBLICATION LIST ABOUT AGING

CHAPTER 35
Publication list from the National Institute of Child Health and Human Development on aging related issues 1999-2005

Joav Merrick

The National Institute of Child Health and Human Development in Israel has over the years published papers related to adults and aging as part of our work and in collaboration with many partners in Israel and around the world. We also in 2005 established collaboration with with the Center for Multidisciplinary Research in Aging at the Faculty of Health Sciences, Ben Gurion University of the Negev and in 2005 we also initiated a one semester course on "Aging with disability" as part of the master of science (MSc) program in Gerontology. Original articles (peer review). Below a list of publications during the 1999-2005 period.

ORIGINAL PEER REVIEWED ARTICLES

- Kessel S, Merrick J, Kedem A, Borovsky L, Carmeli E.
  Use of group counseling to support aging-related losses in older adults with intellectual disabilities.
  J Gerontol Soc Work 2002;38(1/2):241-51.

- Lifshitz H, Merrick J.
  Ageing and intellectual disability in Israel: A study to compare community residence with living at home.
  Health Soc Care Community 2003;11(4):364-371.

- Carmeli E, Bar-Chad S, Lotan M, Merrick J, Coleman R.
  Five clinical tests to assess balance following ball exercises and treadmill training in adult persons with intellectual disability.
  J Gerontol A Biol Sci Med Sci 2003;58(8):M767-M772.

- Carmeli E, Merrick J, Kessel S, Mashrawi Y, Carmeli V.
  Elderly persons with intellectual disability: A study of clinical characteristics, functional status and sensory capacity.
  ScientificWorldJournal 2003;3:298-307.

- Carmeli E, Cahana C, Merrick J.
  The assimilation of assistive technology in residential care centers for people with intellectual disabilities.
  ScientificWorldJournal 2004;4:178-85.

- Lifshitz H, Merrick J.
  Aging among persons with intellectual disability in relation to type of residence, age and etiology.
  Res Dev Disabil 2004;25:193-205.

- Morad M, Gringols M, Kandel I, Merrick J.
  Vitamin B 12 deficiency in persons with intellectual disability in a vegetarian residential care community.
  ScientificWorldJournal 2005;5:58-61.

- Carmeli E, Kessel S, Bar-Chad S, Merrick J.
  A comparison between older persons with Down syndrome and a control group: Clinical characteristics, functional status ans sensori-motor function.
  Down Syndr Res Pract 2004;9(1):17-24.

- Merrick J, Davidson PW, Morad M, Janicki MP, Wexler O, Henderson CM.
  Older adults with intellectual disability in residential care centers in Israel: Health status and service utilization.
  Am J Ment Retard 2004;1009(5):413-20.

- Carmeli E, Merrick J, Berner YN.
  Effect of training on health and fundtional status in older adults with intellectual disability.
  Int J Ther Rehab 2004;11(10):481-5.

- Carmeli E, Zinger-Vaknin T, Morad M, Merrick J.
  Can physical training have an effect on well-being in adults with mild intellectyual disability?
  Mech Ageing Dev 2005;126:299-304.

CASE REPORTS AND SHORT COMMUNICATIONS (PEER REVIEW)

- Merrick J, Ventegodt S.
  What is a good death ? To use death as a mirror and find the quality of life.
  BMJ   2003   October   31   online   at
  http://bmj.com/cgi/eletters/327/7406/66#39303

- Merrick J, Morad M, Kandel I, Ventegodt S.
  Prevalence of Helicobacter pylori infection in residential care centers for people with intellectual disability.
  BMJ   2004   Jul   23   on-line   at
  http://bmj.bmjjournals.com/cgi/eletters/329/7459/204#68360

- Morad M, Halperin I, Shupac A, Merrick J.
  Health policy and intellectual disability.
  BMJ   2004   Aug   21   on-line   at
  http://bmj.bmjjournals.com/cgi/eletters/329/7463/414#71691

- Ventegodt S, Morad M, Merrick J.
  Challenge of chronic disease is the challenge of understanding life. The social medicine of our time.
  BMJ 2005 Mar 18 on-line at
  http://bmj.bmjjournals.com/cgi/eletters/330/7492/657#100776

- Merrick J.
  Anti-psychotic drugs for older persons.
  Med Dir Bull 2005;35:4.

REVIEW ARTICLES (PEER REVIEW)

- Merrick J, Aspler S, Schwarz G.
  Should adults with phenylketonuria have diet treatment ?
  Mental Retardation 2001;39(3):215-7.

- Merrick J.
  Health aspects of aging in persons with intellectual disability.
  Elwyn Israel J 2001;4:2-4,18. (Hebrew).

- Kessel S, Merrick J.
  The benefits of Jewish mourning rituals for the grieving individual with intellectual disability.
  J Religion Disabil Health 2001;5(2/3):147-56.

- Merrick J, Kandel I, Morad M.
  Health needs of adults with intellectual disability relevant for the family physician.
  ScientificWorldJournal 2003;3:937-45.

- Merrick J, Kandel I.
  Medical services for persons with intellectual disability in Israel.
  Public Health Rev 2003;31(1):45-68.

- Merrick J, Arda H, Kandel I.
  Nursing aspects of services for persons with intellectual disability in
  Israel.
  Int J Nurs Intell Dev Disabil 2004;1(1):4.
  Available at: http://journal.hsmc.org/ijnidd

- Merrick J, Merrick E, Lunsky Y, Kandel I.
  Suicide behavior in persons with intellectual disability.
  ScientificWorldJournal 2005;5:729-35.

- Ventegodt S, Merrick J.
  Suicide from a holistic point of view.
  ScientificWorldJournal 2005;5:759-66.

- Flensborg-Madsen T, Ventegodt S, Merrick J.
  Why is Antonovsly's sense of coherence not correlated to physical
  health? Analysing Antonovsky's 29-item sense of coherence scale
  (SOC-29).
  ScientificWorldJournal 2005;5:767-76..

CHAPTERS IN BOOKS

- Cahana C, Merrick J, Carmeli E.
  The involvement of physiotherapists in the implementation of
  assistive technology for persons with intellectual disability in Israel.
  A National Survey.
  In: Marincek C, Buhler C, Knops H, Andrich R, eds. Assistive
  technology. Added value to quality of life. Amsterdam: IOS Press,
  2001:677-80.

- Kessel S, Merrick J.
  The benefits of Jewish mourning rituals for the grieving individual
  with intellectual disability.
  In: Gaventa WC, Coulter DL, eds. Spirituality and intellectial
  disability. International perspectives on the effect of culture and
  religion on healing body, mind and soul.
  New York: Haworth Press, 2001:147-56.

INVITED PAPERS (PEER REVIEW)

- Cahana C, Tishler SC, Merrick J.
  Active-Passive-Trainer (APT). Experience from Israel with severe
  nursing patients.
  First International APT Meeting, Kibbutz Tzora, January 1999.

- Merrick J.
  Medical and psychiatric services for persons with mental retardation in Israel.
  Seminar in honor of professor Ludwig Szymanski, MD, Harvard School of Medicine, The Israel Child and Adolescent Psychiatry Association, Chaim Sheba Medical Center, Tel Hashomer, April 1999.

- Ezra E, Merrick J, Wientroub S, Josef B, Steinberg DM.
  Associated medical disorders in persons with Down Syndrome.
  International Conference on Down syndrome, Jerusalem, 19-21 October, 1999.

- Koslowe K, Merrick J, Yinon U.
  Visual anomalies in a Down syndrome population in comparison with a varied population of retarded subjects.
  International Conference on Down syndrome, Jerusalem, 19-21 October, 1999.

- Schwarz G, Merrick J.
  Phenylketonuria discovered in an adult with intellectual disability.
  International Seminar on Phynylketonuria, Ministry of Health, Ramat Gan, Chaim Sheba Medical center, March 7, 2000.

- Arda H, Merrick J.
  Aging and intellectual disability.
  Seminar on service for persons with intellectual disability, Ministry of Labour and Social Affairs, Neurim, Tel Mond, May 16, 2000. [Hebrew]

- Kessel S, Merrick J.
  Aging and intellectual disability.
  Roundtable arranged by the Association for the Planning and Development of Services for the aged in Israel, JDC-Brookdale Institute, Jerusalem, November 20, 2000. [Hebrew]

- Merrick J, Kessel S.
  Aging and intellectual disability.
  Seminar on service aspects in the Division for Mental Retardation in Israel, Ministry of Labour and Social Affairs, Yad Lebanim, Ranana, January 2001. [Hebrew]

- Merrick J, Weintroub S, Steinberg DM, Ezra E, Josef B, Hendel D.
  The adult with Down syndrome.
  RRTC-ADD Research symposium on aging with developmental disability, University of Illinois at Chicago, Department of Disability and Human Development, Chicago, United States, November 14-15, 2001.

- Morad M, Merrick J, Nasri Y.
  Vitamin B12 deficiency in persons with developmental disability in a vegetarian residential care community.
  RRTC-ADD Research symposium on aging with developmental disability, University of Illinois at Chicago, Department of Disability and Human Development, Chicago, United States, November 14-15, 2001.

- Kessel S, Arda H, Cahana C, Goshen ZD, Havusha H, Merrick J, Murover M, Shalem G, Shalom G.
  Government committee on aging and persons with developmental disability in residential centers in Israel.
  RRTC-ADD Research symposium on aging with developmental disability, University of Illinois at Chicago, Department of Disability and Human Development, Chicago, United States, November 14-15, 2001.

- Lifshitz H, Merrick J.
  Adults with developmental disability in community residence versus living at home.
  RRTC-ADD Research symposium on aging with developmental disability, University of Illinois at Chicago, Department of Disability and Human Development, Chicago, United States, November 14-15, 2001.

- Merrick J, Gat H.
  Dental treatment of adults with developmental disability in residential care in Israel.
  RRTC-ADD Research symposium on aging with developmental disability, University of Illinois at Chicago, Department of Disability and Human Development, Chicago, United States, November 14-15, 2001.

- Kessel S, Merrick J, Muraver M, Carmeli E, Cahana C, Dvir R.
  Falls in persons with developmental disability.
  RRTC-ADD Research symposium on aging with developmental disability, University of Illinois at Chicago, Department of Disability and Huma Development, Chicago, United States, November 14-15, 2001.

- Merrick J, Morad M.
  Health policy for persons with developmental disability in Israel.
  RRTC-ADD Research symposium on aging with developmental disability, University of Illinois at Chicago, Department of Disability and Human Development, Chicago, United States, November 14-15, 2001.

- Merrick J, Morad M, Kessel S.
  Health profile of persons with developmental disability aged 40 years and older in residential care in Israel.
  RRTC-ADD Research symposium on aging with developmental disability, University of Illinois at Chicago, Department of Disability and Human Development, Chicago, United States, November 14-15, 2001.

- Kessel S, Merrick J, Kedem A, Borovsky L, Carmeli E.
  Older adults with developmental disability and loss of physical abilities.
  RRTC-ADD Research symposium on aging with developmental disability, University of Illinois at Chicago, Department of Disability and Human Development, Chicago, United States, November 14-15, 2001.

- Merrick J, Morad M, Muraver M, Kessel S.
  Age of menopause in women with developmental disability.
  RRTC-ADD Research symposium on aging with developmental disability,
  University of Illinois at Chicago, Department of Disability and Human Development, Chicago, United States, November 14-15, 2001.

- Merrick J.
  Mortality studies in persons with developmental disability in Israel.
  RRTC-ADD Research symposium on aging with developmental disability,
  University of Illinois at Chicago, Department of Disability and Human Development, Chicago, United States, November 14-15, 2001.

- Kessel S, Merrick J.
  Mourning and the adult with developmental disability.
  RRTC-ADD Research symposium on aging with developmental disability,
  University of Illinois at Chicago, Department of Disability andd Human Development, Chicago, United States, November 14-15, 2001.

- Carmeli E, Kessel S, Merrick J, Bar-Chad S, Carmeli V.
  A comparison of clinical characteristics and physical activity of aging adults with and without developmental disability.
  RRTC-ADD Research symposium on aging with developmental disability, University of Illinois at Chicago, Department of Disability and Human Development, Chicago, United States, November 14-15, 2001.

- Merrick J, Schwarz G.
  Phenylketonuria (PKU) in Israel.
  RRTC-ADD Research symposium on aging with developmental disability, University of Illinois at Chicago, Department of Disability and Human Development, Chicago, United States, November 14-15, 2001.

- Merrick J, Crystal-Shalit O, Koslowe K, Yinon U, Gozovsky M.
  Vision project for adults with developmental disability in residential care in Israel.
  RRTC-ADD Research symposium on aging with developmental disability, University of Illinois at Chicago, Department of Disability andd Human Development, Chicago, United States, November 14-15, 2001.

- Merrick J, Morad M, Kessel S.
  Aging and falls in the population of persons with intellectual disability in residential care centers in Israel.
  Conference on falls, Division for Mental Retardation, Ministry of Labour Social Affairs, Hevrat Neurim, Tel Mond, Dsecember 05, 2001. [Hebrew]

- Merrick J, Morad M.
  Adults with Down syndrome. Research results from Israel 1995-2002.
  Seminar on Down Syndrome, Ministry of Health, Tel Hashomer: Chaim Sheba Medical Center, April 08, 2003. [Hebrew]

- Merrick J, Morad M.
  National health provision: Research agenda and perspectives.
  12th IASSID (Int Ass Sci Study Intell Disabil) World Congress, Montpellier, France, June 14-19, 2004.
  Published in J Intell Disabil Res 2004;48(4-5):426.

- Merrick J, Morad M, Davidson PW, Janicki MP, Wexler O, Henderson CM.
  Older adults with intellectual disability in residential care centers in Israel.
  12th IASSID (Int Ass Sci Study Intell Disabil) World Congress, Montpellier, France, June 14-19, 2004.
  Published in J Intell Disabil Res 2004;48(4-5):427.

PAPERS PRESENTED (PEER REVIEW)

- Shapira J, Efrat J, Berkey D, Mann J, Gat H, Merrick J.
  Dental health profile of a population with mental retardation in Israel.
  First National Congress on Mental retardation, Ministry of Labour and Social Affairs, Holiday Inn Crown Plaza, Jerusalem, 13-14 June 1999. [Hebrew]

- Yogev U, Gat H, Merrick J.
  Model for dental treatment in the community. The Levzeller Project.
  First National Congress on Mental retardation, Ministry of Labour and Social Affairs, Holiday Inn Crown Plaza, Jerusalem, 13-14 June 1999. [Hebrew]

- Gat H, Merrick J.
  Dental treatment in general anaesthesia for persons with mental retardation.
  First National Congress on Mental retardation, Ministry of Labour and Social Affairs, Holiday Inn Crown Plaza, Jerusalem, 13-14 June 1999. [Hebrew]

- Merrick J, Gat H.
  Overview of expenses for dental services to the population of the mentally retarded 1985-99.
  First National Congress on Mental retardation, Ministry of Labour and Social Affairs, Holiday Inn Crown Plaza, Jerusalem, 13-14 June 1999. [Hebrew]

- Koslowe K, Yinon U, Arda H, Merrick J, Aminadav C.
  Multidisciplinary assessment of persons with severe mental retardation. Eye examinations.
  First National Congress on Mental retardation, Ministry of Labour and Social Affairs, Holiday Inn Crown Plaza, Jerusalem, 13-14 June 1999. [Hebrew]

- Cahana C, Merrick J.
  Rehabilitation equipment in institutions for persons with mental retardation.
  First National Congress on Mental retardation, Ministry of Labour and Social Affairs, Holiday Inn Crown Plaza, Jerusalem, 13-14 June 1999. [Hebrew]

- Cahana C, Merrick J.
  APT (Active-Passive-Trainer) in the treatment of persons with mental retardation.
  First National Congress on Mental retardation, Ministry of Labour and Social Affairs, Holiday Inn Crown Plaza, Jerusalem, 13-14 June 1999. [Hebrew]

- Merrick J.
  Mortality in the institutionalized population of persons with mental retardation in Israel 1991-97.
  First National Congress on Mental retardation, Ministry of Labour and Social Affairs, Holiday Inn Crown Plaza, Jerusalem, 13-14 June 1999. [Hebrew]

- Cahana C, Merrick J.
  A National Israeli Survey of the use of assistive technology by persons with   mental retardation.
  AAMR (American Association on Mental Retardation) 124th Annual Meeting, Washington, DC, May 30-June 03, 2000.

- Merrick J, Morad M, Levy U.
  Spiritual health in institutions for persons with intellectual disability in Israel. A National Survey.
  11th IASSID (International Association for the Scientific Study of Intellectual   Disabilities) World Congress, Seattle, Washington, August 01-06, 2000.
  Published in the Journal of Intellectual Disability Research 2000;44:393.

- Cahana C, Merrick J.
  Utilization of assistive technology by persons with intellectual disability in institutions in Israel.
  11th IASSID (International Association for the Scientific Study of Intellectual   Disabilities) World Congress, Seattle, Washington, August 01- 06, 2000.
  Published in the Journal of Intellectual Disability Research 2000;44:228.

- Merrick J.
  Mortality in institutions for persons with intellectual disability in Israel 1991-97.
  11th IASSID (International Association for the Scientific Study of Intellectual   Disabilities) World Congress, Seattle, Washington, August 01- 06, 2000.
  Published in the Journal of Intellectual Disability Research 2000;44:393.

- Kerr M, Merrick J, Crowther M.
  An international database for the management of epilepsy in people with an intellectual disability-EUROPIE-ID
  11th IASSID (International Association for the Scientific Study of Intellectual Disabilities) World Congress, Seattle, Washington, August 01-06, 2000.
  Published in the Journal of Intellectual Disability Research 2000;44:345.

- Cahana C, Merrick J, Aminadav C, Koslowe K, Korenbrot F, Tischler SC, Israeli S, Eshel S.
  Multidisciplinary intervention in the treatment of persons with severe and profound intellectual disability and associated physical handicaps in an institution in Israel.
  11th IASSID (International Association for the Scientific Study of Intellectual Disabilities) World Congress, Seattle, Washington, August 01-06, 2000.
  Published in the Journal of Intellectual Disability Research 2000;44:228.

- Merrick J, Lifshitz H, Gabbay Y.
  Judaism and the person with intellectual disability.
  11th IASSID (International Association for the Scientific Study of Intellectual Disabilities) World Congress, Seattle, Washington, August 01- 06, 2000.
  Published in the Journal of Intellectual Disability Research 2000;44:393.

- Kessel S, Merrick J.
  Jewish mourning rituals and bereavement in adults with intellectual disability.
  11th IASSID (International Association for the Scientific Study of Intellectual Disabilities) World Congress, Seattle, Washington, August 01-06, 2000.
  Published in the Journal of Intellectual Disability Research 2000;44:345.

- Kedem H, Borovsky L, Kessel S, Merrick J.
  Loss of physical abilities in older adults with intellectual disabilities
  A grief counseling group support program at a residential center in Israel
  Second National Congress on Intellectual Disability, Ministry of Labour and Social Affairs, David Intercontinental, Tel Aviv, 02-03 May 2001. [Hebrew]

- Kessel S, Merrick J.
  Altzheimer disease in persons with intellectual disability.
  Second National Congress on Intellectual Disability, Ministry of Labour and Social Affairs, David Intercontinental, Tel Aviv, 02-03 May 2001. [Hebrew]

- Greenzweig S, Merrick J, Dvir R, Beider M, Hamama I.
  Quality of care in residential care centers in Israel.
  Second National Congress on Intellectual Disability, Ministry of Labour and Social Affairs, David Intercontinental, Tel Aviv, 02-03 May 2001. [Hebrew]

- Kessel S, Merrick J.
  Jewish mourning rituals helping persons with intellectual disabilities.
  Second National Congress on Intellectual Disability, Ministry of Labour and Social Affairs, David Intercontinental, Tel Aviv, 02-03 May 2001. [Hebrew]

- Mirav G, Merrick J.
  The wheel-chair project of the Division for Mental Retardation.
  Second National Congress on Intellectual Disability, Ministry of Labour and Social Affairs, David Intercontinental, Tel Aviv, 02-03 May 2001. [Hebrew]

- Morad M, Merrick J, Nasri Y.
  Helicobacter pylori studies in the population of persons with intellectual disability.
  Second National Congress on Intellectual Disability, Ministry of Labour and Social Affairs, David Intercontinental, Tel Aviv, 02-03 May 2001. [Hebrew]

- Morad M, Merrick J, Nasri Y.
  Vitamin B-12 deficiency and the persons with intellectual disability.
  Second National Congress on Intellectual Disability, Ministry of Labour and Social Affairs, David Intercontinental, Tel Aviv, 02-03 May 2001. [Hebrew]

- Aspler S, Dubman I, Merrick J.
  Abdominal pain and dyspepsia in persons with intellectual disability.
  Second National Congress on Intellectual Disability, Ministry of Labour and Social Affairs, David Intercontinental, Tel Aviv, 02-03 May 2001. [Hebrew]

- Cahana C, Merrick J, Carmeli E.
  The involvement of physiotherapists in the implementation of assistive technology for persons with intellectual disability in Israel. A National Survey,
  6th European Conference for the Advancement of Assistive Technology, Ljubljana, Slovenia, September 3-6, 2001.

- Morad M, Merrick J.
  The family physician and persons with intellectual disability.
  Israel Medical Ass, Isr Ass Family Physicians, Ramat Gan: Kfar Makabi, March 06, 2002. [Hebrew]

- Lifshitz H, Merrick J.
  Future planning by aging parents of adults with intellectual disability in the Jewish and palastinian population. A comparison between two sectors. Int Roundtable on Aging and Intellectual Disability, Koriyama City, Fukushima, Japan, March 13-15, 2002.

- Lifshitz H, Merrick J.
  Aging and intellectual disability. Differences between living in community residence or living with your own family ? Int Roundtable on Aging and Intellectual Disability, Koriyama City, Fukushima, Japan, March 13-15, 2002.

- Morad M, Merrick J, Kessel S.
  Aging and falls in the population of persons with intellectual disability in residential care centers in Israel.
  Third Int Conf Developmental Disabilities. Tel Aviv: Dan Panorama Hotel, July 2-4, 2002.

- Lifshitz H, Merrick J.
  Aging and developmental disability. Living at home or in community residence.
  Third Int Conf Developmental Disabilities. Tel Aviv: Dan Panorama Hotel, July 2-4, 2002.

- Carlin Y, Ben-Ari Mozes J, Merrick J, Feldberg I.
  A survey of dental hygiene services rendered to the intellectually disabled in Israel.
  16th Int Symposium Dental Hygiene. Madrid, spain: Jul 08-11, 2004.

- Merrick J.
  Health and intellectual disability.
  Pardes Hanna: Ilanit Center, Min Soc Affairs, January 2, 2005.

- Lifshitz H, Davidson PW, Janicki MP, Morad M, Merrick J.
  Older persons with intellectual disability living in community
  residence compared with residential care centers. Aging and health
  concerns.
  Dortmund, Germany: 14th Int Roundtable Aging Intellect Disabil,
  May 17-20, 2005.

- Davidson PW, Merrick J, Morad M, Wang K, Hsieh K, Henderson
  CM, Janicki MP, Robinson LA, Bishop KM, Wexler O, Torrence C.
  Health outcomes with increasing age among adults with intellectual
  disabilities living in the USA, Israel and Tai Taiwan.
  Taipei, Taiwan, June 12-15, 2005.

- Merrick J.
  Health and intellectual disability.
  Pardes Hanna: Ilanit Center, Min Soc Affairs, January 2, 2005.
  [Hebrew]

VARIOUS REPORTS

- Cahana C, Merrick J.
  Survey of physiotherapist and paramedical services in institutions
  for the mentally retarded in Israel.
  Jerusalem: Office of the Medical Director, Division for the Mentally
  Retarded, Ministry of Labour and Social Affairs, 1997. [Hebrew]

- Aminadav C, Merrick J, Arda H, Cahana C.
  A new approach to treating nursing patients with mental retardation
  in institutions.
  Jerusalem: Division for the Mentally Retarded, Ministry of Labour
  and Social Affairs, 1997. [Hebrew]

- Merrick J.
  Pneumococcal vaccine for persons with mental retardation.
  Jerusalem: Office of the Medical Director, Division for the Mentally
  Retarded, Ministry of Labour and Social Affairs, 1999. [Hebrew]

- Merrick J.
  Guidelines for influenza vaccine 1999-2000 to persons with mental
  retardation.
  Jerusalem: Office of the Medical Director, Division for the Mentally
  Retarded, Ministry of Labour and Social Affairs, 1999. [Hebrew]

- Arda H, Merrick J, Habusa H, Cahana C, Murover M, Shalem G, Kessel S.
  Aging in persons with mental retardation in institutions in Israel.
  Jerusalem: Division for the Mentally Retarded, Ministry of Labour and Social Affairs, 1999. [Hebrew]

- Merrick J.
  Trends in the aging of persons with intellectual disability in residential care centers in Israel, 1999-2003.
  Jerusalem: Office of the Medical Director, Division for Mental Retardation, Ministry of Social Affairs, 2004.

- Nissim D, Cahana C, Carmeli E, Dvir R, Goshen A, Kessel S, Merrick J, Morad M, Murover M, Shalom G.
  Falls and its prevention in the aging population of persons with intellectual disability.
  Jerusalem: Div Ment Retard, Min Soc Affairs, 2004.

- Merrick J, Kandel I.
  Trends in number of deaths, mortality rate and average age at death for persons with intellectual disability in residential care centers in Israel, 1991-2003.
  Jerusalem: Office of the Medical Director, Division for Mental Retardation, Ministry of Social Affairs, 2005.

- Merrick J.
  Trends in cause of deaths for persons with intellectual disability in residential care centers in Israel, 1991-2003.
  Jerusalem: Office of the Medical Director, Division for Mental Retardation, Ministry of Social Affairs, 2005.

- Merrick J, Morad M.
  Trends in food strangulation as the cause of deaths in persons with intellectual disability living in residential care centers in Israel, 1991-2003.
  Jerusalem: Office of the Medical Director, Division for Mental Retardation, Ministry of Social Affairs, 2005.

- Merrick J.
  Mortality in residential care centers in Israel for persons with intellectual disability, 2003.
  Jerusalem: Office of the Medical Director, Division for Mental Retardation, Ministry of Social Affairs, 2005.

- Merrick J.
Trends in mortality rate for persons with intellectual disability in residential care centers, 1991-2003.
Jerusalem: Office of the Medical Director, Division for Mental Retardation, Ministry of Social Affairs, 2005.

- Merrick J.
Survey of medical clinics for persons with intellectual disability, 2004.
Jerusalem: Office of the Medical Director, Division for Mental Retardation, Ministry of Social Affairs, 2005.

- Merrick J.
Trends in the population served by the Division for mental retardation, 1985-2004.
Jerusalem: Office of the Medical Director, Division for Mental Retardation, Ministry of Social Affairs, 2005.

- Merrick J.
Trends in the aging of persons with intellectual disability in residential care, 1999-2004.
Jerusalem: Office of the Medical Director, Division for Mental Retardation, Ministry of Social Affairs, 2005.

- Merrick J.
Trends in challenging behavior of residents with intellectual disability in residential care centers in Israel, 1998-2004.
Jerusalem: Office of the Medical Director, Division for Mental Retardation, Ministry of Social Affairs, 2005.

- Merrick J.
Trends in number of persons with intellectual disability in residential care in Israel, 1985-2004.
Jerusalem: Office of the Medical Director, Division for Mental Retardation, Ministry of Social Affairs, 2005.

- Merrick J.
Mortality in residential care centers in Israel for persons with intellectual disability, 2004.
Jerusalem: Office of the Medical Director, Division for Mental Retardation, Ministry of Social Affairs, 2005.

- Merrick J, Merrick E.
Trends in number of deaths, mortality rate and average age at death for persons with intellectual disability in residential care in Israel, 1991-2004.
Jerusalem: Office of the Medical Director, Division for Mental Retardation, Ministry of Social Affairs, 2005.

- Merrick J, Kandel I.
  Trends in mortality rate for persons with intellectual disability in residential care centers, 1991-2004.
  Jerusalem: Office of the Medical Director, Division for Mental Retardation, Ministry of Social Affairs, 2005.

- Merrick J.
  Trends in cause of death for persons with intellectual disability in residential care in Israel, 1991-2004.
  Jerusalem: Office of the Medical Director, Division for Mental Retardation, Ministry of Social Affairs, 2005.

- Merrick J, Morad M.
  Trends in food strangulation as the cause of death in persons with intellectual disability in residential care centers in Israel, 1991-2004.
  Jerusalem: Office of the Medical Director, Division for Mental Retardation, Ministry of Social Affairs, 2005.

INDEX

INDEX

ISBN 142512304-X

9 781425 123048